Day Fighter Aces
of the Luftwaffe

Dedicated to Paul Budden

Day Fighter Aces of the Luftwaffe

Knight's Cross Holders 1943–1945

Jeremy Dixon

'The first rule of all air combat is to see the opponent first. Like the hunter who stalks his prey and manoeuvres himself unnoticed into the most favourable position for the kill, the fighter in the opening of a dogfight must detect the opponent as early as possible in order to attain a superior position for the attack.'

Generalleutnant Adolf Galland

Pen & Sword
AVIATION

First published in Great Britain in 2023 by
Pen & Sword Military
An imprint of Pen & Sword Books Limited
Yorkshire – Philadelphia

Copyright © Jeremy Dixon 2023

ISBN 978 1 39903 073 1

The right of Jeremy Dixon to be identified as
Author of this Work has been asserted by him in accordance
with the Copyright, Designs and Patents Act 1988.

A CIP catalogue record for this book is
available from the British Library

All rights reserved. No part of this book may be reproduced or
transmitted in any form or by any means, electronic or mechanical
including photocopying, recording or by any information storage and
retrieval system, without permission from the Publisher in writing.

Typeset by Mac Style
Printed in the UK by CPI Group (UK) Ltd, Croydon, CR0 4YY.

Pen & Sword Books Limited incorporates the imprints of After the Battle, Atlas,
Archaeology, Aviation, Discovery, Family History, Fiction, History, Maritime,
Military, Military Classics, Politics, Select, Transport, True Crime, Air World,
Frontline Publishing, Leo Cooper, Remember When, Seaforth Publishing, The
Praetorian Press, Wharncliffe Local History, Wharncliffe Transport, Wharncliffe
True Crime and White Owl.

For a complete list of Pen & Sword titles please contact

PEN & SWORD BOOKS LIMITED
47 Church Street, Barnsley, South Yorkshire, S70 2AS, England
E-mail: enquiries@pen-and-sword.co.uk
Website: www.pen-and-sword.co.uk

or

PEN AND SWORD BOOKS
1950 Lawrence Rd, Havertown, PA 19083, USA
E-mail: Uspen-and-sword@casematepublishers.com
Website: www.penandswordbooks.com

Contents

Acknowledgements vi
Introduction vii

1943 1

1944 64

1945 193

Appendix: Top Aces of the Luftwaffe 234
German Awards and Decorations 237
Bibliography 239
Index 243

Acknowledgements

I would like to thank John Preece for proofreading the book and for offering advice and support once again. I must also thank family and friends for their continued support. I would like to thank my mum and dad, my sister and my nephews together with friends, especially Anne and Alan Taylor, Conal Taylor, Ann Driscoll, Jo Robinson, Paul Budden, Josie Hobson, Bev Drew, Jackie Snowling, Nick Isles, Angela Axton-Green, Hazel Kirby, Elizabeth Ross, Jo Jeffries, Gemma Ross, Tracy Dover, Jo Jeffries, Carol Ryan, Lisa Hunt, Laura Fisher, Alex Curran, Colin Harris, Matt Jackman, Nathan Pearce, David Ross, Paul and Claire Fairbrass, and Debra and Dave Mills.

Some of the photographs in the book are from my own collection and some are from the archive of *Deutsches Wehrkundearchiv*.

Introduction

In 1943, despite the disaster at Stalingrad, Hitler decided to launch another offensive which he hoped would turn the tide of war in Germany's favour by eliminating a large Soviet force – this was Operation Citadel, the Battle of Kursk. In support was the *Luftwaffe*, under *Generalfeldmarschall*s Robert Ritter von Greim and Wolfram von Richthofen. The offensive began on 5 July 1943 and *Luftwaffe* fighter aircraft flew between six and seven sorties per day over Kursk. The Soviet air force lost 1,100 aircraft between 5 and 31 July, while the *Luftwaffe* recorded a loss of 687 aircraft. Although the Soviet air force was losing more aircraft than the Germans, their strength appeared unchanged. By October the *Luftwaffe* had been pushed back toward the Dnieper and by December had just 425 operational fighters on the Eastern Front.

In the west the *Luftwaffe* had maintained its defence of its homeland from US and British bombers. During October, the Americans had lost 120 bombers in two raids on Regensburg and Schweinfurt. The Allies for a time had to direct their bombing missions on targets within the range of their own fighters. Raids deep inside Germany would be suspended until long-range fighters became available.

Then in 1944 the US 8th Air Force, flying from bases in Britain, carried out air raids against the German aviation industry throughout occupied Europe. Its new commander, Major General Jimmy Doolittle, changed an important policy that required escorting US fighters to remain with the bombers at all times. Now escorting fighters such as the P-38, P-47 and the P-51 Mustang would from the spring be flying against the German fighters over Europe, independently. *Luftwaffe* losses began to increase, by February 1944 the losses of twin-engined fighter-bombers increased and more worrying for Hitler was the loss of 17 per cent of his fighter pilots: almost 100 had been killed. The tide had turned, and air superiority had at last passed to the Western Allies.

By May 1944, with long-range fighter support now available to the Allies, the *Luftwaffe*'s defensive efforts had been severely damaged. The *Luftwaffe* fighters had no opportunity to attack unprotected bombers. Although by August German aircraft production reached its peak, equalling Soviet and US output, it was too later to alter the outcome of the air war. On 6 June, D-Day, the Allied invasion of Europe, the *Luftwaffe* was unable to offer any serious opposition the Allied landings in France. Only a handful of operations were successful, the best known being that of two fighter aces, *Oberstleutnant* Josef 'Pips' Priller and his wingman, *Hauptmann* Emil Lang. who scored twenty-nine victories against the Western Allies. During Operation Market Garden in late September 1944, the Allies attempted to end the war by forcing a route through the Netherlands and into Germany. The *Luftwaffe* managed to inflict significant losses on Allied aircraft and supplies, but their own losses were serious, including 192 fighter aircraft.

From mid-December 1944 until the end of January 1945 the *Luftwaffe* under took night bombing and flew fighter protection missions during the Battle of the Bulge. The final major *Luftwaffe* operation of the war took place on 1 January 1945, Operation Bodenplatte, an attack against Allied airfields in the Netherlands and Belgium in a bid to establish air superiority – which failed. The Germans lost 271 Messerschmitt Bf 109 and Focke-Wulf Fw 190 fighters and a further 65 were damaged, and they lost 143 pilots killed, 70 taken prisoner and 21 wounded. Later, General of Fighters *Generalleutnant* Adolf Galland, together with *Oberstleutnant* Johannes Steinhoff, planned a massive attack on the Allies with over 800 fighters, hoping to cause devastating losses to Allied bombers. *Reichsmarschall* Hermann Göring was against the idea and they tried to get Hitler to remove him as Commander-in-Chief of the *Luftwaffe* but all their calls were dismissed and they were sent back to their front-line units.

By February and March 1945 the *Luftwaffe* high command had turned their attention to a new aircraft, the Messerschmitt Me 262 jet fighter. It could outrun any Allied aircraft, and had armament that could effectively destroy Allied bombers with a single burst of fire – but it wasn't produced in

Knight's Cross with Oakleaves, Swords and Diamonds. (*Author's collection*)

Knight's Cross with Oakleaves and Swords. (*Author's collection*)

Knight's Cross with Oakleaves. (*Author's collection*)

Knight's Cross. (*Author's collection*)

sufficient numbers to change the outcome of the air war. The *Luftwaffe* was now fighting over a new front line, Germany itself, and was also very short of fuel. Priority was therefore given to the Me 262, with most of Germany's other aircraft grounded with no fuel. By April the German front in the west had disintegrated and the Red Army in the east had encircled Berlin. The *Luftwaffe* was no more. Hitler committed suicide on 30 April and a few days later Germany surrendered.

The *Luftwaffe* was completely disbanded in 1946. During the Second World War, German pilots had achieved about 70,000 aerial victories, while over 75,000 *Luftwaffe* aircraft were destroyed or severely damaged.

The *Luftwaffe*'s five top aces were:

1. Erich Hartmann   352 victories
2. Gerhard Barkhorn 301
3. Günther Rall   274
4. Otto Kittel   265
5. Walter Nowotny   256

The *Luftwaffe*'s five top jet-fighter aces were:

1. Heinrich Bär   18
2. Rudolf Rademacher 16
   Franz Schall   16
   Kurt Welter   16*
5. Hermann Buchner   12

* Some references state that Welter shot down more than twenty aircraft.

Of the 387 German day fighter pilots of the Second World War, a total of 212 were killed either in action or in accidents.

Knight's Cross with Oakleaves, Swords and Diamonds: two were killed.
Knight's Cross with Oakleaves and Swords: ten were killed.
Knight's Cross with Oakleaves: thirty-eight were killed.

Luftwaffe Score System

Single-engined fighter   1 point
Twin-engined bomber   2 points
Four-engined bomber   3 points

Western Front
Iron Cross 2nd Class = 1 point
Iron Cross 1st Class = 3 points
Goblet of Honour = 10 points
German Cross in Gold = 20 points
Knight's Cross = 40 points
Knight's Cross with Oakleaves = 80 points
Knight's Cross with Oakleaves and Swords = 100–149 points
Knight's Cross with Oakleaves, Swords and Diamonds = 150–175 points

Eastern Front
Iron Cross 2nd Class = 2–3 points
Iron Cross 1st Class = 8 points
Goblet of Honour = 20 points
German Cross in Gold = 30 points
Knight's Cross = 45–50 points
Knight's Cross with Oakleaves = 100–120 points
Knight's Cross with Oakleaves and Swords = 160–200 points
Knight's Cross with Oakleaves, Swords and Diamonds = 250 points

The points system varied throughout the war.

1943

Wilhelm 'Willi' FREUWÖRTH

Oberleutnant

Knight's Cross: Awarded on 5 January 1943 as *Feldwebel* and fighter pilot with the 2nd Squadron of the 52nd Fighter Wing for operations over England and the Soviet Union and for claiming his 46th aerial victory.

(Deutsches Wehrkundearchiv)

Wilhelm Freuwörth claimed forty-eight aerial victories and flew a total of 254 combat missions mainly over the Eastern Front during the Second World War. He was born on 14 November 1917 in Börssum, a district of Wolfenbüttel in Lower Saxony. He joined the *Luftwaffe* in early 1940, and with his training complete he was assigned as a *Gefreiter* and fighter pilot to the 2nd Squadron of the 2nd Fighter Wing in April 1941. He saw brief action over the Channel and claimed his first victory on 26 August, an RAF Blenheim light bomber over north Juist in Lower Saxony, and was awarded the Iron Cross 2nd Class.

In late October his squadron had moved to Ponjatowka in Poland and the following month Freuwörth was promoted to *Unteroffizier*. He claimed two victories later that month and then nothing for a while and then on 9 January 1942 was slightly wounded when his Bf 109F-2 collided with an RAF Lancaster. He was awarded the Iron Cross 1st Class shortly after claiming three more victories during May. By June he was flying the Focke-Wulf Fw 190A-2 and had claimed another two victories that month, and was awarded the *Luftwaffe* Honour Goblet on 6 July. He claimed a total of nine more victories during August, claiming his 20th and 21st victories on 2 September, and claimed two more the following day – by the end of the month he had achieved his 31st victory. He was promoted to *Feldwebel* towards the end of October 1942 and claimed another nine victories that month, giving him a total of forty. On the 24th his Fw 190 was severely damaged by British fighters but he managed to land safely at his home base. On 1 November he claimed four more victories, all Lavochkin LaGG-3 fighters, and he claimed a single victory on 2 and 3 November. Now with a score of forty-six victories in just seven months, Freuwörth was awarded the German Cross in Gold on 17 November.

On 1 February 1943 he transferred to the 5th Squadron of the 26th Fighter Wing, and was now operating over the Western Front, part of the 2nd Group under the command of *Hauptmann* Wilhelm-Ferdinand Galland, the brother of *Generalmajor* Adolf Galland. He claimed an RAF Spitfire over Dungeness on 24 March and the next day he shot down another Spitfire over Dover, his 48th and last victory. Some sources state it wasn't a Spitfire he shot down over Dover but a Typhoon flown by Flight Lieutenant J.R. Baldwin of 609 Squadron, who bailed out unhurt and who was destined to become the highest-scoring Typhoon ace of the war.

Freuwörth was wounded on 24 October when his aircraft was damaged by British fighters and then on 21 December he was attacked by Spitfires over the St. Omer-Arques area of Northern France and this time was seriously wounded. His injuries were so severe that he never returned to combat. Instead he spent the final 12 months or so of the war as a flight instructor following time in hospital and convalescence. He died on 5 December 1970 in Wetzlar, Hesse.

Johannes WIESE

Major

Knight's Cross: Awarded on 5 January 1943 as *Hauptmann* and *Staffelkapitän* of the 2nd Squadron of the 52nd Fighter Wing for operations over the Soviet Union and for claiming his 46th aerial victory. It was presented to him by the Commander-in-Chief of *Luftwaffe* Command Don, *Generalleutnant* Günther Korten, in Rossosh on the Eastern Front.

Knight's Cross with Oakleaves: He became the 418th recipient on 2 March 1944 as *Major* and commander of the 1st Group of the 52nd Fighter Wing and for claiming his 118th aerial victory. He was presented with his award by Hitler at the Berghof on 4 April 1944 together with *Hauptmann* Gerhard Barkhorn, *Leutnant* Erich Hartmann, *Oberleutnant* Walter Krupinski, *Major* Kurt Bühligen, *Hauptmann* Horst Ademeit, *Major* Reinhard Seiler, *Hauptmann* Hans-Joachim Jabs, *Major* Dr Maximilian Otte, *Major* Bernhard Jope, *Major* Hansgeorg Bätcher and anti-aircraft *Oberwachtmeister* Fritz Petersen.

Johannes Wiese is credited with 118 aerial victories from 480 combat missions over the Eastern Front, which included sixty-two Ilyushin Il-2 ground-attack aircraft, with another twenty-seven aircraft listed as unconfirmed victories. Wiese was born on 7 March 1915 in Prussia, in present-day Wrocław in Western Poland, the son of a minister.

He joined the Army in 1934 and was assigned to the 6th Infantry Regiment, under the command of *Oberst* Kuno-Hans von Both. He transferred to the *Luftwaffe* in 1936 as an *Oberfähnrich*, an officer cadet, and trained as an aerial observer. He was commissioned as a *Leutnant* on 1 April 1937, and in September the following year he transferred to the 17th Air Replacement Unit in Quedlinburg and began his training as a fighter pilot. He was assigned to Air Training Regiment 62 under *Oberst* Heinz Funke from April 1939. He attended fighter school and

(Deutsches Wehrkundearchiv)

from 1940 served as a reconnaissance pilot until June 1941 when he transferred to the 52nd Fighter Wing. He was promoted to *Oberleutnant* and served as an adjutant with the 3rd Group in Russia under the command of *Major* Albert Blumensaat. He flew the Bf 109F during combat missions and claimed his first aerial victory, an Ilyushin DB-3 bomber, on 23 September, and four days later was awarded the Iron Cross 2nd Class. Wiese flew more combat missions and was awarded the Flying Clasp for Fighters in Silver on 11 October. He claimed his second victory on 30 March 1942 and two more victories on 19 April, and by the time he had been awarded the Iron Cross 1st Class on 1 May he had achieved seven victories and been promoted to *Hauptmann*.

On 26 June he was appointed *Staffelkapitän* of the 2nd Squadron of the 52nd Fighter Wing and in July he claimed two victories, another being unconfirmed. On 13 July he was awarded the Flying Clasp for Fighters in Gold after claiming another eight victories, and on 3 September he claimed four victories, but only one was ever officially confirmed. He claimed his 20th victory two days later and by the end of September he had claimed his 25th aerial victory, a Lavochkin LaGG-3 fighter over Stalingrad. On 6 November he was awarded the *Luftwaffe* Honour Goblet after claiming his 38th victory, another fighter over Stalingrad. On 5 December he was awarded the German Cross in Gold. He hadn't scored any more victories but had flown a number of dangerous combat missions. On 16 December he claimed five aerial victories to become an 'ace-in-a-day' but post-war investigations have since ruled these victories as unconfirmed. He scored his 40th victory on 21 December, and by the 29th had claimed another six victories. He was awarded the Knight's Cross for operations over the Soviet Union and in recognition of his 46th aerial victory.

Following a lengthy period of leave Wiese returned to combat and claimed two victories on 7 and 9 May before taking over as Acting *Gruppenkommandeur* of the 1st Group of the 52nd Fighter Wing on 11 May. He shot down four aircraft on 26 May which included his 50th aerial victory and continued to score victories during June. On 5 July Wiese shot down twelve aircraft to become a double 'ace-in-a-day', all Il-2 ground-attack aircraft. Shortly after this he was himself shot down over the Kuban Bridgehead and had to make an emergency landing at his airfield. He claimed a further six victories on 7 July, but these have also been proven as unconfirmed. Between 16 and 27 July he claimed another thirteen victories, he had now officially shot down ninety-six Soviet aircraft. During the month of August Wiese did not take part in active service as he was in bed ill.

On 1 October 1943 Wiese was promoted to *Major* and on the 20th he became an 'ace-in-a-day' again when he claimed six victories which included his 100th victory. By the end of the month he had achieved 111 aerial victories and on 13 November was appointed *Gruppenkommandeur* of the 1st Group of the 52nd Fighter Wing in Rostov. Wiese claimed another five victories during January 1944 and claimed his last two on 22 February. He was awarded the Knight's Cross with Oakleaves on 2 March and received the award from Hitler personally. He travelled to Berchtesgaden to Hitler's headquarters at the Berghof by train with eleven others, including Erich Hartmann, Walter Krupinski and Gerhard Barkhorn. On the train they drank cognac and champagne and could hardly stand when they arrived at the Berghof. *Major* Nikolaus von Below, Hitler's *Luftwaffe* adjutant, was shocked and had to sober them up. After some coffee they were still intoxicated and Hartmann took an officer's hat from the hatstand and put it on, but it was too large. Von Below became agitated and told him to take it off and put it back on the stand as it belonged to the *Führer*. They all then received their awards without any more fuss and left.

After a few days' leave Wiese returned to the Front and on 19 May he was severely wounded. Once recovered he was posted to the Training School for Unit Leaders of the General of Fighters at Königsberg, thus ending his service on the Eastern Front. He participated in test flights at the *Luftwaffe*'s main testing ground at Rechlin and was later appointed commander of the school. In November he was posted to the Western Front and took part in 'Defence of the Reich' missions and from 7 November was *Kommodore* of the 77th Fighter Wing, the first jet-fighter wing in the world – replacing *Oberstleutnant* Johannes Steinhoff. On 16 December Germany launched its last major offensive of the war in the Ardennes, which became known as the Battle of the Bulge. It failed to achieve its objectives – to split the British and American line in half so the Germans could encircle and destroy them. On Christmas Day 1944, Wiese was seriously wounded in a training flight and his wingman *Feldwebel* Hansch was killed. Wiese, whose parachute did not open correctly, landed heavily and was taken to hospital with concussion and a fractured skull. He spent the rest of the winter in hospital and was replaced by *Major* Siegfried Freytag.

When Germany surrendered in May 1945 Wiese was handed over to the Soviets by the Americans and spent four years in prison, being released on 28 November 1949. He later joined the *Bundeswehr* and worked for the Military History Research Office. He retired on 10 November 1970, with the rank of *Oberstleutnant* and died on 16 August 1991 in Kirchzarten, a town in Baden-Württemberg in south-western Germany.

Eugen-Ludwig ZWEIGART

Oberleutnant

Knight's Cross: Awarded on 22 January 1943 as *Oberfeldwebel* and pilot attached to the 9th Squadron of the 54th Fighter Wing '*Grünherz*' for operations over England and the Soviet Union and for claiming his 53rd aerial victory.

(Deutsches Wehrkundearchiv)

Eugen-Ludwig Zweigart claimed sixty-two aerial victories during the Second World War of which fifty-two were claimed over the Eastern Front and the remainder, which included ten four-engined bombers, over the Western Front. He was born on 3 May 1914 in Saargemünd, Lothringen, the western part of Alsace-Lorraine and he joined the Army in October 1935 and later transferred into the *Luftwaffe*.

Zweigart trained as a fighter pilot and was assigned to the 9th Squadron of the 54th Fighter Wing as an *Unteroffizier* in October 1940. During this time his squadron was converted to a fighter-bomber unit and flew over southern England, and from late October he flew missions over Holland and the Dutch North Sea coast. On 10 November he claimed his first victory, a Blenheim twin-engined bomber over De Kooy, and was shortly after awarded the Iron Cross 2nd Class. In early December his Group relocated to Dortmund to be refreshed and in early 1941 they moved to Charleville and from 9 February flew from Le Mans in France. In March his Group relocated to Cherbourg and later flew missions over the Channel and from early April Zweigart flew as part of the attack on the Balkans, flying over Yugoslavia. He flew the Messerschmitt Bf 109F-2 during this time, later flying from Bucharest and then from Stolp-Reitz, and during the campaign his Group claimed seven victories, but Zweigart failed to add to his score.

From 22 June he flew as part of the German invasion of the Soviet Union, flying in support of Army Group North, and on that day he claimed his second aerial victory, a Polikarpov I-153 fighter. On 14 July he claimed his fifth victory and on 1 August he was promoted to the rank of *Feldwebel*. By mid-September his Group was flying operations over the Demyansk and Leningrad areas and Zweigart claimed a MiG-1 on 11 September and was awarded the Iron Cross 1st Class shortly afterwards. By mid-December operations had been affected by the extreme weather conditions and because of the lack of flying Zweigart only claimed two more victories before the end of the year.

At the beginning of 1942 his squadron was in Siverskaya, about 45 miles south of Leningrad, then on 20 January it was temporarily relocated to the Demyansk area, returning a week later. On 9 February Zweigart claimed two victories and on 6 March his squadron moved to Jessau where he claimed four victories during April and was promoted to *Oberfeldwebel*. On 13 August he claimed his 20th victory, a P-40 Warhawk, and by the end of the month had claimed six more victories. In September he claimed a total of thirteen victories and claimed his 40th victory on 26 October, and that same day he was awarded the *Luftwaffe* Honour Goblet. He claimed two more victories on 30 October and shot down two P-40s on 7 November, being awarded the German Cross in Gold the same day. In December he was flying from Smolensk and claimed four victories on the 29th, which included his 50th victory, and on 22 January 1943 he was awarded the Knight's Cross.

From early February 1943 his Group was withdrawn from the Soviet Union and relocated to Vendeville in France. From mid-February he served as a fighter instructor on the Western Front, returning later to his old squadron of the 54th Fighter Wing in May and from 23 June he was flying from Deelen in the Netherlands. Here he flew against Allied bombers, flying protection missions over industrial areas and ports. He claimed a B-17 Flying Fortress over south-west Dorfen, Germany on

25 June and a P-51 Mustang on 18 July, his 55th victory. On 27 July he was shot down during combat with RAF Spitfires over Schipol and was forced to bail out but was only slightly wounded.

From 16 October he was flying as part of the 7th Squadron, with the rank of *Leutnant* on 'Defence of the Reich' missions. He claimed another B-17 on 29 November near Cloppenburg and from the beginning of 1944 he was flying from Ludwigslust near the town of Mecklenburg-Vorpommern. In February his Squadron moved to Lüneburg and on the 20th Zweigart claimed two more B-17s, and on 6 March he claimed three more. He claimed another on the 18th near Lahr-Biberach, Germany and from April he was flying with the 8th Squadron. In early May he took over as *Staffelkapitän* of the Squadron and was promoted to *Oberleutnant*, and flew as part of the Staff Squadron attached to the 3rd Group, and claimed a B-24 Liberator on 19 May and another B-17 on the 27th.

On 8 June during aerial combat with P-51 Mustangs he was shot down near La Cambaux, Normandy and although he managed to bail out of his stricken aircraft he was shot whilst hanging from his parachute and killed. He now lies in the German Military Cemetery in St. Desir-de-Lissieux, in Block 1, Row 45, Grave No. 984.

Herbert FRIEBEL

Leutnant

Knight's Cross: Awarded on 24 January 1943 as *Oberfeldwebel* and fighter pilot in the 12th Squadron of the 51st Fighter Wing '*Mölders*' for claiming his 54th aerial victory over the Soviet Union.

(Deutsches Wehrkundearchiv)

Herbert Friebel claimed fifty-seven aerial victories whilst flying combat missions over the Eastern Front during the Second World War. He was born on 28 July 1915 in Berlin and from September 1939 served with the *Luftwaffe* during the Polish campaign as a reconnaissance pilot.

He retrained as a fighter pilot and joined the 10th Squadron of the 51st Fighter Wing in mid-1940, seeing action over France. In June 1941, with the rank of *Feldwebel*, he was assigned to the 12th Squadron and took part in the invasion of the Soviet Union. He claimed his first aerial victory on 28 June, an Ilyushin DB-3 bomber, and claimed another DB-3 the following day. He was awarded the Iron Cross 2nd Class shortly afterwards and by the end of July he had claimed his 10th aerial victory and had been awarded the Iron Cross 1st Class. The month of August was a very successful time for Friebel, and by the 22nd he had achieved twenty victories. He claimed two more victories on the 22nd itself, three on the 27th and two on the 30th. On 2 September he shot down two Il-2 ground-attack aircraft and on the 9th he claimed three victories and was later wounded when his Bf 109F-2 was hit by anti-aircraft fire near Novgorod-Seversky. Whilst recovering, he was awarded the *Luftwaffe* Honour Goblet on 20 October 1941.

He returned to combat with the 51st Fighter Wing in early 1942 and was promoted to *Oberfeldwebel* and continued to fly with the 12th Squadron. He claimed his 35th victory on 4 August and he was awarded the German Cross in Gold on 8 September when he achieved his 40th victory on 8 December. He claimed four victories on 16 December and two more on the 17th, and in mid-December he was commissioned as a *Leutnant*. He shot down another on Christmas Day and claimed two more on the 29th, which included his 50th victory and on 6 January 1943 he shot down three Soviet aircraft. Friebel had now claimed a total of fifty-four victories and on 24 January he was awarded the Knight's Cross.

In early May he was appointed *Staffelführer* of the 10th Squadron of the 51st Fighter Wing and on the 15th he led his first combat mission. During that day he claimed a Yakovlev Yak-9 north-west of Tarnopol, his 57th and last victory. Then later that afternoon he took off again to lead a *Schwarm* of four aircraft against enemy aircraft, and became involved in a dogfight with ten Lavochkin La-5 fighters. At an altitude of almost 3,300ft he tried to follow an enemy aircraft through a diving turn, but it resulted in him hitting the ground behind the front lines south-west of Tarnopol, and his aircraft burst into flames and was totally destroyed. Friebel was killed. The area near Poland where Friebel crashed reveals just how far the 51st Fighter Wing had been forced to retreat on the central sector of the front. The *Luftwaffe* had once stood at the very gates of Moscow and was now fighting along the Polish border.

Friedrich Albert Ragnar RUPP

Oberleutnant

Knight's Cross: Awarded on 24 January 1943 as *Leutnant* and fighter pilot attached to the 7th Squadron of the 54th Fighter Wing for operations over the Soviet Union.

Friedrich Rupp claimed fifty-one aerial victories of which all but one were achieved over the Eastern Front during the Second World War. He was born on 26 November 1917 in Freiburg im Breisgau near the Black Forest. After the completion of his pilots training he was assigned to the 1st Squadron of Reconnaissance Group 31 in September 1939.

Rupp flew reconnaissance flights for the VIII Army Corps during the Polish campaign, flying the Henschel HS 126 two-seater aircraft. He retrained as a fighter pilot from October 1940 and from April 1941 was assigned to the 9th Squadron of the 54th Fighter Wing, flying from its base in Hungary. He took part in the invasion of the Soviet Union as an *Oberfeldwebel* and claimed his first victory on 24 August, a Polikarpov I-16 fighter, whilst flying from his base in Poland.

(Deutsches Wehrkundearchiv)

At the beginning of 1942 he was flying from Siversky near Leningrad in his Bf 109F-2, and on 2 January claimed two more victories and was shortly afterwards awarded the Iron Cross 2nd Class. A few weeks later he was promoted to *Leutnant* and transferred to the 7th Squadron of the 54th Fighter Wing, claiming eleven victories during March, which included four on the 22nd, and he was awarded the Iron Cross 1st Class. He continued to fly in support of ground troops and from 18 February his Squadron was withdrawn from service so they could convert to the Bf 109F-4 in Insterburg. From mid-March his operational area had moved to the Demyansk area and he claimed a P-40 on 21 March, his 10th victory, and claimed another four on the 22nd and two on the 23rd. He claimed his 20th victory on 2 June, another P-40, and was awarded the *Luftwaffe* Honour Goblet on 1 July in recognition of this achievement.

Rupp was briefly appointed *Staffelführer* of the 7th Squadron on 12 August and claimed three more victories that month before he relinquished his command on 2 September. During September his Group moved several times but he continued to score victories, claiming his 30th to 32nd victories on the 11th and two more the following day. He claimed two more before the end of the month and by the end of October he had won the German Cross in Gold and had claimed his 40th aerial victory. He claimed a Yak-1 on 5 November and the following day he made a belly-landing in his Bf 109 after combat with Soviet P-39s, but he wasn't injured. He claimed three more victories during November and claimed an LaGG-3 on 16 December and two on the 29th and three on the 30th. He had now claimed fifty victories and on 24 January 1943 his success was recognised when he was awarded the Knight's Cross.

On 12 February his Group was withdrawn and relocated to France where they were re-equipped with the Bf 109G-4. He remained in France until 25 March when his Group moved to Bad Zwischenahn in Germany to strengthen the air defences over the Reich. He claimed a B-24 Liberator four-engined bomber on 14 May – his only victory over the Western Front. The following day Rupp was shot down and killed during combat with B-17 bombers. His aircraft crashed into the sea near Heligoland, Germany. His body was washed up on the beach at Cuxhaven on 19 June 1943.

Herbert BRÖNNLE

Leutnant

Knight's Cross: Awarded on 14 March 1943 as *Oberfeldwebel* and fighter pilot in the 2nd Squadron of the 54th Fighter Wing for operations over the Soviet Union.

Herbert Brönnle flew 387 combat missions and claimed fifty-eight aerial victories of which fifty-seven were over the Eastern Front and he claimed a B-17 four-engined bomber over the Western Front. He was born on Christmas Day 1920 in Munich-Pasing and applied to join the *Luftwaffe* and learnt to fly in 1939. In September 1940 Brönnle was assigned to the 2nd Squadron of the 54th Fighter Wing in Jever where he continued his training and gained combat experience. On 27 May 1941 he had to make an emergency landing in his Messerschmitt Bf 109F fighter at Wangerooge, an island in the North Sea, due to engine damage and was injured.

(Deutsches Wehrkundearchiv)

In June 1941 his unit was sent east at the start of Operation Barbarossa, the invasion of the Soviet Union. As an *Unteroffizier* he flew his first combat mission on 23 June, claiming a Tupolev SB-2 bomber, then on 6 July he claimed three victories and was awarded the Iron Cross 1st and 2nd Classes. By the end of the month he had claimed eight victories, and on 12 August he claimed his 10th victory. Five days later his Bf 109F-2 was struck by enemy fire and he had to make an emergency landing near Tschertskowad some 12 miles behind enemy lines. Only slightly wounded he walked back to his own lines, evading capture. He was promoted to *Feldwebel* in September and was awarded the *Luftwaffe* Honour Goblet on 7 October after achieving his 20th aerial victory. He was wounded during a dogfight on 17 March 1942 near Pogosstjue by return fire and claimed his 30th victory on 18 April. On 14 May he claimed two Tupolev SB-2 twin-engined bombers and was shortly afterwards attacked by several Soviet fighters over Krasnogvardeysky, near Leningrad, he was severely wounded and was absent from combat duty for several months whilst recovering in hospital and was awarded the German Cross in Gold on 15 June.

Brönnle returned to combat in October and was shortly afterwards promoted to *Oberfeldwebel*. On 12 January 1943 he shot down three Il-2 ground-attack aircraft, and the following day he claimed two more, which included his 40th victory. He claimed his 50th victory on 24 January and was awarded the Knight's Cross on 14 March soon after his 53rd victory. In May he was commissioned as a *Leutnant* and was transferred to the 53rd Fighter Wing and was attached to the 3rd Squadron of the 1st Group, stationed in Catania, Sicily. On 26 May south-west of the island of Gozo, off the coast of Sicily he claimed a B-17 Flying Fortress, his only aerial victory over the Western Front. In June he was transferred to France where he joined the 3rd Squadron of Fighter Replacement Group South as an instructor. On 4 July whilst engaged in aerial combat with RAF Spitfires over Sicily his Bf 109G-6 was struck by several bullets in its engine. Brönnle attempted to return to base but the engine seized and he crashed vertically and was killed north of Lago Lentini. It is thought that he may have been shot down by New Zealand ace Squadron Leader Evan 'Rose' MacKie of RAF 243 Squadron.

Gustav DENK

Oberleutnant

Knight's Cross: Awarded posthumously on 14 March 1943 as *Oberleutnant* and fighter pilot on the Staff of the 2nd Group of the 52nd Fighter Wing for operations over England and the Soviet Union.

Gustav Denk claimed sixty-seven aerial victories and all but one were scored over the Eastern Front, flying a total of almost 500 combat missions during the Second World War. He was born on 24 January 1915 in Soest in Westfalen, Germany, serving with the 52nd Fighter Wing at the outbreak of war. He saw action during the Polish campaign and took part as an *Oberfeldwebel* in the invasion of France. He served with the 6th Squadron and claimed an RAF Blenheim over north-west Borkum on 13 July 1940, his first and only victory over the Western Front. He claimed another Blenheim on 1 May 1941 but this remains an unconfirmed victory. Even so, he was awarded the Iron Cross 2nd Class.

(Deutsches Wehrkundearchiv)

In mid-1941 Denk was commissioned as a *Leutnant* and saw action over the Soviet Union, claiming his first victory on the Eastern Front on 25 August, shooting down a MiG-1 fighter. By May 1942 he was still serving with the 52nd Fighter Wing but was attached to the Staff Squadron of the 2nd Group, under the command of *Hauptmann* Johannes Steinhoff. By this time Denk had claimed a total of six victories and had been awarded the Iron Cross 1st Class. He claimed three victories during August, and claimed three more on 9 September, claiming his 20th victory on the 25th near Tuapse. After claiming his 21st victory Denk was awarded the *Luftwaffe* Honour Goblet on 23 October. He claimed a total of twelve victories during November and claimed another fifteen in December, which included his 50th victory. As a result of his success he was awarded the German Cross in Gold on 23 December.

Denk was promoted to *Oberleutnant* and appointed *Staffelführer* of the 5th Squadron of the 52nd Fighter Wing in January 1943. He claimed four victories in January and two on 2 February, a single victory on the 7th and two more, which included his 60th, four days later. On 12 February he transferred to the 6th Squadron, and on that day he claimed five victories to become an 'ace-in-a-day'. He claimed a Boston bomber on the 13th, and that same day during an attack on a Soviet airfield at Tschernigow he destroyed two aircraft on the ground. However, just as his Bf 109G-2 was turning it was struck by anti-aircraft fire and exploded, killing Denk instantly. He was posthumously awarded the Knight's Cross on 14 March 1943. He is currently buried in Prikubansky a rural area of Takhtamukaysky in Russia.

Günter FINK

Hauptmann

Knight's Cross: Awarded as *Oberleutnant* and fighter pilot in the 8th Squadron of the 54th Fighter Wing on 14 March 1943 after claiming his 48th aerial victory over the Soviet Union.

(Deutsches Wehrkundearchiv)

Günter Fink had a relatively short career as a fighter pilot. In just over two years he claimed forty-eight victories, all on the Eastern Front, before he was reported as missing. He was born on 17 March 1918 in Spandau, Berlin, joined the *Luftwaffe* in 1939 and trained as a fighter pilot. He was initially attached to the 1st Group of the 77th Fighter Wing and flew over southern Germany and later briefly during the Polish campaign.

In late 1940 *Leutnant* Fink transferred to the 3rd Group of the 54th Fighter Wing with its base in Döberitz, but saw little action. During April 1941 he flew escort missions for Stuka dive-bombers during the Balkan campaign, and in May he flew similar missions over Crete. Promoted to *Oberleutnant* in June he saw action during the opening phase of Operation Barbarossa, the invasion of the Soviet Union, and claimed two victories on 5 July. He then briefly served with the Supplementary Squadron of the 54th Fighter Wing, claimed his third victory on 20 August and shortly afterwards was awarded the Iron Cross 2nd Class.

In early 1942 he returned to the 3rd Group where he stayed until the end of April, claiming another three victories. In May he transferred to the 8th Squadron where he was appointed Acting *Staffelkapitän* until August when the position was confirmed. He claimed two victories over the Baltic Sea on 7 and 8 June, and claimed another four on the 10th, during this time he was awarded the Iron Cross 1st Class. By the end of June he had achieved nineteen victories, and was awarded the *Luftwaffe* Honour Goblet in early August, and by the end of the month he had achieved his 26th victory. He continued to fly combat missions over the Baltic Sea, and claimed three victories on 2 September and claimed his 30th nine days later. In recognition of this and missions flown he was awarded the German Cross in Gold on 27 October and by 30 December had claimed his 35th victory.

On 1 January 1943 his Squadron moved to Smolensk and he claimed three victories on 5 January over Velikiye-Luki south-west of the Baltic Sea and four the next day, which included his 40th victory. On 17 January he claimed his 48th and last victory. Later that day, during an intercept mission against US bombers over the North Sea in the area around Helgoland his Bf 109G-4 fighter disappeared. Fink was officially listed as missing in action on 1 August 1944 and his body has never been recovered.

Herbert KAISER

Leutnant

Knight's Cross: Awarded on 14 March 1943 as *Oberfeldwebel* and fighter pilot with the 9th Squadron of the 77th Fighter Wing for operations over Poland, France, the Balkans, Crete, the Soviet Union and North Africa. It was presented to Kaiser on 14 March 1943 by the commander of Supplementary Fighter Group South, *Oberstleutnant* Alfred Müller.

Herbert Kaiser claimed at least fifty aerial victories of which thirty-nine were achieved over the Eastern Front during the Second World War. He was born on 16 March 1916 in Jessen, Herzburg in Saxony and flew on virtually every front in 1,200 missions with his operational career beginning in 1938, when he served with the 132nd Fighter Wing under a very young *Staffelkapitän* called Johannes Steinhoff.

From October 1938 he flew with the 2nd Group of Fighter Training Group 186 and saw action over Poland as an *Unteroffizier* and later during the Battle of France. On 5 May he claimed his first victory, a Blenheim over Tschelling, and his second was a Fokker DXXI, shot down on 10 May and shortly afterwards he was awarded the Iron Cross 2nd Class. From July his unit became the 8th Squadron of the 77th Fighter Wing and he took part, briefly, in the Battle of Britain before being transferred to the Balkans and claimed a Hurricane over Greece on 16 May 1941 and from June he took part in the invasion of the Soviet Union. Now an *Oberfeldwebel* he claimed seven victories during July, which included four on the 7th, and his 11th victory. He was awarded the Iron Cross 1st Class on 9 August and he claimed his 20th victory on 19 October.

(Deutsches Wehrkundearchiv)

At the beginning of 1942 he flew his Bf 109F-4 over the Crimea, where he flew missions over Sevastopol but mainly over the eastern part of the Peninsula. He claimed his 25th victory on 5 January, a DB-3 long-range bomber, and on 20 March his Group was relocated to Germany for a rest. He was awarded the German Cross in Gold on 30 March after achieving twenty-eight victories and Kaiser returned with his Group to the Soviet Union in May and flew from Kharkov and claimed two victories on 12 May, which included his 30th victory. Towards the end of June he transferred to the 9th Squadron and had claimed his 35th victory on 6 July, and he claimed his 40th victory on 23 July.

In October his Group moved to North Africa where on the 27th he was listed as missing when he was shot down during combat with RAF Kittyhawks. He managed to make a belly-landing at Mersa Matruh, Egypt and soon returned to his unit. He claimed two victories in November, both P-40s, and in late January 1943 he was posted as an instructor with Fighter Group South. He was awarded the Knight's Cross in March in recognition of his 44th victory, and Kaiser returned to the 3rd Group of the 77th Fighter Wing in June, where he flew over Sicily and then moved to Italy with the 3rd Squadron. On 10 July, the day the Allies landed in Sicily, his Group was non-operational due to the lack of useable aircraft and because of air raids by the 17th they had moved operational bases three times. During this time most pilots became ill with malaria and stomach problems and very few missions were flown, so in August the Group moved again and were deployed across the Strait of Messina. Kaiser saw action during the Allied landing near Salerno but by September his Group had been withdrawn and transferred to Cecina where they flew protection missions over Corsica. From early October he flew missions over Volturno in support of the 10th Army and by the end of November the Group had moved and relocated to northern Italy.

In January 1944 he transferred to the 7th Squadron of the 1st Fighter Wing and flew 'Defence of the Reich' missions but was rushed to Normandy in June following the D-Day landings. Despite being considered a combat veteran by his fellow pilots, Kaiser later recalled that the fighting on the invasion front was some of the toughest he had experienced. He later claimed a Spitfire on 12 July and a Typhoon the next day, his 50th aerial victory – some sources state he claimed many more victories but there are records missing. On one occasion he was leading four Bf 109G-6s on a mission to intercept a formation of Allied bombers in the Normandy area. They flew as low as they could, hedge-hoping, taking advantage of natural camouflage whilst flying a few feet above the ground. His formation spotted the bombers and began to climb when they were attacked by a formation of Norwegian-flown Spitfires of 331 Squadron and three of the four aircraft were shot down. Kaiser was also attacked and was seriously wounded and opened his canopy of his burning fighter and bailed out, but his right leg became entangled in his parachute and he collided with his rudder. He landed behind German lines with multiple fractures to his right thigh and was hospitalized until February 1945.

He joined Adolf Galland's *Jagdverband* 44 flying the Me 262 but there is no record of Kaiser claiming a victory whilst flying this jet fighter. He survived the war and died in Felde near Kiel on 5 December 2003.

Günther RÜBELL

Hauptmann

Knight's Cross: Awarded on 14 March 1943 as *Leutnant* and fighter pilot with the 2nd Group of the 51st Fighter Wing '*Mölders*' for operations over the Soviet Union and North Africa.

Gunther Rübell claimed at least forty-seven aerial victories during the Second World War of which forty-one were achieved over the Eastern Front. He was born on 4 May 1921 in Traden-Trarbach, Berkastel-Cues in the district of Rhineland-Palatinate in Germany and joined the *Luftwaffe* in 1940.

On completion of his training in January 1941, *Leutnant* Rübell was assigned to the 6th Squadron of the 51st Fighter Wing and was attached to the 2nd Group. He flew the Bf 109F and from February flew coastal protection missions just west of Dunkirk. On 25 February he crashed at Mardyck after being shot down by a Spitfire of 611 Squadron and was slightly injured, and on 30 March he crash-landed again at Mardyck, although not due to combat damage, but wasn't hurt.

(Deutsches Wehrkundearchiv)

From early June he flew from Dortmund and from 22nd moved to Siedlce in Poland and took part in the invasion of the Soviet Union. He flew on fighter protection missions during the bombing of Soviet airfields and on 24 June he claimed his first victory, a SB-2 twin-engined bomber, and followed this with his second the next day. In early July his Group moved to Bobruisk and on the 3rd he claimed two victories, both Pe-2 twin-engined dive-bombers. His Squadron moved a number of times during July and August and by the end of August Rübell had claimed six victories and had been awarded the Iron Cross 2nd Class. On 10 September his Squadron moved again to Novgorod-Seversky and from 1 October flew ground support missions for the army on its march to Moscow. By the end of October Rübell had achieved a total of fourteen victories and had been awarded the Iron Cross 1st Class.

From early 1942 his Group was in Bryansk, equipped with the Bf 109F-2, and Rübell flew in support of the 4th Army and the 2nd Panzer Army south-west of Moscow. He claimed three victories during January and three during February which included his 20th victory and by the end of March he had claimed his 31st aerial victory. From mid-April operations came to an end due to mud. The fighters could not take off and spent the next few weeks grounded. By May the mud had cleared and he claimed two more victories and on the 22nd he was awarded the German Cross in Gold in recognition of his 25th victory. During early August his Group flew in support of another Squadron in the Rzhev area and by the end of the month he had achieved his 40th victory, an Il-2 ground-attack aircraft over Belyov. In October his Group was withdrawn from the front and moved to Jesau to be rested and re-equipped and converted to the Fw 190A, but by early November the order was given for them to convert back to the Messerschmitt Bf 109G-1 and they were moved to the Mediterranean. By 14 November his Squadron had reached Sidi Ahmed near Bizerte in Tunisia and on the 27th Rübell claimed a Spitfire, and the Group moved to Tunis in late November where it remained. Before the end of the year Rübell claimed two P-38 Lightnings on 2 and 4 December, his 43rd and 44th victories.

On 3 February 1943 Rübell was promoted to *Oberleutnant* and appointed *Staffelkapitän* of the 5th Squadron of the 51st Fighter Wing, still operating over Tunisia. On 14 March he was awarded the Knight's Cross in recognition of claiming forty-five victories. He claimed a P-40 on 20 March and two days later he claimed a B-25 Mitchell twin-engined bomber north of Medenine. His Squadron later saw action during the Allied landings in Sicily in July and his Group was evacuated soon after the Allied advance and by early August he had moved to Munich. His Group flew support missions during the German withdrawal of Italy in 1944 and later moved to Bulgaria.

In August 1944 Rübell was promoted to *Hauptmann* and appointed *Gruppenkommandeur* of the 1st Group of the 104th Fighter Wing and flew over Germany during the last months of the war. Captured by the Western Allies in late April 1945 and released later that year, he had flown approximately 820 combat missions during the war and had been shot down five times. A few years later he moved to Vancouver in British Columbia where he died on 1 November 1985.

Bruno STOLLE

Hauptmann

Knight's Cross: Awarded on 17 March 1943 as *Hauptmann* and *Staffelkapitän* of the 8th Squadron of the 2nd Fighter Wing '*Richthofen*' for operations over France and England.

Bruno Stolle claimed twenty-eight aerial victories, including three four-engined bombers, all whilst flying combat missions over the Western Front during the Second World War. He was born in Münster in North Rhine-Westphalia on 13 April 1915, joining the *Luftwaffe* in 1935.

In November 1936, on completion of his training *Leutnant* Stolle was assigned to the 1st Group of the 1st Training Wing. From September 1939 he flew with the 3rd Squadron of the 51st Fighter Wing stationed in Speyer in Bavaria, but by early March 1940 Stolle, now an *Oberleutnant*, had been transferred to the 8th Squadron of the 2nd Fighter Wing in Frankfurt-Rebstock. From May, at the time of the invasion of France, his squadron was relocated to Bastogne in

(*Author's collection*)

Belgium, and on the 21st his *Gruppenkommandeur Major* Dr Erich Mix was shot down and taken prisoner but later returned unharmed. From 5 June Stolle flew in support of the 6th and 9th Armies on the Somme and on the 21st his Group was withdrawn to be refreshed.

From August 1940 he took part in the Battle of Britain and claimed his first two victories of the war on the 11th, both Spitfires over Portland, Dorset. Shortly afterwards he was awarded the Iron Cross 2nd Class and later flew over London protecting bombers and he claimed his third victory about 15 miles south-west of the Isle of Wight on 26 September. On 20 October his Group transferred to Mont de Marsan in south-western France from where he flew escort missions protecting Hitler's command train.

At the beginning of 1941 his Group was in Bernay, Northern France, flying the Bf 109E-1 and E-4. In April they were converted to the Bf 109F and he resumed operations, flying surveillance missions over the French coastal area. Stolle then from July flew from St. Pol Brais, in the Pas-de-Calais area where he claimed a Spitfire on the 2nd and claimed another on 23 July. During the summer he flew defensive missions against British bombers, and claimed two Spitfires on 14 and 16 August and was awarded the Iron Cross 1st Class. He was appointed *Staffelkapitän* of his Squadron on 7 September and five days later he was awarded the *Luftwaffe* Honour Goblet and claimed his 10th victory, another Spitfire, on 17 September. From November he flew protection missions over the Normandy area and by the end of the year he had claimed fourteen victories.

At the beginning of 1942 he flew missions over Cherbourg and in February his Group relocated to Koksijde in Belgium on the North Sea coast. It was at this time that his Group made ready for the Channel breakout of the warships *Scharnhorst*, *Gneisenau* and *Prinz Eugen*. From April he led his Squadron in protection missions over the port of Brest and from May his Squadron had been converted to Focke-Wulf Fw 190s. On 19 August his Group was used to repel the Allied landings at Dieppe and then he flew from Brest and was used to repel British submarines off Lorient and St. Nazaire. He claimed his 15th victory on 21 September, an Armstrong Whitworth Whitley twin-engined medium bomber. He was awarded the German Cross in Gold on 29 October and had by this time claimed a total of seventeen victories, which had included a B-17 Flying Fortress claimed on the 21st, and by the end of the year Stolle had claimed a total of twenty-four victories.

In early January 1943 he was promoted to *Hauptmann* and on 1 July was appointed *Gruppenkommandeur* of the 1st Group of the 11th Fighter Wing. From June he flew protection missions over the U-boat bases in the Atlantic ports and he had by this time claimed twenty-eight victories and on 17 March Stolle had been awarded the Knight's Cross. In 1944 he flew from Cormeilles-en-Verxi, northern France and on 26 July his Group was withdrawn to Mönchengladbach to be refreshed.

From August he flew with the Operational Test Command 152 (*Erprobungskommando* 152) at Rechlin where he helped to develop the new Focke-Wulf Ta 152. It was a high-altitude fighter-interceptor and entered service with the *Luftwaffe* in January 1945. However, it was produced far too late in the war to make any difference and not in sufficient numbers to have a significant role in the war. It was among the fastest piston-engined fighters of the war, with a top speed of almost 470 mph, but by February all production of this new aircraft had ceased.

After the war Stolle had a number of jobs and in 1956 he joined the *Bundesluftwaffe* and retired on 31 March 1972 with the rank of *Oberstleutnant*. He died on 22 January 2004 in Rheinbach, a town in the Rhein-Sieg district of North Rhine-Westphalia.

Heinz SCHUMANN

Oberleutnant der Reserve

Knight's Cross: Awarded as *Hauptmann* and *Staffelkapitän* of the 10th Squadron of the 2nd Fighter Wing '*Richthofen*' on 18 March 1943 for operations over England and the Soviet Union.

Heinz Schumann claimed at least thirteen aerial victories during the Second World War with the majority claimed over the Eastern Front. He was born on 29 November 1914 in Leipzig, Germany and saw action during the Spanish Civil War where he won the Spanish Cross in Gold with Swords on 14 April 1939, but failed to score any victories.

On 15 July 1939 *Oberleutnant* Schumann was appointed as *Staffelkapitän* of the 1st Squadron of the 71st Fighter Wing in Schlessheim and from 1 September it was redesignated the 4th Squadron of the 52nd Fighter Wing. His squadron was attached to the 2nd Group and flew from Böblingen, equipped with the Bf 109E-1 and E-3 fighters. At the beginning of 1940 he flew missions over Germany

(Deutsches Wehrkundearchiv)

and from February his unit moved to the French border, and during the Western campaign in May he flew combat missions over the Rhine area and later over Metz. On 14 May Schumann claimed his first victory, an RAF Fairey Battle light bomber near Sedan, and he later flew missions over the Rhine area and was awarded the Iron Cross 2nd Class. Towards the end of May his Group transferred to Luxembourg where he saw very little action and from June his Group flew from its base in northern France in support of Army Group A, and from August flew missions over the Channel against British aircraft. Schumann transferred to the Staff Squadron of the 52nd Fighter Wing in late August, and from mid-November he transferred as *Staffelkapitän* to the 1st Group of the 51st Fighter Wing. In early 1941 his Group was relocated to Mannheim and converted to the Bf 109F-1. In February it moved again, this time to Abbeville to take over coastal protection duties, and on 15 May 1941 Schumann claimed his second victory, a Spitfire near Folkestone. From June his Group flew from Stara Wieś in Poland and prepared for the invasion of the Soviet Union.

On 22 June, the first day of the invasion, he flew fighter-bomber missions from his base in Poland and later flew missions against airfields near the Soviet border. From late June he was flying over the Minsk area and claimed at least five victories, which included three on 25 June – shortly afterwards he was awarded the Iron Cross 1st Class. On 2 July his Group moved to Bobruisk where Schumann claimed two victories that day. He claimed another five victories that month, which included three on the 24th but exact figures are unknown. He was awarded the *Luftwaffe* Honour Goblet on 15 September and was now flying missions north of Smolensk. In October his group flew fighter-bomber missions in support of the army in its attack on Moscow. Schumann continued to fly missions over the Soviet Union and on 22 January 1942 he was awarded the German Cross in Gold.

He transferred to the 2nd Fighter Wing in late 1942 and in January 1943 was appointed *Staffelkapitän* of the 10th Squadron. On 20 January his unit was based in France and he took part in a bombing mission over England in his Focke-Wulf Fw 190A-4 with a 1,100lb bomb attached to his aircraft. Once over England he dropped his bomb on a school on Sandhurst Road in Catford, south-east London, killing thirty-eight children and six staff, and injuring another sixty. Many of the children were buried for hours under the rubble. It has been debated whether Schumann deliberately targeted the school or simply attacked what looked like a large factory – the school was several storeys high. At that same time a block of flats was also targeted and destroyed. A later report stated that the RAF had bombed Berlin three days previously so was this raid by the *Luftwaffe* in retaliation? A few weeks later he flew fighter protection missions over the Atlantic ports and U-boat bases, and on 18 March he was awarded the Knight's Cross in recognition of his success as a fighter and fighter-bomber pilot. From May his command was redesignated 2nd Group of the 10th Ground-Attack Wing (*Schnellkampfgeschwader*) and operated over France. A few weeks later he was promoted to *Hauptmann* and transferred to the 4th Group flying fighter-bomber missions over France and Italy.

On 16 July 1943 he was appointed *Kommodore* of the 10th Ground-attack Wing, flying over Italy. In early August he was promoted to *Major* and in October his command was redesignated the 10th Battle Wing or *Schlachtgeschwader* 10, and flew over France and Luxembourg. On 8 November Schumann was killed when his Fw 190G-3 was shot down by RAF Spitfires over a region of Paris. Some accounts state that he died in a crash that was accidental, stating it was in thick fog whilst flying back from a conference in Berlin. He was officially credited with fourteen aerial victories, although some records state it could have been more than twenty! He is buried today in Champigny German War Cemetery in Block 6, Row 9, Grave No. 787.

Wolfgang BÖWING-TREUDING

Oberleutnant

Knight's Cross: Awarded posthumously on 24 March 1943 as *Oberleutnant* and *Staffelkapitän* of the 10th Squadron of the 51st Fighter Wing '*Mölders*' in recognition of claiming his 46th aerial victory during operations over the Soviet Union.

Wolfgang Böwing-Treuding claimed forty-six aerial victories, all whilst flying combat missions over the Eastern Front during the Second World War. His victory score included fifteen Ilyushin Il-2 ground-attack aircraft and fourteen Petlyakov Pe-2 dive-bombers.

He was born on 28 January 1922 in Hamburg and joined the *Luftwaffe* in early 1941. As a *Leutnant* he was assigned to the 8th Squadron of the 51st Fighter Wing from July, based in Orsha in Belarus where he scored his first victory on 13 July, an Ilyushin DB-3 long-range bomber. He scored his second victory on 29 July and shortly after was transferred to the 12th Squadron and four weeks later scored his third victory and was soon awarded the Iron Cross 2nd Class. By the end of December he had scored eleven victories and had been awarded the Iron Cross 1st Class.

(Deutsches Wehrkundearchiv)

In January 1942 he scored two victories and by the end of July had scored nineteen and was transferred to the Staff Squadron of the 4th Group, still with the 51st Fighter Wing. He claimed his 20th victory on 1 August, and shot down two Petlyakov Pe-2 twin-engined dive-bombers the following day. His 25th victory came on 9 August and the day after that he was appointed *Staffelkapitän* of the 11th Squadron, and on 13 September he was awarded the *Luftwaffe* Honour Goblet in recognition of his 30th victory and on 15 October was awarded the German Cross in Gold. He claimed three Il-2 ground-attack aircraft on 30 October, including his 36th victory, and he shot down two more aircraft on 17 December. The next day he was confirmed as *Staffelkapitän* of the 10th Squadron based in Vitebsk, Soviet Union. On 6 January he claimed four victories, which included three Pe-2 dive-bombers and he also shot down a Lavochkin La-5 fighter the next day. He claimed his 46th, and what would be his last victory on 3 February, another Pe-2 west-north-west of Jelnja. On the 11th Böwing-Treuding took part in a ground-attack mission on Soviet motor vehicles north-west of Velikiye Luki, when his Fw 190A-4 was shot down by anti-aircraft fire and he was killed. He was posthumously promoted to *Oberleutnant* and awarded the Knight's Cross on 24 March 1943.

Walter BRANDT

Oberleutnant

Knight's Cross: Awarded on 24 March 1943 as *Oberfeldwebel* and fighter pilot in the 2nd Squadron of the 77th Fighter Wing for operations over England, Malta, the Soviet Union and North Africa.

Walter Brandt was credited with forty-two aerial victories and flew 527 combat missions over the Eastern Front during the Second World War. He was born on 24 March 1917 in Bad Salzuflen, a spa resort in the Lippe district of North Rhine-Westphalia. At the outbreak of the Second World War Brandt was serving in the 2nd Fighter Squadron of the 2nd Training Wing. He claimed his first aerial victory on 13 March 1941, when he shot down an RAF Spitfire north of Cap Gris Nez in the Pas-de-Calais area of France. In June his unit transferred to Russia where he claimed his second victory, a SB-2 twin-engined bomber. He was awarded the Iron Cross 2nd Class after claiming his third victory on 16 October and after shooting down his sixth victory in November Brandt was awarded the Iron Cross 1st Class. In January 1942 his unit was renamed the 2nd Squadron of the 77th Fighter Wing and he was promoted to *Feldwebel* in May and by the end of June had claimed twenty victories, and had flown a total of 100 ground-attack missions.

In July his unit moved to the Mediterranean, flying out of Comiso in Sicily and claiming four Spitfires over Malta that month. He was awarded the *Luftwaffe* Honour Goblet on 5 September in recognition of his 25th victory and by the end of October Brandt had claimed his 30th victory, ten of which were Spitfires. Promoted to *Oberfeldwebel* in December he claimed another Spitfire and three Curtiss P-40s, being awarded the German Cross in Gold on 18 December after achieving his 34th victory. On 14 January 1943, having claimed another P-40, his 37th victory, Brandt was seriously wounded by return fire. He managed to land his aircraft and was immediately taken to hospital where he underwent surgery and would later lose a leg. Whilst recovering in hospital news came through that he had been awarded the Knight's Cross and it was presented to him a few days later.

(Deutsches Wehrkundearchiv)

He returned to active duty in August 1944, complete with an artificial leg, having been appointed *Staffelführer* of 2nd Squadron of the 3rd Fighter Wing, operating out of Paderborn airfield in North Rhine-Westphalia. On 26 November, his squadron was ordered to take off. It was a very hazy afternoon and radio contact with the ground had been lost. During these conditions the *Gruppenkommandeur*, *Hauptmann* Horst Haace collided with his wingman, *Leutnant* Hans Fritz. Both aircraft crashed and both pilots were killed. Brandt assumed command and decided to abandon the mission and led the remaining aircraft back to Paderborn. However, he was later charged with cowardice and was arrested. He explained that he had no contact with the enemy and could not reach ground control because the radios weren't working and saw little point flying 'blind' looking for an enemy that might not be there anyway. His explanation was believed and all charges were dropped.

Brandt was charged with cowardice after his *Gruppenkommandeur* was killed in an accident when he collided with his wingman. Brandt took over command and felt it was better to return to base. It was later found that he had no way of making contact with ground control because of faulty radios, and all charges against him were dropped. (Deutsches Wehrkundearchiv)

The following month he was promoted to *Leutnant* and led a successful mission against a formation of RAF Lancaster bombers making a daylight raid on Essen and claiming one of the bombers himself. He suffered injuries during an accident when his Bf 109G overturned during take-off on 25 December. His injuries were serious enough to require hospital treatment and kept him from taking part in Operation Bodenplatte – the aerial attack on Allied airfields in Holland, Belgium and France on 1 January 1945. On the 22nd his unit was relocated to Stettin-Altdamn for operations on the Eastern Front. His mission was to fly low-level attacks in support of the army in the Bromberg-Posen area. Additionally he flew escort missions for Fw 190 ground-attack and Ju 87 bomber missions, and in February his unit was moved again to Pinnau near Kolberg. On 3 March Brandt shot down three Soviet aircraft, destroyed three tanks and twenty trucks on the ground. He was then forced to make a belly-landing with his Bf 109 at Augustwalde following combat with Il-2 ground-attack aircraft and was again wounded. On 22 March he took over as *Staffelkapitän* of the 7th Squadron of the 3rd Fighter Wing, a post he held until the end of the war. Brandt died on 28 January 1977 in Bottrop on the Rhine-Herne Canal in North Rhine-Westphalia from complications of his many wartime wounds and injuries.

Willi 'Altvater' NEMITZ

Leutnant

Knight's Cross: Awarded on 24 March 1943 as *Oberfeldwebel* and fighter pilot attached to 5th Squadron of the 52nd Fighter Wing for operations over the Soviet Union.

Willi Nemitz claimed a total of eighty-two aerial victories during the Second World War, all achieved whilst flying combat missions over the Eastern Front. He was born on 1 November 1910 in Greifenhaegn in Pommern and flew with the 4th Squadron of the 52nd Fighter Wing during the Battle of Britain in 1940.

From June 1941 *Unteroffizier* Nemitz saw action with the 5th Squadron during the beginning of Operation Barbarossa, the invasion of the Soviet Union. On 3 July he claimed his first two victories, both Ilyushin DB-3 bombers, whilst flying missions over Vitebsk and Polotsk in Belarus. He claimed his third victory on 23 July, a Pe-2 dive-bomber, and on the 26th he claimed two more victories and a day later

(Deutsches Wehrkundearchiv)

he claimed his sixth victory and was awarded the Iron Cross 2nd Class. From August he flew combat missions over Leningrad and claimed two victories that month and claimed another two in September, all over the same area, being awarded the Iron Cross 1st Class at the end of the month. By 2 October his Group had moved south to Staba near Smolensk and later moved to Vyazma near Smolensk and on 14 November he claimed two MiG-1 fighters but with the start of the Soviet winter offensive in December his group was hampered by persistent bad weather. By 14 December his Group moved to Dugino and could not operate due to the weather and handed over their Bf 109s to another Group.

On 20 January 1942 his Group was re-equipped and refreshed but didn't fly combat missions until May when on the 11th *Feldwebel* Nemitz claimed a Polikarpov R-5 light reconnaissance aircraft. On 26 May he claimed his 15th victory and by 24 June he had claimed twenty victories. In early July his group moved to Sswoy south of Kursk in support of the 6th Army and continued to see action during the German summer offensive, and by the end of July he had claimed his 27th victory. During August he flew combat missions over Stalingrad and by the end of the month he had claimed seven more aerial victories and on 7 September he was awarded the *Luftwaffe* Honour Goblet. He now flew missions in support of the 1st Panzer Army, flying as far out as the Caucasus, and was awarded the German Cross in Gold on 27 October. He was promoted to *Oberfeldwebel* at this time and flew in support of the 6th Army at Stalingrad, claiming his 40th victory on 28 November. In December his Group had moved to Kotelnikovo from where he flew missions in support of the LVII Panzer Corps attack on Stalingrad. He achieved his 50th aerial victory on 18 December and by the end of the month had claimed a total of fifty-four victories.

At the beginning of 1943 his Group flew from Gigant in the Rostov district and was now equipped with the Bf 109G fighter. He claimed two victories on 22 January, both Il-2 ground-attack aircraft, and he claimed his 60th victory on 5 February. Towards the end of February he was appointed *Staffelkapitän* of the 6th Squadron of the 52nd Fighter Wing and claimed his 70th victory on 14 March. He claimed another victory two days later and on the 17th he claimed three Il-2s, and the following day he claimed three Lavochkin LaGG-3 fighters.

On 24 March Nemitz was awarded the Knight's Cross and by the end of the month he had claimed eighty-one victories. On 9 April he claimed his 82nd victory, but it was to be his last. Two days later he was shot down by Soviet fighters near Nishe-Bakinskaja. Apparently two infantrymen reported seeing a single Bf 109 dive out of the clouds and head straight for the ground without making any attempt to level out. They didn't see the pilot parachute out and the aircraft buried itself about 12ft into the ground. The pilot's identity was established when a recovery team discovered a photo and his Knight's Cross. Nemitz flew over 500 combat missions and was posthumously promoted to *Leutnant*, and is today buried in Anapa, Russia, his body having not yet been moved to a military cemetery.

Kurt EBENER

Oberleutnant

Knight's Cross: Awarded on 7 April 1943 as *Feldwebel* and fighter pilot in the 4th Squadron of the 3rd Fighter Wing '*Udet*' for operations over the Soviet Union and for claiming his 51st aerial victory.

Kurt Ebener flew 159 combat missions and claimed a total of fifty-one aerial victories over the Eastern Front during the Second World War. He was born on 4 May 1920 in Könitz in the Saalfeld region of Thüringen, and he joined the *Luftwaffe* on 17 November 1939. On completion of his training he was posted to the 3rd Fighter Wing in December 1941 with the rank of *Unteroffizier*.

(Deutsches Wehrkundearchiv)

He was attached to the 4th Squadron in Wiesbaden-Erbenheim, Germany, part of the 2nd Group, and from early 1942 he flew missions over Malta and North Africa before being relocated to the Eastern Front. He claimed his first two victories on 23 May, both MiG-3 fighters, then four days later he claimed his third victory, a MiG-1. By July his Group had moved into Russia itself and was flying from Millerowo and Ebener had been awarded the Iron Cross 2nd Class. He claimed seven victories during July, which included his 10th, and was awarded the Iron Cross 1st Class. Promoted to *Feldwebel* towards the end of the year from mid-December until mid-January he flew missions over the Stalingrad area. He claimed two victories on 3 and 17 December and a single victory on the 18th, an Ilyushin Il-2 ground-attack aircraft. Two days later he became an 'ace-in-a-day' when he shot down five aircraft, and claimed a further two on Christmas Day and another four on the 30th to score his 36th victory. He claimed a further fifteen victories during January, which included two on the 7th, four on the 10th, three on the 12th and four on the 15th. He emerged as the leading German fighter pilot over the Stalingrad area, claiming thirty-one victories at this time and with a total of fifty-one victories since May 1942.

On 1 March 1943 he was transferred to the Supplementary Fighter Group East where he carried out instructional duties teaching his skills with new and young fighter pilots. On 15 March he was awarded the *Luftwaffe* Honour Goblet and just three days later was awarded the German Cross in Gold for his outstanding achievements over Stalingrad. Awarded the Knight's Cross on 7 April he was shortly afterwards promoted to *Leutnant*. On 31 March 1944 he was transferred to the 5th Squadron of the 11th Fighter Wing and in July he became *Staffelkapitän* of his squadron, based from August in France. He claimed five US fighters in August but these remain unconfirmed victories. On 23 August his Bf 109G-14 was shot down by US fighters south-east of Paris and although he bailed out he was severely wounded. He was captured by Allied troops and transferred to a local hospital.

In January 1945 he was repatriated due to his wounds and ended the war in a German hospital. He had two brothers, both serving as officers in the army, and both were killed on the Eastern Front. Ebener died on 7 May 1975 in Kelkheim, a town in Main-Taunus, Germany due to complications of his war wounds.

Otto SCHULTZ-WITTMER

Hauptmann

Knight's Cross: Awarded on 14 April 1943 as *Oberfeldwebel* and fighter pilot with the 4th Squadron of the 51st Fighter Wing '*Molders*' for operations over the Soviet Union.

Otto Schultz-Wittmer claimed seventy-nine aerial victories during the Second World War, of which thirty-nine were achieved over the Eastern Front and the remainder were claimed over the Western Front and North Africa. He was born on 31 May 1920 in Dannenberg, Elbe and with his training complete he joined the 2nd Group of the 51st Fighter Wing on 1 April 1940.

(Deutsches Wehrkundearchiv)

He flew as part of the 4th Squadron based in Böblingen, Germany, and from late May he was flying from Emptinne in Belgium. From June he flew in support of Army Group B during the second phase of the Western campaign and from 9 June his squadron was relocated to Abbeville. His squadron moved several times before taking over protection duties over the Channel coast where his Group won fourteen victories, without loss. Schultz-Wittmer had yet to score a victory. In August his Group was taken out of action and relocated to Jever where they were refreshed and flew protection missions over Denmark and later moved back to France and from December was relocated to Mannheim via Cologne.

From early 1941 Schultz-Wittmer was flying coastal protection missions from his base in Mardyck, northern France. In June his Group converted to the Bf 109F-2 and on the 22nd he saw action during the invasion of the Soviet Union. He claimed his first two victories on the opening day of the invasion, both Tupolev SB-2 twin-engined bombers, and he claimed a third on the 29th and two more the next day, and shortly after he was awarded the Iron Cross 2nd Class. In July his Group moved to Bobruisk to keep up with the advancing army units and he claimed his 10th victory on 26 July and was awarded the Iron Cross 1st Class. He claimed his last three victories of the year in late October and during the last weeks of 1941 he flew fighter protection missions over Moscow in support of ground troops. He was awarded the *Luftwaffe* Honour Goblet on 3 November in recognition of gaining eighteen victories.

At the beginning of 1942 his Group was in Bryansk and Schultz-Wittmer had been promoted to *Oberfeldwebel*. He was flying the Bf 109F-2 in support of the 4th Army and the 2nd Panzer Army south of Moscow. He flew over the Yukhnov area during April and then operations came to a standstill due to the mud and the wet weather conditions. On 23 June he gained his 20th victory and in July his Group moved north, and by August he was flying combat missions over the Rzhev area. During the month of August he claimed a total of twelve aerial victories, which included two on the 22nd and 25th and three on the 27th. On 24 September he was awarded the German Cross after claiming thirty-six victories.

On 14 November his Group moved to Tunisia, based near Bizerta, and it was here that Schultz-Wittmer demonstrated his abilities as a fighter pilot. The task of his Group was to escort air and sea transports over the Tunisian bridgehead. During December he claimed five victories, which included his 40th on the 4th, and continued to fly escort duties into January 1943. He claimed a total of nine victories that month, which included six P-38 Lightnings, and he achieved his 50th victory on 30 January. In February he claimed three more victories of which one was a B-25 Mitchell twin-engined bomber and the other was a B-17 Flying Fortress. On 14 April he was awarded the Knight's Cross after claiming fifty-four victories. In July his Group left Tunisia and flew for a time from Munich and then briefly flew over Sicily. In September his Group moved again, back to the Reich where he flew air defence missions and was promoted to *Leutnant*.

He was transferred to Italy and joined the 5th Squadron in late December and there claimed his 60th victory, a Boston medium bomber on 16 January 1944 six miles north-east of Civitavecchia. On 4 February he was appointed *Staffelkapitän* of the 6th Squadron and claimed six more victories, which included five B-24 bombers, and he was promoted to *Hauptmann* around the same time. He was wounded on 28 June when his Bf 109G-6 was shot down by a P-51 Mustang east of Sofia. On Christmas Eve he was appointed *Gruppenkommandeur* of the 2nd Group of the 51st Fighter Wing.

At the beginning of 1945 his Group was flying from Veszprèm in Hungary and here he claimed his 70th victory on 3 January. He claimed his final victory on 2 February, a Boston twin-engined bomber. From March his group was posted to Fels am Wagram in Austria and on 12 April it was dissolved and most of the personnel, including Schultz-Wittmer, surrendered to the Allies. He had flown 800 combat missions during the war and he joined the *Bundeswehr* after the war, retiring as an *Oberstleutnant* on 30 September 1976. He died in Fürstenfeldbruck, a town located about 20 miles west of Munich, on 28 July 2013.

Horst 'Adomaitis' ADEMEIT

Major der Reserve

Knight's Cross: Awarded on 16 April 1943 as *Leutnant* and fighter pilot in the 1st Group of the 54th Fighter Wing after achieving his 53rd aerial victory over the Soviet Union.

Knight's Cross with Oakleaves: Awarded on 2 March 1944 to become the 414th recipient as *Hauptmann* and commander of the 1st Group of the 54th Fighter Wing in recognition of his 130th aerial victory. He was presented with his award by Hitler at the Berghof, Obersalzburg on 4 April 1944 together with *Major* Kurt Bühlingen, *Leutnant* Erich Hartmann, *Oberleutnant* Walter Krupinski, *Major* Reinhard Seiler and *Major* Johannes Wiese.

(Deutsches Wehrkundearchiv)

Horst Ademeit spent his entire wartime career with the 54th Fighter Wing, seeing action over France, England and the Soviet Union, where he scored all of his victories. Ademeit was born on 8 February 1912 in Breslau, Prussia, now part of western Poland. He studied at the Königsberg Albertina University and went onto study chemistry at the Technical University of Berlin and in Braunschweig. He joined the *Luftwaffe* in August 1936 and learnt to fly as a reservist, before being made an officer cadet in December 1938.

In the spring of 1940 he was transferred to the 3rd Squadron of the 54th Fighter Wing with the rank of *Unteroffizier*. He took part in the Battle of France and the Battle of Britain and was awarded the Iron Cross 2nd Class on 7 September. He claimed an aerial victory on 18 September 1940 over England but this has never been confirmed. That same day, however, he was himself shot down but was unhurt and was later rescued from the Channel. With the German invasion of the Soviet Union in June 1941 Ademeit left for the Eastern Front as part of the 1st Group of the 54th Fighter Wing. He claimed his first official aerial victory on 23 June 1941, a Tupolev SB-2 twin-engined bomber, and his second came on 6 July, a Tupolev SB-3 bomber. By the end of September Ademeit had achieved eight aerial victories. By the start of 1942 he had achieved sixteen aerial victories, and was appointed *Staffelkapitän* of the 6th Squadron and by the end of May he had achieved his 27th victory. It's fair to say that Ademeit found success hard to come by especially when other pilots were achieving far more against the poorly equipped Soviet air force. His success rate slightly improved in 1943 by the end of February that year he had achieved his 45th victory. On 16 April he was awarded the Knight's Cross in recognition of his 53rd aerial victory, a Yakovlev Yak-1 twin-engined bomber. Ademeit was promoted to *Oberleutnant* in June and continued to score victories through the next few months and by the end of September had achieved his 98th victory. He was more successful the following month: on 11 October he claimed two victories, on the 12th he claimed another six, and by the end of the month had claimed his 120th aerial victory over the Soviet Union.

In December 1943 the 54th Fighter Wing was given new fighters, the Bf 109s being replaced by Fw 190s, and Ademeit much preferred these aircraft. He could now show his true skills and his score rate began to rise quite dramatically. He was appointed *Gruppenkommandeur* of the 1st Group of the 54th Fighter Wing in January 1944 and was promoted to *Hauptmann* on 4 February. On 2 March Ademeit was awarded the Knight's Cross with Oakleaves in recognition of his 130th aerial victory. In fact by the end of March he had increased his score to 142 victories. On 2 July he claimed three aerial victories, with another two the following day, and by the end of the month he had achieved 160 aerial victories. On 1 August he was made temporary *Kommodore* of the 54th Fighter Wing, but it was a short assignment, just seven days later he was reported as missing in action. In a rare occurrence, his Fw 190 had succumbed to infantry fire over Dünaburg in south Latvia. His aircraft was last seen going down behind enemy lines, and he was never seen again. He was posthumously promoted to the rank of *Major*.

Edwin Ludwig THIEL

Hauptmann

Knight's Cross: Awarded on 16 April 1943 as *Oberleutnant* and *Staffelkapitän* of the 2nd Squadron of the 51st Fighter Wing '*Mölders*' for operations over the Soviet Union after claiming his 51st aerial victory.

Edwin Thiel claimed seventy-one victories over the Eastern Front and flew over 300 combat missions during the Second World. He was born on 19 June 1913 in Höcherberg near Oberbexbach in Hamburg and before the war he flew for Lufthansa.

He joined the *Luftwaffe* in 1939 as an instructor before being assigned to the 1st Squadron of the 51st Fighter Wing in September 1941. He flew over the Soviet Union in support of the attack on Moscow and claimed his first two victories on 2 and 3 October and in early November his Group relocated to Staraya and his deployment over the Moscow area was over. He continued to claim victories and before the end of the year he had shot down over twenty enemy aircraft and had been awarded the Iron Cross 1st and 2nd Classes.

(Deutsches Wehrkundearchiv)

In February 1942 he briefly flew fighter-bomber missions and later flew over the Lake Ilmen area where he claimed another seven aerial victories. He transferred into the 2nd Squadron and from April flew missions over Demyansk and Cholm areas. On 16 June he was awarded the *Luftwaffe* Honour Goblet and he claimed his 28th aerial victory eleven days later. On 6 July he claimed three more victories, which included his 30th, and in August his Group moved to the area of Army Group Centre and Thiel was now flying the Fw 190A. By September he had claimed his 35th victory and his Group had moved to the area of Ljuban and he saw action over the Leningrad area. He was awarded the German Cross in Gold on 9 September in recognition of claiming thirty-five victories and on 17 October his Group was withdrawn and relocated to South Vyazma and almost two weeks later he claimed two more victories. On 4 December he claimed four Ilyushin Il-2 ground-attack aircraft and a P-40 fighter.

In January 1943 his group moved to Smolensk and from there he flew over Velikye Luki and in February he was promoted to *Oberleutnant* and on the 23rd claimed four Petlyakov Pe-2 twin-engined dive-bombers. The following day Thiel became an 'ace-in-a-day' when he claimed five aircraft, which included his 50th victory, another Il-2 ground-attack aircraft. From March he was flying from Bryansk and on 16 April he was awarded the Knight's Cross. He claimed his 55th victory on 6 July and by the middle of the month had claimed his 64th victory and had been transferred as *Staffelkapitän* to the 1st Squadron of Fighter Replacement Group East.

In May 1944, now a *Hauptmann*, Thiel transferred to the Staff Squadron of the 51st Fighter Wing and claimed five victories on the 23rd to become an 'ace-in-a-day' for the second time. He claimed his 70th and 71st and last victories on 25 June. On 14 July his aircraft took a direct hit in the right wing from Soviet anti-aircraft fire, at a height of only 650ft. His Focke-Wulf Fw 190 immediately flipped over and plunged straight into a wood east of Volkovysk and he was killed. He had bailed out but was far too low and his parachute had no time to open. His body has never been officially located but it is possible that his remains have been recovered but not identified in spite of all efforts and that he is buried at the Military Cemetery Berjasa as an unknown soldier.

Wilhelm-Ferdinand 'Wutz' GALLAND

Major

Knight's Cross: Awarded on 18 May 1943 as *Hauptmann* and as commander of the 2nd Group of the 26th Fighter Wing '*Schlageter*' for claiming his 42nd aerial victory over the Soviet Union. The nomination for the award had been submitted following his 34th aerial victory and the presentation was made at Vitry-en-Artois airfield by Chief of the 3rd Air Fleet *Generalfeldmarschall* Hugo Sperrle.

(Deutsches Wehrkundearchiv)

Wilhelm-Ferdinand Galland was one of four brothers of whom three became fighter aces and his brother Adolf became a *Generalleutnant* and General of Fighters. Paul, the youngest, became a fighter pilot and Fritz, the least known, was a reconnaissance and later a fighter pilot who claimed one victory. Wilhelm-Ferdinand was credited with fifty-six aerial victories of which thirty-nine were Spitfires and nine were four-engined bombers, flying a total of 186 combat missions over the Western Front. Galland was born on 23 October 1914 in Bochum, North-Rhine Westphalia and he joined the *Luftwaffe* in 1935.

He served in an anti-aircraft artillery regiment during the Battle of France and in late 1940, as a *Leutnant*, he began his flight training. From June 1941 he finished his supplementary fighter pilot training whilst attached to the 2nd Group of the 26th Fighter Wing. In July he was appointed *Staffelkapitän* of the 6th Squadron and claimed his first victory on 23 July, a Spitfire, and was awarded the Iron Cross 2nd Class. He was promoted to *Oberleutnant* shortly afterwards and claimed his second victory, another Spitfire, on 27 September over Boulogne, and after claiming his third victory over Calais on 6 November he was awarded the Iron Cross 1st Class.

On 28 March 1942 Galland's unit was called into action when there was an attack on Boulogne. The RAF attacked the headquarters of the 26th Fighter Wing and the 2nd Group between Cap

Gris-Nez and Calais. During the attack Galland claimed another Spitfire, his fourth victory. On 10 April the RAF flew two diversion missions to cover a bomber attack on Boulogne. That day, Galland, under the command of *Hauptmann* Joachim Müncheberg, claimed another Spitfire, but his group lost three aircraft and two pilots were killed. On 4 May he transferred to the 5th Squadron where he later replaced *Oberleutnant* Wolfgang Kosse as *Staffelkapitän* on 10 June. He claimed another Spitfire over Guînes in northern France on 20 June, and two more on 31 July near the Somme estuary.

During the Dieppe raid on 19 August, the 5th Squadron was scrambled and led by Galland they engaged enemy fighters and he claimed another Spitfire. Later that same afternoon he led a flight of Fw 190*s* again to Dieppe where he sank a small steamer laying offshore and he also spotted another vessel which tried to escape north but he sank that too. By 5 September he had claimed his 17th victory and on 12 October was awarded the *Luftwaffe* Honour Goblet. On 31 October his younger brother Paul, who was also serving as a fighter pilot with the 26th Fighter Wing, was killed when he was shot down and crashed about 15 miles west of Calais. Galland claimed his 20th victory on 12 December, a Spitfire over Boulogne. Three days later the 2nd and 3rd Groups began experimenting with the new Bf 109F-4 – there had been a number of changes to the earlier variants and the 2nd Group had been scheduled to be fully re-equipped with the new fighter in early 1943. However *Gruppenkommandeur Hauptmann* Conny Meyer and later Galland stalled the change-over, and they retained their Focke-Wulf Fw 190 fighters, which they much preferred, until the decision was revoked.

On 2 January 1943 and with a promotion to *Hauptmann* Galland was appointed *Gruppenkommandeur* of the 2nd Group by his brother, General of Fighters, *Generalmajor* Adolf Galland. Just a week later on 9 January Galland claimed yet another Spitfire part of the 340 Free French Squadron. Then there was a tragic incident four days later when Galland accidentally shot down and killed *Unteroffizier* Johann Irlinger from the 6th Squadron, having mistaken his aircraft for a Spitfire over Abbèville airfield. The incident was witnessed by *Unteroffizier* Peter Crump but the records were altered to show no blame towards Galland. He led his Group in a mission against RAF bombers and fighters on 22 January, and he claimed a Spitfire that day from 350 Belgian Squadron, north-north-west of Gravelines. Six days later Galland was awarded the German Cross in Gold in recognition of achieving his 24th aerial victory.

On 3 February Galland claimed three victories, two Spitfires and a Hudson A-29 bomber north of Fort Philipp, northern France. He claimed two more Spitfires on the 13th and two days later he claimed his 30th aerial victory. On 8 March RAF Bomber Command attacked Rennes, Brittany and Galland claimed a B-24 bomber that day. He led twenty-four Fw 190s against B-24s and his unit suffered no losses but they did claim four bombers over Tôtes, France, of which Galland claimed one. He claimed three victories on 4 April, two Spitfires and one B-17 Flying Fortress over Fécamp near Normandy. He claimed another B-17 the following day and a third on the 17th, over the Somme estuary, and that same day he also claimed a P-51 Mustang, but since there were no P-51s operating in that area it is highly likely that his opponent was a Typhoon which was reported to have crashed with engine failure and was not credited to him. On the 21st Galland led his flight against eleven Lockheed Ventura medium bombers from 21 Squadron attacking Abbeville.

On 17 August 1943 Galland was shot down in his Fw 190A-6, about three miles west of Maastricht, Netherlands. His wingman *Unteroffizier* Heinz Gomann yelled out a warning over the radio but it was too late. Galland disappeared after the first P-47 fighter attacked, and his body was found still in his aircraft two months later in north Liège, Belgium. He is now buried at the Military Cemetery in Lommel, Block 21, Grave No. 200. (*Author's collection*)

Galland was credited with two Venturas and on 18 May he was awarded the Knight's Cross for claiming a total of forty-two victories.

Galland claimed two B-17s on 22 June and two P-47 Thunderbolts four days later. On the afternoon of the 4 July he claimed a Spitfire and five days later he was promoted to the rank of *Major* and claimed another Spitfire that same day. On the 14th he claimed a P-47 Thunderbolt over west Étaples and the following day he claimed two more victories, a Boston medium bomber and another P-47 over the Somme estuary. On the 30th the US Army Air Force targeted the Fiesler aircraft manufacturing factories located in Kessel, and Galland led the 2nd Group during the counter-attack. He claimed a B-17 bomber east of Apeldoorn, his 54th victory and on 12 August during a US bombing mission against the Ruhr and Rheine area he claimed his last two victories of the war, both B-17s.

On 17 August Galland was shot down by a P-47 Thunderbolt piloted by Walker 'Bud' Mahurin of the US 56th Fighter Group, and his body remained missing for two months.

Wolf-Udo ETTEL

Oberleutnant

Knight's Cross: Awarded on 1 June 1943 as *Leutnant* and fighter pilot in the 4th Squadron of the 3rd Fighter Wing '*Udet*' for actions over the Soviet Union and Italy. The presentation was made in Berlin when Ettel was on leave, by General of Fighters *Generalmajor* Adolf Galland personally.

Knight's Cross with Oakleaves: He became the 289th recipient posthumously on 31 August 1943 as *Oberleutnant* and *Staffelkapitän* of the 27th Fighter Wing in recognition of his 121st aerial victory, a US B-24 Liberator.

(Deutsches Wehrkundearchiv)

Wolf-Udo Ettel claimed 121 victories, and all but three were whilst flying combat missions over the Soviet Union in just over 250 combat missions during the Second World War. He was born on 26 February 1921 in Hamburg in the Weimar Republic, and was the son of a representative of the Junkers aircraft manufacturer. Due to his father's work, the family lived in Tehran and in Colombia where he attended the German school. When his parents divorced in 1934 he returned to Germany with his two younger brothers and attended boarding school at Potsdam.

Ettel joined the *Luftwaffe* in November 1939 and following various training courses, he attended flying school in January 1941. Once he received his pilot's licence he then attended the Fighter Pilot School based in Paris, France. In September he was posted to the Supplementary Fighter Group based in Denmark and in April 1942, *Leutnant* Ettel was posted to the 4th Squadron of the 3rd Fighter Wing. At this time he was part of the 2nd Group which was placed under the command of the 53rd Fighter Wing and was based at San Pietro Clarenza, Sicily, flying combat missions during the siege of Malta. However, in May his Group was moved to the Eastern Front in preparation for Hitler's invasion of the Soviet Union. Ettel arrived in Pilsen from Sicily on 27 April and his Group, whilst under the command of *Hauptmann* Kurt Brändle, was having a refit for the summer campaign. After three weeks of rest, the 2nd Group, part of the 8th Air Corps, arrived at its new base at Chuguyev on 19 May. On 24 June it moved to Schigry, a forward airfield about 31 miles east of the front lines, near Kursk. On that day Ettel claimed his first two aerial victories, both Ilyushin Il-2 ground-attack aircraft. He claimed his third victory on 28 June, another Il-2, and his fourth on 30 June.

On 9 July Ettel claimed two more victories but the following day he was shot down himself, about nine miles north of Voronezh, managing to bail out of his damaged Bf 109F-4 behind Soviet lines. He swam across the Don River and returned to his unit four days later. On 24 July he claimed three more Soviet aircraft and also that day received the Iron Cross 2nd Class. Ettel claimed three more aerial victories on 26 July and by the end of the month had claimed a total of seventeen victories. Awarded the Iron Cross 1st Class on 2 August, he continued to claim victories throughout the following month and by the end of August had achieved his 22nd aerial victory. He continued to score victories in September, claiming two on the 13th, the 15th and the 23rd, and then on 7 October he claimed two LaGG-3 fighters. He claimed three more victories on 31 October but one remains unconfirmed. He was awarded the German Cross in Gold on 23 December in recognition of his success and for scoring thirty-two victories.

Following the German defeat at Stalingrad in February 1943 the 4th Squadron was relocated to the Kuban Bridgehead, and there followed months of intensive operations and Ettel claimed twenty-eight Soviet aircraft shot down in March and thirty-six more in April, including five shot down on 11 April, achieving 'ace-in-a-day' recognition. In fact between 22 and 28 April he claimed a total of eighteen aerial victories and by the end of the month had claimed his 98th aerial victory. On 6 May he claimed four victories, which included his 100th, making him the 38th *Luftwaffe* fighter pilot to achieve the century mark. He continued to add to his score in May, on the 8th he claimed four victories, on the 9th he claimed three and on the 10th he claimed six victories, becoming an 'ace-in-a-day' for the second time. On 11 May he shot down two LaGG-3s to claim his 117th and 118th victories, his last of the Eastern Front. Whilst returning to base he was shot down by Soviet anti-aircraft fire and had to make a forced landing, west of Anastassiewskaja. Once back to his own lines he then led a patrol, the same day, to his damaged aircraft to salvage important equipment.

On 1 June Ettel was awarded the Knight's Cross in recognition of his 118th aerial victories and his success as a fighter pilot on the Eastern Front and the same day was promoted to *Oberleutnant*. On 5 June he was appointed *Staffelkapitän* of the newly created 8th Squadron of the 27th Fighter Wing, which at the time was based in Tanagra, Greece. While there his squadron was re-equipped with the new Bf 109G-4 and G-6 series. In June he led his squadron out on training missions so his pilots could familiarise themselves with the new aircraft. At the end of the month his unit was moved to an airfield at Argos in Peloponnese, there they were tasked with flying combat air patrol missions over the Aegean Sea. However, the Allied invasion of Sicily resulted in the relocation of the 3rd Group to Brindisi in southern Italy in July 1943.

On 15 July the 3rd Group flew its first mission in support of German ground forces south-east of Catania, Sicily and because of the distance the Bf 109s had to be equipped with drop tanks. The fighters engaged in aerial combat north of Mount Etna where Ettel claimed his first victory in the Mediterranean theatre, an RAF Spitfire over south-east Noto. The following day he claimed three B-24 Liberators, although one remains unconfirmed. On 17 July his Group was tasked with flying ground-support missions against British forces in the area around Catania. Whilst flying over the area of Lentini the Group encountered strong defences which included anti-aircraft guns. Out of the ten aircraft sent, five were lost and these included Ettel who was shot down and crashed north-east of Lago di Lentini. He was posthumously awarded the Knight's Cross with Oakleaves on 31 August. He was buried at the German cemetery at Motta Saint Anastasia, Catania.

Stefan LITJENS

Oberfeldwebel

Knight's Cross: Awarded on 21 June 1943 as *Oberfeldwebel* and pilot with the 4th Squadron of the 53rd Fighter Wing for operations over France, England, the Soviet Union, Malta and North Africa.

Stefan Litjens claimed sixteen aerial victories over the Eastern Front and sixteen over the Western Front whilst flying a total of 444 missions during the Second World War. He was born on 13 October 1913 in Hasselt, Kleve and joined the *Luftwaffe* in 1935. He trained as a pilot and was assigned to the 334th Fighter Wing from early 1937.

By May 1939 his squadron had merged with other Groups to form the 53rd Fighter Wing and *Feldwebel* Litjens was assigned to the 4th Squadron, part of the 2nd Group based in Mannheim-Sandhofen. He flew the Bf 109E-1 and later the E-4 and during the opening stages of the war he flew protection missions over the Reich. He claimed his first aerial victory, but later unconfirmed, on 7 April 1940, a Morane-Sauliner M.S. 406 fighter over Saarbrücken. Three days later he claimed a Hawk 75 over Metz, his first official victory, and he was awarded the Iron Cross 2nd Class. Later in May he flew fighter protection missions over the area of the advance of Army Group A near Reims, Réthel, Clermont and Amiens. He claimed his second victory, a Potez 630 twin-engined fighter on 8 June, and he claimed a Spitfire on 13 August over Dorchester and shortly after was awarded the Iron Cross 1st Class. On 8 October Litjens crashed his Bf 109 on take-off from Berck-sur-Mer in France but wasn't injured.

(Deutsches Wehrkundearchiv)

He claimed an RAF Spitfire on 11 November and was shortly after promoted to *Oberfeldwebel* and flew fighter bomber missions until the end of the year. He claimed two Spitfires on 11 November but in late December his Group was withdrawn after heavy losses and relocated to Cologne. On 22 June 1941 his Group was sent to the Soviet Union as part of the German invasion force during Operation Barbarossa. On the first day of the campaign he claimed two SB-2 bombers and on 1 July he claimed two SB-3 bombers, his 9th and 10th victories. He claimed two more SB-3s on 10 July and on the 21st he was awarded the *Luftwaffe* Honour Goblet after achieving thirteen confirmed victories and another three unconfirmed. From early August his Group flew the new Bf 109F-4, and on the 25th Litjens claimed five victories to become an 'ace-in-a-day' and by the end of the month had claimed his 20th victory. On 11 September he claimed two more victories and later that day he was shot down during combat with I-16 fighters, and was forced to bail out of his aircraft severely wounded, losing his right eye. Whilst recovering he was awarded the German Cross in Gold on 24 April in recognition of his bravery and achieving twenty-two aerial victories.

He returned to duty in October 1942 in North Africa and claimed two victories in November, a Spitfire and a P-38 Lightning. From early November his Group was relocated to Sardinia and then to Tunis and he claimed two victories over Mateur on 4 December and claimed a Spitfire over south Teboura two days later. His Group remained in the Mediterranean area throughout 1943 and he claimed three more victories during this time and flew fighter protection missions against the Allied landings in Salerno. On 21 June Litjens was awarded the Knight's Cross after achieving his 30th aerial victory. From early 1944 he flew missions against the American four-engined bombers and claimed two on 22 February but these were later reclassified as unconfirmed. He claimed another on the 24th and this was confirmed and then on 23 March he claimed another B-17 over Brandes. That same day his own aircraft was damaged by return fire from a Flying Fortress and he was wounded in his left eye. He belly-landed his Bf 109 at Gifhorn and never returned to combat.

He joined the *Bundeswehr* in January 1956 and retired with the rank of *Hauptfeldwebel* in March 1966. He died on 25 February 2002 in Kalkar-Wissel in Germany.

Franz 'Nawratil' SCHIESS

Hauptmann

Knight's Cross: Awarded on 21 June 1943 as *Oberleutnant* and *Staffelkapitän* of the 8th Squadron of the 53rd Fighter Wing for operations over the Soviet Union, Malta, North Africa and Italy and for claiming his 54th aerial victory, an RAF Spitfire.

Franz Schiess claimed sixty-eight aerial victories during the Second World War of which fifty-four were achieved over the Western Front and included three four-engined bombers. He was born on 25 February 1921 in Worth, St. Pötten in Austria and saw action with the army during the Polish campaign in 1939 before transferring to the *Luftwaffe* to train as a fighter pilot in 1940.

(Deutsches Wehrkundearchiv)

Leutnant Schiess was assigned to the Staff Squadron of the 53rd Fighter Wing, based on the Channel front from March 1941, and from December served as adjutant. On 22 June, the opening day of Operation Barbarossa, the invasion of the Soviet Union, Schiess claimed two aerial victories, a Polikarpov I-153 fighter and an Ilyushin DB-3 long-range bomber. Two days later he claimed two more victories, both SB-2 twin-engined bombers, and Schiess was awarded the Iron Cross 2nd Class. He established a close friendship with the *Kommodore* (Wing Commander) *Major* Günther von Maltzahn and became his wingman. After claiming another nine victories during July and being awarded the Iron Cross 1st Class, Schiess and the rest of the Wing left the Soviet Union for Germany to be refreshed and refitted.

In December his unit was deployed to the Mediterranean, operating from Sicily, and Schiess flew combat missions over Malta where on 25 January 1942 he claimed an RAF Hurricane and another one on 24 February. Schiess was now flying the new Bf 109G-2 and by 14 July he had scored twenty victories and had outscored his *Kommodore*, claiming his 22nd victory, a Spitfire, on 26 August. On 7 September he was awarded the *Luftwaffe* Honour Goblet in recognition of scoring twenty victories. From November he flew from Tunisia and claimed his 25th victory on the 17th, another Spitfire, and continued his success during December, scoring another five victories, claiming his 30th victory on the 6th. He claimed his 35th victory on 17 January 1943, a P-38 Lightning about 18 miles north-east of Beja, Portugal and was awarded the German Cross in Gold on the 23rd. He claimed a B-17 Flying Fortress, his first four-engined bomber, and another P-38 in the same area six days later.

On 16 February, now promoted to *Oberleutnant*, Schiess took over as *Staffelkapitän* of the 8th Squadron of the 53rd Fighter Wing, and was by now was regarded as one of the most aggressive and enthusiastic pilots in the Mediterranean area. He claimed his 40th victory on 5 April and on the 18th whilst flying escort missions for transport aircraft evacuating troops from Africa he claimed a Spitfire but twenty-four fully-loaded transport aircraft were shot down by Allied fighters and thirty-five more were damaged, in what became known as the 'Palm Sunday Massacre'. Shortly after this his unit evacuated to Sicily after the fall of Tunis but he continued to fly missions over Sicily, sometimes at night, and claimed his 50th victory on 21 May. He was awarded the Knight's Cross on 25 June after claiming his 54th victory, a Spitfire north-east of the Island of Pantelleria, and the same day his award was confirmed he claimed his second B-17 four-engined bomber over the Island of Stromboli.

He was sent on leave for two months and missed the air battles over Sicily, returning to his command in mid-August, his Squadron now flying out of southern Italy. He claimed thirteen victories during August, which included another B-17 bomber, three B-26 twin-engined bombers, one B-25 Mitchell and seven P-38 fighters. On 1 September together with Jürgen Harder he was promoted to the rank of *Hauptmann*. The next day he led his Squadron into action against a large formation of B-26 bombers that were attacking railway marshalling yards north-east of Naples as part of the softening-up process prior to the Salerno landings. At approximately 13:45 pilots heard Schiess over the radio say, '… at them again, everyone get ready'. However, just as this happened his wingman was forced away by two P-38 Lightnings and lost sight of his *Staffelkapitän*. Ten of the P-38s were shot down by Schiess in his Bf 109G-6 before it crashed into the Mediterranean about 20–30 miles south-south-west of Ischia in the Gulf of Salerno. His body was never recovered. His *Kommodore* and friend von Maltzahn wrote to his parents praising their son as a good friend and pilot. He said that he could not have wished for a better officer and that he had lost his best friend, on whom he could always depend. He had flown a total of 657 combat missions, and of his sixty-eight victories, seventeen were P-38 Lightnings, making him the highest-scoring 'Lightning-Killer' of the war.

Albert BRUNNER

Oberfeldwebel

Knight's Cross: Awarded posthumously on 3 July 1943 as *Oberfeldwebel* and fighter pilot with the 6th Squadron of the 5th Fighter Wing for operations over the Soviet Union.

Albert Brunner flew 135 combat missions and claimed at least fifty-three victories over the Eastern Front during the Second World. He was born on 17 July 1918 in Mergentheim-Dortel in Franconia, north-east of Baden-Württemberg, and he joined the *Luftwaffe* in 1939. He trained as a pilot and was attached to Fighter Group West and on completion of his training he served as an instructor.

In early April 1942, now a *Feldwebel*, he was posted to the Arctic Front whilst attached to the 2nd Group of the 5th Fighter Wing, serving with the 6th Squadron in Pori, Finland. He soon became one of the best pilots of his squadron, scoring his first victory on 29 May, an RAF Hurricane south of Nautsi. He claimed another Hurricane, his second victory, on 24 June 1942 and after claiming his third victory, another Hurricane on 7 July, he was awarded the Iron Cross 2nd Class. On 21 August during combat with another aircraft Brunner was hit by return fire and had to bail out of his Bf 109F-4, landing safely and unhurt. The following day he claimed his 10th victory a P-39 fighter and was awarded the Iron Cross 1st Class, and claimed victories regularly. On 5 September he claimed two victories and shortly after he was shot down and had to bail out of his aircraft. He landed in enemy territory and it took him four days to get back to the safety of his own lines, being eventually rescued by a German reconnaissance patrol.

(Deutsches Wehrkundearchiv)

Now an *Oberfeldwebel*, his exact score is unknown, and details of all his victories have not come to light. But on 4 April 1943 he did claim four victories, one Hurricane and three P-40s over the area of Pechenga in Murmansk, Soviet Union. On 10 April Brunner was awarded the *Luftwaffe* Honour Goblet after claiming approximately forty-two victories. He later claimed four victories, three Hurricanes and a P-40, over the Murmaschi area on 13 April. On the 19th he claimed two victories and on 22 April he claimed his 50th victory. Shortly after claiming his 52nd victory he was shot down by a US fighter. Although he managed to bail out of his Bf 109 he was too low and was killed when his parachute failed to open. Brunner was posthumously awarded the German Cross in Gold on 4 June 1943, and on 3 July, a month later, was finally awarded the Knight's Cross. He is buried today in the cemetery in Petschenga, Russia. He is officially credited with fifty-three victories, but he probably shot down more. His victories included nine Hurricanes and eleven P-40 Warhawk ground-attack aircraft.

Friedrich-Wilhelm STRAKELJAHN

Hauptmann

Knight's Cross: Awarded on 19 August 1943 as *Hauptmann* and *Staffelkapitän* of the 14th Fighter-Bomber Squadron of the 5th Fighter Wing for operations over Poland, France, England, the Balkans and the Soviet Union.

Friedrich-Wilhelm 'Strakes' Strakeljahn was a fighter-bomber pilot who claimed nine aerial victories as well as sinking 5,000 tons of shipping whilst serving on both the Eastern and Western Fronts during the Second World War. He was born on 7 September 1914 in Lübeck, northern Germany and was a policeman before joining the *Luftwaffe* in 1935.

With his training complete, *Leutnant* Strakeljahn was assigned to the 2nd Fighter-Bomber Squadron of the 2nd Instruction Wing and saw action over Poland, France and England. On 19 May 1940 he was shot down by a French M.S. 406 fighter, having to make an emergency landing near Compiègne and was listed as missing, but returned wounded three

(Deutsches Wehrkundearchiv)

days later. On 19 May he claimed a Westland Lysander liaison aircraft and a Hurricane near Le Cateau in the Lille area and was awarded the Iron Cross 2nd Class a few days later. On 24 August he claimed his third victory, an RAF Spitfire, and six days later he claimed another Spitfire and was that same day appointed *Staffelkapitän* of his squadron. He claimed a Spitfire on 20 October and was awarded the Iron Cross 1st Class towards the end of 1940, and continued to fly fighter-bomber missions over England into early 1941. From June he flew with his Squadron as part of the invasion force over the Soviet Union and claimed an I-15 on 6 June and an I-16 on 17 July, his seventh victory.

In January 1942 his unit was renamed the 2nd Squadron of the 77th Fighter Wing and he stayed as its *Staffelkapitän*. The entire Group moved to Stalino and he flew fighter-bomber missions over the operational area of the 17th Army in the Donets area. Promoted to *Oberleutnant* in March Strakeljahn claimed a Petlyakov Pe-2 dive-bomber on 15 March. From April he flew over the oil fields in Ploesti, Romania and on 16 May he took over as *Staffelkapitän* of the 7th Squadron of the 77th Fighter Wing. His Squadron was relocated to Kharkov and on 1 July he claimed a Yak-1 fighter and then took over as *Staffelkapitän* with the 4th Group of the 5th Fighter Wing. From August he flew the Focke-Wulf Fw 190A-2 fighter and on 21 September he was awarded the German Cross in Gold in recognition of his nine victories and his successful fighter-bomber missions.

From mid-February 1943, *Hauptmann* Strakeljahn transferred again as *Staffelkapitän* of the 14th Fighter-Bomber Squadron with the 5th Fighter Wing. He soon became a very successful fighter-bomber pilot, flying missions over Arctic waters, sinking ten ships which included a 2,000-ton auxiliary ship and a 3,000-ton freighter. He was awarded the Knight's Cross on 19 August for his part in the success of his Wing, and his Group was sent congratulations from the Commander-in-Chief of the 5th Air Fleet, *General der Flieger* Josef Kammhuber: 'The *Führer* has expressed his recognition of the attacks on shipping … and further conveys his wishes that these operations be continued with all available means.'

In February 1944 he became *Staffelkapitän* of the 4th Squadron of the 5th Ground-attack Wing and flew missions attacking Soviet positions on the Fischer Peninsula, against targets in the Arctic Ocean and shipping in the port of Murmansk. From 4 May he was *Gruppenkommandeur* of the 2nd Group of the 4th Ground-attack Wing and flew over the Eastern Front. He was killed when his Fw 190A-2 was shot down by anti-aircraft fire over Daugavpils, Latvia on 6 July 1944. During his career he had flown a total of 300 fighter and fighter-bomber missions.

Rudolf TRENKEL

Hauptmann

Knight's Cross: Awarded on 19 August 1943 as *Oberfeldwebel* and pilot attached to the 2nd Squadron of the 52nd Fighter Wing for operations over the Soviet Union and for achieving seventy aerial victories.

Rudolf Trenkel claimed 132 aerial victories and all but one were achieved over the Eastern Front during the Second World War. He was born on 17 January 1918 in Neudorf, Quedlinburg just north of the Harz Mountains in the west of Saxony-Anhalt and he joined the Army in 1936, transferring to the *Luftwaffe* three years later.

From February 1942 Trenkel trained as a fighter pilot and was assigned to the 7th Squadron of the 77th Fighter Wing. Promoted to *Feldwebel* he claimed his first victory on 26 March, an I-153 fighter. In May he transferred to the Staff Squadron of the 52nd Fighter Wing and flew from his base in the Ukraine, claiming his second victory on 2 June and his third on the 22nd, a Yak-1 fighter. Towards the end of June he transferred to the 2nd Squadron of the 52nd Fighter Wing, and

(Deutsches Wehrkundearchiv)

by 10 September Trenkel had claimed ten victories and had been awarded the Iron Cross 2nd Class. He then flew combat missions over the Stalingrad area, and by 27 September he had claimed his 20th victory and had been awarded the Iron Cross 1st Class. Trenkel claimed three victories in November and towards the end of the month his Group moved to Nikolajevka and he continued to fly in support of the troops in the Stalingrad area. He claimed four victories on 21 December and was promoted to *Oberfeldwebel* a few days later and by the 29th he had claimed his 30th victory.

At the beginning of 1943 he was operating from Rossosch and flying the Messerschmitt Bf 109G-2, and on the 15th he was awarded the German Cross in Gold in recognition of achieving twenty-five victories. On 25 January his Group moved to Kursk and from there he flew escort missions for Junkers Ju 87s and in early February he was flying from Kharkov and had been awarded the *Luftwaffe* Honour Goblet. Over the next few months his Group moved a number of times and from early April he was flying over the area of Kursk. Trenkel became an 'ace-in-a-day' on 16 April when he claimed five victories, all Lavochkin LaGG-3 fighters. He claimed more victories towards the end of April and on 7 May he claimed three more victories which included his 50th victory. He claimed his 60th victory on the 26th and claimed four victories on 2 June and on 19 August he was awarded the Knight's Cross in recognition of achieving seventy victories and for his skill as a fighter pilot. Shortly after he was transferred and appointed as an instructor with Fighter Replacement and Training Group East, under the command of *Major* Werner Andres.

Trenkel returned to the 52nd Fighter Wing in October and continued to claim victories. He claimed three victories on the 13th, two on the 14th and three more on the 15th and continued his success throughout the month. He claimed his 75th victory on 15 October and his 80th was achieved on the 22nd and he claimed his 90th victory on 28 October. He was shot down on 1 November during combat with Yakovlev Yak-9s and Ilyushin Il-2s and was severely wounded, just about managing to land his Bf 109G-6 near Dzhankoi. Whilst recovering he was promoted to *Leutnant* and by the time he had returned to duty in July he had been promoted to *Oberleutnant*. He claimed his 100th victory on 17 July, north-west of Busk and he became an 'ace-in-a-day' for the second time on the 19th when he claimed another five victories. On 5 August he was appointed *Staffelkapitän* of the 2nd Squadron of the 52nd Fighter Wing and on 12 September he claimed two Il-2 ground-attack aircraft and the following day he claimed a B-17 Flying Fortress over Cracow, Poland.

From late September his Group moved many times and from 14 October he was flying from Ebenrode and he claimed his 115th victory that same day. He claimed six victories the following day to become an 'ace-in-a-day' for the third time and by the end of the month he had claimed 126 aerial victories. His Group moved several times from November to February and he claimed his 130th victory on 20 February 1945. He claimed his last victory on 11 March, a Yak-9, and four days later he was shot down by Soviet anti-aircraft fire. He bailed out of his Bf 109G-14 near Strehlen. Just before the end of the war he was promoted to *Hauptmann* and on 8 May he surrendered to troops of the 90th US Infantry Division near Pisek. He was initially interned at a POW camp at Strakonice, Czechoslovakia where on 14 May Trenkel married his fiancée Ida Sehnal who was among the civilian refugees at the camp. The wedding ceremony was conducted by the *Kommodore* of the 52nd Fighter Wing, *Oberst* Hermann Graf. The witnesses to the wedding were *Major* Adolf Borchers, his former *Gruppenkommandeur*, and his successor *Hauptmann* Erich Hartmann. However, Trenkel was handed over to the Soviets, together with Hartmann but due to his wounds he was released in June 1945 and returned to Germany.

He died in Vienna, Austria on 26 April 2001, at the age of 83. He was credited with over 500 combat missions and why he wasn't awarded the Oakleaves or even recommended for them seems a mystery, considering the number of aircraft he claimed.

Emil BITSCH

Hauptmann

Knight's Cross: Awarded on 29 August 1943 as *Oberleutnant* and *Staffelkapitän* of the 8th Squadron of the 3rd Fighter Wing '*Udet*' for operations over the Soviet Union.

Emil Bitsch claimed 106 aerial victories during the Second World War of which all but one were over the Eastern Front. The exception was a B-17 four-engined bomber shot down over the Innsbruck area in December 1943 – his final victory. Bitsch was born in Bad Griesbach, Baden on 14 June 1916, and he joined the *Luftwaffe* in early 1941. With his training complete he was assigned to the 8th Squadron of the 3rd Fighter Wing and from July took part in Operation Barbarossa, the invasion of the Soviet Union, being attached to the 3rd Group under *Hauptmann* Walter Oesau.

(Deutsches Wehrkundearchiv)

His squadron operated from an airfield in north-western Ukraine, and Bitsch claimed his first victory, an Ilyushin Il-2 ground-attack aircraft, on 2 July 1941. He claimed his second victory on 10 July, a Polikarpov I-16 fighter south of Sabelotschje, and on 20 September he claimed his third victory and was awarded the Iron Cross 2nd Class a few days later. By the end of the year he had scored six victories, and he claimed his seventh victory on 26 February 1942. In March he was awarded the Iron Cross 1st Class and scored two more victories on 24 June. By the end of July he had claimed his 27th victory and continued to score at a tremendous rate throughout August. He claimed his 30th victory on 13 August and his 35th victory on the 20th and was promoted to *Oberleutnant* soon afterwards. Bitsch claimed his 44th victory on 31 August and that same day was awarded the *Luftwaffe* Honour Goblet.

On 4 September, shortly after claiming his 46th victory, Bitsch was shot down by anti-aircraft artillery north-west of Stalingrad. He bailed out of his Bf 109F-4 and landed safely, suffering only slight injuries and soon made a return to combat duty. He claimed his 50th victory on 16 March and continued to claim victories at a fast rate. He claimed his 55th victory on 20 April and just seven days later claimed his 60th victory, when he shot down three Lavochkin LaGG-3 fighters. In June he succeeded *Oberleutnant* Franz Beyer as *Staffelkapitän* of the 8th Squadron of the 3rd Fighter Wing. He claimed his 70th victory on 10 June, and his 75th on 2 July. He became an 'ace-in-a-day' on 5 July when he shot down six aircraft, and continued to claim victories throughout July. He claimed his 90th victory, an La-5 fighter, on 13 July, a Pe-2 dive-bomber on the 15th, two victories on the 16th, another one the following day and four on the 19th and two on the 20th, to record his 100th aerial victory.

Bitsch flew his last mission on the Eastern Front on 1 August 1943. The following day his Group was ordered to Tschassof-Jar and then back to Germany. He arrived with together with his Group at Münster-Handorf airfield on 3 August and was placed under the command of *Gruppenkommandeur Major* Walther Dahl. Bitsch now flew 'Defence of the Reich' missions and on 29 August was awarded the Knight's Cross in recognition of 105 victories. His group then relocated to Bad Wörishofen in southern Germany and on 1 October the USAAF attacked German aircraft production, targeting Wiener Neustadt and other such targets. Bitsch and his Group were scrambled and intercepted about fifty to sixty B-24 Liberator bombers and twenty-five B-17 Flying Fortresses. His Group claimed four victories without loss, Bitsch claiming a B-17.

The last resting place of *Hauptmann* Emil Bitsch. *(Author's collection)*

On 15 March, 344 bombers and 588 fighters of the US 2nd and 3rd Air Division took off to attack the German aircraft factories at Braunschweig. The 3rd Group, including Bitsch, took off to intercept these US bombers and fighters returning from the target area. In the area of Volkel in North Brabant, Netherlands the 3rd Group came under attack by P-47 Thunderbolts. During the engagement they lost six Bf 109 fighters, including Bitsch, who was shot down and killed about 2½ miles west of Schijndel. He was posthumously promoted to *Hauptmann*. He is buried today at the German War Cemetery at Ysselsteyn, Netherlands, located in Block Z, Row 6, Grave No. 148. In 1994 a Dutch researcher, Thijs Hellings, discovered the crash site and with some help he found the remains of Bitsch's aircraft and recovered among other things the radio, armoured glass and the compass.

Adolf 'Addi' GLUNZ

Oberleutnant

Knight's Cross: Awarded on 29 August 1943 as *Oberfeldwebel* and fighter pilot in the 4th Squadron of the 26th Fighter Wing *'Schlageter'* for operations over England, the Soviet Union and the Western Front.

Knight's Cross with Oakleaves: He became the 508th recipient on 24 June 1944 as a fighter pilot with the 6th Squadron of the 26th Fighter Wing *'Schlageter'* for continued operations over the Western Front, after achieving his 62nd aerial victory. He was presented with the Oakleaves personally by Hitler at the Wolf's Lair on 2 August 1944 together with *Major* Anton Hackl, *Oberleutnant* Erich Hartmann and *Oberstleutnant* Josef Priller who were receiving their Swords.

Adolf Glunz was credited with sixty-nine aerial victories, all but three in the West, of which seventeen were four-engined bombers and over

(Deutsches Wehrkundearchiv)

thirty were Spitfires. Although his victory tally was nothing exceptional, what was unusual was that out of nearly 575 combat missions in which he encountered the enemy on 238 occasions he was never once shot down or wounded.

Glunz was born on 11 June 1916 in Bresegard, in the district of Ludwigslust, Mecklenburg-Vorpommern, the son of Karl Glunz, a civil servant of the *Deutsche Reichsbahn* or German National Railways. Due to his father's job, the family moved to Hamburg and in 1934 to Heide. Following his schooling he began training as a mechanical engineer and worked for a company that built gliders, which acted as the catalyst for his own interest in flying. In 1934 he began to build his own glider and became a flight instructor with the National Socialist Flyers Corps, teaching members of the Hitler Youth to fly. He attended compulsory *Reichsarbeitsdienst* (RAD – Reich Labour Service) from November 1938 and joined the *Luftwaffe* on 1 September 1939, the day Germany invaded Poland.

He served with the 2nd Company of the 61st Flight Training Regiment and on 30 September was transferred to 1st Squadron of the 4th Fighter Pilot School in Fürth. Glunz, a *Gefreiter*, was briefly posted to the training unit of the 52nd Fighter Wing and then on 9 September 1940 he transferred to the Wing's 4th Squadron and was attached to the 2nd Group who were undergoing a period of rest and refitting in Mönchengladbach following the Battle of Britain. The Group was then commanded by *Hauptmann* Erich Woitke and the 4th Squadron was commanded by *Oberleutnant* Johannes Steinhoff. On 22 December the 2nd Group was ordered to Leeuwarden airfield where it was made responsible for patrolling the North Sea coast in the Netherlands. The Group stayed briefly at Haamstede and moved to Berck-sur-Mer on 10 February 1941 and then on 27 April the Group moved again, this time to an airfield at Katwijk. On 7 May Glunz claimed his first victory, an RAF Spitfire near Deal in Kent, and on 19 May he shot down his second, another Spitfire over Canterbury. Seven days later he was awarded the Iron Cross 2nd Class and on 8 June he received the Iron Cross 1st Class.

On 13 June the 4th Squadron moved east to Suwalki about 19 miles south-west of the Lithuanian border, ready for the invasion of the Soviet Union. During the opening phase of the campaign his Group was part of the 52nd Fighter Wing, attached to the 8th Air Corps covering the northern area of Army Group Centre. Glunz claimed his third victory on 26 June, an Ilyushin DB-3 bomber, and he claimed two more on 3 July over north-east Borisov. On 8 July he transferred to the 2nd Group of the 26th Fighter Wing commanded by *Hauptmann* Walter Adolph and based at Moorsele, Belgium. *Feldwebel* Glunz flew his first combat mission with his new unit on 29 July and on 21 August he made an emergency landing at Saint-Omer but was unhurt. Together with his wingman, *Unteroffizier* Josef Sieker, Glunz chased two Spitfires that had passed over their airfield at low altitude. They caught them but the American pilots outmanoeuvred them and after a brief dogfight Sieker's Fw 190 was hit, snap-rolled and crashed into the Channel and Sieker was lost. Glunz went on to claim one of the Spitfires before returning home. On 28 June he achieved his 18th aerial victory and was awarded the *Luftwaffe* Honour Goblet on 4 July. On 31 July he claimed two more Spitfires west of Berck-sur-Mer but only one was confirmed, and he scored his 20th victory on 19 August. He was awarded the German Cross in Gold on 15 October 1942 in recognition of achieving his 21st aerial victory of the war.

Glunz achieved his 25th aerial victory on 8 March 1943, a Spitfire over Rouen, northern France. On 12 August he claimed two B-17 bombers of which one was unconfirmed; this would be the first of many four-engined bomber victories. During the Schweinfurt Raid of 17 August he claimed a B-17. He had managed to dodge the fighter escorts and his victory was the only bomber success of that day. On 14 November his skill as a pilot led directly to his 43rd victory it was during the nuisance raids by single Mosquitoes. They did little actual damage but by triggering air-raid warnings across the Reich they caused considerable disruption to industry. Glunz took off alone, directed by ground control, and climbed to 28,000ft and he soon came in contact with the Mosquitoes skimming along below him.

Slowly he closed in and when he had them in his sights he pressed the firing button and claimed at least three of them.

On 15 January 1944, Glunz was appointed *Staffelführer* of the 5th Squadron when its former *Staffelkapitän Hauptmann* Johann Aistleitner had been killed in action. The appointment of Glunz to a position of such responsibility, although only a non-commissioned officer, showed how desperate the *Luftwaffe* was for fighter leaders. It should also be noted that these men received no officer training, as it was believed that command of a squadron was a matter of instinct. On 11 February Glunz claimed a B-17 and on 22 February came his greatest day in combat when he led his squadron against US heavy bombers. In the first mission of the day he shot down two B-17s and forced a third out of formation. That same afternoon he claimed another two B-17s and also shot down two P-47 Thunderbolts, although two of the B-17s were later reported as unconfirmed victories. On 3 March, Glunz was appointed *Staffelkapitän* of the 6th Squadron, replacing *Leutnant* Friedrich Lang who had been killed the day before. On 1 April Glunz was finally commissioned as a *Leutnant*.

On 11 May Glunz claimed a B-24 Liberator four-engined bomber, his 59th aerial victory, and he claimed three P-47s on 10 June. He had now claimed his 62nd aerial victory and was awarded the Knight's Cross with Oakleaves on 24 June. On 13 October 1944, shortly after claiming his 66th aerial victory, Glunz, now an *Oberleutnant* nearly lost his first and only aircraft when a broken oil pipe caused his engine to seize during a dogfight with two Thunderbolts. He managed to evade the American fighters by hard turns, followed by a near-vertical dive into cloud. On 24 December he claimed his 67th and 68th aerial victories over Liège, Belgium, then on 1 January 1945 Glunz led his Squadron in its attack on Brussels-Evere airfield during Operation Bodenplatte, an attempt to gain air superiority during the Battle of the Bulge. Whilst south of Brussels Glunz claimed his last victory of the war, an RAF Spitfire flown by Flight Lieutenant David Harling who was killed in the encounter. In addition, Glunz made nine strafing attacks on the Brussels-Evere airfield, claiming five aircraft destroyed, plus two further damaged.

On 18 March 1945, Glunz left the 26th Fighter Wing and was transferred to the 3rd Group of the Fighter Replacement Training Wing, equipped with the Me 262 jet fighter. However, because of the general chaos at the time he never flew the Me 262 in combat. He was captured by US troops in May 1945 and was released a month later and returned home. During the post-war years Glunz was a Formula 3 racing driver, competing in nine races and had a second and a third placing. He died on 1 August 2002 in Lüdenscheid in North Rhine-Westphalia, Germany.

Berthold KORTS

Leutnant

Knight's Cross: Awarded on 29 August 1943 as *Leutnant* and pilot with the 9th Squadron of the 52nd Fighter Wing for operations over the Soviet Union.

Berthold Korts claimed 108 aerial victories during the Second World War and all of them over the Eastern Front, achieved in just 383 days! He was born on 21 May 1912 in Karlsruhe, a city in south-western Germany, and he joined the artillery in 1938, transferring to the *Luftwaffe* two years later.

He began his pilots training during the summer and in June 1942, and with the rank of *Feldwebel* he joined the 9th Squadron of the 52nd Fighter Wing on the Eastern Front. At this time his Squadron was attached to the 3rd Group under the command of *Hauptmann*

(Deutsches Wehrkundearchiv)

Hermann Graf, a future fighter ace and Diamonds recipient. In early August 1942 Korts was based about 35 miles west-south-west of Salsk near Rostov in the Soviet Union. Now with the rank of *Unteroffizier*, he flew in support of the 1st Panzer Army and on 6 August he claimed his first victory, an LaGG-3 fighter. Korts claimed two Soviet Boston bombers on the 14th, and another on the 23rd and a few days later he was awarded the Iron Cross 2nd Class. He then flew in support of the 17th Army across the Kuban River and during September he claimed a further six victories and was awarded the Iron Cross 1st Class. By the end of the year he had achieved twenty-one aerial victories and had been awarded the *Luftwaffe* Honour Goblet on 1 February 1943.

During the spring he served with the Staff of the 52nd Fighter Wing and achieved more victories over the Kuban bridgehead area. Commissioned as a *Leutnant* in April he claimed four more victories on the 15th and by the end of the month had claimed his 31st victory. He went on to claim another eighteen victories during May, which included three on the 8th, and five on the 26th and 27th to become an 'ace-in-a-day' two days in a row. On 1 June he claimed his 50th victory, and had by the end of the month claimed a total of fifty-six victories. He claimed four victories on 5 July, which included his 60th and was awarded the German Cross in Gold on 12 July.

In late July he was appointed *Staffelkapitän* of the 9th Squadron, still with the 52nd Fighter Wing, and flew combat missions during the fighting near Oryol. On 28 July during a Soviet air attack on German positions Korts claimed an LaGG-3 fighter shot down west of Bolkhov. He claimed his 70th victory on 1 August and claimed four victories on the 3rd and nine on the 4th, which included his 80th victory. This made him an 'ace-in-a-day' for the third time, and his Group claimed a total of forty-two victories that day. On 19 August he shot down five victories to become an 'ace-in-a-day' yet again and this included his 100th victory, an Il-2 ground-attack aircraft over north-east Kuteinikowo in the Ukraine. He claimed his 108th and last victory on 23 August, then six days later it was announced that he had been awarded the Knight's Cross. However, that same day he went missing together with his wingman *Unteroffizier* Hans-Otto Müller. They were last seen during combat with a Soviet P-39 fighter in the area of Amvrosiivka, Ukraine and their bodies have never been found.

Heinz-Edgar BERRES

Hauptmann

Knight's Cross: Awarded as *Oberleutnant* and *Staffelkapitän* of the 1st Squadron of the 77th Fighter Wing, posthumously on 19 September 1943 for operations over the Soviet Union, Malta, North Africa and Italy.

Heinz-Edgar Berres claimed forty-nine aerial victories in over 354 missions during the Second World War and all but three were on the Western Front. He was born in Koblenz, Germany on 10 January 1920, and he joined the *Luftwaffe* as a pilot and after his training was posted to the 3rd Squadron of the 2nd Training or Instruction Wing in August 1941. He was briefly assigned to the Staff Squadron of the 1st Group of the 77th Fighter Wing. He claimed his first victory on 29 November 1941, a Tupolev SB-3 twin-engined bomber. In December his unit was redesignated the 1st Squadron and on the 29th he claimed another victory and then another on 28 February 1942 but both were

(Deutsches Wehrkundearchiv)

unconfirmed. He was commissioned as a *Leutnant* and on 9 March he claimed his second official victory and was awarded the Iron Cross 2nd Class. He claimed his third victory on 24 March, then shot down a USAAF B-24 Liberator bomber on 12 June over the Romanian oilfields near Ploesti, and was shortly after awarded the Iron Cross 1st Class.

In early July his squadron was relocated to the Mediterranean and he flew from Comiso in Sicily and claimed ten Spitfires and one P-40 over Malta between July and October. On 8 November Operation Torch began and Allied forces invaded Vichy French Morocco and Algeria. The Germans and Italians sent in large forces to prevent the Allied advance into Tunisia. It was a success, and the fall of the country into Allied hands was prevented and the 77th Fighter Wing played an important part. Berres together with the Staff Squadron was now based in North Africa and by the end of the year he had claimed twenty-two victories. On 25 January 1943 Berres was awarded the *Luftwaffe* Honour Goblet after claiming his 24th victory. He claimed five more during February and was awarded the German Cross in Gold on 16 February. On 13 March he was appointed *Staffelkapitän* of the 1st Squadron of the 77th Fighter Wing, based in Fatnassa, Tunisia. On 24 March he claimed two P-40s and one B-25 Mitchell medium bomber west of Fatnassa and on 22 April he shot down a Spitfire to claim his 40th aerial victory. He didn't claim another victory until 2 July when he shot down four aircraft, two Spitfires and two P-40s, and on the 24th he claimed what would be his last victory, a P-51 Mustang south of Cesaro.

Seven Bf 109s from the 77th Fighter Wing, including Berres, took off and were ordered to provide fighter escort to ten Junkers Ju 52 transport aircraft which had been tasked with resupplying the German forces on the northern coast of Sicily. About 12 miles east of Milazzo, the escort fighters came under attack by about thirty RAF Spitfires. During this encounter all ten Junkers transport aircraft were shot down and four Bf 109s were also shot down, one being Berres. It was reported that he had no time to react and his aircraft when hit went into a steep dive and crashed. Berres was posthumously awarded the Knight's Cross on 19 September and promoted to *Hauptmann*.

Hans Heinrich DÖBRICH

Oberleutnant

Knight's Cross: Awarded on 19 September 1943 as *Feldwebel* and fighter pilot with the 6th Squadron of the 5th Fighter Wing for operations over the Soviet Union and for achieving sixty-five aerial victories.

Hans Döbrich claimed a total of sixty-five victories in 244 combat missions, all flown over the Eastern Front during the Second World War. He was born on 24 March 1916 in Sonneberg, Thüringen, in Central Germany and he joined the *Luftwaffe* in January 1940. He served with Air Training Regiment 72 at Fels am Wagram in Austria and from there he transferred to air school to train as a pilot.

In August 1941 he was transferred to Fighter Pilot School 2 in Zerbst and in January 1942, now qualified as a fighter pilot he joined the 1st Squadron of the 5th Fighter Wing in Kjevik, Norway. In March *Unteroffizier* Döbrich transferred to the 6th Squadron in Petsamo, Murmansk in the Soviet Union where on 19 July he was shot down.

(Deutsches Wehrkundearchiv)

His Bf 109F-4 was struck in the radiator after an aerial engagement with a Soviet Yak-1 fighter and his aircraft caught fire and Döbrich had to bail out. He found himself about 12 miles behind enemy lines and spent the next seven days walking back to the German lines.

On 24 April 1942 Döbrich claimed his first aerial victory, a Hurricane west of Murmansk, and five days after he claimed his second victory, a Polikarpov I-153 fighter. He claimed another seven aerial victories during May and was awarded the Iron Cross 1st and 2nd Classes after claiming his ninth victory. During June 1942 he shot down nine aircraft and was awarded the *Luftwaffe* Honour Goblet on 17 August 1942 after claiming his 20th victory. By 9 September he had achieved his 30th aerial victory, and on 15 October was awarded the German Cross in Gold after claiming his 39th victory, a Yakovlev Yak-1 fighter near Murmaschi. In early 1943 he was promoted to *Feldwebel* and claimed two victories on 23 March, which included his 50th, a P-40 fighter. He claimed a P-39 on 3 June and shot down four Soviet Hurricanes on 5 June, claiming his 60th victory on the 20th, another Hurricane shot down over the region of Kandalakscha. He claimed two more victories on 21 June, an Il-2 ground-attack aircraft on 9 July and he claimed two victories on 16 July. A few minutes later he was himself shot down near Fiskerhalzen, and bailed out into Petsamofjord and was rescued by a German ship. He was severely wounded and as a result was taken off flying duties and sent to hospital in Kirkenes.

He spent many months recovering in hospital and was awarded the Knight's Cross on 19 September 1943, shortly afterwards was promoted to *Leutnant*. He never returned to operational duty and before the end of the war he was promoted to *Oberleutnant* whilst still in hospital. He was put in a prisoner-of-war camp near Traunstein in May 1945 by US troops and was released in April the following year. After the war he was employed by a fashion company in Vienna, rising to factory controller in January 1948. Döbrich died of heart-related problems in Vienna on 6 April 1984.

Erich Alfred 'Bubi' HARTMANN

Major

Knight's Cross: Awarded on 29 October 1943, whilst *Leutnant* and attached to the 7th Squadron of the 52nd Fighter Wing, after achieving his 148th victory over the Soviet Union. It was presented personally to Hartmann by Hitler at his headquarters the *Wolfschanze*, East Prussia,

Knight's Cross with Oakleaves: *Leutnant* Hartmann became the 420th recipient on 2 March 1944, as *Staffelkapitän* of the 9th Squadron of the 52nd Fighter Wing, whilst still flying combat missions over the Soviet Union. The award was presented to him by Hitler at the Berghof in early April 1944.

Hartmann whilst serving as *Staffelkapitän* of the 9th Squadron of the 52nd Fighter Wing, the youngest recipient of the Knight's Cross with Oakleaves and Swords. (Deutsches Wehrkundearchiv)

Knight's Cross with Oakleaves and Swords: On 2 July 1944, he became the 75th recipient of the Swords, in recognition of his 266th victory, whilst an *Oberleutnant* and still serving as *Staffelkapitän* of the 9th Squadron of the 52nd Fighter Wing. Hartmann was the youngest recipient of the Swords, and it was presented to him by Hitler on 2 August at *Führer* Headquarters in East Prussia, together with Friedrich Lang and Heinz-Wolfgang Schnaufer, the night-fighter ace.

Knight's Cross with Oakleaves, Swords and Diamonds: On 25 August 1944, he became the 18th and the youngest pilot to receive the award after achieving 303 victories, whilst still serving as *Staffelkapitän* with the 52nd Fighter Wing. The presentation was made by Hitler at his Military Headquarters in East Prussia.

Erich Hartmann was the most successful fighter pilot of the Second World War, claiming 352 aerial victories. Known by his nickname 'Bubi' which means boy or lad in German, he always looked ten years younger than his actual age. In his glory days, he was handsome with blond hair and blue eyes; he epitomized the German Nordic man. He was born on 19 April 1922, at Weissbach in the district of Böblingen in Baden-Württemberg. He spent much of his childhood in China, where his father Alfred Erich, a physician, practised during the 1920s. His mother, Elisabeth Wilhelmine Machthof, was once a pilot of some repute and was responsible for Hartmann's early interest in flying. The family returned to Germany in 1928 when the Chinese Civil War broke out. His younger brother Alfred served in the *Luftwaffe* as a gunner on a Junkers Ju 87 in North Africa. He was captured by the British and spent four years as a prisoner of war. Hartmann was educated at the *Volksschule* in Weil im Schönbuch from April 1928 to April 1932. He later attended the Gymnasium in Böblingen until April 1936 and finally at the local school in Korntal, where he met his future wife, Ursula 'Usch' Paetsch. Frau Hartmann was originally a sports flyer, but after the Nazis came to power, gliding clubs were encouraged. She helped to establish a flying club at Weil in Schönbuch near Stuttgart in 1936. The young Hartmann was well-versed in the way of flying by his mother whilst still in his teens and gained his pilot's licence in 1937.

On 15 October 1940, he joined the *Luftwaffe* and entered Military Training Regiment 10 at Neukurn, at the Air Academy School at Berlin-Gatow, qualifying as a fighter pilot in August 1941. From October 1941 to February 1942 he attended Fighter Pilot School 2 at Lachen-Speyerdorf, and later attended the Pilots School at Zerbst. He was commissioned as a *Leutnant* in March and in July was posted to Supplementary Group East at Gleiwitz for operational training, which he completed in October 1942. As a young pilot he wanted to impress and show off to his colleagues and on at least one occasion he ignored regulations and performed aerobatics over the airfield at Zerbst, where he was training. His senior officer at the airfield wasn't impressed and as a result, Hartmann was confined to his quarters for a week. Hartmann later wrote that 'The week in confinement saved my life'. His roommate and friend took a flight in an aircraft Hartmann should have been on. The aircraft developed engine problems and crashed, his room-mate was killed. He joined the 7th Squadron of the 52nd Fighter Wing on the Eastern Front on 10 October 1942, and *Leutnant* Hartmann found himself under the guidance of *Oberfeldwebel* Edmund 'Paule' Rossmann, considered one of the best pilots on the Eastern Front. During this time he learnt from several other accomplished aces, including *Oberfeldwebel* Alfred Grislawski and *Leutnant* Walter Krupinski. He flew his first combat mission on 14 October, which ended without shooting down any enemy aircraft when he ran out of fuel and had to make a crash landing. He was not injured apart from his pride and his commanding officer had a few choice words to say to the young pilot.

Hartmann recorded his first victory, a Soviet Il-2 ground-attack aircraft, shot down on 5 November 1942. Together with three other fighters he had attacked a force of twenty-eight Soviet fighters. Hartmann was hit by return fire and had to make a belly landing, and was picked up by an Army car and taken back to his base. This first encounter with the enemy made him a better pilot, but he had nevertheless lost his aircraft. Two days later he was stricken with fever and hospitalized for two weeks, and on 17 December Hartmann was awarded the Iron Cross 2nd Class. He didn't score another victory until 27 January 1943, a Soviet MiG-1, and on 7 March he was awarded the Iron Cross 1st Class after claiming his fourth victory. By the end of April, his victory total stood at eleven. Hartmann had painted a bleeding heart on the fuselage of his Bf 109; this he would later say symbolized his anguish he

Hartmann with his crew chief and friend Heinz 'Bimmel' Mertens. (Deutsches Wehrkundearchiv)

felt when he was away from his wife, Ursula. On 23 May 1943, he claimed his 17th victory, but two days later he had to make a forced landing after colliding with an LaGG-3 fighter. After a period of leave, he returned to duty in late June. By the end of July, his victory total had reached forty-two, including seven aircraft shot down on 7 July. In August, he claimed forty-eight victories, including five on the 1st, 4th, 5th and 7th, and on 20 August, following his 90th victory, Hartmann was shot down and captured. Hartmann feigned injury, and when his captors weren't looking he managed to escape and after two days reached his unit. On 2 September, Hartmann was appointed *Staffelkapitän* of 9th Squadron of 52nd Fighter Wing, and he claimed his 100th victory on 20 September, and in October he claimed another 33 victories.

After Kursk the demands on fighter pilots increased. The Germans had suffered huge losses and Kursk was certainly a turning point in the war on the Eastern Front. Germany had now begun to lose control of the skies. In early August 1943, Hartmann flew twenty missions. By the end of the month, he had ninety aerial victories. On the 19th, his aircraft was badly damaged after aerial combat with a Soviet fighter and Hartmann had to make an emergency landing, setting down in a large field of sunflowers. As he unbuckled the parachute and prepared to climb out he could see through his dirty windscreen a German truck approaching. He was relieved because he was unsure if he had landed in enemy territory or not. However, as the truck came closer, two soldiers got out and Hartmann didn't recognize their uniform as German. He soon realized to his horror they were Russian uniforms, he had crashed behind enemy lines. He knew that if he made a run for it, they would shoot him, so he decided if he was to have any chance of escape he would have to fake an injury. Two Red Army soldiers climbed onto the wings of his aircraft and Hartmann pretended to be unconscious. The Russians pulled him from the cockpit and Hartmann screamed out in 'pain', they let him go and said, 'War over. Hitler kaput'. They then carefully helped Hartmann out of the aircraft and carried him on a makeshift stretcher to their truck. After a brief examination by a doctor, he was amazed to find himself back in the truck heading for a hospital. He knew he had to escape. While Hartmann considered what to do, some German Stukas were heard overhead and the two Russian soldiers kept looking up at the sky. Hartmann took his chance and jumped the one in the back with him, and pushed him; he struck his head on the inside of the truck and collapsed. Hartmann jumped from the truck and ran. Bullets flew past his head, but he kept running. After many hours he eventually made it to the German lines and was nearly shot by a sentry. But he had made it back alive. However, he was then told that his mechanic *Feldwebel* 'Bimmel' Mertens had gone looking for him. For over 24 hours Mertens was missing but eventually turned up, hungry and exhausted but alive.

The two men were so pleased to see each other. He was awarded the *Luftwaffe* Honour Goblet on 13 September and the German Cross in Gold on 17 October.

Hartmann wearing his Knight's Cross with Oakleaves and Swords and dressed in his usual *Luftwaffe* black leather jacket. (Deutsches Wehrkundearchiv)

During October Hartmann claimed another thirty-three victories. On 11th he claimed his 125th victory, and on 29 October was awarded the Knight's Cross. He recorded his 150th victory on 13 December, a Soviet La-5. On 30 January 1944, he shot down six aircraft and claimed another five on 1 February. During the first two months of 1944, Hartmann claimed over fifty Soviet aircraft, which included his 175th aerial victory on 23 January an La-5, and his 200th, on 26 February, one of ten shot down that day! By this time, the Soviet pilots were familiar with Hartmann's radio sign of 'Karaya 1', and a price of 10,000 roubles was put on his head for anyone who shot down his aircraft. On 2 March Hartmann was awarded the Oakleaves and together with three other recipients, Gerhard Barkhorn, Walter Krupinski and Johannes Wiese, all arrived at Hitler's headquarters in early April still drunk on cognac from the night before. Hartmann was reprimanded by Hitler's adjutant Nikolaus von Below, for intoxication and for handling Hitler's hat. Hartmann had taken the *Führer*'s hat off a hat stand thinking it was his own. He put it on which created some laughter among his friends and then said Hitler must have a large head! Von Below was not impressed.

On 21 March 1944, it was Hartmann who claimed the 3,500th aerial victory of the 52nd Fighter Wing. For a brief time, he operated over Romania, intercepting the American daylight bombing raids on the Romanian oilfields. On 1 May Hartmann was promoted to *Oberleutnant* and his squadron had been resisting the Soviet Crimean Offensive and recording many aerial victories. On 21 May, Hartmann engaged fighters from the USAAF during the defence of the Ploiesti oilfields, over Romania. He claimed six aircraft on 1 June, two of which were P-39s, and on 4 June he claimed his 250th aerial victory, another P-39, one of seven shot down that day by Hartmann. He claimed his 265th victory on 24 June 1944, a USAAF P-51 Mustang. In late June a Soviet counter-offensive took Hartmann's unit back to the Crimea and he accounted for 60 Soviet aircraft, to bring his total score to 267. In August he claimed thirty-five victories, including eight on 23 August. On 24 August, he became the first fighter pilot to record 300 victories, on a day when he shot down eleven enemy aircraft. The following day Hartmann was awarded the Diamonds to his Knight's Cross, and the following month was promoted to *Hauptmann*. He said later in a post-war interview that when he arrived at Hitler's headquarters he was asked to surrender his sidearm – an extra security precaution after the failed assassination attempt on Hitler in July 1944. Hartmann refused and threatened to decline the Diamonds if he were not trusted to carry his pistol. After consulting with Hitler's *Luftwaffe* adjutant it was decided that Hartmann could keep his pistol and he accepted the Diamonds. During his meeting with Hitler, Hartmann discussed at length the shortcomings of fighter-pilot training. He also stated that Hitler told him that he believed that, militarily, the war was lost, and that he wished the *Luftwaffe* had more like him. He was then granted extended leave and ordered not to fly.

Hartmann was now assigned to a test squadron, and he flew the new Me 262 jet fighter. In October his prohibition on combat flying was lifted and after a request to return to combat duty *Generalleutnant* Adolf Galland cancelled his assignment. Galland could see the advantages of keeping such an ace in combat. Hartmann was then ordered to go on holiday to the *Luftwaffe* resort for fighter pilots in Bad Wiessee. There on 10 September 1944, he married his long-time love, 'Usch' Paetsch. Witnesses to the wedding included his friends, Gerhard Barkhorn and Wilhelm Batz. On returning to combat duty Hartmann was appointed *Staffelkapitän* of 4th Squadron of 52nd Fighter Wing, based in Hungary. By the end of 1944, he had raised his victory tally to 331. From 1 to 14 February 1945, Hartmann briefly led the 1st Group of 53rd Fighter Wing. He was only the acting *Gruppenkommandeur* and he relinquished the command to *Hauptmann* Helmut Lipfert on 15 February. In mid-February, Hartmann was given command of the 1st Group of the 52nd Fighter Wing, and in March he was transferred to Lechfeld for training on the Me 262 fighter. On 17 April 1945, he became the only man to achieve 350 aerial victories and was later that same month promoted to the rank of *Major*. On 8 May 1945, the last day of the war in Europe, Hartmann shot down his 352nd and last victory, a Soviet Yak-9 fighter over Brünn, Czechoslovakia.

After the collapse of the Reich, Hartmann marched westward across Czechoslovakia with his staff, together with other *Luftwaffe* fighter aces, including Adolf Galland, to avoid capture by the advancing Red Army. They marched right into the arms of Patton's 3rd US Army. Hartmann became a prisoner of the Americans. However, under an agreement made by Roosevelt and Stalin at the Yalta Conference, Hartmann was soon transferred to Soviet custody. Hartmann was incarcerated in various Soviet prisons for 10½ years, stripped of his human rights, treated badly and half-starved. He rarely received letters from his wife, sometimes one a month if he was lucky. He had a son, conceived on his final leave, but he never met him. When little Peter Erich died in 1948, Hartmann was unaware of this until 1950. Originally Hartmann had been sentenced to 25 years hard labour, but he refused to work.

He was eventually put into solitary confinement, which enraged his fellow prisoners. They began a revolt, overpowered the guards and freed him. Hartmann made a complaint to the commandant's office, asking for a representative from Moscow and an international inspection to visit the prison and acquit him. This was refused, and he was transferred to a camp in Novocherkassk, where he spent five more months in solitary. Eventually, he was granted a tribunal, but it upheld the original sentence and he was transferred to another camp, this time at Diaterka in the Ural Mountains. Also, his captors tried to convince Hartmann to cooperate with them and asked him to spy on his fellow officers. Hartmann refused and was given ten days of solitary confinement in a four-by-nine-by-six-foot chamber. He slept on a concrete floor and was given only bread and water. Another time during an interrogation he was asked more and more about the Me 262 jet fighter and during the interrogation he was struck by a Soviet officer with a cane across the face, prompting Hartmann to slam his chair over the head of the officer, knocking him out. Expecting to be shot, Hartmann was taken back to the small bunker. In 1955, Hartmann's mother wrote to the new West German Chancellor, Konrad Adenauer, to whom she appealed the release of her son. A trade agreement between West Germany and the Soviet Union was reached, and Hartmann was released along with 16,000 German military personnel.

When Hartmann finally returned to West Germany, he re-entered military service in the *Bundeswehr*, and he became an officer in the West German *Luftwaffe*, where he commanded West Germany's first all-jet unit, 71st Fighter Wing '*Richthofen*' (still active today). It was equipped with the Canadair Sabre jet fighters, and later with Lockheed F-104 Starfighters. Hartmann also made several trips to the United States, where he was trained on US Air Force equipment. However, Hartmann considered the F-104 a fundamentally flawed and unsafe aircraft and strongly opposed its adoption by the *Luftwaffe*. His outspoken criticism proved unpopular among his superiors, even though the aircraft had crashed 282 times and 115 German pilots had been killed. However, Hartmann was forced into early retirement in 1970. From 1971 to 1974 he worked as a flight instructor in Hangelar, near Bonn. In 1980 he became ill with angina pectoris – the condition that killed his father. By 1983 he had recovered and was clear to fly again, and he resumed flying as an instructor at various airfields. But, fearing a second attack, he decided to appear less at public events and went into semi-retirement. On 20 September 1993, he died at the age of 71 in Weil, Schönbuch, and is buried together with his wife, who died on 3 February 1996.

Otto 'Bruno' KITTEL

Oberleutnant

Knight's Cross: Awarded on 29 October 1943 as *Oberfeldwebel* with the 1st Group of the 54th Fighter Wing for exceeding 120 aerial victories over the Russian Front. He was presented with his award by *Oberst* Franz Reuss, a staff officer from the 6th Air Corps.

Knight's Cross with Oakleaves: He became the 449th recipient on 11 April 1944 as *Leutnant* whilst still serving with the 1st Group of the 54th Fighter Wing for claiming over 150 aerial victories, again over the Russian Front. The award was personally presented by Hitler on 5 May 1944, at the Berghof, Obersalzburg together with *Hauptmann* Alfred Grislawski, *Leutnant* Anton Hafner, *Hauptmann* Erich Rudorfer and *Leutnant* Günther Schack who were also presented with their Oakleaves.

(Deutsches Wehrkundearchiv)

Knight's Cross with Oakleaves and Swords: Awarded on 25 November 1944, to become the 113th recipient as *Oberleutnant* and *Staffelkapitän* of the 2nd Squadron of the 54th Fighter Wing in recognition for achieving 265 aerial victories. The award was presented by Hitler at the Reich Chancellery in Berlin in late November 1944.

Otto Kittel was born on 21 February 1917 in Kronsdorf, Jägerndorf, Austria-Hungary, now in the Moravian-Silesian region of the Czech Republic. He was a small in stature, very quiet and some say too serious, speaking slowly and with some hesitation. After working briefly as a car mechanic he joined the *Luftwaffe* at the age of 21 in January 1939. He began his pilot training towards the end of 1939 and once passed he attended various training courses and was transferred to the 1st Group of the 54th Fighter Wing '*Grünherz*' in February 1941, under the command of *Hauptmann* Hubertus von Bonin.

Kittel's first operations were escort mission in support of the German invasion of Yugoslavia, including the bombing of Belgrade, which killed almost 17,000 civilians. On 31 May 1941 he transferred as an *Unteroffizier* to the 2nd Squadron of the 54th Fighter Wing and from June took part in Operation Barbarossa, the Invasion of Russia. On 24 June he shot down his first two aerial victories, both Tupolev SB-2 twin-engined bombers. He claimed two Ilyushin I-2s near Dünaberg on 30 June, which remain unconfirmed, and that same day he was awarded the Iron Cross 2nd Class. He claimed a MiG-1 fighter on 18 August and the following day claimed a DB-3 bomber. By the end of 1941 he had claimed twelve aerial victories and had been awarded the Iron Cross 1st Class in October.

He shot down his first aircraft of 1942 on 27 February, a Polikarpov I-16, and on 20 March he claimed two P-40s and on 14 May he claimed two SB-2 twin-engined bombers. On 21 December Kittel was awarded the *Luftwaffe* Honour Goblet in recognition of his 12th aerial victory. On 12 January 1943 he became an 'ace-in-a-day' when he shot down six enemy aircraft to give himself a total of twenty-seven aerial victories, and by the end of the month his score had increased to thirty-one. When Kittel claimed his 39th aerial victory on 19 February it was the 54th Fighter Wing's 4,000th victory. On 15 March he was shot down approximately 40 miles behind Soviet lines in the vicinity of Dzukte, in the Courland area, and it took him three days to get back to the German lines.

Kittel took part in the spring battles over the Crimea Peninsula, Vyazuma-Bryansk, Vitebsk, Kharkov, Orsha and Orel regions, and was awarded the German Cross in Gold on 18 March, in recognition of his 45th aerial victory. During the Battle of Kursk, Kittel's squadron escorted Junkers Ju 87 Stukas of the Dive-Bomber Wing commanded by *Oberleutnant* Hans-Ulrich Rudel. In June he was promoted to *Oberfeldwebel* and claimed a total of six aerial victories that month and on 5 July he claimed four victories and on 7th he claimed another three. On 13 July he shot down four Ilyushin I-2 ground-attack aircraft and claimed three Lavochkin La-5 fighters on the 16th, and claimed two more aircraft on 17 July. On 2 August he shot down three aircraft and the following day he became an 'ace-in a day' again when he claimed seven aerial victories. On 14 September he claimed three more victories which included his 100th victory, a Yak-9 fighter shot down east of Karacev. He was the 53rd Luftwaffe pilot to achieve his century.

On 5 October he claimed two victories and on 12th he claimed three, another on the 13th, two more on the 14th and four on the 15th. On 29 October he was awarded the Knight's Cross in recognition of exceeding 120 aerial victories over Russia. On 1 November Kittel was commissioned as a *Leutnant*, and four days later he claimed three more aerial victories to give him a total of 126. In March he claimed a total of fifteen victories and on 4 April he claimed his 150th aerial victory and on the 14th was awarded the Knight's Cross with Oakleaves. Kittel continued to score regularly, claiming five aerial victories on 28 June, one on the 29th and four on the 30th. By the end of July 1944 he had achieved 190 aerial victories. In August Kittel was appointed *Staffelführer* which later became *Staffelkapitän* of the 3rd Squadron with the 54th Fighter Wing. He claimed eighteen aerial victories in

August and on 14 September he shot down six aircraft and his pace never faltered. He claimed three victories on 10 October, four on the 16th, six on the 27th, six on the 29th and three on 30 October to give himself a score of 264 aerial victories. On 25 November Kittel was awarded the Knight's Cross with Oakleaves and Swords and was promoted to *Oberleutnant*.

On 16 February 1945, Kittel took off in his Fw 190A to engage a formation of Soviet aircraft over the Courland Pocket. During an attack at low-level Kittel was seen to attack a Soviet Il-2 and then turn on another when his own aircraft was hit by return fire from another Il-2. His aircraft burst into flames and plummeted towards the ground, trailing a long sheet of flame, where it crashed. Kittel had no chance. The crash was believed to have been almost 4 miles south-west of Dzukste in Latvia. The death of Kittel seemed to trigger an end to the *Luftwaffe*'s resistance in the Courland Peninsula, and one squadron commander said, 'When Kittel was killed, for us darkness fell in the Courland Pocket'. It was not long before the German units caught up in the pocket were flying west to surrender to the Western Allies. Kittel was the most successful *Luftwaffe* fighter pilot to be shot down and killed during the Second World War. In the summer of 2013 his aircraft and his remains were found by two amateur researchers in Latvia.

Günther SCHACK

Hauptmann

Knight's Cross: Awarded on 29 October 1943 as *Leutnant* and fighter pilot in the 9th Squadron of the 51st Fighter Wing '*Mölders*' for operations over the Soviet Union and for claiming his 114th aerial victory over the Smolensk area of the Soviet Union.

Knight's Cross with Oakleaves: He became the 460th recipient on 20 April 1944 as *Leutnant* and *Staffelkapitän* of the 9th Squadron of the 51st Fighter Wing '*Mölders*' for continued actions over the Soviet Union and for claiming his 131st aerial victory. He was presented with his award by Hitler on 5 May 1944 at the Berghof together with *Hauptmann* Alfred Grislawski, *Leutnant* Anton Hafner, *Leutnant* Otto Kittel, *Oberleutnant* Emil Lang and *Hauptmann* Erich Rudorffer.

(Deutsches Wehrkundearchiv)

Günther Schack is credited with approximately 174 aerial victories during the Second World War, all of them whilst flying 780 combat missions over the Eastern Front. Schack was born on 12 November 1917 in Bartenstein, at the time in East Prussia, present-day Bartoszyce. Following his graduation from school he studied metallurgy at the University of Stuttgart and the Technical High School in Aachen. In 1937 he attempted to join the *Luftwaffe* but was not accepted as he was deemed unsuitable for military service due to a sports injury. Then on 1 September 1939, German forces invaded Poland which marked the beginning of the Second World War. Again Schack volunteered for military service and this time he was accepted.

On joining the *Luftwaffe* Schack began his training as a fighter pilot with the rank of *Gefreiter*. In March 1941 he was posted to the 7th Squadron of the 51st Fighter Wing, and was attached to the 3rd Group based at Saint-Omer in northern France and equipped with the Bf 109F-1 fighter aircraft. At this time his Squadron was fighting against the British, then on 26 May it was withdrawn from France and moved to Düsseldorf where it was replenished, the aircraft were serviced and made ready for new orders. By 15 June his unit was given orders to move and make ready for the incoming invasion of the Soviet Union and were based at airfields in Siedlco, Stara Wiés and Halasy, close to the Soviet border with Germany. On the 22nd Germany invaded the Soviet Union and the 51st Fighter Wing began flying fighter patrols along the Bug River. In July Schack's Group moved to an airfield at Orscha, about 62 miles south-west of Smolensk, and flew combat air patrols along the Dnieper in the area between Mogilev and Zhlobin. Flying near Orscha, Schack claimed his first aerial victory on 23 July and was soon afterwards awarded the Iron Cross 2nd Class.

In October the German forces launched a new offensive, Operation Typhoon, which resulted in the Battle of Moscow. On the 10th Schack claimed his second aerial victory, a Pe-2 Petlyakov dive-bomber north-east of Juchnov. Then on the 23rd Schack had to bail out from his stricken Bf 109 following aerial combat near Ugoskosawed. He claimed his third victory after one missions on 10 November, over Serpukhov and was awarded the Iron Cross 1st Class on 15 June 1942, after claiming five victories. By the end of August he had claimed his 11th victory and was promoted to *Feldwebel* soon after. He claimed two Pe-2 dive-bombers on 3 September and shot down another two a week later, and then on the following day he claimed a single LaGG-3 fighter.

During October the 3rd Group flew combat air patrols mainly over the area of Rzhev where the German 9th Army was deployed. On 10 November his Group received orders that their aircraft was to be converted to the Focke-Wulf Fw 190 at Jesau, south-east of Königsberg. One squadron at a time was converted, mainly because the *Luftwaffe* fighter units were already stretched in the combat area and were covering Army Group Centre. The first units converted were the staff Squadron and the 7th, while the 8th and 9th Squadrons were still engaged in combat. On 17 December Schack flew his first mission in his Fw 190 and claimed five Pe-2 aircraft near Sychyovka, making him an 'ace-in-a-day' for the first time. On 1 January 1943 Schack was commissioned as a *Leutnant* and on the 16th was awarded the *Luftwaffe* Honour Goblet in recognition of achieving his 23rd aerial victory. On 23 February he claimed another five aircraft, becoming an 'ace-in-a-day' for the second time, and the following day he claimed his 38th victory and was awarded the German Cross in Gold. Two days later he claimed three more victories on 8 March and claimed another three the next day, giving him a total of forty-four victories. He claimed two more on 11 March and on 1 April and was then transferred to the Replacement Fighter Group East where he served as an instructor. More often than not fighter aces were taken off front-line duty to share their experiences and skill with new fighter pilots destined for the Eastern Front.

Schack returned to the front on 5 July and was posted to the 8th Squadron of the 51st Fighter Wing. He returned just in time for the start of the German offensive Operation Citadel, the Battle of Kursk. During the operation his squadron was part of the 3rd Group supporting the 9th Army on the northern flank of the offensive. The Soviets launched their own offensive on 12 July, with its objective being to collapse the Orel salient to cut behind the 9th Army and annihilate it. The 3rd Group flew its first missions on 15 July, during the early afternoon in the vicinity north of the Orel salient. Schack claimed four aerial victories, which included his 50th, and went onto claim another on the 19th, and two more on the 20th. By the end of July he had claimed his 56th victory, continuing to score victories throughout August, claiming his 80th aerial victory east of Jelnja on the 19th, and by the 27th he had achieved his 90th victory. The following day his aircraft was struck by friendly fire and he was forced to land at Glukhov but wasn't injured. In mid-August Schack had been appointed *Staffelführer* of the 7th Squadron a position he held until 15 October.

On 3 September, whilst flying from Konotop escorting Junkers Ju 87s on their mission to attack Soviet forces south-east of Ssewsk, west

Schack became the 460th recipient of the Oakleaves on 20 April 1944, and was presented with the award personally by Hitler at the Berghof on 5 May 1944. (*Author's collection*)

of Kursk, Schack claimed an La-5 fighter. On 6 September he claimed two victories, which included his 100th aerial victory, a Yak-7 shot down over Buda. He became the 47th *Luftwaffe* fighter pilot to achieve his century. He continued to claim aerial victories throughout September and October, and was awarded the Knight's Cross on 29 October in recognition of his 114th victory. In early December Schack was appointed *Staffelkapitän* of the 9th Squadron, replacing *Oberleutnant* Maximilian Mayerl who had been transferred. Schack claimed seven victories during January and another seven during February. The German forces began to be pushed out of the Soviet Union and Schack and his squadron covered the retreat of Army Group Centre, moving from Orscha to Terespol and then back to Minsk and Kaunas. On 20 April Schack was awarded the Knight's Cross with Oakleaves after claiming his 131st aerial victory. A few days later he was promoted to *Oberleutnant* and continued to claim victories. On 7 July he claimed his 140th, and on 17 August he became the 25th fighter pilot to achieve his 150th aerial victory. On 16 September he shot down four Yak-9 fighters over east Libau and by the end of the month had claimed his 165th victory.

In December 1944 Schack was promoted to *Hauptmann* and appointed *Gruppenkommandeur* of the 1st Group of the 51st Fighter Wing, succeeding *Major* Erich Leie. At the end of January 1945, the 1st and 4th Groups were moved to an airfield at Danzig-Langfuhr where the two units were supplied with new pilots. Here it was placed under the control of the 2nd Air Corps and fought in support of the evacuation of East Prussia. However, because of serious fuel shortages Schack was never able to fly missions with more than a few aircraft at a time. Unfortunately this created the false impression that his Group was over-staffed, with many pilots staying on the ground seemingly without a job, so Schack was ordered to transfer some of his personnel, which included pilots, to the infantry! He was even threatened with a court martial by *Oberst* Otto Weiss if he did not comply. He reluctantly gave up some of his ground personnel. From February to March his Group flew in the area of Elbing and sources vary with respect to the number of aerial victories Schack claimed.

On 12 April the 1st Group had just one serviceable aircraft remaining, which Schack had to bail out of following damage during aerial combat. He suffered burns to his face and had to be flown out. Soon after this his Group was disbanded. On 1 May, whilst still recovering from his injuries, he was named *Gruppenkommandeur* of the 4th Group of the 3rd Fighter Wing, based at Rerik. Three days later the German forces in north-west Germany surrendered to the Allies. After the war Schack met with Lieutenant Hollis 'Bud' Nowlin, the US fighter pilot who had shot him down over East Prussia. They met again a few years later and in 1991 they met for a third time in America at the 357th Fighter Group reunion in Georgia. Schack spent the last few years of his life in a cabin in the middle of a forest and he died on 14 June 2003 in Nideggen-Schmidt, North Rhine-Westphalia.

Heinrich JUNG

Hauptmann

Knight's Cross: Awarded posthumously on 12 November 1943 as *Hauptmann* and commander of the 2nd Group of the 54th Fighter Wing for operations over the Soviet Union.

Heinrich Jung claimed a total of sixty-five aerial victories whilst flying combat missions over the Eastern Front during the Second World War. He was born on 15 August 1912 in Offenbach am Main in Hesse and during the Spanish Civil War *Leutnant* Jung flew reconnaissance missions as part of the Condor Legion where he won the Spanish Cross in Gold with Swords in April 1939.

He joined the 1st Group of the 54th Fighter Wing in November 1940 and was assigned to the 3rd Fighter Wing. From June 1941, now a *Hauptmann*, he saw action in Russia as part of Operation Barbarossa, claiming his first aerial victory on 13 October, a Boston twin-engined bomber north of

Wojlakata. He claimed his second victory on the 30th, a MiG-1, and on 13 November he claimed two victories over Leningrad and was shortly after awarded the Iron Cross 2nd Class. From early January 1942 his squadron was based at Krasnogvardeysky south-west of Leningrad and he flew the Bf 109F-2. He couldn't fly in combat until 19 January because of bad weather and then flew in support of the army during the Soviet winter offensive and claimed two more victories that month, and was awarded the Iron Cross 1st Class. In February his Group moved to Siwerskaja about 45 miles south of Leningrad and he claimed three victories on the 23rd and two on the 28th, which included his 10th victory.

From April he flew as part of the 4th Squadron over Demyansk in support of ground troops and by 14 August he had claimed his 25th victory. He claimed three more victories on 22 August and in early October he was awarded the *Luftwaffe* Honour Goblet, and after

(Deutsches Wehrkundearchiv)

claiming his 30th victory he was awarded the German Cross in Gold on 17 November. From early 1943 he was flying the Focke-Wulf Fw 190A, and from 22 February he flew as *Gruppenkommandeur* of the 2nd Group of the 54th Fighter Wing. He claimed his 45th victory on 6 March and his 50th on 21 March and from May he flew from Orel. In July he became really successful, claiming a total of twelve aircraft but then his luck ran out! He had claimed an La-5 fighter on 29 July and during the very early hours of the next day he was shot down and killed just east of Mga in the Kirovsky District of Leningrad Oblast. He was eventually posthumously awarded the Knight's Cross on 12 November 1943, four months after his death.

Hubert STRASSL

Oberfeldwebel

Knight's Cross: Awarded posthumously on 12 November 1943 as *Oberfeldwebel* and fighter pilot with the 8th Squadron of the 51st Fighter Wing '*Mölders*' for operations over the Soviet Union.

Hubert Strassl claimed sixty-seven aerial victories during the Second World War in just 12 months over the Eastern Front. He was born on 24 May 1918 in Linz, Austria-Hungary and with his pilot training completed he was assigned to the 9th Squadron of the 51st Fighter Wing as an *Unteroffizier* in December 1941.

He first saw combat during the start of the Soviet winter offensive and on 17 December his Group, having moved to Juchow-South, lost a large part of their equipment due to the extreme weather conditions. At the beginning of 1942 he was in Dugino flying the Bf 109F-2, where his Group was in a desperate condition and only flew very few missions. On 5 April his Group moved to Smolensk and from 4 May and was deployed near to the operational area of the 9th Army. On 6 July he

(Deutsches Wehrkundearchiv)

claimed his first aerial victory, a Petlyakov Pe-2 dive-bomber, and he claimed two more victories on 4 August. By the end of the month Strassl had claimed a total of eleven victories, which included four on 19 August, and had been awarded the Iron Cross 1st and 2nd Class. His Group's mission ended in November when his Group was converted to the Focke-Wulf Fw 190A-2 fighter.

On 28 January 1943 his Group moved from Dugino to Orel, and from early February moved again to Krasnogvardeysky and converted to the Bf 109G. His Group returned to Orel in late May and from June Strassl began to score many victories, he claimed two on 1 May, and three the following day. On 6 June he transferred into the 8th Squadron and continued to fly from Orel and added to his victory tally, and in fact he claimed his 20th victory that same day. On the 8th he became an 'ace-in-a-day' when he claimed six victories and three days later he claimed another three, which included his 30th victory, a MiG-3 fighter. A few days later he was promoted to *Feldwebel* and continued to claim victories. On 5 July he claimed an amazing fifteen victories in a single day to become a triple 'ace-in-a-day', and the following day he claimed four more victories, mainly over Maloarkhangelsk and near Trosna. On the 7th he claimed six victories to become an 'ace-in-a-day', and the next day he did the same, claimed another six victories. In fact he claimed a total of thirty aerial victories in just four days and during this time he was promoted to *Oberfeldwebel*.

However on 7 July shortly after claiming his sixth victory of the day his luck ran out. He was being hunted by Soviet LaGG-3 fighters and was unable to get out from under them, and he found himself forced ever lower, and tried to gain height. The fighters attacked and a burst from one of them shredded his wing. He bailed out near Ponyri, north of Kursk, but was less than 100ft from the ground. His parachute failed to open in time and he was killed. He was posthumously awarded the Honour Goblet on 9 August 1943, the German Cross in Gold seven days later and the Knight's Cross on 12 November 1943.

Karl-Heinz 'Benjamin' WEBER

Hauptmann

Knight's Cross: Awarded on 12 November 1943 as *Oberleutnant* and *Staffelführer* of the 7th Squadron of the 51st Fighter Wing '*Mölders*' for operations over the Soviet Union and for claiming his 100th aerial victory.

Knight's Cross with Oakleaves: Awarded posthumously on 20 July 1944, as the 529th recipient as *Hauptmann* and *Staffelkapitän* in the 51st Fighter Wing '*Mölders*' for continued operations over the Soviet Union after claiming his 132nd aerial victory.

(Deutsches Wehrkundearchiv)

Karl-Heinz Weber volunteered for the *Luftwaffe* at the age of only 17 and flew over 500 combat missions during the Second World War, achieving 132 aerial victories in less than three years, all of them over the Eastern Front. Weber was born on 30 January 1922 in Heringsdorf in the province of Pomerania, Prussia. He flew gliders in his teens and volunteered to join the *Luftwaffe* in late 1939. He was posted to the 7th Squadron of the 51st Fighter Wing in October 1940 with the rank of *Leutnant*, and was stationed at Peuplingues, France.

In June 1941, whilst attached to the 2nd Group, Weber and his Squadron were transferred to the Eastern Front in preparation for Operation Barbarossa, the invasion of the Soviet Union. From June Weber flew from Kobryn in Belarus and on the 24th he claimed his first aerial victory, a Tupolev SB-2 bomber. He claimed another SB-2 on 30 June and claimed his third victory, an Il-2 ground-attack aircraft, the following day and was awarded the Iron Cross 2nd Class on 6 July. He claimed another four victories during the following 33 days and was awarded the Iron Cross 1st Class on 17 August.

From November 1941 Weber was attached to a fighter testing unit and he returned to his squadron in July 1942. He claimed two Pe-2 twin-engined dive-bombers on 5 July, both shot down over Sychyovka, and he claimed a further five victories during August but on 3 September he was wounded when his Bf 109F-2 was shot down whilst attacking a Pe-2 north-west of Dugino. While he was recovering from his injuries the 3rd Group of the 51st Fighter Wing was relocated to Jesau, near Königsberg for conversion training to the Focke-Wulf Fw 190A-2. On 3 September he claimed his 21st aerial victory and in recognition of this was awarded the *Luftwaffe* Honour Goblet in September.

On 19 November, the Soviets launched the Velikiye Luki Offensive Operation, part of the northern pincer of the Rzhev-Sychevka Strategic Offensive Operation, known as Operation Mars, in an effort to liberate the Soviet city. During the operation Weber claimed a MiG-3 fighter east-south-east of Zubtsov on 15 January 1943, and claimed two Pe-2 dive-bombers on the 29th. He claimed three Il-2s on 3 February, and shot down two aircraft on the 23rd and the 24th to claim his 31st aerial victory and was awarded the German Cross in Gold on 16 March. Weber claimed another four victories in May, and on 5 June was appointed *Staffelführer* of the 7th Squadron, replacing *Hauptmann* Herbert Wehnelt who had fallen ill.

On 5 July, during the Battle of Kursk he claimed five aerial victories to become an 'ace in a day' and which included his 40th victory, claimed four victories the following day and on 8 July he claimed his 50th victory, a MiG-3 fighter. On 12 July Weber together with his wingman *Unteroffizier* Heinrich Dittlmann shot down Soviet fighter aces Nikolay Zhukov and Nikolay Safonov. He claimed his 75th aerial victory on 3 August and the next day he became an 'ace-in-a-day' for the second time when he shot down five aircraft to claim his 80th victory. On 11 August he shot down an Ilyushin Il-2 to claim his 90th victory and on the 13th he was appointed *Staffelkapitän* of his Squadron. On 22 October he claimed his 100th aerial victory, a Yak-9 fighter over Lojew, Poland, and as a result of his success was finally awarded the Knight's Cross on 12 November. Weber claimed two more victories on 22 November and then fell ill, and was away from the front for four weeks. He returned to combat on 23 December and continued to add to his score, claiming his 110th victory on 6 February 1944, and claimed his 120th victory on 22 February. In March 1944 he was promoted to *Hauptmann* and on 5 April he claimed his 130th victory, and 12 days later he claimed an LaGG-3 single-engined fighter over North Kovel, which would be his last victory of the war.

On 3 June Weber was appointed *Gruppenkommandeur* of the 3rd Group of the 1st Fighter Wing, succeeding *Major* Hartmann Grasser. Then only four days later Weber was shot down whilst leading his Group from Beauvais-Tille, France against Allied fighters south of Rouen on his first mission over the invasion front. It is assumed he had been shot down and killed when he failed to return from the mission, and later it was reported that his Messerschmitt Bf 109G-6 had been shot down by P-51 Mustangs from 315 Polish Fighter Squadron. As a result his command of the 3rd Group was temporarily given to *Hauptmann* Alfred Grislawski. Weber was posthumously awarded the Knight's Cross with Oakleaves on 20 July 1944. His body has never been recovered and he was officially declared dead by a German court in 1959.

Adolf BORCHERS

Major

Knight's Cross: Awarded on 22 November 1943 as *Hauptmann* and *Staffelkapitän* of the 11th Squadron of the 51st Fighter Wing '*Mölders*' for claiming his 77th aerial victory whilst flying operations over Poland, France, England and the Soviet Union.

Adolf Borchers claimed 132 aerial victories during the Second World War, of which all but two were over the Eastern Front. He was born in Wendhausen near Lüneburg, Germany on 10 February 1913, and he had two brothers who both fought during the war. Borchers joined the *Luftwaffe* in 1937 and underwent pilot training, and on its completion he joined the 1st Squadron of the 88th Fighter Group, known as the Condor Legion and took part as an *Unteroffizier* in the Spanish Civil War.

At the beginning of the Second World War he flew over Poland with the 2nd Squadron of the 77th Fighter Wing as a *Feldwebel* and later saw action during the Battle of France and the Battle of Britain. He claimed an RAF Hurricane over Le Cateau, France on 19 May 1940, his first victory of the war. Later his aircraft was damaged during an attack and he had to ditch in the Thames Estuary, but was rescued. He was awarded the Iron Cross 2nd Class a few days later and claimed at least another three aircraft over France, but these remain unconfirmed. Soon after his second, confirmed, aerial victory on 5 March 1941, a Spitfire shot down over the Boulogne area he was awarded the Iron Cross 1st Class.

(Deutsches Wehrkundearchiv)

On 15 June his squadron was moved to 45 miles west of Brest-Litovsk and from 22nd he took part in the invasion of the Soviet Union, whilst attached to the 4th Group of the 51st Fighter Wing. He claimed two Ilyushin DB-3 long-range bombers on 24 June and claimed three more victories on 30 June. Borchers claimed his 10th victory on 14 July and his 15th came on 31 August. He claimed seven more victories during October and was awarded the *Luftwaffe* Honour Goblet on 13 October after achieving sixteen victories. He claimed his 23rd victory on 24 October and in early August 1942 he was commissioned as a *Leutnant*, and was quickly promoted to *Oberleutnant*. By the beginning of September Borchers had achieved thirty-one victories, and on 9 October he was appointed *Staffelkapitän* of the 11th Squadron, replacing *Leutnant* Wolfgang Böwing-Treuding. On 15 October he was awarded the German Cross in Gold after achieving his 31st victory. By the end of the year he had claimed his 38th victory, an Il-2 ground-attack aircraft over Orel.

In 1943 he married the famed skier Christl Cranz, who had won a gold medal at the 1936 Winter Olympic Games and twelve gold and three silver medals in pre-war World Championships. Borchers continued to claim victories during 1943 and by 2 June had claimed his 50th victory and by the end of September he had claimed seventy-five victories and had been promoted to *Hauptmann*. On 22 November Borchers was awarded the Knight's Cross for his success as a fighter pilot and for claiming his 77th aerial victory. In fact he claimed a victory that same day and two more on 29 November, which included his 80th. By the end of May he had claimed his 86th victory. When *Hauptmann* Johannes Wiese had been seriously wounded he took temporary command of the 1st Group of the 52nd Fighter Wing, and the position was confirmed on 11 June and he was named as the new *Gruppenkommandeur*. On 11 July he claimed three victories, all Yakovlev Yak-9 fighters, and he went onto claim another eight victories in July. He claimed three victories on 22 August which included his 100th, and he claimed another three on the 26th and four more on the 31st – his 112th victory. He claimed his 118th victory on 22 September and this was in fact the 52nd Fighter Wing's 10,000th aerial victory of the war!

By the end of the year Borchers had scored his 122nd victory and in January 1945 was promoted to *Major*. On 1 February he was appointed *Gruppenkommandeur* of the 3rd Group of the 52nd Fighter Wing, and he claimed his last two victories of the war on 22 March, both Pe-2 dive-bombers. On 8 May he surrendered to the Americans at Pisek, Brün and was shortly after handed over to the Soviets. His wife had also been arrested by the Soviets because of her collaboration with the Nazis and was forced to work on a farm for 11 months. She fled to the American Occupation Zone in 1947 and later founded a skiing school with Borchers. He died on 9 February 1996 and his wife died on 28 September 2004 in Oberstaufen, Allgäu. Borchers had two brothers who were both awarded the Knight's Cross. Walter served as a *Major* and *Gruppenkommandeur* of the 3rd Group of the 5th Night Fighter Wing, winning the award on 29 October 1944. His other brother Hermann was a *SS-Sturmbannführer* and was also awarded the Knight's Cross that same month, as leader of the 1st Battalion of the 19th SS-Panzer Grenadier Regiment.

Joachim 'Achim' BRENDEL

Hauptmann

Knight's Cross: Awarded on 22 November 1943 as *Oberleutnant* and *Staffelkapitän* of the 1st Squadron of the 51st Fighter Wing '*Mölders*' for claiming his 95th aerial victory whilst flying combat missions north-east of Biala-Cerkiew, Ukraine.

Knight's Cross with Oakleaves: He became the 697th recipient on 14 January 1945 as *Hauptmann* and commander of the 3rd Group of the 51st Fighter Wing '*Mölders*' for claiming his 154th aerial victory. The award was presented to him personally at the Air Ministry in Berlin at the end of March by *Reichsmarschall* Hermann Göring.

(Deutsches Wehrkundearchiv)

Joachim Brendel claimed all but six of his 189 aerial victories over the Eastern Front, flying more than 950 combat missions, including 162 ground-support missions. He was born in Ulrichshalben near Weimar on 27 April 1921, the son of a police *Hauptmann*. He attended the local Gymnasium or secondary school and after graduating he joined the *Luftwaffe* in November 1939. He trained as a pilot before he joined the 2nd Squadron of the 51st Fighter Wing '*Mölders*' on the Russian Front. Brendel claimed his first aerial victory on 29 June 1941, and two days later was commissioned as a *Leutnant*. He was also awarded the Iron Cross 2nd Class on 3 July in recognition of his first aerial victory. Usually a fighter pilot, having achieved his first victory, would follow with another soon afterwards but Brendel had to wait until 31 March 1942 before he could add to his score. On 5 April he claimed his third aerial victory and then flew a number of ground-support missions for which he was awarded the Iron Cross 1st Class on 21 April. He claimed another four victories in July and by 14 December had only achieved eleven victories. Considering the amount of aircraft over Russia at that time and the superiority of the German aircraft and pilots, Brendel was a slow starter.

However, 1943 would be a turning point. On 24 February he scored his 20th aerial victory and was awarded the *Luftwaffe* Honour Goblet on 15 March. He claimed another three victories on 18 March and by the beginning of May had claimed his 30th. From May he led the 1st Squadron of the 51st Fighter Wing '*Mölders*', replacing *Oberleutnant* Hans Boos who had been killed in a mid-air collision on 21 April. Brendal was awarded the German Cross in Gold on 17 May after claiming his 35th aerial victory, an Ilyushin Il-2 ground-attack aircraft, and on 10 June he claimed his 40th victory and was promoted to *Oberleutnant* on 1 July 1943. Four days later on the first day of the Battle of Kursk Brendel claimed two Ilyushin Il-2s, and his wingman *Unteroffizier* Oskar Romm was credited with the destruction of a third. On 6 and 8 July he claimed two more victories, claimed another three on the 9th and claimed five on the 12th, to become an 'ace-in-a-day', and claimed his 70th aerial victory on 25 July. On 28 July, he was shot down by anti-aircraft fire and managed to bail out of his Fw 190 but not without serious injury. In mid-September 1943, he returned to duty and continued to be successful, achieving his 75th victory on 15 September. By the end of October he had achieved his 92nd victory. On 22 November Brendel was awarded the Knight's Cross as *Staffelkapitän* of the 1st Squadron, in recognition of his 95th victory, and that same day he claimed six aerial victories to become an 'ace-in-a-day' for the second time and now had a total of 101 victories, the 60th Luftwaffe pilot to achieve the century mark.

On 29 March 1944, he was once again shot down but was able to make an emergency landing without injury. He was promoted to *Hauptmann* in early April and on 27th, after an attack by Soviet fighters he had to bail out of his aircraft, sustaining only minor injuries. On 29 July he claimed a Yakovlev Yak-9 fighter whilst flying a combat mission over Bialystok and his opponent may have been Vladimir Shchegolev from the 162nd Fighter Aviation Regiment, a fighter ace credited with fourteen victories, who was killed in action that day. In September he was appointed commander of the 3rd Group of the 51st Fighter Wing, and the following month he achieved his 150th aerial victory, a Yakovlev Yak-3 fighter shot down east of Trakehnen. During the last months of the war, Brendel did not give up. Although the situation was hopeless, he continued to achieve more aerial victories. In 1945 he shot down a total of thirty-seven aircraft, and on 14 January he became the 697th recipient of the Oakleaves after achieving his 153rd aerial victory. His last aerial victory, his 189th, was achieved on 25 April 1945, a Yak-9 fighter. He died on 7 July 1974 in Cologne, West Germany and was buried in Salzburg, Austria.

Wilhelm 'Willy' KIENTSCH

Oberleutnant

Knight's Cross: Awarded on 22 November 1943 as *Leutnant* and as fighter pilot in the 2nd Group of the 27th Fighter Wing for operations over North Africa, Italy and the Western Front, and for claiming his 40th aerial victory, an American B-17 Flying Fortress.

Knight's Cross with Oakleaves: Awarded posthumously on 20 July 1944, to become the 527th recipient as *Oberleutnant* and *Staffelkapitän* of the 6th Squadron of the 27th Fighter Wing for operations over the Western Front and for claiming his 47th victory.

Wilhelm 'Willy' Kientsch was one of the top four-engined bomber aces of the *Luftwaffe* during the Second World War, and was one of the most successful pilots during the campaign in Sicily. He was born on 12 May 1921 in Kisslegg, a district in Baden-Württemberg, Germany, and after service in the RAD he joined the *Luftwaffe* in 1940, just after his 18th birthday.

(Deutsches Wehrkundearchiv)

After pilot training, in May 1941 he was assigned to the Supplementary Training Squadron of the 27th Fighter Wing, where he learnt basic combat skills. In early 1942 *Oberfähric* Kientsch was attached to the 2nd Group based in North Africa, and flew in support of Rommel's *Afrika Korps*. He claimed his first two victories of the war, both P-40 fighters, shot down near Tobruk on 18 March 1942. Shortly afterwards he was awarded the Iron Cross 2nd Class, and on 7 April claimed his third aerial victory, another P-40 shot down over Ain el Gazal. By 17 June he had shot down seven aircraft, all P-40s. Just a few days later he transferred to the 5th Squadron and was awarded the Iron Cross 1st Class. Kientsch claimed an RAF Hurricane south of El Alamein on 21 July and a few weeks later was commissioned as a *Leutnant*. Between 20 and 26 October he claimed five P-40s, and on 18 November he claimed another one east-north-east of Sidi Ahmed el Magram. He shot down his 15th aerial victory on 27 November, an RAF Spitfire south-west of Agedabia.

He transferred to the 6th Squadron of the 27th Fighter Wing in early 1943, and flew out of Vienna, before moving to Bari in southern Italy. During April he claimed six aircraft, four P-38 Lightnings, one Spitfire and a B-17 Flying Fortress, his first four-engined bomber. On 21, 22 and 25 May he claimed a B-17 bomber, on 28 May he shot down two P-38s. On 1 June he was appointed *Staffelführer* of the 6th Squadron and was now operating out of Italy as the *Luftwaffe* had been defeated in North Africa. On 9 June he shot down two P-38s over Pantelleria near Sicily, and the following day he claimed two Spitfires, shot down over the same area. He was particularly successful over Sicily and southern Italy during the spring and summer of 1943 where he claimed twenty-five aerial victories. He claimed his 30th victory on 30 June and on 19 July he claimed his 40th victory, a B-24 Liberator shot down near Spartivento. In August 1943 his squadron relocated back to Germany and he now flew combat missions in 'Defence of the Reich'. He was awarded the *Luftwaffe* Honour Goblet on 9 August and on the 16th he was awarded the German Cross in Gold in recognition of his success as a fighter pilot.

On 22 November Kientsch was awarded the Knight's Cross in recognition of his 40th aerial victory. A few days later he claimed his 41st and 42nd victories, both four-engined bombers. He shot down two more bombers on 1 December, one over Bonn and another over Cologne. Kientsch claimed his 47th and last victory on 11 January 1944 a few days after being promoted to *Oberleutnant*. On 29 January he was killed in his Bf 109G-6 aircraft when he became disoriented when he entered heavy cloud during aerial combat and crashed into the ground near Würrisch-Hunstrück in the Rhineland-Palatinate, Germany. He was posthumously awarded the Knight's Cross with Oakleaves on 20 July and is buried in Neu-Ulm, Germany, War Grave No. 44.

Emil 'Bully' LANG

Hauptmann

Knight's Cross: Awarded on 22 November 1943 as *Leutnant* and *Staffelführer* of the 9th Squadron of the 54th Fighter Wing for operations over the Soviet Union and for claiming his 116th aerial victory.

Knight's Cross with Oakleaves: He became the 448th recipient on 11 April 1944 as *Oberleutnant* and *Staffelkapitän* of the 9th Squadron of the 54th Fighter Wing for continued operations over the Soviet Union and for claiming his 141st aerial victory. He was presented with his award by Hitler on 5 May 1944 at the Berghof during a special ceremony in the Great Hall.

(Author's collection)

Emil Lang claimed a total of 172 aerial victories in 403 combat missions during the Second World War, including seventeen aircraft in one day, a record which has never been equalled and was achieved in less than 18 months. He was born on 14 January 1909, in Thalheim, now part of Frannberg in the Isar Region, Bavaria. Before the Second World War he qualified as a civil pilot and flew with Lufthansa. Lang earned his nickname 'Bully' from his bulldog-like looks, characterised by his barrel-chested physique. He joined the *Luftwaffe* as a member of the Reserve Transport Unit, and from 8 May to 3 June 1939, and served with the 8th Squadron of the 51st Bomber Wing.

When war broke out in September 1939, Lang was put on active duty, serving as a transport pilot with the airfield company at Gablingen. From April 1940 he flew as part of Aviation Equipment Group 7 and flew missions to Norway, France, Crete and North Africa. In November 1941 he was commissioned as a *Leutnant* and from April to July 1942 Lang was attached to Aircraft Ferrying Wing Prenzlau, being responsible for flying finished aircraft from the factories to the front-line units. On 3 July he was accepted for fighter pilot training and transferred to the Advanced Fighter School, under *Oberstleutnant* Otto-Friedrich von Houwald, in Jever. From 15 August he was attached to Advanced Fighter School 5 at Villacoublay-Nord in France and from there transferred to Replacement Fighter Training Group East in January 1943.

In March 1943 Lang transferred to 54th Fighter Wing as a fully trained fighter pilot and was attached to the 5th Squadron of the 2nd Group operating out of Kalinin initially and from May he flew out or Orel in the Soviet Union. He claimed his first aerial victory on 23 March, a MiG-3 over the area near Pushkin. He claimed his second and third victories on 30 May, both P-40s shot down over the Schlüsselburg region. On 13 June he was awarded the Iron Cross 2nd Class, and he claimed another nine victories during July. By the time he was awarded the Iron Cross 1st Class on 2 August he had claimed sixteen victories. From late July he served as *Staffelführer* and on 20 August he was appointed *Staffelkapitän* of the 5th Squadron, succeeding *Oberleutnant* Max Stotz after he had been listed as missing. Lang now began to claim victories at a fast rate. On 7 October he became an 'ace-in-a-day' when he claimed five victories, then between 8 and 25 October he claimed fifty-nine victories. This included ten on the 13th, twelve on the 21st, eight on the 22nd, six on the 23rd and five on the 24th. He was awarded the *Luftwaffe* Honour Goblet on 27 October 1943 in recognition of his 30th aerial victory The victories didn't stop: on 2 November he claimed eight more, and on the 3rd he claimed an amazing seventeen victories, a record that has never been equalled. He had become an 'ace-in-a-day' eight times and had claimed a total of 115 enemy aircraft in just eight months and for this he was awarded the German Cross in Gold and the Knight's Cross.

Lang's rate of victories was astounding and between the time of the recommendation for the Knight's Cross and the actual presentation he had doubled his score and was probably being considered for the Oakleaves. His achievements led to him appearing on the cover of the 13 January 1944 *Berliner Illustrirte Zeitung* ('Berlin Illustrated Magazine'). Lang was featured inside receiving his Knight's Cross, an article telling of his amazing seventeen victories achieved on 3 November 1943 during the Battle of Kiev. In March he was promoted to *Oberleutnant*, and on 9 April was appointed *Staffelkapitän* of the 9th Squadron in Landau, and flying over Germany in 'Defence of the Reich' missions. By 6 April Lang had achieved his 141st victory and five days later was awarded the Knight's Cross with Oakleaves, presented by Hitler personally at the Reich Chancellery. Promoted to *Hauptmann* in May, the following month he was flying missions out of Villacouby in northern France, claiming victories against pilots of the United State Air Force. On 14 June he claimed three P-47s Thunderbolts, and on the 20th he shot down four P-51 Mustangs, which included his 150th victory.

On 9 June he succeeded *Hauptmann* Hans Naumann as *Gruppenkommandeur* of the 2nd Group of the 26th Fighter Wing, based in Guyancourt, north-central France, flying the Focke-Wulf Fw 190A. He claimed three Spitfires on 9 July over Caen, two P-47s over Rambouillet on 15 August, and by 26th he had claimed his 172nd and last aerial victory. On 3 September Lang took off from Melsbroek together with his wingman *Unteroffizier* Hans-Joachim Borreck. Lang experienced some mechanical problems, having had difficulty raising the undercarriage of his aircraft. Ten minutes later Allied fighters (probably Mustangs or Thunderbolts) intercepted Lang's' flight. Suddenly Borreck called out over the radio, that there were fighters on Lang's tail. Lang broke upward, to the left and a round struck his aircraft in the hydraulic system causing the wheels to drop. His aircraft went into a steep dive and crashed into the ground and exploded near St. Tronf, Belgium, killing Lang instantly.

After some extensive research it seems very likely that Lang was shot down by Lieutenant Darrell Cramer who had reported hitting a Focke-Wulf in that area. Later *Kommodore* Josef Priller submitted a recommendation for a posthumous promotion for Lang, but it was refused. Lang is buried at the German Military Cemetery at Lommel, Belgium. in a communal grave.

Maximilian MAYERL

Hauptmann

Knight's Cross: Awarded on 22 November 1943 as *Oberleutnant* and *Staffelkapitän* of the 9th Squadron of the 51st Fighter Wing '*Mölders*' for operations over France, England and the Soviet Union and in recognition of claiming seventy-five aerial victories.

(Deutsches Wehrkundearchiv)

Maximilian Mayerl claimed seventy-five aerial victories, of which all but four were achieved over the Eastern Front during the Second World War. He was born on 28 May 1917 in Aigen, Liezen in Austria-Hungary and joined the *Luftwaffe* in November 1937. After the completion of his training Mayerl was assigned to the 2nd Squadron of the 20th Fighter Wing.

Unteroffizier Mayerl flew combat missions during the Polish campaign and claimed his first victory on 8 June 1940, an RAF Blenheim near Allery in France, and was awarded the Iron Cross 2nd Class. He later saw action over England during the Battle of Britain, and on 19 July he claimed a Spitfire six miles off Dover and on 8 August he claimed another Spitfire almost in the same area. On the 13th after combat with RAF fighters his Bf 109 was damaged and he crash-landed at Calais-Marck, but was unhurt. He claimed a third Spitfire over London on 18 August and was awarded the Iron Cross 1st Class soon afterwards.

He was promoted to *Leutnant* in December 1940 and transferred to the Eastern Front in July 1941 where on 26 July he claimed two Petlyakov Pe-2 twin-engined dive-bombers south of Dorogobush, his 5th and 6th aerial victories. He claimed another seven victories during September, which included two on the 19th and three on the 22nd. With the start of the Soviet winter offensive in December there was an increase in aerial fighting but Mayerl didn't add to his score at this time. Bad weather kept some pilots grounded and some equipment was lost due to the weather and on 22 December his Group moved to Dugino. At the beginning of 1942 the weather was even worst and very few missions were flown, however during February Mayerl flew missions mainly over the area near Rzhev and claimed his 20th victory on 22 March, a MiG-3 fighter. From April his Group flew from Smolensk and in May returned to Dugino where they were deployed in the operational area of the 9th Army. Mayerl claimed two more victories in May and during early August the Group's airfields were attacked by Soviet aircraft and they lost seven aircraft with ten being badly damaged. On 7 August he was appointed *Staffelkapitän* of the 9th Squadron and continued to fly combat missions, claiming his 25th victory on 13 August, an Il-2 ground-attack aircraft. In November his squadron converted to the Focke-Wulf Fw 190A-2 and after the start of the Soviet offensive the Group's operational activity increased. By the end of October Mayerl had claimed a total of thirty-four victories and had been awarded in June the *Luftwaffe* Honour Goblet and on 27 November was also presented with the German Cross in Gold.

Now an *Oberleutnant*, Mayerl and his Group had returned to Dogino in Januray 1943 and he claimed his 40th victory on 8 March, a Pe-2 over south Zalegoshch and ten days later he had claimed his 45th victory. On 7 May his Fw 190 was hit by ground fire about 10 miles west north-west of Spas-Demensk but he was only slightly wounded. In early July he was promoted to *Hauptmann* and on the 6th claimed four victories, and two days later he claimed two more, which included his 50th victory. By the end of July he had claimed a total of sixty-one victories and claimed two victories on 4th and 9 August, three on the 10th, which included his 70th victory and he claimed his 75th on 27 August. That same day he became seriously ill and was hospitalized for almost seven months.

On 22 November 1943 he was awarded the Knight's Cross in recognition of his aerial victories and determination as a fighter pilot.

In early December 1943 he flew with the 1st Group of the 1st Supplementary Fighter Wing and from June 1944 he was *Staffelkapitän* of the 1st Squadron of Supplementary Fighter Group East, serving as an instructor. From 1 September he was transferred as *Gruppenkommandeur* of Replacement Fighter Group North, which from November 1944 was redesignated the 1st Group of the 1st Supplementary Fighter Wing. By the end of the war Mayerl had flown a total of 647 combat missions and forty-two ground-attack and fighter-bomber missions, and had flown more than 100 missions over England during the Battle of Britain. Mayerl died on 11 February 2010 in Nimes, France at the age of 92.

Albin WOLF

Oberleutnant

Knight's Cross: Awarded on 22 November 1943 as *Oberfeldwebel* and fighter pilot in the 2nd Group of the 54th Fighter Wing for operations over the Soviet Union and for claiming his 114th aerial victory.

Knight's Cross with Oakleaves: Awarded posthumously on 25 April 1944, to become the 464th recipient as *Leutnant* and *Staffelkapitän* of the 6th Squadron of the 54th Fighter Wing for continued operations over the Soviet Union.

(Deutsches Wehrkundearchiv)

Albin Wolf claimed a total of 142 aerial victories and flew 416 combat missions during the Second World War, all of them over the Eastern Front. He was born in Neuhaus, now part of Selbitz in the district of Hof, Bavaria, on 28 October 1920.

After leaving school in 1940 he joined the *Luftwaffe* and upon completion of his flight training in May 1942 was assigned to the 6th Squadron of the 54th Fighter Wing as an *Unteroffizier*. At this time his squadron was operating over the Eastern Front and began to fly combat missions with his wingman *Leutnant* Hans Beisswenger whilst attached to the 2nd Group which was one of the *Luftwaffe* units flying in support of Army Group Centre in the Cholm and Demyansk Pockets. Wolf claimed his first victory on 6 August over Kamischtchewo, an Il-2 ground-attack aircraft, and he claimed his second on 23 August, a Yak-1 fighter south-south-east of Suchinia. He claimed his third and fourth victories in September and on 1 October was awarded the Iron Cross 2nd Class. He claimed four victories during December and was awarded the Iron Cross 1st Class on 22 January 1943, and only days later he claimed his 10th victory. On 23 March his victory score had risen to eighteen, and on 22 April he was awarded the *Luftwaffe* Honour Goblet.

During Operation Kutuzov, the Soviet counteroffensive against the German operations in Kursk, Wolf claimed three aerial victories on 13 July and by the end of the month had claimed his 35th victory. He claimed six further victories during the first week of August and on the 16th claimed his 50th, and he continued to score at a fast rate during the next few days. He claimed two victories on 21st, four on the 22nd, a single P-39 on the 23rd and claimed four on the 24th and by the end of the month Wolf had claimed his 74th victory. He continued to score rapidly during September, claiming two on the 1st, 4th and 5th, and became an 'ace-in-a-day' on 7 September when he claimed five Yak-9 aircraft. On the 15th he claimed another five to become an 'ace-in-a-day' for the second time and this included his 90th victory. On 17th he was awarded the German Cross in Gold after recording his

94th victory. He claimed three victories on 23 October, and shot down two more on the 25th, which included his 100th victory.

Between 1st and 6 November Wolf claimed another ten victories, which included becoming an 'ace-in-a-day' for the second time. On 22 November he was finally awarded the Knight's Cross in recognition of achieving 114 victories. A week later he shot down two Yak-9 fighters in three minutes over Zeleogorsk, claiming another five victories during December. On 24 December, following the German retreat during the Battle of the Dnieper, Soviet forces began the Zhitomir-Berdicher Offensive and threatened the German airfields at Bila and Tserka and the 2nd Group of the 54th Fighter Wing was ordered to relocate to Tarnopol. The skies were full of Soviet aircraft and on the 29th Wolf was seriously wounded when he was shot down in his Fw 190A-6, crashing in a field north-north-east of Nemirow. He returned to combat just over two weeks later and claimed three victories on 15 January 1944, and by the end of the month he had achieved his 129th victory, seeming to be back to his old self.

On 11 March Wolf was appointed *Staffelkapitän* of the 6th Squadron, and on the 19th he claimed three more victories. On 23 March he claimed his 135th victory which was the 54th Fighter Wing's 7,000th aerial victory of the war. By the end of the month Wolf had claimed his 141st victory. On 2 April, shortly after claiming his 142nd victory, a Yak-9 fighter 12 miles south-east of Pskov, at 09:27 he was attacked by a Lieutenant Ivanov, but post-war investigations have concluded that Wolf was shot down and killed by a direct hit from anti-aircraft fire from the ground. His body has not been recovered and Wolf was posthumously awarded the Knight's Cross with Oakleaves on 25 April 1944.

Jürgen Hans Eberhard HARDER

Major

Knight's Cross: Awarded on 5 December 1943 as *Oberleutnant* and *Staffelführer* in the 3rd Group of the 53rd Fighter Wing for operations over the Soviet Union, Malta, North Africa and Italy, and for claiming his 39th aerial victory, a B-17 Flying Fortress over Granitola Toretta, Italy.

Knight's Cross with Oakleaves: He became the 727th recipient on 1 February 1945 as *Major* and *Kommodore* of the 11th Fighter Wing for continued operations over Italy and the Eastern Front and for claiming his 56th aerial victory. Harder was killed before he could be presented with the award.

(Deutsches Wehrkundearchiv)

Jürgen Harder claimed over fifty-six aerial victories, mainly on the Western Front, including ten four-engined bombers, flying approximately 500 missions during the Second World War. He was born on 13 June 1918 in Swinemünde, Pomerania, and had two brothers. Rolf served in the Army and was listed as missing on the Eastern Front in August 1943, while Harro, who was older, served in the *Luftwaffe* claimed eleven aircraft during the Spanish Civil War and was killed in September 1940 when he was shot down by a Spitfire over the Isle of Wight. Jürgen unfortunately would share the same fate as his two brothers.

Harder joined the *Luftwaffe* in October 1939 as a *Fahnenjunker* and for his training was attached to the 3rd Group of the 53rd Fighter Wing at the beginning of 1941. His *Gruppenkommandeur* at this time was *Hauptmann* Wolf-Dietrich Wilcke who had succeeded Harder's brother who had been killed in August 1940. He added the name 'Harro' to the cockpit of his Bf 109, in honour of his brother. On 1 April 1941 he was commissioned as a *Leutnant*, and on 4 May he made an emergency landing at Maldeghem damaging his aircraft but was unhurt. Three days later his Bf 109 was hit by anti-aircraft fire, twice, and was then struck by a bullet from a Spitfire flown by Squadron Leader M. Lister-Robinson. Harder managed to get his aircraft back to base, however, and was unhurt.

In June his unit prepared for Operation Barbarossa, the invasion of the Soviet Union, and on the first day of the invasion, 22 June, Harder achieved his first aerial victory when he claimed a MiG-1 fighter. He claimed his second aerial victory on 25 June, a SB-3 bomber, shortly after he was awarded the Iron Cross 2nd Class. On 14 July Harder claimed two Polikarpov I-16 fighters over Smolensk and by the end of September he had achieved his 10th victory and was awarded the Iron Cross 1st Class. On 25 September his Bf 109 ran out of fuel and he had to make a belly landing near Novgorod, but he wasn't hurt. In November his unit moved to the Middle East where he flew combat missions over North Africa, Tunisia and Sicily. He claimed an RAF Spitfire on 10 March 1942, and a few days later transferred to the 7th Squadron. Harder claimed two Spitfires over Malta on 30 April, and by the end of May had claimed his 15th victory. He claimed a total of ten P-40 Warhawk ground-attack aircraft during October, which included four on the 9th and two on the 13th. On 9 November he achieved his 30th aerial victory and was awarded the *Luftwaffe* Honour Goblet a few days later.

Harder was promoted to *Oberleutnant* in early 1943, and on 12 January was awarded the German Cross in Gold. Three days later he was appointed *Staffelführer* of the 8th Squadron, claiming a Spitfire on 8 February. He claimed his first four-engined bomber, a B-17 Flying Fortress, shot down over Cap Vito, on 22 March. On 8 May he claimed two Spitfires and his second B-17 the following day. Promoted to *Hauptmann* later that month he was officially grounded soon after when it was reported that his brother Rolf had been listed as missing on the Russian Front. With his other brother Harro having been killed in 1940, the High Command issued what was known as the 'last surviving son' rule, as he was the family's only son left. To keep him safe he was grounded and given a staff position with the 2nd Air Corps under *Generalleutnant* Martin Harlinghausen based near Messina. On 5 December Harder was awarded the Knight's Cross in recognition of his 39th aerial victory, which had been achieved back in May!

In February 1944 his ban on flying was lifted, the *Luftwaffe* needing as many pilots as they could find, and Harder was only too pleased to return, having lost none of his enthusiasm. He claimed another Spitfire on 7 February, his 40th victory, and seven days later he claimed a P-38 south of Rome. On the 15th he was appointed *Gruppenkommandeur* of the 1st Group of the 53rd Fighter Wing and claimed his third four-engined bomber 10 days later, when he shot down a B-24 Liberator south of Villach, Austria. On 10 March he was wounded when his Bf 109G-6 was damaged during combat with B-17s and he had to bail out, then on the 28th he claimed two P-47s shot down over Fano, Italy, to claim his 45th victory. He claimed another five victories in April, which included two B-24s shot down over Italy on the 25th. He was promoted to *Major* in May and continued to claim victories. On 25 April he shot down a B-24 and about 30 minutes later he was wounded when he rammed a second B-24 bomber which crashed but Harder's own aircraft was badly damaged and he crashed near Strada Cassentino, Tuscany.

In June 1944 Harder was given the task of improving the *Luftwaffe*'s defensive performance in protecting Romanian's vital oil industry from Allied bombing. He formed the *Gesfechtsverband Harder* (Combat Command Harder), combining several units which included the 2nd Group of the 51st Fighter Wing, the 3rd Group of the 77th Fighter Wing and his 1st Group of the 53rd Fighter Wing. But such measures were almost useless because of the growing strength of the US 15th Air Force. *Luftwaffe* losses rose rapidly, culminating on the last day of the month, which in Harder's own words had been, 'Critical – twenty-three of my thirty-two aircraft were shot down. Terrible, we were opposed by over 150 enemy fighters!' In fact during a bombing raid by B-24s on 9 July, Harder had to make a forced landing in his Bf 109 at Mizil after combat with a P-51 over the Ploesti area, but he was unhurt.

On 2 January 1945, Harder was appointed *Kommodore* of the 11th Fighter Wing, based in Biblis, Germany and from 23 January based in Strausberg, Brandenburg. He was now flying combat missions in 'Defence of the Reich' against Allied fighters. He claimed an La-5 Soviet fighter on 14 January, his last aerial victory. On 17 February near Strausberg his Bf 109G-14 suddenly developed engine failure and crashed, killing Harder instantly. Later technical experts analyzed the wreckage and came to the conclusion that the piston cylinder had penetrated the engine block and the escaping toxic fumes had filled the cockpit and poisoned Harder who lost consciousness and crashed. Harder is buried at the Military Cemetery in Strausberg, Germany in Block 10, Row 6, Grave No. 6. He had been awarded the Knight's Cross with Oakleaves on 1 February but was killed before he could be presented with it.

Josef 'Pepi' JENNEWEIN

Leutnant

Knight's Cross: Awarded posthumously on 5 December 1943 as *Oberfeldwebel* and fighter pilot with the 1st Group of the 51st Fighter Wing '*Mölders*', for operations over England and the Soviet Union.

Josef Jennewein claimed eighty-three aerial victories, of which all but five were achieved over the Eastern Front, totalling 271 combat missions during the Second World War. He was born on 21 November 1919 in St. Anton am Arlberg in the Tyrolean Alps of Austria, and he enjoyed skiing. He became a professional skier, winning the world combined championship in 1939 and the world combined and downhill championships in 1941.

(Deutsches Wehrkundearchiv)

He began his flight training in 1940 and on completion he was transferred to the 4th Training Squadron of the 5th Fighter Air School based in Le Havre on the Channel Front in the summer of 1941. Here he flew in support of the 2nd and 26th Fighter Wing where he claimed three victories, all Spitfires, on 20 September over Fécamp and was awarded the Iron Cross 2nd Class. On 15 October he was transferred to the 2nd Squadron of the 51st Fighter Wing and the same day he claimed another Spitfire and a Bristol Blenheim twin-engined bomber and soon after was awarded the Iron Cross 1st Class. He also flew in support of ground forces during the attack on Moscow and from December during the start of the Soviet winter offensive there was an increase in aerial battles. From early 1942 he flew escort missions over Lake Ilmen for fighter-bomber aircraft and operations began to suffer during the spring because of mud, but he did manage to fly a few missions over the Demyansk and Cholm areas. He claimed three victories in March and on 5 April he claimed two MiG-3 fighters which included his 10th victory.

From January 1943 his Group moved to Vyazma-South and on 18 January a formation of nine Petlyakov Pe-2 bombers had attacked his base on the 'Great Ivan Lake' near Velikiye Luki. Jennewein was flying with *Leutnant* Joachim Brendal and were in a perfect position to attack the Soviet bombers. Brendal claimed three while Jennewein claimed five to become an 'ace-in-a-day' – the ninth aircraft got away. Promoted to *Oberfeldwebel* in mid-January, on the 30th he claimed his 20th victory and on 22 February he claimed three victories and he claimed another five on the 23rd, making him an 'ace-in-a-day' again, and was awarded the *Luftwaffe* Honour Goblet on 1 March. Jennewein claimed seven more victories on the 24th, which included his 40th victory, becoming an 'ace-in-a-day' for the third time. He was awarded the German Cross in Gold on 12 April after claiming his 45th aerial victory. From May his Group moved to Orel and he claimed five victories on 6th, which included his 50th, making him an 'ace-in-a-day' for the fourth time, claiming another four on 8 May.

Jennewein claimed two victories over west Maloarkhangelsk on 2 June 1943, which included his 60th victory and he claimed a total of twenty-three victories in 13 days, which included his 70th and 80th victories. He claimed five on 21 July to become an 'ace-in-a-day' for the fifth time. On 26 July his Fw 190A-6 was shot down by Soviet fighters east of Orel and was never seen again. He was listed as officially missing and posthumously awarded the Knight's Cross and promoted to *Leutnant*. He was a gifted pilot who was a great loss to his Group and who had shot down twenty-two Il-2 ground attack aircraft.

Günther SCHEEL

Leutnant

Knight's Cross: Awarded posthumously on 5 December 1943 as *Leutnant* and fighter pilot attached to the 3rd Squadron of the 54th Fighter Wing for operations over the Soviet Union.

Günther Scheel claimed seventy victories in seventy combat missions over the Eastern Front during the Second World War. He was born on 23 November 1921, in Dannenberg, Lower Saxony and after completing his flight training he was posted to the 2nd Squadron of the 54th Fighter Wing, arriving in January 1943.

(Deutsches Wehrkundearchiv)

Scheel was attached to the 1st Group, under the command of *Major* Hans Philipp, based at Krasnogvardeysk, about 25 miles from Leningrad, and soon gained a reputation as a deadly shot. Promoted to *Leutnant* in February he flew the Focke-Wulf Fw 190A-4, and took part in combat over south-east and east Leningrad. He claimed his first two fighters on 9 February over Schlüsselburg, both Lavochkins, an La-5 and an LaGG-3, and because of the weather conditions had to wait until the 14th to claim two more. By 16 April he had claimed ten victories and had been awarded the Iron Cross 1st and 2nd Class. The weather conditions played a part in combat operations for both sides and Scheel was the only pilot of his Group to claim a victory on 1 May, an Ilyushin Il-2 ground-attack aircraft over Leningrad. By the 5th weather conditions had improved slightly and Scheel claimed two more victories over south Leningrad, and on the 24th he was deployed over the combat area of the 16th Army, east of Soltsy where he claimed two more Il-2 aircraft. He was on bomber escort duty, escorting Heinkel He 111s on the 30th when he claimed another four victories over the Volkhov River. On 5 June he claimed his 20th and 21st victories and his group saw little action during the following weeks due to the weather – it was again only Scheel who claimed a victory on 10 June. By the end of the month he had claimed twenty-nine victories and his reputation of being a deadly shot was earning him great respect.

From early June he flew missions over the southern sector of Army Group Centre, where it fought during Operation Citadel, the beginning of the Battle of Kursk. On 2 July his Group relocated to a makeshift airfield in Panikowo and three days later the German Army launched Operation Citadel, with Scheel and his Group flying in support of the 9th Army, escorting bombers. On the 5th Scheel claimed eight victories to become an 'ace-in-a-day' for the first time. He claimed a single victory on the 6th but the following day he became an 'ace-in-a-day' again when he shot down seven aircraft over Dmitrovsk and Arkhangelsk. He claimed another three victories on 8 July and three more the following day which included his 50th victory. But the German advance on the ground had come to a halt as the 9th Army were facing a tough enemy as well as difficult conditions. Scheel however managed to claim five victories on 10 July, and the next day he added another three to his total. On the 13th he became an 'ace-in-a-day' for the fourth and final time. The next day the Soviets attacked the 2nd Panzer Army which forced the 9th Army to strengthen its defences – Operation Citadel had effectively failed on the northern sector of the front, as the Soviets began to launch their own offensive.

Bad weather had once again grounded most aircraft and visibility was poor. On the 16th Scheel claimed three victories. Shortly after claiming his third victory he collided with another Fw 190 and crashed. He managed to escape with minor injuries but was captured by Soviet troops and never seen again. His fate remains unknown but he was probably executed a few days later. He claimed seventy victories in just over five months and was posthumously awarded the German Cross in Gold on 31 May 1943; the *Luftwaffe* Honour Goblet on 13 September 1943 and the Knight's Cross on 5 December 1943.

Heinrich 'Bazi' STERR

Oberleutnant

Knight's Cross: Awarded on 5 December 1943 as *Oberfeldwebel* and fighter pilot of the 6th Squadron of the 54th Fighter Wing for operations over the Soviet Union and for claiming his 83rd aerial victory.

Heinrich Sterr claimed 108 aerial victories, all but two over the Eastern Front during the Second World War. He was born on 24 September 1919 in Ortenburg, Vilshofen in Bavaria and unlike many fighter aces he wasn't a member of the pre-war *Luftwaffe* as he had only reached the age of 20 when the war broke out, and missed the fighting in Poland and France and the first year of the campaign in the East.

After completing his pilot training in early 1942, he was assigned as an *Unteroffizier* to the 6th Squadron of the 54th Fighter Wing. At the time it was based at Ryelbitzi, west of Lake Ilmen, and he flew in the battles near the Demyansk Pocket as the Soviets continued to try and break through the German lines at Leningrad where he scored his

(Deutsches Wehrkundearchiv)

first victory on 6 April 1942, a MiG-3 fighter. He claimed his second victory, a Petlyakov Pe-2 twin-engine dive-bomber, on 9 June and was awarded the Iron Cross 2nd Class on 30 June. He claimed his fourth and fifth victories on 28 September and by the end of the year had claimed a total of twelve. His Group had converted to the Focke-Wulf Fw 190A and moved to Kalinin in December, and Steer was awarded the Iron Cross 1st Class on 8 January 1943.

He claimed his 20th victory on 28 February and by the end of March his score had risen to thirty one. He was awarded the *Luftwaffe* Honour Goblet on 30 April, and in July, most other fighter Groups were assembled around the Kursk salient for Operation Citadel, the next German offensive but most of the 54th Fighter Wing were kept back to guard Leningrad. It appears, however, that several of its pilots, including *Oberfeldwebel* Sterr, went with the 1st Group to Orel and he claimed another ten victories in two weeks to add to his tally and on 17 July he claimed his 50th aerial victory. On 23 July he was awarded the German Cross in Gold in recognition and appreciation of his skill as a fighter pilot, and by the end of the month his score had risen to sixty victories.

In August his Group moved to Kiev and he claimed seven victories on the 2nd, becoming an 'ace-in-a-day', and claimed his 70th victory on 11 August over Leningrad. On 12 September his Group Commander, *Hauptmann* Erich Rudorffer wrote in Sterr's file: '*Oberfeldwebel* Sterr is a trustworthy, balanced, calm character. His attitude in every respect is immaculate. He is fully rooted in National

Socialist ideology. As a fighter pilot he is excellent.' On 8 October he became an 'ace-in-a-day' for the second time when he claimed six victories north of Kiev, and on that day he was shot down in his Fw 190A-6 north-east of Dymer. He managed to bail out but was wounded nevertheless. On 5 December he was awarded the Knight's Cross and sent home for leave and also attended officer training.

In January 1944 he returned to duty in Ukraine as a *Leutnant* and claimed four more victories that month. From March he was transferred to the 4th Squadron and his Group moved to Jakobstadt in Latvia and he claimed seven victories, which included his 90th on 27 March. He continued to claim victories and in early April he returned to the 6th Squadron once again. He claimed his 100th victory on 1 May and after the beginning of the Soviet summer offensive his Group moved to Finland on 9 June. From August he was attached to the 16th Squadron of the 54th Fighter Wing and was now flying over the Western Front, flying from Germany. From mid-September the Allies launched Operation Market Garden, the plan to seize the bridges at Arnhem. This forced the urgent transfer of the ill-prepared 4th Group to the West and Sterr was transferred to the Group as part of the 16th Squadron. He claimed two victories during September, a P-47 Thunderbolt over the Nijmegen area and on the 25th he claimed a B-25 Mitchell twin-engined bomber. From early November Sterr was appointed *Staffelkapitän* of the 16th Squadron and was promoted to *Oberleutnant*. On 26 November he was shot down and killed by a P-47 Thunderbolt piloted by Captain P.L. Larsen of the 78th Fighter Group. He had been nominated for the Oakleaves but it was never awarded, not even posthumously. He is buried in the German Military Cemetery at Hofkirchen in Row 23, Grave No. 6-68.

Kurt TANZER

Leutnant der Reserve

Knight's Cross: Awarded on 5 December 1943 as *Oberfeldwebel* whilst attached to the 12th Squadron of the 51st Fighter Wing '*Mölders*' for operations over the Soviet Union.

(Deutsches Wehrkundearchiv)

Kurt Tanzer claimed at least thirty-five aerial victories over the Eastern Front during the Second World War. He was born on 1 November 1920 and was educated in Germany and entered the *Luftwaffe* in 1940, and two years later on completion of his training he joined the 12th Squadron of the 51st Fighter Wing as a *Gefreiter*.

He was attached to the 4th Group and based in Vyazma and flew the Bf 109F-2 and in May his Group briefly withdrew from combat for maintenance and overhaul in Smolensk. Later his Squadron provided fighter cover over the left flank of Army Group Centre in the area of the 9th Army. At the end of July the Soviets launched the First Rzhev-Sychyovka Operation with the objective of crushing the Rzhev salient held by the 9th Army. On 2 August just west of Rzehev Tanzer claimed his first aerial victory, an Ilyushin Il-2 ground-attack aircraft. Three days later he claimed his second victory, a Petlyakov Pe-2 dive-bomber, and before the end of the month he claimed another Il-2, and soon afterwards he was awarded the Iron Cross 2nd Class. In September he was promoted to *Unteroffizier* and from early October his Group moved to Vitebsk where he flew missions over Army Groups North and Centre. He claimed seven victories in December, six being Il-2s, and shortly after he was awarded the Iron Cross 1st Class.

From January 1943 he was flying the Fw 190A-4 as part of the 4th Group over the Velikiye Luki area and the focus of operations had shifted to the area south-west of the city. He claimed two victories on 5 January, both Il-2s, claimed four on the 6th, and shot down his 20th victory six days later, and by the end of the month he had claimed his 25th victory. His Group was recalled at short notice to Germany in February and on the 15th he was awarded the *Luftwaffe* Honour Goblet. On 19 April he claimed his 30th victory and on 6 May, now with the rank of *Oberfeldwebel*, Tanzer together with his Squadron was alerted to an attack by Soviet Il-2 ground-attack aircraft. He managed to destroy two of the aircraft, attacking despite having been wounded and he continued to attack and shot down two more. After further intensive battles he landed his badly-damaged fighter. His right hand had been seriously injured and he had suffered serious blood loss. He was nominated for the Knight's Cross whilst recovering in hospital but was awarded the German Cross in Gold on 24 June.

After a period of convalescence Tanzer was assigned to the Staff Squadron of the 51st Fighter Wing in November 1943. He was briefly wingman to fighter ace *Major* Karl-Gottfried Nordmann, and flew a number of ground-attack missions and increased his victory tally and on 5 December he was finally awarded the Knight's Cross. In June 1944 he transferred together with *Oberstleutnant* Nordmann to the staff of Fighter Leader 6 in East Prussia. He continued to claim victories but proof of these do not seem to be available. On 10 February 1945, now with the rank of *Leutnant*, he was transferred to the 13th Squadron and became *Staffelkapitän* on 12 March. He was part of the 4th group in Danzig and later Anklam and finally from April 1945 they moved to Eggersdorf where they surrendered.

He had flown a total of 723 combat missions and officially claimed at least thirty-five victories, although some reports put the figure at 128 or even 140. The true figure seems to have been closer to fifty! After the war he joined the *Bundesluftwaffe* and on 25 June 1960, flying as a *Hauptmann*, together with *Oberleutnant* Hans-Ludwig Seseke, their Lockheed T-334 crashed during bad weather in south-west Mallorca and both were killed.

Werner 'Quax' QUAST

Oberfeldwebel

Knight's Cross: Awarded on 31 December 1943 as *Oberfeldwebel* as fighter pilot attached to the 2nd Group of the 52nd Fighter Wing for operations over the Soviet Union.

Werner Quast claimed eighty-four aerial victories in just 350 days, an average of one every four days, and all of them over the Eastern Front during the Second World War. He was born in Thale, Quedlinburg in northern Germany on 21 June 1920 and joined the *Luftwaffe* in early 1940. From mid-1941 he was assigned to the 4th Squadron of the 52nd Fighter Wing as an *Unteroffizier* where he continued his training.

In the autumn of 1942 he was sent to the Soviet Union as part of the 2nd Group of the 52nd Fighter Wing, claiming his first victory, an LaGG-3 fighter over south Stalingrad, on 23 August, claiming his second and third victories just six days later. In September he flew in support of the German army in the Caucasus and claimed two more LaGG-3 fighters on 7 October over north-east Tuapce and was awarded the Iron Cross 2nd Class. His Group flew missions over Stalingrad and due to the Soviet advance had to move airfields to Zimovniki in early December, and then later to Kotelnikovo.

(Deutsches Wehrkundearchiv)

At the beginning of January 1943 his Group was in Gigant, west of Ssalsk, and was equipped with the Messerschmitt Bf 109G. By the 22nd Quast was flying from Rostov and by February had moved again to Nikolayev and now he began to add to his victory tally at an amazing rate. On 11 February he claimed three victories and was awarded the Iron Cross 1st Class a few days later. He claimed another victory the following day, and by the end of the month he had claimed sixteen victories and had been promoted to *Feldwebel*. On 18 April Quast claimed his 25th victory and he claimed two more the next day, two on the 21st, three on the 27th and four on the 29th. By this time his Squadron was flying combat missions from its base in Anapa, a town in Krasnodor Krai on the northern coast of the Black Sea.

Quast claimed his 40th victory on 5 May, a Yakovlev Yak-1 fighter over south Krymsk, and he went on to claim a total of fifteen victories during that month, which included his 50th victory. He became an 'ace-in-a-day' on the 30th when he claimed five victories and he claimed his 60th victory on 8 June. He claimed three more victories on the 10th over the Kalabatka area and was awarded the *Luftwaffe* Honour Goblet on 25 June, and was promoted to *Oberfeldwebel*. On 22 July he became an 'ace-in-a-day' once again when he claimed six victories and the following day he was awarded the German Cross in Gold after achieving sixty victories. By the time he received the award he had achieved just over seventy-five victories! He claimed two victories on 6 August, which included his 80th and he claimed his last three victories the following day. On that day his aircraft was rammed by an Il-2 ground-attack aircraft and he bailed out of his Bf 109 into the Black Sea near Novorossiysk where he was picked up by a Soviet ship and taken prisoner. He was awarded the Knight's Cross on 31 December 1943, but didn't receive it until after the war, being released in 1949.

After the war he joined the *Bundeswehr*, rising to the rank of *Hauptfeldwebel* and became an instructor with Army Air Force School. He was killed in a helicopter crash on 12 July 1962, whilst instructing students near Mittenwald in Bavaria.

1944

Gustav FRIELINGHAUS

Hauptmann

Knight's Cross: Awarded on 5 February 1944 as *Oberleutnant* on the Staff of the 4th Group of the 3rd Fighter Wing for operations over the Soviet Union, Malta and Italy.

Gustav Frielinghaus claimed sixty-nine aerial victories during the Second World War, of which sixty-one were achieved over the Eastern Front. He was born in Osnabrück, Germany on 5 March 1912 and after learning to fly whilst serving with the *Luftwaffe* he became an instructor.

(Deutsches Wehrkundearchiv)

From September 1939 *Gefreiter* Frielinghaus served with Fighter School 5 in Combat Replacement Group Merseberg where in early 1941 he was commissioned as a *Leutnant*. In February he transferred to Fighter School 2 as an instructor and then from June he served with the 6th Squadron of the 3rd Fighter Wing. He took part in Operation Barbarossa, the invasion of the Soviet Union, and he claimed his first victory on 6 July, a Tupolev SB-2 bomber near Polonnoje. He claimed two victories on 25 July and that same day he was wounded when his Bf 109F-2 overturned when he had to make an emergency landing at Stawuszce. Shortly after this he was awarded the Iron Cross 2nd Class and after his rapid recovery he claimed his fourth victory near Dnepropetrovsk on 26 August. By the end of October he had achieved seven aerial victories and had been awarded the Iron Cross 1st Class.

In early January 1942 he served as officer with special duties, still with the 6th Squadron, and saw brief action over Malta. He returned to the Soviet Union with his squadron in May and from early June served as Technical Officer with the 2nd Group of the 3rd Fighter Wing. He claimed his 10th victory on 23 June, and by the end of July he had claimed a total of eighteen victories. On 10 August his Group was moved and was deployed over the Stalingrad area, and on the 17th Frielinghaus claimed his 26th victory and six days later his Group was withdrawn for rest and to take on new aircraft. He was awarded the *Luftwaffe* Honour Goblet on 7 September and on the 24th he was awarded the German Cross in Gold.

In September his Group was relocated to Dedjurewo near Smolensk on the Eastern Front. After the 6th Army at Stalingrad was encircled his Group was ordered in December to that area where they flew to protect transport aircraft that were flying in supplies to the beleaguered and cut-off 6th Army. During this time Frielinghaus claimed a Boston bomber on 21 December and he claimed another victory on the 29th and two more the following day, his 30th victory. Promoted to *Oberleutnant* in late January 1943 he claimed his 40th victory on 25 March, and that same day he was named acting *Staffelkapitän* of the 6th Squadron. On 15 April he claimed three victories and on the 17th he claimed his 50th victory and by the end of the month he had claimed his 55th. He claimed six victories during May and on 1 June he was confirmed as *Staffelkapitän* of the 6th Squadron, and by September had claimed a total of sixty-nine aerial victories.

On 9 September he was seriously wounded and his Bf 109G-6 was destroyed in aerial combat over Foggia with USAAF B-24 bombers. He had barely recovered from his wounds when he was badly injured in a take-off accident at Neubiberg on 19 December. He remained in hospital for a number of weeks and was presented with his Knight's Cross whilst there. He left hospital in April, and was appointed Acting *Gruppenkommandeur* of the 2nd Group of the 3rd Fighter Wing on 1 May with the rank of *Hauptmann*. Even though he would never fly again his Group did take part in defensive action after the Allied invasion of France in June 1944. He transferred as *Staffelkapitän* of the 2nd Squadron of replacement Fighter Group South on 26 June and from November he was *Staffelkapitän* of the 6th Squadron of the 1st Replacement Fighter Wing. His last command was as *Gruppenkommandeur* of the 2nd Group with the 1st Replacement Fighter Wing from 28 March 1945. His headquarters were in Berlin-Gatow until 22 April and then moved to Garz, a small town in Mecklenburg-Vorpommern where he surrendered in early May 1945. Frielinghaus lived in retirement in Düsseldorf until his death at the age of only 51 on 11 September 1963.

Kurt GOLTZSCH

Oberleutnant

Knight's Cross: Awarded on 5 February 1944 as *Leutnant* and whilst attached to the 5th Squadron of the 2nd Fighter Wing for operations over England, North Africa and the Western Front.

Kurt Goltzsch claimed a total of forty aerial victories, which included five four-engined bombers, whilst flying a total of 130 missions over the Western Front during the Second World War. He left school unemployed and then became an apprentice car mechanic before joining the *Luftwaffe* in 1935. He began his pilot training in 1939 as an *Unteroffizier* and joined the 8th Squadron of the 2nd Fighter Wing in March 1940. He saw little action during the opening stages of the invasion of France in May and it wasn't until his Group was transferred to France that he started to claim victories.

(Deutsches Wehrkundearchiv)

Goltzsch claimed his first victory as a *Feldwebel* on 11 August, an RAF Hurricane over Bournemouth. On the evening of 7 September he shot down a Spitfire and seven days later claimed a reconnaissance Spitfire near Le Havre. On 30 September he was awarded the Iron Cross 2nd Class and on 30 October he was presented with the Iron Cross 1st Class personally by *Reichsmarschall* Göring during a visit to the 2nd Fighter Wing. His progress as a fighter ace came to a standstill when he was transferred as an instructor. He flew instruction missions over south-western France from May 1941 and passed the time rabbit hunting and fishing, when he wasn't flying. There was a nearby resort town of Arcachon which provided a welcome break for Goltzsch and his comrades.

Promoted to *Oberfeldwebel* in August 1941, he returned to combat duty a year later with the 4th Squadron of the 2nd Fighter Wing. The 2nd Group was the first in the Wing to convert from the Bf 109 to the new Focke-Wulf Fw 190 in March 1942. On 31 May he claimed a Spitfire on the Channel Front, and claimed another on 5 and 6 August (the one on the 5th was later reclassified as unconfirmed). He claimed two more Spitfires on 19 August during the failed Allied landing at

Dieppe. During this time he also carried out dangerous reconnaissance missions to the south coast of England and on one such mission he attacked a British patrol boat in the Channel. On 6 September he claimed a Stirling four-engined heavy bomber. He claimed his 10th victory on 12 November, a B-26 Marauder twin-engined bomber over south-east Les Pieux, France which had apparently become lost en route to North Africa.

In late November 1942 the 2nd Group was transferred to Tunisia following the Allied landings in Vichy French North-west Africa. During this time Goltzsch claimed a total of thirteen aerial victories over North Africa, the third highest score of the 2nd Group at this time. He had now claimed his 23rd victory and had also displayed excellent ground-attack abilities in Tunisia when he destroyed a landing-craft, anti-aircraft positions and on one occasion twenty fully-loaded trucks. In March during the Allied retreat in North Africa, the 2nd Group was pulled out and returned to the Channel Front. Goltzsch now flew the Bf 109G-6 fighter and on 4 April in recognition of his success he was awarded the *Luftwaffe* Honour Goblet. In May he was transferred to the 5th Squadron where he assumed command of the squadron after the death of *Leutnant* Lothar Werner. He claimed two Spitfires later that month, which included his 25th victory, and he claimed two victories on 26 June, which included a B-17 Flying Fortress. He claimed two more victories on 4 July, which included his 30th victory. On 18 July he shot down a Spitfire of the RAF's 41 Squadron near the mouth of the Somme River to record his 35th victory. It had been flown by 21-year-old South African Flying Officer Rycherde H.W. Hogarth, who was killed.

In early August Goltzsch was promoted to *Leutnant* and claimed a B-17 bomber on the 15th and 17th. He claimed a Spitfire on the 19th and the 31st and another on 2 September and he claimed a B-17 Flying Fortress the next day. On the 4th the British and Americans launched bombing operations over France, which included Mitchells, Bostons, Marauders and Venturas escorted by Spitfires and P-47s. The 2nd Fighter Wing had no successes that day and lost two pilots, and one of them was Goltzsch. It's very likely that he was shot down by Norwegian fighter pilot Captain Svein Heglund. Goltzsch managed to nurse his aircraft towards his airfield just outside Vitry-en-Artois and had to make an emergency landing in an open field. He suffered serious spinal cord compression, and would never fly again. He spent the final 13 months of his life paralysed in a hospital bed. He was awarded the Knight's Cross on 5 February 1944, and unfortunately seven months later he died at the Reserve Hospital in Glanchau, close to his birthplace and also near the home of his wife and son. He was posthumously promoted to *Oberleutnant* on 1 October 1944.

Günther JOSTEN

Oberleutnant

(Deutsches Wehrkundearchiv)

Knight's Cross: Awarded on 5 February 1944 as *Oberfeldwebel* and fighter pilot in the 1st Squadron of the 51st Fighter Wing '*Mölders*' for operations over the Soviet Union and for claiming his 82nd aerial victory, a Lavochkin La-5 fighter.

Knight's Cross with Oakleaves: He became the 810th recipient on 28 March 1945 as *Oberleutnant* and *Staffelkapitän* of the 2nd Squadron of the 51st Fighter Wing '*Mölders*' for operations over the Eastern Front and the Soviet Union and for claiming his 160th aerial victory.

Günther Josten flew 420 combat missions during the Second World War and claimed 178 aerial victories, all over the Eastern Front, just outside the top twenty top aces of the *Luftwaffe*. He was born on

7 November 1921 in Rhynern, today part of Hamm, in the Province of Westphalia, Germany. He was the second son of Johannes Josten, a Pastor, and his wife Gertraud. His older brother Reinhard, who was also a fighter pilot, was killed in April 1942 when his Bf 109 crashed in the Soviet Union. In October 1935 an airfield was built near to where he lived and this influenced the young Günther and his brother to become aviators. Josten attended a boarding school which had been established to educate a new generation for the political, military and administrative leadership of the Third Reich. He joined the National Socialist Flyers Corps (NSFK) and made his first flight in a glider at Naumburg on 25 May 1938.

In September 1939 Germany invaded Poland and within a few days of the start of hostilities Josten volunteered for military service with the *Luftwaffe*. He was accepted in January 1940, and after his initial training he was posted, in April, to the 61st Training Regiment in Oschatz. His desire was to become a fighter pilot, but at first he feared he might become an air gunner. Much to his delight he was posted to flight school for pilot training, and in August 1940 was granted leave to return to school to take his *Abitur* or School Diploma exam, a precondition to becoming an officer. He returned to his training a few months later, and made his first solo flight on a Fw 44 'Stieglitz' on 18 October. He received his pilot's licence in July 1941 and was promoted to *Unteroffizier*, the only student in his class to receive such a promotion.

On 1 August 1941, with his pilot training complete Josten was sent to the *Jagdfliegervorschule* (Fighter Pilot Pre-School) in Kamenz. With his training over he was transferred into Fighter Group Drontheim, based in Denmark. There on 9 January 1942, he flew the Bf 109 fighter for the first time, and in July was posted to the Supplementary Fighter Group East, based in Cracow, Poland. At the end of August he was sent to the Eastern Front where he was assigned to the 1st Squadron of the 51st Fighter Wing. Josten claimed his first aerial victory on 23 February 1943, when he shot down an Ilyushin Il-2 ground-attack aircraft north-east of Shisdra. In March his squadron was equipped with the Focke-Wulf Fw 190A-4 and a few days later he claimed his second victory, another Il-2, shot down near Glazunowka. He was awarded the Iron Cross 2nd Class on 4 April and two weeks later was granted some leave and visited Dresden where he met Alice Schmidt for the first time. The two were to marry in June 1944.

On 8 June 1943, Josten claimed his third victory, and two days later he shot down three more aircraft, all Il-2s. By 12 July he had claimed his 10th aerial victory, and the same day was awarded the Iron Cross 1st Class. The following day 13th Josten became an 'ace-in-a-day', when he shot down five aircraft, again all Il-2s, and a sixth remains unconfirmed. By the end of July he had claimed his 25th victory. He claimed another five victories on 2 August, but two remain unconfirmed. He claimed his 40th aerial victory on 14 August, and by the 30th he had recorded his 50th aerial victory, an La-5 fighter shot down south-west of Nikitino. On 4 September he claimed four victories and on the 7th he became an 'ace-in-a-day' for the second time when he shot down seven aircraft. He claimed his 70th victory on 14 September and the following day he became an 'ace-in-a-day' yet again when he claimed seven more aircraft. By the end of September Josten had claimed a total of eighty-two victories, and had been awarded the *Luftwaffe* Honour Goblet on 31 August and on the 17 October he was awarded the German Cross in Gold.

Shortly after some leave he was transferred to Air War School 4 at Fürstenfeldbruck where he passed on his skill and experience to younger, less experienced pilots. He returned to his squadron on 3 February 1944 where two days later he shot down two Boston bombers near Paritschi and was awarded the Knight Cross in recognition of his success and was promoted to *Leutnant*. On 30 April he claimed his 90th aerial victory, and he claimed his 94th and 95th victories on 25 June. He was appointed *Staffelkapitän* of the 3rd Squadron of the 51st Fighter Wing on 18 July, and two days later he achieved his 100th victory when he shot down an Il-2 east of Rawa Ruska. By the end of August he had claimed his 113th victory, and during September he added another ten victories to his total, which included a B-17 four-engined bomber, shot down over Warsaw. This was the B-17 known by her crew as 'Til we meet again', piloted by Lieutenant Francis Akins, who was killed during the attack when a burst of bullets from Josten's aircraft hit him in the face. The attack killed all but two members of the crew, who managed to bail out of the stricken aircraft.

On 9 October Josten shot down three aircraft, followed by another two on the 16th, three on the 18th and the 20th, and by the end of the month he had achieved his 139th victory. He was promoted to *Oberleutnant* on 1 November, and claimed his 150th aerial victory on 17 February 1945. On 28 March he was awarded the Knight's Cross with Oakleaves in recognition of his 160th aerial victory, and it should be noted that he never received the Oakleaves either from Hitler or Göring and he never received the award documentation either. On 2 April he was presented with the Oakleaves by the commanding general of *Luftwaffe* Command in East Prussia, *Generalmajor* Klaus Uebe, and received a telegram from Göring congratulating him on his award.

On 12 April, Josten was appointed *Gruppenkommandeur* of the 4th Group of the 51st Fighter Wing, equipped with Fw 190s. That day, *Hauptmann* Günther Schack, the *Gruppenkommandeur* of the 1st Group, was seriously wounded in combat, so Josten briefly took command of the 1st Group which delayed his taking command of the 4th Group until 18 April. Josten claimed two more victories on 22 April and the following day his command received a visit from the commander of the *Luftwaffe* in the North East, *General der Flieger* Martin Fiebig who told the Group that he was asking for volunteers to make suicide attacks against the Soviet Oder crossing. The idea was to fly Junkers Ju 88 bombers loaded with explosives into the Oder bridge. None of Josten's pilots volunteered for the missions. On 25 April, Josten claimed nine victories, to become an 'ace-in-a-day' yet again! The following day he claimed his last victory of the war when he shot down a Yak-3 fighter over Berlin.

On 6 May Josten was taken prisoner by British forces of the RAF Second Tactical Air Force in Flensburg. The British wanted to compare the Fw 190's performance against a Hawker Tempest. On 25 June, Josten and Heinz Lange flew the Fw 190D-13 in mock combat against the Tempest piloted by a British pilot. They proved to be evenly matched. Josten was released from captivity on 31 October 1945, and later became a joiner and worked at a furniture factory. His wife gave birth to a son, Meinhard Gero, on 2 July 1946. They divorced in November 1955 and Josten later worked for an industrial wood supplier in Cologne. In 1950 he was invited by friends to a New Year's Eve party and he met Ursula from Erfurt. They later got married and had two sons. In April 1956, Josten rejoined the *Luftwaffe* in the *Bundeswehr* and was promoted to *Hauptmann* in November 1956. He later served as *Staffelkapitän* in the 73rd Fighter Wing and was promoted to *Major* in March 1959. In May 1962 he succeeded Erich Hartmann as *Kommodore* of the 71st Fighter Wing, and there was promoted to *Oberstleutnant* in June and to *Oberst* in June 1965. Two years later he was appointed commander of the 4th *Luftwaffe* Division. He retired from service on 31 March 1981, and lived in retirement in Aurich, Lower Saxony until his death on 7 July 2004.

Gerhard LOOS

Oberleutnant

Knight's Cross: Awarded on 5 February 1944 as *Leutnant* whilst attached to the 1st Squadron of the 54th Fighter Wing for operations over the Soviet Union and the Western Front.

Gerhard Loos claimed eighty-four aerial victories and all but one, a four-engined bomber, were scored over the Eastern Front during the Second World War. He was born on 21 August 1916 in Kommern, Brüz in Austria-Hungary and entered the *Luftwaffe* in early 1939 and qualified as an instructor with a fighter pilot school.

From December 1942 *Leutnant* Loos was with the 1st Group of the 54th Fighter Wing flying the Bf 109F-4 over the Soviet Union. From February 1943 he was with the 1st Squadron, flying the Fw 190A, scoring his first victory, a Petlyakov Pe-2 twin-engined dive-bomber north-east of Luban on 19 February. He claimed his second victory, an LaGG-3 fighter, on the 22nd and on 8 April he claimed his fifth victory over Leningrad and was awarded the Iron Cross 2nd Class. From May he flew from Nikolskoye and on the 24th he claimed four aerial victories, three being Il-2 ground-attack aircraft, and he was awarded the Iron Cross 1st Class. By June he flew from Orel and on 5 July he claimed five victories to become an 'ace-in-a-day', three LaGG-3s and two Il-2s. By 10 July he had claimed his 20th aerial victory, and he claimed two Il-2s on 2 August which included his 30th victory. He claimed three more victories on the 3rd and became an 'ace-in-a-day' for the second time on the 4th when he claimed six victories, which included his 40th victory. On 12 August he claimed four victories, which included his 50th and six days later he claimed his 60th victory. On 23 August he claimed six victories to become an 'ace-in-a-day' for the third time and now had claimed a total of seventy-nine victories. On 20 September he was awarded the *Luftwaffe* Honour Goblet in recognition of his 60th victory and by the end of September he had achieved his 83rd victory and was awarded the German Cross in Gold on 17 October.

(Deutsches Wehrkundearchiv)

On 28 September his Wing left the Eastern Front and flew 'Defence of the Reich' missions as part of the 9th Squadron of the 54th Fighter Wing. He now flew the Bf 109G out of Schwerin and from December he flew from Ludwigslust and he claimed a four-engined bomber over the Bremen area on 20 December. From February 1944 he flew from Lüneburg and in early March he was promoted to *Oberleutnant* and made *Staffelkapitän* of his squadron. On 6 March he was shot down during combat with P-51 fighters over Germany and bailed out of his Bf 109 near Soltau in Lüneburg Heath. He found that he was drifting toward electric pylons and so decided to drop out from his parachute from an altitude of 65ft and was killed. However, accounts do differ as to exactly what happed – one source describes his parachute harness as coming apart as soon as his canopy opened.

Hans-Peter 'Dackel' WALDEMANN

Oberleutnant

Knight's Cross: Awarded on 5 February 1944 as *Feldwebel* and pilot attached to the 6th Squadron of the 52nd Fighter Wing for operations over the Soviet Union and for claiming his 85th aerial victory.

Hans-Peter Waldmann claimed 131 aerial victories during the Second World War, of which 121 were achieved over the Eastern Front. He also claimed ten victories over the Western Front, of which two were four-engined bombers, and claimed two victories whilst flying the Me 262 jet fighter. He was born on 24 September 1922 in Braunschweig, Lower Saxony and was the second son of Ludwig Waldmann, a bank manager, and his wife Maria.

Waldemann applied to join the *Luftwaffe* in 1938 but at only 16 he was too young. He graduated from school in 1940 and was accepted into the *Luftwaffe* in July and undertook a 12-week basic training

(Deutsches Wehrkundearchiv)

course. From early October he attended flight school and in August 1941 he completed his flight training and was transferred to the 6th Fighter Pilot School at Lachen-Speyerdorf near Neustadt an der Weinstrasse. He was finally assigned to front-line duty on 17 August 1942, serving with the 2nd Group of the 52nd Fighter Wing on the Eastern Front. Waldmann flew his first combat mission as an *Unteroffizier* on 31 August 1942, piloting his Bf 109G-2 as wingman to *Hauptmann* Johannes Steinhoff over Stalingrad. Steinhoff was impressed by Waldmann's first performance. He claimed his first victory on 7 September, an LaGG-3 fighter near Makowkin, and two days later he claimed his second victory and on the 10th he claimed his third, both LaGG-3s. On 25th September after gaining his sixth victory he was awarded the Iron Cross 2nd Class. The same day his Bf 109G-2 sustained damage during combat and Waldmann had to make a forced landing at Maikop. He wasn't hurt and on 3 November claimed his 10th victory and eight days later was awarded the Iron Cross 1st Class. He claimed ten more victories during December, and two were later reclassified as unconfirmed.

In early January 1943 he transferred to the 6th Squadron of the 52nd Fighter Wing, and on 12 February he claimed four victories and by the 25th he had achieved his 32nd victory. On 15 March he was awarded the *Luftwaffe* Honour Goblet and the German Cross in Gold on 17 April. On the 30th he claimed his 35th victory near Usun and on 7 May, just after claiming his 40th victory, he had to make a forced landing at Taman due to engine failure. By the end of May he had claimed forty-eight victories and continued to be successful during the next two months. He was promoted to *Feldwebel* in early June and claimed his 60th and 61st victories on 26 July. He claimed four victories on 4 August, his 70th on the 7th, and his 75th on the 10th and by the end of the month he had claimed his 84th victory, an Ilyushin Il-2 ground-attack aircraft.

In September Waldmann was promoted to *Leutnant* and assigned to the Supplementary Fighter Group East, and he was credited with the destruction of a B-17 Flying Fortress on 5 January 1944. This victory was actually a 'separation-shot', a severely-damaged heavy bomber which had been forced to separate from the other aircraft from its 'combat box' and this counted as a victory. On 5 February he was rewarded for his skill as a pilot and for his tally of eighty-five victories when he was awarded the Knight's Cross. In late February he returned to his old squadron with the 51st Fighter Wing and was appointed *Staffelkapitän*. He claimed six more victories during March and claimed his 95th to 97th victories on 11 April, and on the 18th he claimed two victories, his 100th and 101st. On 4 May Waldmann and his squadron intercepted twenty-four Ilyushin Il-2 ground-attack aircraft from the 8th Guards Ground-attack Aviation Regiment, escorted by twenty-three fighter aircraft over the Black Sea. Pilots from the 2nd Group claimed six victories, including an Il-2 and a Yak-7 by Waldmann without any losses. On 6 May he claimed three more victories near Sevastopol, which included his 110th victory, and the following day he became an 'ace-in-a-day' when he claimed six victories over the Black Sea. By 31 May his score had risen to 122 victories.

In early July the 2nd Group of the 52nd Fighter Wing, which included Waldman's squadron, was transferred to the Invasion Front in Normandy. The Group was under the command of *Major* Gerhard Barkhorn and was tasked with ground-support missions. In one of these missions against Allied invasion forces Waldmann claimed a P-51 Mustang on 31 July, but it was never confirmed. During this period he was credited with the destruction of numerous trucks and he claimed his first confirmed aerial victory on the Western Front on 6 August when he shot down a B-24 Liberator over Méry in southern France. The following day he claimed a British Auster observation aircraft and on the 14th he shot down two P-47s, his 125th and 126th victories. On 18 August he transferred as *Staffelkapitän* to the 8th Squadron of the 3rd Fighter Wing flying from Athis in northern France, and claimed two more P-47s on 18 August and another the following day. From November he flew as an *Oberleutnant* and *Staffelführer* of the 3rd Squadron of the 7th Fighter Wing, flying the Messerschmitt Me 262 jet fighter. He claimed two Mustangs on 22 February 1945, whilst flying with his wingman *Oberfähnrich* Günter Schrey, one was shot down over Berlin and the other over north-west Brocken.

On 18 March, a Sunday and with low cloud cover at Kaltenkirchen, not ideal weather conditions for the Me 262, Waldmann's squadron was ordered to take off by *Reichsmarschall* Göring and engage heavy bombers approaching. The weather conditions worsened and as a result both Waldmann and his wingman Schrey were killed. Waldmann was killed when he was involved in a mid-air collision with *Leutnant* Hans-Dieter Weihs shortly after take-off and Schrey was killed in combat with US fighters. Waldmann's body was recovered the next day almost a mile from the crash site of his Me 262, having managed to bail out but had failed to deploy his parachute in time. Schrey was found dead. He had bailed out with his parachute but his body was riddled with machine-gun bullets. Both men were buried with full honours, including a flypast by a Me 262 above the cemetery in Kaltenkirchen. Waldmann had flown a total of 527 combat missions and was posthumously recommend for the Oakleaves but it was never approved.

Heinz LEBER

Leutnant

Knight's Cross: Awarded posthumously on 29 February 1944 as *Oberfeldwebel* and pilot attached to the 1st Group of the 51st Fighter Wing '*Udet*' for operations over the Soviet Union.

Heinz Leber claimed fifty-two aerial victories during the Second World War, all of them whilst flying combat missions over the Soviet Union. He was born on 14 May 1920 in Ahlendorf, Thüringen in Central Germany and after his flight training he was assigned to the 51st Fighter Wing from March 1941.

From June he saw action during Operation Barbarossa, the invasion of the Soviet Union, whilst assigned to the 2nd Squadron of the 51st Fighter Wing as an *Unteroffizier*. He began the campaign flying fighter-bomber missions against airfields and by early July was flying from the Bobruisk area. He claimed his first aerial victory on 2 July, a Polikarpov I-16 fighter east of Bobruysk, and claimed his second victory on 28 July, an Ilyushin Il-2 ground-attack aircraft. During

(Deutsches Wehrkundearchiv)

August his group moved a number of times and from September flew from an area near Smolensk, and claimed his third victory on 6 September, an I-16 fighter. From October his unit flew missions in support of the army in its attack on Moscow and he claimed two victories on 5 October, both DB-3 bombers. He claimed another victory the following day and two more later that month. He continued to fly in support of ground forces attacking Moscow and claimed his ninth victory and his last for 1941 on 13 November.

From the beginning of 1942 his Group was stationed in Staraya Russa and was equipped with the Bf 109F-2. Again his Squadron was used for fighter-bomber missions and by the end of January he was equipped with the Bf 109E-7 and had moved airfields to Solzy about 25 miles west of Lake Ilmen. From here he flew hunting protection missions and he began to score victories again in February, claiming three that month and claimed four during March which included his 16th victory. From the end of March to the beginning of April the entire Group had problems with mud but still managed to fly missions over the Demyansk and Cholm areas.

In late April he claimed his 21st victory and in early May he was awarded the *Luftwaffe* Honour Goblet. From May until early June he briefly joined Fighter School East as an instructor, returning as a *Feldwebel*. On 17 June he was awarded the German Cross in Gold after claiming his 20th aerial victory. In August his Group had moved and was supporting Army Group Centre and in mid-August his Group left the front to be upgraded and equipped with the Focke-Wulf Fw 190A fighter. Leber and his Group returned to action in mid-September, being relocated via Riga and Rjelbitzi to Ljuban. Later in October the Group was withdrawn and relocated to Vyazma South and Leber began to score victories once again. He claimed a MiG-3 on 26 October and during December he claimed three more aircraft, which included his 26th victory.

From the beginning of January 1944 his Group was flying from the frozen Lake Ivan about 30 miles from Velikiye Luki. In March the Group moved to Bryansk and in May to Orel and it was around that time that Leber began to increase his rate of victories. He claimed five victories in April and in contrast he claimed a total of five on 5 May to become an 'ace-in-a-day' mainly over the area of Kursk. The following day he did one better and claimed six victories, five of them Il-2s, and he became an 'ace-in-a-day' for the second day running. He claimed four more victories on 7 May and two on the 8th, the same day he was promoted to *Oberfeldwebel*. He claimed his 50th victory on 12 May near Zolotuchino and he claimed his 52nd and last aerial victory on 1 June. That same day his aircraft was struck by anti-aircraft fire at an altitude of 650ft and he crashed and was killed, having had no time to parachute to safety. He was posthumously awarded the Knight's Cross on 29 February 1944 and soon after he was also posthumously promoted to *Leutnant*. He is buried at Mszensk in the Soviet Union near to where he crashed and his remains have not yet been removed to a military cemetery.

Viktor PETERMANN

Oberleutnant

Knight's Cross: Awarded on 29 February 1944 as *Leutnant* and whilst attached to the 6th Squadron of the 52nd Fighter Wing for operations over the Soviet Union.

Viktor Petermann claimed sixty-four aerial victories from over 550 missions over the Eastern Front during the Second World War, with four being achieved after losing his left arm. He was born on 26 May 1916 in Weipert, Austria-Hungary and after leaving school he studied engineering and worked for a time in the textile industry. He learnt to fly gliders before the war and joined the *Luftwaffe* in July 1939, receiving his basic training at Strabing in East Prussia and attended pilot course between April 1940 and March 1941.

In October 1941 Petermann was assigned to the 2nd Squadron of the Advanced Training Group whilst attached to the 52nd Fighter Wing. He flew as an *Unteroffizier* over the Eastern Front from 15 June 1942, and was attached to the Staff Squadron. He achieved his first victory on 1 July, an LaGG-3 fighter over the area of Volokonovka, and he followed that with a MiG-1 the next day. He flew as wingman to *Kommodore Major* Herbert Ihlefeld and claimed his fifth victory on 25 August and a few days later Petermann was awarded the Iron Cross 2nd Class. He claimed three more victories during September, and was awarded the Iron Cross 1st Class on 16 October after claiming his ninth victory.

(Deutsches Wehrkundearchiv)

In February 1943 Petermann was promoted to *Feldwebel* and by 19 March he had claimed fourteen victories. He went on to claim a total of twelve victories during April, and claimed his 30th victory on 4 May, a Yak-1 over the Black Sea. He claimed a further three victories the following day and by the end of the month he had achieved his 44th victory. On 6 June he sank a gunboat, but the same day he was attacked by a Soviet fighter and his aircraft was badly damaged and he had to make an emergency landing behind enemy lines. He managed to sneak through the Soviet positions and reached his own lines three days later. After a few weeks' rest in hospital he returned to duty and was awarded the German Cross in Gold on 23 July and three days later he claimed his 50th victory. Shortly after he was promoted to *Leutnant* and on 9 August was awarded the *Luftwaffe* Honour Goblet. On 14 September he claimed his 55th victory, and claimed four more victories on the 25th and claimed his 60th victory the following day. On 1 October he was again shot down, this time by 'friendly fire'. His Bf 109 was hit by a German anti-aircraft shell and he made an emergency landing at Novo-Zaporozhye. He was seriously wounded and had to have his left arm and his fourth toe from his left foot amputated. He was awarded the Wound Badge in Silver on 22 December.

After being in hospital yet again, this time for a number of months, he was awarded the Knight's Cross on 29 January before being reassigned to the Military Science Branch of the *Luftwaffe* in May 1944, but was keen to get back to flying. On 22 July he finally received permission to fly again and joined the Staff Squadron of the 52nd Fighter Wing, with a prosthetic left arm. He flew his first mission with his false arm on 24 September but found it difficult and failed to score another victory until 16 January 1945 when he claimed a Yakovlev Yak-9 fighter. He claimed another Yak-9 on 11 February and claimed a P-39 and a Yak-9 in March, his 63rd and 64th victories. On 31 March he joined the 7th Fighter Wing and trained with the Me 262 jet fighter, but failed to score any victories, and found it tough and he returned to his old Squadron in the 52nd Fighter Wing on 11 April.

He was promoted to *Oberleutnant* on 1 May and seven days later he surrendered to US troops at Deutsch Brod in Czechoslovakia. They handed him over to the Soviets the next day, but due to his wounds he was released from captivity on 26 July 1945 and returned to Germany. He became a farm labourer in eastern Germany and from 1954 he worked as a technical advisor and engineer with a farm machine production company. He lived in retirement in Freiburg, Saxony until his death on 19 May 2001.

Oskar ROMM

Oberleutnant

Knight's Cross: Awarded on 29 February 1944 as *Oberfeldwebel* whilst attached to the 1st Group of the 51st Fighter Wing '*Mölders*' for operations over the Soviet Union.

Oskar 'Ossi' Romm claimed eighty-eight aerial victories during the Second World War of which seventy-eight were achieved whilst over the Eastern Front and the remaining ten, which included eight four-engined bombers, were claimed over the Western Front. He was born on 18 December 1919 in Haindorf in Friedland, Czechoslovakia and joined the *Luftwaffe* in October 1939 and trained as a fighter pilot.

With his training complete and with the rank of *Unteroffizier* Romm was assigned to the 1st Squadron of the 51st Fighter Wing in September 1942, seeing action over the Soviet Union. He claimed his first victory on 4 December, an Ilyushin Il-2 ground-attack aircraft, over Oledar and from January 1943 his Group was equipped with the

(Deutsches Wehrkundearchiv)

Fw 190A and had moved to Smolensk. From here Romm flew over the Velikiye Luki area and on 15 January he claimed his second victory, a MiG-3 fighter. On 28 January his Group moved again to Orel-West and on 24 February he claimed an Il-2 over north Zhizdra. By March his Group had moved to Bryansk and from May flew from Orel and by this time Romm had been awarded the

Iron Cross 2nd Class. He claimed his 10th victory on 8 July and by the 13th he had claimed sixteen victories and had been awarded the Iron Cross 1st Class. In August he was promoted to *Feldwebel* and his Group returned to Bryansk briefly before moving to Poltava and during August Romm claimed thirty-five victories which included becoming an 'ace-in-a-day' three times. He claimed five on 2 August, five on the 14th and six on the 20th and was shortly after promoted to *Oberfeldwebel*. In September he claimed thirteen victories and on the 4th became an 'ace-in-a-day' for the fourth time, and had now claimed a total of sixty-six victories.

Towards the end of September Romm transferred as an instructor to Advanced Training Group East, and during his time he was awarded the German Cross in Gold on 17 October 1943 and *Luftwaffe* Honour Goblet on 1 November in recognition of his success, and he returned to his Squadron in January 1944. He was now flying from Bobruisk, equipped with the Bf 109G, and on 5 February he became an 'ace-in-a-day' again when he claimed six victories, which included his 70th, and on 29 February he was awarded the Knight's Cross in recognition of his great success on the Soviet front. In early June Romm transferred to the 4th Group of the 3rd Fighter Wing and took part in the 'Defence of the Reich' and from July he was promoted to *Leutnant* and appointed *Staffelkapitän* of the 12th Squadron. He was now flying over his homeland, defending the skies over Germany, and on 7 July he claimed a B-24 bomber, and on the 18th he claimed two B-17s and a P-51 Mustang over south-east Memmingen. On 27 Septembers he claimed three B-24 Liberators over Eschwege, north-eastern Germany, and the next day he claimed two B-17 Flying Fortresses over west Halberstadt, his 80th and 81st victories.

From November he briefly took command of the 4th Squadron, but soon moved to the 1st Group of the 1st Fighter Replacement and Training Wing where he stayed until February 1945. Promoted to *Oberleutnant* Romm was appointed *Gruppenkommandeur* of the 4th Group of the 3rd Fighter Wing based in Prenzlau, a town in Brandenburg, Germany. He claimed three victories during February and his last three victories in March, his final one an Il-2 ground-attack aircraft on 21 March. On 24 April he belly-landed his Fw 190 at Brussow after running out of fuel and was so badly injured that he did not return to combat.

Romm had flown 283 combat missions during the war and had been recommended for the Oakleaves but the war had ended before it could be awarded. Whilst flying over the Eastern Front between January and September 1943 he had claimed sixty-five victories, just over eight a month, and had become an 'ace-in-a-day' five times. He died on 1 May 1993 in Waldesch, a district of Mayen-Koblenz in Rhineland-Palatinate, Germany.

Walther DAHL

Oberst

Knight's Cross: Awarded on 11 March 1944 as *Major* and *Gruppenkommandeur* of the 3rd Group of the 3rd Fighter Wing '*Udet*' for operation over Malta, the Western Front and the Soviet Union and in recognition of his 54th aerial victory, a B-17 Flying Fortress shot down south-west of Regensburg, Germany.

Knight's Cross with Oakleaves: He became the 724th recipient on 1 February 1945 as *Major* and *Gruppenkommandeur* of the 300th Fighter Wing for actions over the Western Front, where he claimed his 76th aerial victory east of Oppeln.

Walther Dahl is credited with at least ninety aerial victories, including twenty-two four-engined bombers, and led one of the most successful units of the *Luftwaffe* during the 'Defence of the Reich', earning himself a formidable reputation as a tactical expert in the war against the bombers. He was born on 27 March 1916 in Lug near Bad Bergzabern, the son of a teacher who he never knew as he was killed in action in 1918 on the Western Front during the First World War. He served briefly in the Reich Labour Service (RAD) in 1935 and in October he entered the Army, serving with the 35th Infantry Regiment and from October 1936 with the 119th Infantry Regiment. He was commissioned as a *Leutnant der Reserve* in January 1938, and in October he transferred to the *Schutzpolizei*. On 1 May 1939, Dahl resigned from the police and joined the *Luftwaffe* and trained as a fighter pilot. From December he trained with the Aircraft Pilot School in Weimar and in October 1940 he transferred to the Fighter Pilot School in Vienna. Promoted to *Oberleutnant* in early October he transferred to the Advanced Training Group of the 3rd Fighter Wing in April 1941.

(Deutsches Wehrkundearchiv)

In May Dahl was posted to his first operational unit, the 3rd Fighter Wing, which was preparing for the attack on the Soviet Union. He claimed his first aerial victory on 22 June 1941, a MiG-1 fighter east of Lvov, and for this achievement he was awarded the Iron Cross 2nd Class. He achieved his 2nd victory on 16 July, a Polikarpov I-16 fighter shot down over south Koziatyn. He claimed another four victories in August but only the two he claimed on the 24th were confirmed, and he claimed two on 13 September and was awarded the Iron Cross 1st Class. By November he had achieved a total of thirteen victories, another five were unconfirmed, and on 23 December was awarded the *Luftwaffe* Honour Goblet.

From 13 February until 9 April 1942 Dahl commanded the 4th Squadron of the 3rd Fighter Wing, having taken over from *Hauptmann* Georg Michalek. On 10 April he was appointed *Staffelkapitän* of the 1st Squadron of the Fighter Replacement and Training Wing, serving as an instructor. This took him away from front-line duties and it wasn't until August that he returned to the front as a squadron adjutant with the 3rd Fighter Wing. He claimed his 15th victory on 7 September and by the end of the month had claimed his 23rd. Dahl continued to be even more successful in October, which included two victories on the 14th, three on the 25th and four on the 26th. On 2 December achieved his 38th victory and was awarded the German Cross in Gold.

In March 1943 Dahl was promoted to *Hauptmann* and the following month was transferred to the Staff of the General of Fighter Pilots where he commanded a training and instruction squadron. He still managed to fly an occasional combat mission and claimed seven aerial victories during April, and he now had a total of forty-seven victories. On 20 July he was appointed *Gruppenkommandeur* of the 3rd Group of the 3rd Fighter Wing, and on 17 August he made an emergency landing at Cipperath, Eifel when his Bf 109G-6 developed engine problems, landing safely without injury. On 13 August Dahl's Group had been scrambled from its base in Münster-Handorf just after 12:00. However, his group failed to find the force of USAAF B-17 bombers and landed at Woensdrecht in Holland about an hour later. After 90 minutes or so, they took off again determined this time to find the bombers, only to be misdirected by ground control straight into a large formation of RAF Spitfires over northern Belgium. While Dahl and his fighters were otherwise engaged, the B-17s sailed past high overhead some 12 miles away.

On 16 January 1944 a small force of B-17s attacked the Bf 109 components factory at Klagenfurt, Austria but Dahl's Group failed to make contact with them. The US 8th Air Force intended to strike against Frankfurt on 24 January but due to bad weather this was aborted so they tried again on the 29th and this time they succeeded. However, twenty-nine of their number failed to return, mainly due to Dahl's Group which had become one of the most successful units during the 'Defence of the Reich' operations. His Group claimed fifteen bombers of which Dahl himself claimed two, with the loss of only two of their own pilots. Dahl continued to score victories throughout February, which included three on the 23rd; three on the 24th and two more on the 25th, which included another four B-17 bombers. On 11 March Dahl was awarded the Knight's Cross, and not before time. He was now credited with fifty-four aerial victories of which five were B-17s and another three remain unconfirmed victories.

He would claim another four in April and in early May he was promoted to *Major* and approached by *Generalmajor* Adolf Galland who was General of the Fighters and asked if he would command a special fighter wing, the *Jagdgeschwader z.b.V* (Fighter Wing for Special Purposes). Its former *Kommodore*, *Major* Gerhard Michalski, had been seriously wounded on 1 May. Dahl agreed and officially took up his new position on 20 May, and now commanded a special unit made up from III./JG3, II./JG2, III./JG54 and II./JG53. His new Wing flew its first major operation against the enemy on 24 May, Dahl's fighters had to contend with over 400 escort fighters. It was tough and they were engaged in close fighter-versus-fighter engagements but a few of Dahl's aircraft managed to breakthrough to the bombers, in fact they shot down thirty-three B-17s with a further 256 being damaged.

On 27 June 1944, Dahl took over as *Kommodore* of the 300th Fighter Wing, with his headquarters in Ansbach where he planned combined operations with the 3rd Fighter Wing. On 7 July the US 8th Air Force set out from England to bomb aircraft factories in the Leizig area and the synthetic oil plants at Boehlen, Leuna-Merseburg and Lützkendorf. The force consisted of 1,129 B-17 Flying Fortresses and B-24 Liberators, divided into three groups. A series of accidents at the start of the mission allowed the *Luftwaffe* to focus their attacks on the B-24 force. The formation was attacked by a force of Bf 109s led by Dahl, at point-blank range, when the Bomber Group was temporarily without fighter cover. Within a minute or so the entire squadron of twelve B-24s had been annihilated. Dahl lost nine fighters with three damaged, and five of his pilots were killed.

Dahl now focused on forming a new unit from his Wing, he was able to draw on a number of battle-hardened pilots and his new unit was called the *Sturmgruppe* or Assault Group. By 4 August the conversion and training of this new group was complete. It was equipped with heavily-armoured Fw 190s and charged with breaking up the massed ranks of the USAAF daylight bombers. Initially manned by volunteers, each fighter pilot was trained to close with the enemy at very close range and attack from the front and the rear in tight formations, and even to contemplate deliberately ramming the bombers when circumstances permitted. On 15 August Dahl claimed two B-17 bombers over Koblenz, and claimed another two on 11 September. Dahl was unhurt in a mid-air collision and had to make a forced landing at Holzkirchen airfield on 18 December. By this time he had achieved his 72nd aerial victory and had been promoted to *Oberstleutnant*.

On 26 January 1945, Göring appointed him Inspector of Day Fighters but despite this promotion Dahl still continued to fly operationally. He claimed seven victories in January, and on 1 February was awarded the Knight's Cross with Oakleaves in recognition of his 76th victory. Dahl ended the war flying the Messerschmitt Me 262 jet fighter with the 3rd Group of the Supplementary Fighter Wing. In March he was promoted to *Oberst* and claimed two P-47s on 27 March and his last victory was a P-51 shot down near Dillingen an der Donau, Bavaria on 26 April. He surrendered to the Americans in Königsee on 8 May 1945, and was released in September the same year. Following the war he became a member of the German Reich Party and ran, unsuccessfully, in the West German Federal election of 1961. He founded the Reich Association of Soldiers, and many ex-*Luftwaffe* members joined, including the Stuka ace Hans-Ulrich Rudel, who was honorary president for a time. It was a right-wing party and was soon banned. Dahl died on 25 November 1985 in Heidelberg of heart failure.

Wilhelm 'Willi' BATZ

Major

Knight's Cross: Awarded on 26 March 1944 as *Oberleutnant* and *Staffelkapitän* of the 5th Squadron of the 52nd Fighter Wing for achieving his 101st aerial victory, an American P-39 Airacobra fighter.

Knight's Cross with Oakleaves: He became the 526th recipient of the Oakleaves on 20 July 1944 as *Hauptmann* and *Gruppenkommandeur* of the 3rd Group of the 52nd Fighter Wing for achieving 175 aerial victories over the Soviet Union. The award was presented by Hitler at *Führer* Headquarters *Wolfsschanze*, Rastenburg in July/August 1944.

Knight's Cross with Oakleaves and Swords: On 21 April 1945, as *Major* and *Gruppenkommandeur* of the 2nd Group of 52nd Fighter Wing in recognition of his 230th aerial victory over the Eastern Front an Ilyushin Il-2 Sturmovik Soviet ground-attack aircraft. There is no record of Batz ever being presented with the Swords but after the war it was confirmed by the *Gemeinschaft der Jagdflieger* (Association of German Armed Forces Airmen), that he had been officially awarded them.

(Deutsches Wehrkundearchiv)

Wilhelm Batz was born on 21 May 1916 in Bamberg, Bavaria and was the son of a civil servant. After he graduated from school he volunteered for service with the *Luftwaffe*. In November 1935 he began his basic training with the 13th Regiment in Neubiberg, and then being transferred in February 1936 to the flying school in Kaufbeuren and then to the fighter pilot school at Bad Aibling. He was a born pilot, as his instructors observed, and during his months of training his natural ability and confidence proved him to be an obvious choice as an instructor. In 1937 he clocked up over 5,000 flying hours training pilots. He repeatedly requested for a transfer to combat duty but all of his requests were rejected. Commissioned as a *Leutnant* on 1 November 1940, he attended the Air War School in Berlin and in November 1942 he transferred to Fighter Pilot School 1 under *Oberstleutnant* Erich von Stolle. He was finally accepted for combat duty with the 2nd Squadron of Fighter Group East to undergo training on 20 December 1942. On 1 April 1943, Batz was promoted to *Oberleutnant* and appointed adjutant to *Major* Johannes Steinhoff, commander of the 2nd Group of the 52nd Fighter Wing based on the Eastern Front.

He proved to be a natural fighter, but the wait to achieve his first victory almost drove him insane. Finally he scored his first victory on 11 March 1943, an LaGG-3 fighter over Mingrelskaya in the Soviet Union, and his second victory came two days later. Although he was a late starter he made up for it, and by his appointment as *Staffelkapitän* of the 5th Squadron of the 52nd Fighter Wing in May he had already claimed eight victories. On 24 April he was awarded the Iron Cross 2nd Class and on 3 July he won the Iron Cross 1st Class after achieving nine aerial victories. On 9 September he claimed his 20th victory, his 30th came on 15 October, his 40th on 16 November and by 30 November he had achieved his 50th aerial victory and on 13 November he was awarded the *Luftwaffe* Honour Goblet. By the end of the year, Batz had seventy-five victories to his credit and it had taken him just nine months, but he wanted to be more successful.

On 28 January 1944 he was awarded the German Cross in Gold, but the following month he fell ill. In fact he was utterly exhausted and his nerves were shattered and he was grounded for two weeks. He had time to think and revaluate himself, his confidence returned and he couldn't wait to get back to combat and on his return he became spectacularly successful. On 10 February he claimed three victories two days later he claimed three more and on the 14th he shot down another three followed by two more the next day. On 2 March 1944 he claimed his 90th victory and on 22 March his tally rose to 100. He was awarded the Knight's Cross on 26 March and on 1 April was promoted to *Hauptmann*. Almost three weeks later, with 120 victories, Batz was appointed commander of the 3rd Group of the 52nd Fighter Wing, taking over from *Major* Günther Rall. Batz continued to be very successful and throughout the summer of 1944, he was downing three to four Soviet aircraft a day. On 31 May 1944, he shot down fifteen enemy aircraft in a single day a fantastic achievement, giving him a total of 155 aerial victories at that time. On 20 July, Batz was awarded the Knight's Cross with Oakleaves, becoming the 526th recipient. His 200th victory came on 17 August 1944 and by the end of that month his score had risen to 224.

On 31 January 1945 he was transferred to Hungary to take command of the 2nd Group of the 52nd Fighter Wing. On 16 April he shot down his 237th enemy aircraft, but this was to be his last victory. By May 1945, Batz had moved to Zeltweg Air Base but was no longer flying combat missions. On 8 May, *General der Fleiger* Paul Deichmann ordered a cease fire to come into force at mid-day. To avoid capture by Soviet forces, Batz was ordered to fly his aircraft to Munich where he surrendered to American forces. After the war Batz joined the *Bundesluftwaffe* in 1956 with the rank of *Major*. Following training in the United States, he was appointed commander of a training squadron and then a pilot training school in Landsberg. Batz was then appointed commander of *Lufttransportgeschwader* (Air Transport Squadron) 63, stationed in Schleswig-Holstein before commanding a wing from 1961 to 1964. He retired on 30 September 1972 with the rank of *Oberst*. He died on 11 September 1988, in a hospital in Unterfranken. He was buried in Quettingen Cemetery, a district of Leverkusen-Opladen, about 10 miles from Cologne.

His combat record was amazing. He didn't score his first victory until March 1943 and within six months he had only scored his 21st victory. However, from October 1943 until April 1945 he scored 212 aerial victories in just 18 months! Batz, was the sixth most successful *Luftwaffe* fighter pilot of the war and had flown 445 combat missions all on the Eastern Front, he was wounded three times and shot down four times.

Anton 'Toni' DÖBELE

Leutnant

Knight's Cross: Awarded posthumously on 26 March 1944 as *Oberfeldwebel* and fighter pilot with the 1st Squadron of the 54th Fighter Wing for operations over the Soviet Union.

Anton Döbele claimed ninety-three aerial victories during the Second World War whilst flying 458 combat missions over the Eastern Front. He was born on 16 November 1910 in Ehrensberg in the Waldsee region of Württemberg, Germany. He served as a *Gefreiter* during the Spanish Civil War, but as ground crew, not a pilot. On his return to Germany he trained as a fighter pilot and was posted to the Supplementary Group of the 54th Fighter Wing *'Grünherz'* as a *Feldwebel*.

From mid-June 1941 his group was deployed to the Eastern Front where on 28 July he claimed his first victory, a Chyetvenikov Mdr-6 reconnaissance flying-boat over Osel Island, and claimed his second victory, a Polikarpov I-15 fighter, west of Demyansk two days later. On 4 February 1942 he claimed his third victory, a MiG-1, and was promoted to *Oberfeldwebel* and transferred to the 1st Squadron of the

(Deutsches Wehrkundearchiv)

54th Fighter Wing a few weeks later. He claimed his fourth victory on 17 March and shortly after he was awarded the Iron Cross 2nd Class.

On 13 January 1943, Döbele claimed his eighth aerial victory and was awarded the Iron Cross 1st Class on 3 February. He was slow to increase his score, but was to become part of the most famous flight of fighter pilots of the *Luftwaffe*. This famous Group composed of *Oberleutnant* Walter Nowotny, *Oberfeldwebel* Rudolf Rademacher and *Oberfeldwebel* Karl Schnörrer, and together with Döbele they claimed a total of just over 450 enemy aircraft over the Soviet Union. Döbele claimed his 15th victory on 19 March, and his 20th on 8 June, an LaGG-3 fighter south-west of Schlüsselburg. He claimed two victories on 21 June, three on the 24th, a single P-40 on 5 July and became an 'ace-in-a-day' the following day when he shot down five aircraft, which included his 30th victory. There seemed to be no stopping him: by 18 July he had claimed his 40th victory, and on 7 August he claimed three victories, which included his 50th. Döbele claimed his 60th victory on 21 August and by the end of the month he had achieved a total of sixty-seven victories and was awarded the German Cross in Gold. He claimed three victories on 1 September and four more the following day, and then on the 6th he claimed his 75th and 76th victories, being awarded the *Luftwaffe* Honour Goblet a week later.

On 16 September his *Staffelkapitän*, *Oberleutnant* Walter Nowotny submitted a report recommending Döbele for promotion to *Leutnant*. He said, 'Döbele is a mature, experienced fighter pilot … his sense of duty is extremely well-founded … he is correct towards the men under his command and is well-liked by his comrades'. *Major* Hubertus von Bonin, *Kommodore* of the Fighter Wing wrote: '… an outstanding fighter pilot … It is recommended that he be promoted to officer rank.' It seems strange that these endorsements were not acted upon, with the fact that he had also claimed a total of seventy-five aerial victories. Why hadn't he been awarded the Knight's Cross either? During October he claimed another seven victories and on 6 November achieved his 90th victory. He claimed two more victories on 11 November, which would be his last. He was killed during aerial combat north of the Smolensk-Vitebsk highway that same day, when his Focke-Wulf Fw 190A-4 collided with a Soviet Il-2 ground-attack aircraft at an altitude of 980ft, just four minutes after shooting down an aircraft himself. His body was eventually recovered and he lies today in the German War Cemetery in Vilnius-Vingio, Lithuania. He was posthumously promoted to *Leutnant* and received the Knight's Cross posthumously on 26 March 1944.

Otto FÖNNEKOLD

Oberleutnant

Knight's Cross: Awarded on 26 March 1944 as *Fahnenjunker-Feldwebel* and fighter pilot in the 2nd Group of the 52nd Fighter Wing for operations over the Soviet Union and for claiming his 112th aerial victory.

Otto Fönnekold flew over 600 combat missions during the Second World War and shot down 134 aircraft, all of them over the Eastern Front. He was born on 15 February 1920 in Hamburg. He joined the *Luftwaffe* and was assigned to the 5th Squadron of the 52nd Fighter Wing as an *Unteroffizier* in August 1942. He flew from his base at Maykop near the Black Sea and claimed his first victory on 7 September, an LaGG-3 fighter, with his second coming on 6 October, a Ilyushin Il-2 ground-attack aircraft. He shot down another LaGG-3 on 29 October and on 15 November he claimed a third, his fourth victory, and was awarded the Iron Cross 2nd Class.

(Deutsches Wehrkundearchiv)

On Christmas Day he claimed his eighth victory and was shortly after awarded the Iron Cross 1st Class. He claimed two victories on 8 February 1943 and two on the 14th, and was promoted to *Feldwebel* in May. He claimed a total of fourteen victories during May, and on 6 June whilst flying a mission north-west of Krymsk he claimed his 30th victory, an La-5 fighter. He claimed two victories on 7 June and by the end of the month had claimed a total of thirty-nine victories. He claimed his 40th on 2 August, and claimed three more on the 7th and the 9th, when he was awarded the *Luftwaffe* Honour Goblet in recognition of his 40th victory. Shortly after claiming his 46th victory Fönnekold was awarded the German Cross in Gold on 16 August and claimed his 50th victory, an Il-2 ground-attack aircraft, on 6 September. He claimed two victories on 15 October and on the 20th he claimed four victories, of which three were shot down within three minutes, including his 60th victory.

He kept claiming victories throughout the following month, and by 21 November he had claimed his 75th victory and on the 28th he claimed three victories which included his 80th. On 8 December he claimed another two victories which included his 90th and was promoted to *Leutnant*. He continued to score at a fast rate, on 9 January 1944 he claimed two victories, with two more the next day and he claimed his 98th victory on the 11th and the following day he claimed three victories which included his 100th. He claimed his 110th victory on 7 February, and finally awarded the Knight's Cross on 26 March, in recognition of his 112th aerial victory. After some well-deserved leave Fönnekold was appointed *Staffelkapitän* of the 5th Squadron of the 52nd Fighter Wing on 19 April, He led by example and claimed a total of seven victories, becoming an 'ace-in-a-day' on 30 May.

On 9 July 1944 he was wounded when he was shot down over Jassy, Romania by a Soviet Yak-9 fighter. He returned to duty in early August, claiming his 130th victory on the 5th. His victory score now gets a little uncertain, but the most accurate reports found in German archives give the total of 134 confirmed and three victories unconfirmed. The three that are recorded unconfirmed were those three aircraft shot down by Fönnekold on 31 August, the same day he was shot down and killed. He had landed at his base in Budak, Transylvania and was taxiing back to the dispersal when his aircraft came under attack by US P-51 Mustang fighters. Apparently a single bullet by-passed the cockpit armour and pierced his heart. He died immediately – he stood no chance! The following day he was posthumously promoted to *Oberleutnant*. It seems strange that he wasn't ever awarded the Knight's Cross with Oakleaves, not even posthumously.

Rolf-Günther HERMICHEN

Major

Knight's Cross: Awarded on 26 March 1944 as *Hauptmann* and commander of the 1st Group of the 11th Fighter Wing for operations over France, the Soviet Union and the Western Front and for claiming his 45th aerial victory.

Knight's Cross with Oakleaves: He became the 748th recipient on 19 February 1945 as *Major* and commander of the 1st Group of the 11th Fighter Wing for operations over the Western Front and for claiming his 49th aerial victory. Presented by Hitler at the Reich Chancellery, Berlin during one of the last presentations made during the war.

Rolf-Günther Hermichen flew single and twin-engine fighters during the Second World War, and claimed forty-nine aircraft in a total of 629 combat missions over the Eastern and Western Fronts. During the war several German aces had become specialists in facing the large

(Deutsches Wehrkundearchiv)

formations of US bombers and among these was Hermichen, who claimed seventeen four-engined bombers between July 1943 a March 1944.

He was born on 25 July 1918 in Wernigerde, Harz in the Saxony-Anhalt region of Germany during the final stages of the First World War. Hermichen joined the *Luftwaffe* in 1937, and after the completion of his training as a fighter pilot he was assigned to the 6th Squadron of the 1st Fighter Wing, equipped with the Messerschmitt Bf 110 twin-engined fighter. In August 1939 he was commissioned as a *Leutnant* and in September took part in the Polish campaign but failed to score any victories as he was mainly flying fighter-bomber missions. Awarded the Iron Cross 2nd Class on 24 April 1940, he claimed his first aerial victory on 10 May, during the Battle of France, when he shot down a British Fairey Battle light bomber over Waalhaven. He claimed another victory on 15 May but this was unconfirmed, he then shot down an RAF Spitfire on 27 May, his second aerial victory. On 7 June he was awarded the Iron Cross 1st Class and was then transferred to the 3rd Group of the 76th Destroyer Wing and claimed another four victories over France and the Channel between May and August, but they remain unconfirmed.

In February 1941 he claimed his third official victory and from April his unit was redesignated the 2nd Group of the 210th Light Bomber Wing. In June he took part in Operation Barbarossa, the invasion of the Soviet Union, and claimed his fourth aerial victory on 6 September, a Yak-1 fighter. The following month he was promoted to *Oberleutnant* and on 12 October claimed his fifth aerial victory, and his sixth on the 22nd. In November he was transferred to the 7th Squadron of the 26th Fighter Wing, and from March 1942 was appointed as adjutant to the *Gruppenkommandeur* of the 3rd Group, *Hauptmann* Josef Priller. In May he replaced *Oberleutnant* Johannes Schmidt as *Staffelkapitän* of the 3rd Squadron and claimed his 10th victory on 30 July, an RAF Hurricane near Wizernes, France. He claimed a Spitfire on 18 August and the following day he claimed two victories over Dieppe, another Spitfire and a P-39 fighter.

By the end of 1942 Hermichen had claimed sixteen aerial victories and on 1 February 1943 was promoted to *Hauptmann*. His unit had moved to the Eastern Front and on 18 February he shot down an LaGG-3 fighter and the following day he claimed two Il-2 ground-attack aircraft. In March he claimed five victories and on 15th was appointed temporary *Gruppenkommandeur* of the 3rd Group, but he relinquished this command to Klaus Mietusch on 4 July and returned to the 3rd Squadron as *Staffelkapitän*. He shot down a Typhoon fighter-bomber on 28 July and two days later claimed a B-17, his first four-engined bomber. Three minutes later he shot down a P-47. He claimed two more victories in August, which included his second four-engined bomber. On 15 October he was awarded the German Cross in Gold in recognition of his 34th aerial victory, although five would later be ruled as unconfirmed.

He took over as *Gruppenkommandeur* of the 1st Group of the 11th Fighter Wing on 16 October and was stationed at Husum, near Schleswig-Holstein, Germany. On 5 November he shot down a P-47 and claimed a B-17, but this victory remains unconfirmed. On 10 February 1944, Hermichen claimed five victories, one B-17 bomber and four B-24 Liberators, to become an 'ace-in-a-day'. He claimed another B-17 on 3 March and three more victories on the 6th, which included two B-17s and a P-47. On the 8th he claimed three more four-engined bombers, and he shot down another B-17 on the 23rd. On 26 March he was awarded the Knight's Cross in recognition of his 45th aerial victory. He claimed two P-38 Lightnings on 15 April and shot down a P-51 Mustang on the 24th, to claim his 49th and last victory of the war.

Towards the end of April he took command of a squadron attached to the 104th Fighter Wing, which had been created from staff of Fighter Pilot School 4, and here Hermichen helped to train new fighter pilots. On 1 May he was promoted to *Major* and transferred to the staff of *Generalmajor* Josef Ibel, the commander of the 2nd Fighter Division in Stade, Lower Saxony. On 15 October he returned to the 104th Fighter Wing as a *Gruppenkommandeur* and remained there until 10 January

1945. He was awarded the Knight's Cross with Oakleaves on 19 February, which was presented to him personally by Hitler at the Reich Chancellery in Berlin, which must have been one of the last presentations he made during the war.

After some leave Hermichen was transferred to the staff of the General of Fighters and then to the staff of the 2nd Air Division and the commanding general of the *Luftwaffe* in Norway. He was taken prisoner by the British on 20 April 1945, being released on 8 October 1946. After the war he worked for a time as a manager with the German department store Karstdt. He later settled in Essen where he died on 23 May 2014 at the age of 95.

<u>Klaus</u> Dietrich Wilhelm 'Kurt' MIETUSCH

Major

Knight's Cross: Awarded on 26 March 1944 as *Hauptmann* and commander of the 3rd Group of the 26th Fighter Wing '*Schlageter*' for operations over France, England, Malta, North Africa, the Balkans and the Soviet Union.

Knight's Cross with Oakleaves: He became the 653rd recipient posthumously on 18 November 1944 as *Major* and whilst still serving in the 26th Fighter Wing '*Schlageter*' and for continued operations over the Soviet Union and the Western Front.

Klaus Mietusch was one of the most fascinating fighter pilots of the 26th Fighter Wing during the Second World War. Described by some as rather aloof when not flying, he was a true 'death or glory' pilot. When targets were in sight he paid little attention to his own safety or that of the pilots around him, who were expected to keep up the attack until forced by damage, low fuel or low ammunition to break off.

(Deutsches Wehrkundearchiv)

Mietusch flew 452 combat missions during his short career, was shot down ten times and wounded four, and never turned down a mission.

He was born on 5 August 1918 in Posen, part of Prussia, and at birth his last-name was Mitusz which was later changed to Mietusch to sound more German. Following his graduation he entered the *Luftwaffe* in 1936 as an officer cadet and was assigned to the Air War College in Berlin-Gatow. From February 1938 he served, only briefly, with the 254th Bomber Wing before being assigned as a fighter pilot to the 132nd Fighter Wing. From May 1939, now a *Leutnant* he was assigned to the newly-created 26th Fighter Wing in Düsseldorf under the command of *Oberst* Eduard Ritter von Schleich.

In September 1939, when war broke out, Mietusch was serving as a technical officer with the staff of the 26th Fighter Wing and at this time didn't fly combat missions. By May 1940, now an *Oberleutnant*, he took an active role in the Battle of France, claiming his first victory, an RAF Hurricane over Dunkirk on 31 May. On 8 June, after being shot down south-west of Dieppe, he had to make an emergency landing behind enemy lines. When he climbed out of his aircraft he was shot in the buttocks by a French farmer. He was treated in hospital and after the French Armistice he was transferred to a hospital in Germany. His second victory came on 31 August, when he shot down a Spitfire over Chelmsford. Soon after this he was awarded both the Iron Cross 1st and 2nd Classes.

From January 1941 his squadron was relocated to Sicily in support of the 10th Air Corps, for actions against the strategically important island of Malta. On 26 February he shot down an RAF Hurricane south of Malta to claim his third aerial victory. He claimed two more Hurricanes on 22 March over Malta, and by 26 April he had been awarded the *Luftwaffe* Honour Goblet in recognition of eight aerial victories. On 17 June, his squadron flew with the 1st Group of the 27th Fighter Wing and intercepted Hurricane fighters of the South African Air Force covering the British retreat after the operation to re-capture eastern Cyrenaica from German and Italian forces. During this encounter three RAF Hurricanes were shot down, one by Mietusch. On 19 September he was appointed *Staffelkapitän* of the 7th Squadron, taking over from Joachim Müncheberg who he had learnt so much from whilst flying as his wingman and deputy. He claimed two Spitfires on 21 September, and on 8 December whilst flying with his wingman, *Leutnant* Walter Thorn, he shot down a Spitfire over Berch-sur-Mur, France. Just after this victory, his 14th, he and Thorn were attacked out of the sun by two RAF Spitfires. Thorn's aircraft was hit and he bailed out but his parachute failed to open and he fell to his death over the Pas-de-Calais.

On 12 April 1942 he claimed two Spitfires, one over Arques near Calais and the other near Dunkirk. He claimed two more Spitfires during May and claimed another two on 19 August over Dieppe and he shot down two more on the 17th near Calais. On 9 October Mietusch lead an attack over Lille. His first target was an RAF Stirling, and then he attacked a B-17 four-engined bomber, which was only damaged and became the first US bomber to ditch successfully in the Channel. However, both of these victories remain unconfirmed, there being no witnesses. He had achieved by this time twenty-three aerial victories and on 15 October was awarded the German Cross in Gold.

On 20 January 1943, Mietusch claimed his 25th aerial victory, a Spitfire over Ardres. During an attack on B-17 bombers on 8 March, a flight of P-47s from the 352nd Fighter Group went after Mietusch and his wingman. Mietusch's Bf 109 was seriously damaged during the attack by a P-47 and large pieces of his aircraft flew off in a mass of flames. He bailed out, his parachute opened immediately and he landed safely, but with injuries severe enough to keep him hospitalized for the next few weeks. He returned to combat in April with his squadron which had been transferred to the Eastern Front as part of the 3rd Group of the 16th Fighter Wing. He shot down four Soviet aircraft on 21 May, and by the end of the month he had claimed his 33rd victory. He claimed five aircraft on 18 June to become an 'ace-in-a-day' and on the 22nd he shot down two LaGG-3 fighters. On 29 June he received word that he had been appointed *Gruppenkommandeur* of the 3rd Group and he left for the Western Front. He was replaced by his own deputy, *Hauptmann* Günther Ketch. On 25 July he claimed his first B-17 north of Hamburg and by August 1943 the 3rd Group was operating out of Amsterdam-Schiphol airfield. On the 17th, Mietusch shot down two B-17s and claimed another the following day.

In November the 3rd Group was separated from the rest of the Wing, and in response to the American attacks on northern Germany it was ordered to Mönchen-Gladbach as part of the 1st Fighter Corps under *Generalmajor* Paul Deichmann. On 1 December he shot down a P-38 Lightning of the 20th Fighter Group, his 50th aerial victory. On 8 March 1944, he claimed his 57th aerial victory and on the 26th was awarded the Knight's Cross, and spent a week on leave. On 12 April he hit a bomb crater upon landing and suffered concussion and was in hospital for three weeks. He was promoted to *Major* on 1 May and claimed his 60th aerial victory on 8 June, a P-47 Thunderbolt over Le Havre. He claimed two more victories on 14 June and by the end of the month had claimed his 66th victory. His 70th aerial victory was another P-47, shot down over Rouen in northern France.

On 17 September, the first day of Operation Market Garden, the operation to secure a bridgehead over the River Rhine, he claimed his 72nd and last victory, a P-51 Mustang near the German border to the Netherlands. Just after this he was attacked by a P-51, piloted by Lieutenant William R. Beyer of the 361st Fighter Group. He did not fire on Mietusch until he pulled out of his dive, just above the ground. Mieutsch's Bf 109 was hit full-on by Beyer's first burst of fire, hit the ground and broke up. Mietusch was killed instantly. He was posthumously awarded the Knight's Cross with Oakleaves on 18 November. He is buried at the Düsseldorf Northern Cemetery, Field 112, Section O, Grave No. 117.

Jakob 'Jockel' NORZ

Leutnant

Knight's Cross: Awarded on 26 March 1944 as *Oberfeldwebel* and fighter pilot attached to the 3rd Group of the 5th Fighter Wing for operations over the Soviet Union and for claiming his 57th aerial victory.

Jakob Norz claimed 104 aerial victories, all of them over the Eastern Front whilst flying 322 combat missions during the Second World War. He was born on 20 October 1920 in Saulgrub, Garmisch-Partenkirchen in Bavaria and began his career with the *Luftwaffe* as a long-range intruder pilot over England with the 1st Group of the 2nd Night Fighter Wing.

(Deutsches Wehrkundearchiv)

In early 1942 he was reassigned as a day fighter pilot and in the spring after completing the relevant training he transferred to the 11th Squadron of the 1st Fighter Wing in Norway. On 10 March his Squadron was redesignated the 8th Squadron of the 5th Fighter Wing and from April his new Squadron moved to an airfield at Petsamo in Murmansk in the Soviet Union where *Unteroffizier* Norz flew operations over the Arctic Ocean. He claimed his first victory on 15 May 1942, a Soviet Hurricane over south Ura-Guba near Murmansk, and his second came on 10 August, another Hurricane. He claimed two more victories during September and was awarded the Iron Cross 2nd Class and he claimed his fifth and sixth victories on 28 February 1943, now with the rank of *Feldwebel*. He claimed an Ilyushin Il-2 ground-attack aircraft on 1 March and four days later shortly after claiming two more victories he was shot down and had to make a forced landing on a frozen lake in no man's land. Norz returned to a German-held position after an eight-hour walk in heavy snow. Soon after this he was presented with the Iron Cross 1st Class by *Generaloberst* Hans-Jürgen Stumpff during the General's visit to Pechenga.

He claimed his 20th victory on 27 June 1943 and two days later he claimed three more victories and was promoted to *Oberfeldwebel*. During July he claimed another six victories, and his 30th victory on 20 August. On 6 September he claimed three victories and a week later he was awarded the *Luftwaffe* Honour Goblet. By the end of the month his victory score had increased to forty-two and on 17 October Norz was awarded the German Cross in Gold. On 25 November, following about ten days of no action, the Soviet air force launched an attack on Titovka and the airfields of Høybuktmoen at Kirkenes and Luostari near Pechenga. On that day Norz claimed two Il-2 aircraft, to increase his score to forty-five.

He claimed his 50th victory, another Il-2, on 5 March 1944, and on the 13th he claimed two more aircraft and on 17 March he became an 'ace-in-a-day' when he shot down five aircraft over Havningsberg and Pechenga and on the 26th he was awarded the Knight's Cross in recognition of achieving over fifty aerial victories. On 2 April he shot down two Yak-7 fighters and one Yak-9, which included his 60th victory, and a few weeks later he was promoted to *Leutnant*. On 27 June he became an 'ace-in-a-day' again when he claimed five victories over Kirkenes and the next day he claimed seven more victories, over the same area to become an 'ace-in-a-day' yet again. Norz claimed five victories on 4 July and four more on the 9th and on the 17th he became an 'ace-in-a-day' for the fifth time. He claimed his 90th victory on 22 July and on 17 August he claimed five more victories to become an 'ace-in-a-day' again and six days later he did the same again when he shot down four Petlyakov Pe-2 dive-bombers and one P-39 fighter, which included his 100th victory.

On 16 September Norz attacked and shot down a Douglas Boston bomber but his aircraft was hit in the engine by return fire. Norz reported that his cabin was full of smoke and his wingman urged him to bail out but Norz had decided that he was going to avoid capture by the Soviets and return to his base and try and land his stricken aircraft. By the time he reached his base Norz was intoxicated by the smoke and reported that he couldn't control his aircraft properly, and was now too low to bail out. He attempted a crash-landing in the tundra but his Bf 109G-6 struck a rock, disintegrated and Norz was killed instantly. He was buried with full military honours and lies today at the German War Cemetery in Pechenga.

Friedrich OBLESER

Oberleutnant

Knight's Cross: Awarded on 26 March 1944 as *Leutnant* and *Staffelführer* of the 8th Squadron of the 52nd Fighter Wing for operations over the Soviet Union and for claiming his 91st aerial victory.

Friedrich Obleser claimed at least 112 aerial victories all of which were achieved over the Eastern Front during the Second World War. He was born on 21 February 1923 in Pottenstein in the district of Baden in Austria and he volunteered for service in the *Luftwaffe* in 1940. Following his flight training he joined the 3rd Group of the 52nd Fighter Wing and was assigned to the 8th Squadron in April 1942 flying from Zürichtal in the Crimea.

(Deutsches Wehrkundearchiv)

In January 1943 he flew from Gigant airfield in Salsk, still with the 52nd Fighter Wing, and he flew as wingman to his *Staffelkapitän* Günther Rall. At the time the Soviets had launched Operation Koltso, the final phase of the Battle of Stalingrad, and on 12 January Obleser flew his first combat mission over the Soviet Union and claimed his first victory on 28 March, a P-39 over Tichanowskaja. He claimed his second victory on 11 April, another P-39, and he claimed his third on 20 April and the following day he claimed three victories. By the end of the month Obleser had claimed a total of eleven victories and had been awarded both the Iron Cross 1st and 2nd Classes. At one time he questioned the claims made by Erich Hartmann, the talented fighter ace who later became the top-scoring ace of the war. Hartmann had asked Rall to transfer Obleser to be his wingman so he could observe his victories. Rall agreed and Obleser observed Hartmann 'at work' and saw for himself some of his claims and witnessed his skill as a fighter pilot. He was soon convinced that Hartmann's claims were legitimate. Obleser continued his success into May and by the 11th had claimed another ten victories, and on the 28th shortly after claimed his 26th victory he was shot down by anti-aircraft fire, was wounded and crashed near Kijewskoje in the Soviet Union, and was away from the front line for the next two months.

On 6 June he was appointed *Staffelkapitän* of his Squadron and had claimed his 30th victory by 4 August and he had claimed another seventeen victories by the end of the month. he claimed his 50th victory on 18 September, and the next day he became an 'ace-in-a-day' when he claimed five aerial victories over the Dnepropetrovsk area. On 25 September he claimed his 60th victory and he claimed his 70th on 3 October over north-west Beloserka, Ukraine. He claimed three victories on 7 October, which included his 75th, and on 8 November he was awarded the *Luftwaffe* Honour Goblet and just six days later he was awarded the German Cross in Gold in recognition of his 75th victory.

He continued to score at a steady rate and on 7 December claimed his 80th victory, an Il-2 ground-attack aircraft over north New Praga in Warsaw. On 26 March 1944 Obleser was awarded the Knight's Cross and had by this time claimed a total of ninety aerial victories. In late May he was promoted to

Oberleutnant and he claimed his 100th victory on 21 July, a P-39 about 12 miles south of Rava-Ruska, Ukraine. By the end of August he had shot down 108 aircraft and was now *Staffelkapitän* of the 10th Squadron of the 52nd Fighter Wing. On 30 December he was wounded whilst using a *Panzerfaust* (a hand-held anti-tank weapon) when it exploded in his hands near Zagore in Poland and as a result he never returned to combat duties. In addition to the claims made over the Eastern Front Obleser also claimed nine victories of which seven were US fighters and two were US bombers, but as he didn't see these aircraft actually crash they cannot be classed as definite victories.

He flew over 500 missions during the war and later in post-war Germany he worked for a recycling company which had to dismantle and dispose of bomber aircraft. In 1956 he joined the *Bundesluftwaffe* as a *Hauptmann* and following various assignments to fighter units he was appointed *Kommodore* of the 72nd Fighter Wing in Leck, later known as the 43rd Fighter Wing. He held various positions within the German Air Staff and was later appointed manager of the NATO Management Agency. He then served as Chief of the *Luftwaffe* Staff and was commanding General of the *Luftwaffe* Support Command. From October 1978 until his retirement in March 1983 he was Inspector of the Luftwaffe in the *Bundeswehr* with the rank of *Generalleutnant*. He died of natural causes on 5 June 2004 in Neukirchen-Selscheid, Siegburg in North Rhine-Westphalia area of Germany.

Wilhelm PHILIPP

Oberfeldwebel

Knight's Cross: Awarded on 26 March 1944 as *Oberfeldwebel* and pilot attached to the 1st Group of the 54th Fighter Wing for operations over France, England and the Soviet Union.

Wilhelm Philipp claimed a total of at least seventy-nine victories whilst flying approximately 500 combat missions over the Eastern and Western Fronts during the Second World War. He was born on 31 January 1916 in Böhla, Saxony in Germany and after his training as a fighter pilot he joined the 4th Squadron of the 26th Fighter Wing in late 1939.

From May 1940 he fought during the Battle of France as an *Unteroffizier* and claimed his first victory on 27 May, a Spitfire over Ostend. He claimed his second victory the following day and his third on the 29th, both Spitfires, and was awarded the Iron Cross 2nd Class.

(Deutsches Wehrkundearchiv)

On 7 June shortly after claiming an RAF Hurricane, his fourth victory, he was shot down and slightly wounded but managed to bail out of his Bf 109 over Dieppe. He then fought in the Battle of Britain and claimed two Spitfires over Dover in August and was shortly after awarded the Iron Cross 1st Class. At the beginning of 1941, now with the rank of *Feldwebel* he was flying from Abbeville and he claimed a Spitfire on 5 February and two days later the Group was relocated to Düsseldorf to be refreshed and converted to the Bf 109F. When his group returned to France there task was to protect the port of Brest and the surrounding coastal areas. In July his group was the first *Luftwaffe* unit to be converted to the Focke-Wulf Fw 190A-1, and a few weeks later he was briefly assigned to the 2nd Supplementary Squadron of the 26th Fighter Wing and he claimed two Blenheim light bombers on 12 August, his 9th and 10th aerial victories.

By early 1942 he was back with his old Squadron and was flying against Allied bombers and trying to secure the coastal areas. He also flew protection missions at the time of the breakout of the battleships *Scharnhorst* and *Gneisenau* together with the heavy cruiser *Prinz Eugen* through the

English Channel. He was promoted to *Oberfeldwebel* in June and by the end of July Philipp had claimed a total of seventeen aerial victories and during August flew combat missions over Dieppe. He claimed a Spitfire on 17 August and two more on the 19th, which included his 20th victory, and before the end of the month he had claimed another two victories. He was awarded the *Luftwaffe* Honour Goblet on 24 August and was awarded the German Cross in Gold on 27 October.

In November 1942 he transferred to the Eastern Front attached to the 3rd Squadron of the 54th Fighter Wing. From early 1943 he was based in Krasnoyarsk flying the Bf 109 and during January 1943 he claimed six aerial victories. In February his group converted to the Fw 190 and during February Philipp claimed another ten aerial victories, of which six were Ilyushin Il-2 ground-attack aircraft. He claimed three victories on 15 March, which included his 40th victory, and five days later he claimed two more. In May he saw action over Nikolskoye and from June he flew combat missions over Orel, and his Group relocated to Poltava in August. During that time he claimed five more victories and on 1 September he shot down four Il-2s which included his 50th victory and by the 6th he had claimed his 60th. Then on 7 September he was wounded during combat with Soviet Yak-9s, and was away from combat for the remaining few months of the year.

At the beginning of 1944 his Group was flying from Orsha and then later moved to Wesenberg in Estonia. On 26 March he was awarded the Knight's Cross in recognition of his sixty aerial victories and for operations over the Western and Eastern Fronts. By the end of July Philipp had claimed his 65th victory and he claimed four victories, all Il-2s, and by the end of the month his total was at least seventy-six, although the exact number is not known. From December he flew as part of the 11st Squadron of the 54th Fighter Wing flying from Nasielsk in Poland and claimed two Soviet B-26s and on the 29th he claimed, what would be his last victory, a Typhoon fighter-bomber. Shortly after that he was himself shot down by British aircraft and bailed out north of Nordhorn, Germany severely wounded and never returned to combat. He died on 10 January 1966 in Duisburg, Germany.

Günther 'Hupatz' SEEGER

Oberleutnant

Knight's Cross: Awarded on 26 March 1944 as *Leutnant* and fighter pilot attached to the 7th Squadron of the 53rd Fighter Wing for operations over France, England, North Africa and Italy.

Günther Seeger claimed fifty-one aerial victories, which included eight four-engined bombers, whilst over France, England, Italy and North Africa during the Second World War. He was born on 9 September 1918 in Offenbach am Main, a city in Hesse, Germany. He joined the *Luftwaffe* in 1937 and underwent fighter-pilot training at Werneuchen.

In late February on the completion of his training, *Unteroffizier* Seeger was assigned to the 3rd Squadrons of the 2nd Fighter Wing. He saw action during the Battle of France and claimed his first victory on 8 June, a French Morane M.S. 406 fighter near Soissons. Soon after he was awarded the Iron Cross 2nd Class and from July took part in the Battle of Britain, being based at Beaumont-le-Roger. On 7 September he claimed two Spitfires near Heyfield and in October he was promoted to *Feldwebel*. He claimed his fourth victory near the Isle of Wight, another Spitfire, on 28 November and shortly afterwards was awarded the Iron Cross 1st Class.

(Deutsches Wehrkundearchiv)

From 27 March to 19 June 1941, Seeger was attached to the Training Squadron of the 51st Fighter Wing as an instructor. He returned to regular duty with the Staff Squadron towards the end of June and claimed his fifth victory on the 25th, another Spitfire this time over Calais. It was during this time that he flew as wingman to various famous fighter aces who included Wilhelm Balthasar, Walter Oesau, Rudolf Pflanz and Erich Leie. He claimed seven victories during July, which included three Spitfires on the 23rd and was awarded the *Luftwaffe* Honour Goblet on 9 August and shortly after was promoted to *Oberfeldwebel*. On 13 October Seeger claimed his 19th victory and the following month he began his second stint as a fighter instructor with the Wing's training squadron. It was during this time, on 21 October, that he ran out of fuel and belly-landed his Bf 109 at Blendeques near Pas-de-Calais but he wasn't hurt.

Seeger returned to the 3rd Squadron in January 1942, located in northern France where his Group was tasked with protecting the port of Brest and the heavy *Kriegsmarine* units stationed there. In early February his Group flew protection missions over the warships *Scharnhorst*, *Gneisenau* and *Prinz Eugen*, first to Abbèville and Caen and then on 11 February to Calais-Marck in preparation for the Channel breakout. In June his Group converted to the Focke-Wulf Fw 190A-2 and on 19 August he flew against the Allied landings near Dieppe where he claimed three Spitfires. He was awarded the German Cross in Gold on 29 October after achieving twenty-two victories. He was shot down himself that same day but escaped without injury and was shortly after called back to serve briefly in the Staff Squadron, and whilst on attachment he claimed another Spitfire on 31 October. On 4 November he joined the 11th Squadron of the 2nd Fighter Wing and was sent to Tunisia where his unit was later absorbed by the 6th Squadron of the 53rd Fighter Wing where he claimed three victories on 3 January.

On 22 March, now with the 7th Squadron, he claimed a B-17 Flying Fortress over Cap Vito and nine days later he claimed a B-25 Mitchell twin-engined bomber. On 10 May he claimed a P-38, his 30th victory and whilst operating over Sicily and southern Italy he added another ten victories to his score, which included three Spitfires on 12 July as well as a four-engined bomber. He claimed his 40th victory on 22 August, a B-26 Marauder twin-engined bomber, and in September he was sent back to Germany to recuperate from a bout of Malaria. In October his mother was killed and his father injured when their house was destroyed during an Allied air raid on Offenbach. He returned to combat in November and his Group was equipped with the Bf 109G-6, armed with 20mm and 30mm cannon and even with rockets to intercept US bombers flying over Italy. Promoted to *Leutnant* in December by the end of January 1944 he was flying ground-support missions against the recent Anzio landings by the Allies. On 26 March he was awarded the Knight's Cross after gaining over forty aerial victories and was soon after promoted to *Oberleutnant*.

In April Seeger was appointed *Staffelkapitän* of the 4th Squadron of the 53rd Fighter Wing and now flew over his homeland. During combat against US fighters on 13 May he was shot down near Pritzerbe near Brandenburg and crashed, suffering minor head wounds. He claimed his 47th victory, a Spitfire near Caen, France on 2 July and later that month his Group was withdrawn to Germany once again. In August his Squadron was renamed the 7th Squadron and in October he claimed his 49th victory. He was slightly injured in a car accident shortly afterwards and did not take part in Operation Bodenplatte, the attack on Allied airfields in Holland, Belgium and France on New Year's Day 1945 – he was on leave getting married. He remained with the Squadron until the end of the year but chronic fuel shortages limited his flying time and he only claimed another two victories before the end of the war.

He avoided capture by the Allies, making his way home to his wife in Offenach on foot. He had flown 500 combat missions during the war, and joined the *Bundesluftwaffe* in 1956, rising to the rank of *Oberstleutnant*, before his retirement in 1974. He died in Germany on 6 September 2013, three days before his 95th birthday.

Heinrich 'Heinz' STURM

Hauptmann

Knight's Cross: Awarded on 26 March 1944 as *Leutnant* and *Staffelführer* of the 4th Squadron of the 52nd Fighter Wing for operations over the Soviet Union.

(Deutsches Wehrkundearchiv)

Heinrich Sturm claimed 123 aerial victories, all of them achieved over the Eastern Front during the Second World War. He was born on 12 June 1920 in Dieburg, a small town in southern Hessen, joined the *Luftwaffe* in 1940 and trained as a fighter pilot.

In the summer of 1941 *Feldwebel* Sturm was assigned to the 6th Squadron of the 52nd Fighter Wing and from July he was based on the central sector of the Eastern Front. On 2 October the German forces in the Soviet Union launched Operation Typhoon, the strategic offensive to capture Moscow which ultimately failed. In support of the offensive Sturm and his Group moved to an airfield west of Kalinin on 16 October and two days later Sturm claimed his first aerial victory, a Petlyakov Pe-2 bomber. Shortly after Sturm was removed from the Front and returned to Germany as an instructor at a fighter-pilot school.

He returned to the Eastern Front in May 1942, flying the Bf 109F-4 over the Crimea and later over south Kharkov. He claimed his second victory on 28 May, an Ilyushin Il-2 ground-attack aircraft, and he claimed his third victory, a Lavochkin LaGG-3 fighter, on 3 June. In early July he was flying south of Kursk in support of the 6th Army and he claimed his fourth victory on 28 August and was shortly after awarded the Iron Cross 2nd Class. From September he flew from Maikop in support of the 1st Panzer Army and he claimed his fifth victory on 30 October. Towards the end of October his Group moved to Ssoldatskaya, but returned to Maikop on the 27th, and later withdrawing to Morozovskaya-West due to a Soviet counter-attack. From there he flew missions over the area south-west of Stalingrad and on 17 December his Group covered the counter-attack against Stalingrad whilst supporting the LVII Panzer Corps – during this time he claimed two victories.

From early 1943 Sturm was assigned to the headquarters unit of the 2nd Group and towards the end of January was flying from Rostov. He claimed three victories in February and was awarded the Iron Cross 1st Class. On 5 March he claimed two more victories and shortly afterwards Sturm was promoted to *Leutnant*. By the end of April he was flying combat missions over the Black Sea area and on the 17th he claimed his 25th victory. He claimed five victories on the 20th to become an 'ace-in-a-day', and he continued to claim more victories and on 6 June he claimed his 40th victory and was awarded the German Cross in Gold on 23 July, and three days later he was presented with the *Luftwaffe* Honour Goblet.

On 1 August he was named as *Staffelführer* of the 4th Squadron, replacing *Leutnant* Helmut Lipfert, and his leadership of the Squadron was until now temporary but he was confirmed as the new *Staffelkapitän* exactly a month later. Strum claimed seventeen more victories during September and on 13 October he celebrated his 50th victory with the rest of his Squadron. By the end of the month he had claimed fifty-eight victories and on 4 November he claimed his 60th victory. The following day he became an 'ace-in-a-day' for the second time when he claimed six victories, and the following day he repeated his success with another six victories. On 30 November Sturm claimed his 75th victory, a Yak-1 over Kerch,

From early 1944 he was flying from Bagerov in the Crimea and he claimed his 90th victory on 15 February over East Kerch. Finally on 26 March Sturm was awarded the Knight's Cross after gaining ninety victories. He was promoted to *Oberleutnant* the following month and on 7 April he claimed two victories and the next day he became an 'ace-in-a-day' again when he claimed eight victories, which included his 100th victory. On 16 April he was severely wounded by shrapnel during a bombing raid whilst on leave. He returned to combat on 1 September as a *Hauptmann* and *Staffelkapitän* of the 5th Squadron of the 52nd Fighter Wing. Now flying from an air base in Nagyrábé in Hungary, he had claimed his 110th. By the end of October Sturm had claimed another eight victories and during November he added another three victories to his total.

On 22 December it is thought that he claimed at least two more victories and on the day he was killed during a squadron 'scramble'. His Bf 109G-6 collided with a vehicle on Csor airfield, somersaulted and burst into flames. Sturm was killed. He had claimed a total of 123 victories although some reports state the figure could have been as high as 160, but post-war examinations make this claim seem too high. His own wingman thinks the figure is more likely to be between 123 and 125, but there are fifty-two victories of the 2nd Group of his fighter wing that have no name attributed to them during the period November to December 1944. Sturm is buried in the Military Cemetery at Pápa in Hungary in Block B, Row 4, Grave No. 1.

Fritz TEGTMEIER

Oberleutnant

Knight's Cross: Awarded on 26 March 1944 as *Oberfeldwebel* and pilot attached to the 1st Squadron of the 54th Fighter Wing for operations over the Soviet Union and for claiming his 96th aerial victory.

Fritz Tegtmeier claimed a total of 146 aerial victories, all over the Eastern Front during the Second World War. Born on 30 July 1917 in Lübbeke, a town in north-east Rhine North-Westphalia in northern Germany. Upon joining the *Luftwaffe* he trained as a fighter pilot and in October 1940, at the end of the Battle of Britain, he was assigned to the 2nd Squadron of the 54th Fighter Wing.

On 17 November 1940 he was wounded when his Bf 109E-1 crashed at Jever airfield after his engine caught fire. After he had recovered *Unteroffizier* Tegtmeier saw action over the Soviet Union from June 1941, flying in support of Army Group North. He claimed his first victory, a Tupolev SB-2 twin-engined bomber, on 22 June, and

(Deutsches Wehrkundearchiv)

two days later he claimed two more SB-2s and was awarded the Iron Cross 2nd Class a few days later. His Squadron was later deployed north of Lake Peipus in the area near Leningrad and by mid-October he was flying over Moscow. Promoted to *Feldwebel* in early November, he claimed a MiG-1 fighter on the 15th and was later awarded the Iron Cross 1st Class.

From early 1942 he was based at Krasnogvardeysky south-west of Leningrad, but couldn't fly until 19 January due to bad weather. Operations suffered again from April due to the thaw and during this time his Group was converted to the Bf 109F-4. Tegtmeier claimed two victories during June and July, and by the end of August he had achieved his 20th victory. On 11 September he claimed his 23rd victory and was awarded the *Luftwaffe* Honour Goblet on 5 October. From early 1943 he began to score more regularly. He claimed an LaGG-3 fighter over Leningrad on 7 January, his 25th victory. He claimed two victories on the 12th and two days later he became an 'ace-in-a-day' when he claimed five victories over Mga, all Ilyushin Il-2 ground-attack aircraft. He was awarded the German Cross in Gold on 23 January in recognition of his 25th victory and by the end of the month he had claimed his 38th victory. From early February his Group moved to Heiligenbeil where they were refreshed and converted to the Focke-Wulf Fw 190A. He claimed his 40th victory on 17 February and in April he was promoted to *Oberfeldwebel* and transferred into the 1st Squadron and from May his Group moved to Nikolskoye. On 5 May he claimed his 50th victory, and shortly after he was transferred to the Advanced Training Group East as an instructor, remaining there until September when he returned to the 54th Fighter Wing.

He had moved to Poltava by August and on 26 September he claimed his 60th victory, a Yak-9 fighter near Schatalowka. He later moved to Vitebsk where he claimed fourteen victories during October and on 6 November he claimed his 75th victory. In late January 1944 he claimed five victories, all Lavochkin La-5 fighters, to become an 'ace-in-a-day' for the second time. On 6 March he claimed two more victories, which included his 90th victory, and on the 26th he was awarded the Knight's Cross in recognition of his skill as a fighter pilot and for claiming over ninety victories. He was promoted to *Leutnant* on 20 April and a month later he claimed his 100th victory, a Yak-1 over the Baltic Sea. He continued to claim victories during June a July and by mid-August had claimed his 120th.

On 14 September he transferred to the 3rd Squadron of the 54th Fighter Wing and on that day claimed six victories to become an 'ace-in-a-day' for the third time! He claimed his 130th victory on 15 September and in October he was appointed *Staffelkapitän* of the Squadron and claimed his 139th victory at the end of the month. In March 1945 he transferred to the 7th Fighter Wing and was promoted to *Oberleutnant*. Here he flew the Me 262 jet fighter and claimed seven victories whilst flying this new aircraft, and he surrendered to Allied forces in May 1945. He had flown 530 combat missions and claimed almost 150 aerial victories during the war and had been recommended for the Oakleaves, but they were never awarded. Tegtmeier died on 8 April 1999 in Greven, a town in the district of Steinfurt in the state of North Rhine-Westphalia and close to the city of Münster.

Rudolf WAGNER

Leutnant

Knight's Cross: Awarded on 26 March 1944 as *Leutnant* and fighter pilot with the 10th Squadron of the 51st Fighter Wing '*Mölders*' for operations over the Soviet Union.

Rudolf Wagner claimed seventy-nine victories during the Second World War whilst flying combat missions over the Eastern Front. He was born on 29 October 1921 in Esslingen, Baden-Württemberg in southern Germany. He joined the *Luftwaffe* and on completion of his fighter-pilot training was assigned to the 51st Fighter Wing in early 1942.

Wagner was sent to the Soviet Union as part of the 10th Squadron of the 4th Group and during the first few months flew as a wingman to *Obergefreiter* Otto Gaiser. During his first few months he didn't fly many operations due to bad weather. It wasn't until the end of March that Wagner and his squadron could fly regular missions, flying the Bf 109F-2. From May he flew air defence missions over the 9th Army at Rzhev, and from early June his Group was relocated to Orel and then to Heiligenbeil. From there his Group flew over Rzhev and in July *Unteroffzier* Wagner moved with his Group to the Tatsinskaya airfield and was later deployed again over the Rzhev area. On 10 August he claimed his first victory, an LaGG-3 fighter, near Rzhev

(Deutsches Wehrkundearchiv)

and from late September into early October was deployed over the area of Army Groups North and Centre. He later took part in the Soviet winter offensive and he claimed another victory at this time, an Ilyushin Il-2 ground-attack aircraft on 16 December.

From early 1943 his Group was in Vitebsk and equipped with the Bf 109F-6 and he flew over the area around Velikye Luki. He claimed his third victory on 9 February 1943, a Pe-2 twin-engined bomber, and just after that was awarded the Iron Cross 2nd Class. Later in February his Group was equipped with the Focke-Wulf Fw 190A-4 and moved briefly to Germany before returning to Orel and the Eastern Front. He claimed two victories on 16 March and by 24 April Wagner had claimed his 10th victory and had been awarded the Iron Cross 1st Class. By now his Group had been converted again and he was flying the Bf 109G, and he claimed four more victories on 5 July and the following day he became an 'ace-in-a-day' when he claimed five victories. By the 17th Wagner had claimed his 30th victory and in early August his Group had moved to Bryansk and then to Poltava. He claimed his 40th victory at the end of August and on 20 September he was awarded the *Luftwaffe* Honour Goblet after claiming his 45th victory and the following day he claimed a Yak-9 fighter, his 50th victory. Wagner shot down two Pe-2 dive-bombers on the 24th and two days later he claimed five victories to become an 'ace-in-a-day' for the second time. The next day he claimed six more aircraft to become an 'ace-in-a-day' for the third time, which included his 60th victory. He claimed three more victories on 29 September and by the time he was awarded the German Cross in Gold on 17 October, Wagner had claimed seventy-six victories.

On 11 October he was involved in a mid-air collision with another Bf 109G-6, flown by *Unteroffizier* Helmut Neu, who was killed. Wagner was injured and didn't fly for almost four weeks. In mid-November, now with the rank of *Leutnant*, Wagner claimed his last victory on 13 December (although some records state the date was 11 December) and shortly after he went missing, he was last seen flying over the area of Zhitomir in combat with Soviet fighters. His body has never been recovered and he was posthumously awarded the Knight's Cross on 26 March 1944.

Robert 'Bazi' WEISS

Hauptmann

Knight's Cross: Awarded on 26 March 1944 as *Oberleutnant* and *Staffelkapitän* of the 4th Group of the 54th Fighter Wing for operations over England and the Soviet Union.

Knight's Cross with Oakleaves: He became the 782nd recipient posthumously on 12 March 1945 as *Hauptmann* and commander of the 3rd Group of the 54th Fighter Wing for operations over the Western Front.

(Deutsches Wehrkundearchiv)

Robert Weiss began his military career as an anti-aircraft gunner with the *Luftwaffe* and later became a fighter pilot. He scored 122 aerial victories during his career, ninety-six on the Eastern Front and twenty-six on the Western Front after flying a total of 471 combat missions. Weiss was born on 21 April 1920 in Baden near Vienna, Austria, the eldest son of a *Stadtobersekretär* (Higher City Secretary), and later a police inspector. In 1939 Weiss joined the *Luftwaffe* and was assigned to the 22nd Anti-Aircraft Regiment before applying to become a fighter pilot, beginning his training in early 1940.

He must have impressed because he won the Iron Cross 2nd Class in August 1940, and in January 1941 Weiss was attached to the 6th Squadron of the 26th Fighter Wing. He was part of the 2nd

Group stationed in Abbeville-Drucat, France and in April, shortly before he began flying combat missions on the Channel Front, he was commissioned as a *Leutnant*. He was a relatively 'slow starter' and didn't score his victory until 21 September, an RAF Spitfire over Dunkirk. From October his group was relocated to Wevelgem south-west of Courtrai, Belgium, and in December the Group was relocated to Abbeville, the reason being that five pilots had been killed in a major accident when they crashed into the hills surrounding the airfield in thick fog. Awarded the Iron Cross 1st Class in December 1941, Weiss claimed his second aerial victory in March 1942 over Boulogne, another RAF Spitfire. In May he was transferred and briefly served in the 7th Squadron of the 26th Fighter Wing, claiming his third aerial victory, another Spitfire, over Abbeville.

In September 1942 Weiss was transferred to the 1st Squadron of the 54th Fighter Wing, part of the 1st Group serving in Krasnogvardeysky on the Russian Front. Here he flew operations over Leningrad, and in January 1943 he claimed a total of nine victories. In early March he was promoted to *Oberleutnant* and claimed his 20th victory on the 14th, by the end of the month had claimed his 28th aerial victory. He claimed his 30th victory on 8 April, an LaGG-3 fighter, shot down near Leningrad. Weiss was awarded the *Luftwaffe* Honour Goblet on 8 May, but soon after he became ill and was hospitalized until July when he was awarded the German Cross in Gold. When he returned he took over as *Staffelkapitän* of the 3rd Squadron with the 54th Fighter Wing, after *Oberleutnant* Franz Eisenach had been wounded in action.

On 2 August Weiss claimed two victories, both Il-2 ground-attack aircraft, and he claimed another six victories over the course of the next eleven days. He shot down four aircraft on 14 August, which included his 40th aerial victory, and was gaining victories now at a greater pace, claiming another two on 17 August and three more two days later. He claimed a MiG-3 fighter on the 20th, and claimed two victories on the 22nd, which included his 50th victory. On 2 September he claimed his 60th victory, an LaGG-3 fighter over Jelnja. In September he handed his command of the 3rd Squadron back to Eisenach, and by the end of the year had claimed a total of eighty aerial victories.

In January 1944 Weiss claimed a total of fifteen more victories, which included four on the 25th, which included his 95th. He claimed four more victories on 15 February and was finally awarded the Knight's Cross on 26 March 1944. After some leave he returned to his squadron and in May was transferred to the 8th Squadron which was shortly after relocated to the Western Front, near Normandy. During early May Weiss was promoted to *Hauptmann* and on the 19th shot down a P-38 Lightning over south-east Oschersleben, Germany – his 100th victory. On 27 May he claimed a B-17 Flying Fortress over Colmar, and went on to claim nine victories during June, of which six were RAF Spitfires. On 21 July he was appointed *Gruppenkommandeur* of the 3rd Group of the 54th Fighter Wing, flying the Focke-Wulf Fw 190A from Villacoublay, during the German retreat following the invasion of Normandy. By this time Weiss had recorded his 113th victory, and on 23 July he added two more victories to his score when he claimed two P-38s over Arpajorn. On the 28th he claimed a B-26 Marauder twin-engined medium bomber over Vimoutiers, north-western France, and on 6 August he shot down two B-24 Liberators. His Group was withdrawn from combat operations on 5 September, and was relocated to Oldenburg where he flew the new Fw 190D-9. On 28 September Weiss shot down an RAF photographic reconnaissance Spitfire, flown by Flight Lieutenant Duncan McCuaig who was killed during the confrontation near Apelstadt, near Bremen. His body and his aircraft weren't discovered until the early 1990s.

On Christmas Day his Group became fully operational, with three squadrons flying from Varrelbusch airfield. On 27 December the 3rd Group engaged in fighters from 486 Squadron, a New Zealand squadron of the RAF. Two days later Weiss led his Group in combat against Allied fighters of the RAF Second Tactical Air Force. In return the Germans claimed eight aircraft, with Weiss claiming a Spitfire over Gerstein, his last victory. Later that day, Weiss led his Group into a large formation of RAF Spitfires from 331 and 501 Squadrons, with the loss of seventeen aircraft and thirteen pilots, including Weiss. He was shot down and killed by Flight Sergeant K.F. Haanes of the Norwegian 331 Squadron. Weiss was posthumously awarded the Knight's Cross with Oakleaves on 12 March 1945, and was initially buried in Lingen, but in 1958 his remains were moved and reinterred to the war cemetery at Baden. They were later moved to the family grave.

Rudolf EHRENBERGER

Oberfeldwebel

Knight's Cross: Awarded posthumously on 5 April 1944 as *Oberfeldwebel* and fighter pilot in the 6th Squadron of the 53rd Fighter Wing for operations over France, England, the Soviet Union, North Africa and Italy.

Rudolf Ehrenberger claimed forty-seven aerial victories during the Second World War including thirty-seven over the Western Front of which three were four-engined bombers. Ehrenberger was born on 25 August 1915 at Erbesthal in the Bruck an der Leitha region of Austria, and he joined the *Luftwaffe* in 1939 as an *Unteroffizier*.

(Deutsches Wehrkundearchiv)

He saw action during the Battle of Britain while assigned to the 6th Squadron of the 53rd Fighter Wing and claimed his first victory on 27 September 1940, a Spitfire over north London, and was awarded the Iron Cross 2nd Class soon after. In June 1941, now a *Feldwebel*, he flew with the 4th Squadron during the opening stages of Operation Barbarossa and claimed his second victory, a Tupolev SB-3 twin-engined bomber, on 4 July. Four days later he claimed another SB-3 and on 27 August he claimed two more victories and was awarded the Iron Cross 1st Class. By the end of September he had claimed his 11th victory and was awarded the *Luftwaffe* Honour Goblet on 19 October.

In late autumn of 1941 he transferred to the 6th Squadron based in Bergen aan Zee, a town on the North Sea coast of northern Holland. By December his squadron had moved to Sicily and on the 29th he claimed his 12th victory, an RAF Hurricane. He saw action over Malta and on 24 December together with *Leutnant* Hans Möller they attacked two British submarines off the coast of Malta and claimed them as sunk, but post-war records show neither were lost. At the beginning of 1942, now promoted to *Oberfeldwebel*, Ehrenberger flew as part of the 2nd Group of the 53rd Fighter Wing from his base in Sicily. He claimed three victories in March, and shot down a Spitfire on 5 April and three Hurricanes over Malta on the 10th. He claimed his 20th victory on 21 April, a Curtiss P-40, and the following day he shot down a Spitfire. In mid-July his Group moved to North Africa and flew missions against the Allied offensive near El Alamein. On the 14th Ehrenberger claimed an RAF Spitfire, then a week later his squadron returned to Sicily and from August he flew escort missions against Allied convoys. From September he flew escort missions for ships and transport aircraft to North Africa and was awarded the German Cross in Gold on 9 September. He claimed four Spitfires on 16 October, his 28th victory and on the 20th his Group was withdrawn from the Malta missions and only flew protective mission over North Africa.

At the beginning of 1943 Ehrenberger's squadron was flying from Tunisia and on 20 March he claimed two P-38 Lightnings, his 30th victory. On 7 May his Group moved to Sicily and that same day he claimed his 34th victory, another Spitfire. In early July, during the Allied landings in Sicily, his Group reassembled in Ramacca, and he flew missions over the Allied landing areas. He claimed his 38th victory on 8 July, a P-40 near Scianna, but on the 13th Ramacca had to be evacuated as the

Allies were fast approaching. His Group moved to Leverano and then onto Scalea. By the end of the month most of his Group had moved north-west of Naples, and Ehrenberger continued to fly combat missions. He claimed six victories in August, which included a B-17 Flying Fortress, shot down on 19 August, his 40th victory. He claimed a P-38 Lightning over Ventotene on 2 September and from the 10th flew operations against the Allied landings near Salerno.

His Group moved to Vienna in early 1944 and Ehrenberger flew missions over Germany as part of the 'Defence of the Reich' campaign. On 30 January he claimed a B-24 Liberator over south-east Udine, and despite the difficult weather conditions he claimed another B-17 bomber over South Wels on 24 February. On 8 March he engaged US bombers and fighters over Wittenberg, a town in Saxony and during the subsequent aerial combat his Bf 109G-6 was hit. He bailed out and whilst descending from his parachute he was machine-gunned by US fighters over Jüterbog and was killed. He was posthumously awarded the Knight's Cross on 5 April 1944.

Diethelm von EICHEL-STREIBER

Major

Knight's Cross: Awarded on 5 April 1944 as *Hauptmann* and *Staffelkapitän* of the Staff Squadron of the 51st Fighter Wing for operations over the Soviet Union and for claiming his 69th aerial victory.

Diethelm von Eichel-Streiber claimed ninety-one aerial victories during the Second World War, all but one over the Eastern Front. He was born on 10 August 1914 in Oppershausen in the Mühlhausen region of Thüringen into an aristocratic family and his uncle, *Major* von Winterfeldt, was later implicated in the July 1944 plot to kill Hitler.

(Deutsches Wehrkundearchiv)

Eichel-Streiber joined the *Luftwaffe* in 1935 and served as an observer pilot in the Condor Legion on a Heinkel He 111 during the Spanish Civil War. He was awarded the Spanish Cross in Gold with Swords on 14 April 1939 and commissioned as a *Leutnant* about the same time. In the spring of 1940, after completion of his fighter training, he joined the 3rd Group of the 52nd Fighter Wing, moving to the 77th Fighter Wing in 1941 as adjutant. He flew during the Balkans campaign as an *Oberleutnant* and shortly after claiming an RAF Hurricane over Crete his Bf 109E-7 was damaged by anti-aircraft fire but he was unhurt when he had to make an emergency landing. He later commanded the 1st Supplementary Squadron of the 77th Fighter Wing, which was later renamed the 10th Squadron of the 1st Fighter Wing. Just before he took part in the invasion of the Soviet Union his unit was renamed again this time as the 1st Squadron of the 5th Fighter Wing. He claimed four Ilyushin DB-3 bombers on 26 June over the Lasi area, and flew in support of the 11th Army over the Vossnosensk area in August. After the breakout of the German units from the Dnieper Bridgehead his Group moved to Tschaplinka in September where he flew in further missions in support of the 11th Army. He later flew missions over the Crimea and in December flew during operations around Sevastopol and from the 26th his Group moved to the Eastern part of the Crimean Peninsula.

On 31 January 1942, Eichel-Streiber was appointed *Staffelkapitän* of his squadron, flying from Brest-South. He was promoted to *Hauptmann* on 1 February and later led missions in support of the breakout of the German warships *Scharnhorst*, *Gneisenau* and *Prinz Eugen* through the English Channel. On 21 March he was appointed *Staffelkapitän* of the 1st Squadron of the 5th Fighter Wing in Herdla, Norway. It was a brief assignment as in May he was transferred to the Staff Squadron of the

26th Fighter Wing in Saint-Omer, France where he flew the Focke-Wulf Fw 190A1 and his squadron was deployed over the Dieppe area where they attacked the Allied troops who had landed. On 4 October he took over as *Staffelkapitän* of the 6th Squadron of the 51st Fighter Wing based in Jesau, Germany, and the following month he took command of the Staff Squadron. From the beginning of 1943 he led his Squadron in action over the Eastern Front where in March he claimed three victories and now began to score at a greater rate. He claimed three victories in May, and shot down four aircraft on 8 June and claimed his 25th victory on 19 July. The following day he claimed another two victories and two more on 3 August and three on the 4th, which included his 30th. Eichel-Streiber claimed four more victories on 11 August, three on the 18th, 19th and 20th over the Demyansk area, all Ilyushin Il-2 ground-attack aircraft.

He claimed his 50th victory on 2 September when he shot down two Il-2s over west Yelnja, but nine days later he had to make an emergency landing and was slightly injured when his Fw 190A-6 developed a technical problem. On the 13th he was awarded the *Luftwaffe* Honour Goblet and on 17 October, shortly after claiming his 52nd victory he was awarded the German Cross in Gold. From October his squadron relocated to Orsha and in December moved to Bobrusik and he was now flying the Bf 109G fighter. He claimed nine victories on 15 December, to become an 'ace-in-a-day', which included his 60th victory (two were later reclassified as unconfirmed). On 10 January 1944 he claimed three victories and on 3 April he claimed his 70th and 71st victories and was awarded the Knight's Cross two days later.

He was appointed *Gruppenkommandeur* of the 3rd Group of the 51st Fighter Wing on 1 May, continuing to fly combat missions over the Eastern Front. By 21 June his Group had moved to Bobruisk and on the 24th he claimed two victories, and claimed a single victory, a Yak-7, the next day. He claimed his 75th victory on 4 July over Kursk and claimed seven more during July which included three on the 30th. Eichel-Streiber claimed his 90th victory on 17 August.

On 24 August he took over as *Gruppenkommandeur* of the 1st Group of the 27th Fighter Wing where he flew from his new base in Hoya, Lower Saxony in 'Defence of the Reich' missions. He claimed a P-47 in the Aachen area on 28 November, but this remains unconfirmed. On the 30th he was replaced by *Hauptmann* Johannes Neumayer and underwent training on the new Me 262 jet fighter at Lechfeld. He later went on to supervise the jet-fighter conversion courses for bomber pilots from the IX Air Corps. Promoted to *Major* in April 1945 he transferred to *Jagdverband* 44, under the command of *Generalmajor* Adolf Galland. Then tragedy struck: he was informed that almost his entire family had been killed during the Allied bombing of Dresden in February. He spent the last weeks of the war recuperating from the shock and he had also found out that his uncle had been implicated in the plot to kill Hitler and had been sentenced to death.

After the war Eichel-Streiber joined the *Bundeswehr* and retired as an *Oberst* in the 1960s and then went to live in the United States where he became a successful Volkswagen distributor in Modesto, California. He died on 13 May 1996 in Bonn, having returned to Germany a few years earlier.

Helmut LIPFERT

Hauptmann

Knight's Cross: Awarded on 5 April 1944 as *Leutnant* and *Staffelführer* of the 6th Squadron of the 52nd Fighter Wing for operations over the Soviet Union and for claiming his 88th aerial victory.

Knight's Cross with Oakleaves: He became the 837th recipient on 17 April 1945 as *Hauptmann* and commander of the 1st Group of the 53rd Fighter Wing for operations over the Eastern Front and for claiming his 198th aerial victory. The presentation was made by the commander of the 18th Air Division, *Generalleutnant* Paul Deichmann, that same day.

Helmut Lipfert was credited with 200 aerial victories during the Second World War, almost all of them over the Eastern Front. He flew in 687 combat missions and was shot down fifteen times, without being wounded. He was also responsible for destroying two torpedo boats and thirty trucks during ground-attack missions and is very likely the highest scoring pilot of the war of any nation during 1945.

Lipfert was born on 6 August 1916, in Lippelsdorf near Saalfeld, Thuringia, after compulsory service in the Reich Labour Service he joined Signals Battalion 37, part of the 1st Panzer Division, in November 1937. He saw action during the Polish campaign as an *Unteroffizier*, later taking part in the Battle of France in May 1940. In early 1941 he transferred to the *Luftwaffe* as an officer candidate in June 1942 and was commissioned as a *Leutnant* on 1 August. From September he was attached to the Replacement Fighter Training Group East, based at Saint-Jean-d'Angély, France.

(Deutsches Wehrkundearchiv)

In December 1942 he transferred into the 6th Squadron of the 52nd Fighter Wing, based on the southern sector of the Eastern Front near Stalingrad, under the command of *Hauptmann* Johannes Steinhoff. On the 19th Lipfert made a forced landing near Kotelnikowo, the engine of his Bf 109 having been damaged during a dogfight. He claimed his first aerial victory when he shot down a Lavochkin La-5 fighter on 30 January 1943, his second on 25 February and on the 28th he claimed his third, an LaGG-3 fighter. Lipfert was awarded the Iron Cross 2nd Class on 12 March, and eight days later was appointed *Staffelkapitän* of the 4th Squadron. He had replaced *Leutnant* Wolf-Dieter von Coester, who had been killed in action that day. Lipfert claimed two more LaGG-3s on 30 March and was awarded the Iron Cross 1st Class after his ninth aerial victory on 29 April. Following the death of *Oberleutnant* Karl Ritzenberger on 24 May took command of the 6th Squadron for a time, as well as the 4th. By the end of September he had achieved twenty-five aerial victories and on 7 October he shot down three aircraft and the following day he became an 'ace-in-a-day' when he claimed five. He claimed his 50th victory on 12 November, and was awarded the *Luftwaffe* Honour Goblet two days later. On the 27th he claimed his 60th aerial victory, a P-39 shot down over Gromowka, and on 1 December he shot down his 65th victory. He claimed three more victories on the 2nd, and four more on the 5th and by the end of the year had achieved his 80th victory and was awarded the German Cross in Gold.

In February he went on some well-deserved leave for a few weeks and met *Oberleutnant* Walter Krupinski, who at the time had more than 150 victories. Lipfert later stated that Krupinski '... certainly kept me from getting bored!' Lipfert was however eager to get back to the front but he developed a boil on his neck overnight, which made him unfit for combat for a number of weeks. He finally returned to active duty in late March and on 5 April was awarded the Knight's Cross in recognition of his 88th aerial victory. He was shot down just six days later by a Soviet Il-2 aircraft and had to make a forced landing at Siwasch, but was not hurt. On the 15th he became the 63rd fighter pilot to achieve his 100th aerial victory, an Il-2 ground-attack aircraft, shot down south-east of Sevastopol.

In May Lipfert was promoted to *Oberleutnant*. The Germans were evacuating the Crimea and Lipfert's Group had moved to Kherson. There, the *Luftwaffe* Groups were subjected to near-constant Soviet bombing raids, and Lipfert's Squadron, in particular, lost a number of aircraft. However he continued to add to his score of victories. He claimed two Yak-7 fighters on 4 May, and added three more victories on the 5th; two on the 6th; three (in nine minutes) on the 7th, and by the end of the month had achieved his 120th aerial victory. On 11 June he claimed his first four-engined bomber, a B-17 Flying Fortress, shot down over Tataturi, but post-war examinations have proven this victory to be unconfirmed. He claimed his 130th victory on 16 July, and on the 19th he shot down three Soviet fighters in just five minutes. By the end of August he had achieved 142 victories. On 12 October he crashed his Bf 109 on take-off from Tiszalok airfield but was not injured. He continued to score victories and on 23 October he shot down two Il-2s in just 60 seconds!

On 13 November he claimed his 150th aerial victory, a Yak-3 over Jaszbereny – becoming the 28th pilot to achieve his 150th victory. He claimed three more victories on the 17th and by the end of December had claimed his 163rd victory. In January 1945 he claimed thirteen victories, with his 175th on 22 January. On 15 February Lipfert was appointed *Gruppenkommandeur* of the 1st Group of the 53rd Fighter Wing, now based in Hungary, succeeding his friend *Hauptmann* Erich Hartmann. He wasn't happy about this appointment and said, 'I am supposed to take over as *Gruppenkommandeur* of a Group that has come from a Wing that has long outlived its former glory'. During March he claimed another fourteen victories and on 16 April he became the 12th and last fighter pilot to claim his 200th victory. The following day he was awarded the Knight's Cross with Oakleaves, and unusually they were presented the same day.

On 17 April the 53rd Fighter Wing was disbanded and Lipfert was transferred to the 52nd Fighter Wing and was attached to the 7th Squadron of the 2nd Group based in Austria, under *Hauptmann* Wilhelm Batz. In May he surrendered to the Americans near Munich, and fortunately was not handed over to the Soviets. He later became a schoolteacher, and was seldom seen by his war comrades. Lipfert died on 10 August 1990 in Einbeck, southern Lower Saxony and is buried today in the local cemetery, section 35, Grave No. 30. He was an excellent fighter pilot and should have been awarded the Knight's Cross with Oakleaves and Swords.

Herbert 'Puschi' PUSCHMANN

Hauptmann

Knight's Cross: Awarded posthumously on 5 April 1944 as *Hauptmann* and *Staffelkapitän* of the 6th Squadron of the 51st Fighter Wing '*Mölders*' for operations over the Soviet Union.

Herbert Puschmann claimed fifty-four aerial victories of which thirty-seven were achieved over the Eastern Front whilst flying a total of approximately 650 combat missions during the Second World War. He was born on 18 August 1920 in Bolkenhain in Lower Silesia and joined the *Luftwaffe* in late 1939 and trained to be a fighter pilot.

He was commissioned as a *Leutnant* and assigned to the 6th Squadron of the 51st Fighter Wing shortly before Operation Barbarossa, the invasion of the Soviet Union. On 22 June 1941, the first day of the invasion he claimed his first two victories, both Tupolev SB-2 twin-engined bombers. He claimed his third victory on 4 July, another SB-2, and was awarded the Iron Cross 2nd Class, and he claimed an Ilyushin DB-3 long-range bomber on 14 September. He claimed two victories on 5 October and by the end of the month he had claimed his 10th victory and had been awarded the Iron Cross 1st Class.

(Deutsches Wehrkundearchiv)

At the beginning of 1942 the 2nd Group was in Bryansk and Puschmann was equipped with the Bf 109F-2, flying missions in support of the 4th Army and the 2nd Panzer Army south of Moscow. At the beginning of February his Group was operating over the Juchnow area and during this time he claimed a MiG-3 fighter. In mid-April operations came to a standstill due to mud and in July the Group finally moved to North Orel where on the 2nd Puschmann claimed his 20th victory. On 2 August his Group moved again and on the 5th he claimed three victories and on the 12th he claimed his 30th aerial victory, a Polikarpov I-153 fighter south-west of Kozelsk. On the 14th he was awarded the *Luftwaffe* Honour Goblet and he claimed another victory on the 22nd, and two on 25 and 27 August. On 3 September he was injured when his Bf 109 was hit by a bomb blast at Dugino airstrip, but soon recovered. On 24 September he was awarded the German Cross in Gold and by October his Group had been withdrawn from the area and was moved to Jessau and equipped with the Focke-Wulf Fw 190A.

In late 1942 his Group was rushed out to Tunisia and he was appointed *Staffelkapitän* of the 6th Squadron on 13 January 1943, leading his unit during the retreat into Sicily and Italy. He claimed three victories in January which included two P-40s on the 31st – his 39th and 40th victories – and was promoted to *Oberleutnant* at the beginning of February. He flew over Cagliari in Sardinia where he claimed six more victories and his Group moved to La Fauconnerie in late March and by April the Group had moved to La-Sebala airfield in Tunis in order to take over the fighter protection for incoming shipping. His Group moved several times during the next few weeks and on 18 June he claimed his 50th aerial victory, and after the Allied landings in Sicily on 10 July the Group moved to Trapani where he flew missions against the enemy in the Mediterranean area. He was promoted to *Hauptmann* in early November and from the beginning of 1944 his squadron was in Lavariano, Italy and he claimed a P-38 on 17 January and the following day he shot down a Spitfire about three miles from the small town of Lessa.

On 3 February he claimed a B-26 Marauder medium bomber but he was hit by the rear gunner and his Bf 109 crashed just west of Rome and he was killed. He was posthumously awarded the Knight's Cross on 5 April 1944 and is buried today at the Military Cemetery in Pomezia, Italy, Block N, Grave No. 632.

Herbert ROLLWAGE

Oberleutnant

Knight's Cross: Awarded on 5 April 1944 as *Oberfeldwebel* and fighter pilot with the 5th Squadron of the 53rd Fighter Wing for operations over the Soviet Union, North Africa and Italy, and for claiming his 49th aerial victory.

Knight's Cross with Oakleaves: He became the 713th recipient on 24 January 1945 as *Leutnant* and *Staffelkapitän* of the 5th Squadron of the 53rd Fighter Wing for operations over the Western Front, and for claiming his 65th aerial victory.

(Author's collection)

Herbert Rollwage flew a total of 664 combat missions during the Second World War and is credited with sixty-six aerial victories, including ten four-engined bombers. Early records state his total could be as much as 102 victories but this seems unlikely. Rollwage was born in Gielde near Goslar in Lower Saxony on 24 September 1916. He joined the *Luftwaffe* in 1936 at the age of 19 and began his training as a fighter pilot. In the spring of 1941 he was posted to the 2nd Group of the 53rd Fighter Wing as an *Unteroffizier*, attached to the 5th Squadron stationed in Mannheim-Santhofen.

He saw action during the first day of the German invasion of Russia on 22 June 1941 as a *Feldwebel* and claimed a SB-2 Tupolev twin-engined bomber. On 5 July he was awarded the Iron Cross 2nd Class and on the 11th claimed his second aerial victory, a SB-3 bomber east of Slawkowitschi. By the time he was awarded the Iron Cross 1st Class on 16 September, Rollwage had claimed his eighth aerial victory. By October he had claimed his 10th victory and the 2nd Group was transferred to the Mediterranean theatre in December. He claimed an RAF Hurricane over Maltas Point on 4 January 1942, and by 13 May had claimed his 18th victory. He was promoted to *Oberfeldwebel* at the end of June and continued to score victories, claiming nine Spitfires in July, and by the end of October Rollwage had shot down thirty aircraft, mostly Spitfires shot down over Malta. He was awarded the *Luftwaffe* Honour Goblet on 10 August and on 10 November he was shot down over Konfonisi Island near Greece and had to make a belly-landing in his Bf 109G-2 but was only slightly wounded.

From December he was operating over Tunisia from his new base in Mateur and later Bizerta. He claimed four P-38 Lightnings in December and on the 12th was awarded the German Cross in Gold in recognition of achieving thirty aerial victories. On 2 March 1943 he was shot down by RAF Spitfires in the area of Pontdu Fahs but successfully made an emergency landing. It is thought he was shot down by the British ace Flight Lieutenant Roy Hussey of 72 Squadron. His squadron was relocated to Comisco airfield in Sicily in May 1943, and he claimed a further ten victories, including two four-engined bombers to record his 45th and 46th victories on 10 July. That same day he was seriously wounded when his Bf 109 was shot at during aerial combat near San Pierto, but he managed to land safely although his aircraft was classified as 100 per cent damaged! Rollwage spent the next few months recovering in hospital.

He returned to duty in December 1943, with his squadron now based at Vienna-Seyring and operating in 'Defence of the Reich' duties. On 7 January 1944 he shot down two P-38 Lightnings in just three minutes. In February he claimed two more victories, both being four-engined bombers but these remain unconfirmed as there were no witnesses. He shot down a B-17 bomber over Braunschweig on 23 March, his 49th victory, and in early April he claimed two more victories, both bombers but these remain unconfirmed. He was finally awarded the Knight's Cross on 5 April in recognition of achieving his 49th victory. He finally claimed his 50th aerial victory on 11 April, when he shot down a B-24 Liberator over Halberstadt-Quedlingburg, and almost 50 minutes later he shot down a B-17 near Goslar. Within the next few days Rollwage claimed two more B-17s and in May he claimed a P-51 and two B-17s. On 10 August he was appointed *Staffelkapitän* of the 5th Squadron and was promoted to *Leutnant* at the end of May and claimed his 60th aerial victory on 22 August. The following day he shot down a P-47 Thunderbolt over Mantes-la-Jolie, north-central France and claimed two more on the 28 September and another on 20 October. On 25 November Rollwage claimed his 65th victory, a Piper L-4 Grasshopper reconnaissance aircraft over Hagnenau.

In early December he left his squadron, having been assigned to the 2nd Squadron of the 106th Fighter Wing as an instructor. He was awarded the Knight's Cross with Oakleaves on 24 January in recognition of achieving his 65th victory, and was promoted to *Oberleutnant* in late February or early March. In early April he returned to the 53rd Fighter Wing, and on the 5th claimed a P-47, his last aerial victory of the war. It is thought he never officially returned to his Group. It seems that when the 2nd Group moved to Ulm-Ristissen, the former base of the 106th Fighter Wing, which had been disbanded, Rollwage just attached himself to the 2nd Group and stayed until the end of the war.

After the war he joined the *Bundesluftwaffe*, rising to the rank of *Hauptmann* before retiring in 1968. He died in his home town of Gielde, Goslar on 4 January 1980.

Johannes BUNZEK

Leutnant

Knight's Cross: Awarded posthumously on 6 April 1944 as *Leutnant* and fighter pilot with the 7th Squadron of the 52nd Fighter Wing for operations over the Soviet Union.

Johannes Bunzek claimed a total of seventy-eight victories in just 19 weeks during the Second World War and all were over the Eastern Front. He was born on 22 May 1922 in Gross-Strehlitz, a small town in Upper Silesia, and on completion of his pilot training with Air Combat School 4 in Fürstenfeldbruck, Bavaria he was assigned to the 52nd Fighter Wing. Bunzek was commissioned as a *Leutnant* on 1 December 1942 and was attached to the 7th Squadron from late 1942 as part of the 3rd Group in Mineralnyie Wody in the Caucasus.

(Deutsches Wehrkundearchiv)

He claimed his first victory over east Trojzkaja on 28 May 1943 and on 5 July he claimed two more. He claimed his sixth and seventh victories on 12 July and was awarded the Iron Cross 2nd Class two days later. By the time he had achieved his 10th and 11th victories on 7 August he had already been awarded the Iron Cross 1st Class. On 19 August he claimed three victories, his 15th to 17th, and he claimed a single victory on the 20th, becoming an 'ace-in-a-day' the following day when he shot down five enemy aircraft. He claimed three victories on 22 August, and by the end of the month he had claimed thirty-three victories. On 18 September he claimed his 40th victory and claimed his 50th just nine days later. By the end of the month his victory score had risen to fifty-six.

On 15 October he claimed his 76th victory, a Boston medium bomber south-south-west of Werchnedjeprowak, and on the 27th he was awarded the *Luftwaffe* Honour Goblet. About six weeks later he was awarded the German Cross in Gold and claimed his 78th aerial victory on 7 December 1943. Four days later he was in aerial combat with an Ilyushin Il-2 ground-attack aircraft south-west of Werbjushka near Novgorodka, over the Soviet Union when he was attacked by two La-7 fighters. His Bf 109G-6 took several hits, and some reports say he collided with a Soviet aircraft, but most say that his aircraft exploded in mid-air and he was killed instantly. His body has never been recovered and he is listed as missing in action. Bunzek was posthumously awarded the Knight's Cross on 6 April 1944. His personnel record shows that he was not a good pilot and only just met expectations and had average skills. Nevertheless, he did succeed in claiming seventy-eight victories during a somewhat brief career. It was also reported that he shot down two aircraft the day he was killed but this has never been officially verified.

Walter HOECKNER

Major

Knight's Cross: Awarded on 6 April 1944 as *Hauptmann* and commander of the 2nd Group of the 1st Fighter Wing for operations over England, Crete, the Soviet Union and the Western Front.

Walter Hoeckner claimed fifty-nine aerial victories on the Western Front, including six four-engined bombers over 500 combat missions during the Second World War. He was born on 24 October 1914 in Berlin-Zehlendorf, joined the *Luftwaffe* in 1939 and trained as a fighter pilot.

In September 1940 he joined the 7th Squadron of the 77th Fighter Wing in Döberitz, Germany, flying the Bf 109E-1, whilst continuing with his training. From January 1941 he served with the

Replacement Squadron of the 77th Fighter Wing where he served as a *Leutnant* and instructor. A few months later he transferred to the 6th Squadron and claimed his first victory on 14 March, a Beaufort twin-engined bomber over Brest, and was soon afterwards awarded the Iron Cross 2nd Class. From 6 April his Group took part in the Balkan campaign and he flew escort missions for Stuka dive-bombers and took part in low-level attacks. He claimed his second victory over Larissa in Greece on 15 April, an RAF Spitfire, and he flew missions against shipping off the coast of Athens. At the end of April his time in Greece had ended and his squadron moved to Crete where he flew his first combat patrol on 11 May. On the 26th he claimed three victories, two Blenheim light bombers and a Hurricane, and was awarded the Iron Cross 1st Class.

(Deutsches Wehrkundearchiv)

In June his Group moved east and from the 22nd Hoeckner took part in Operation Barbarossa, the invasion of the Soviet Union, claiming a DB-3 bomber that same day. By the end of July he had claimed his 10th victory and later took part in the attack over the Dniester Bridgehead flying in support of the XI Army Corps. From August he flew missions over the Bug River area and was on the 14th shot down by enemy anti-aircraft fire and had to make a forced landing near Odessa but was unhurt. He claimed a single victory during September but claimed ten victories, including his 20th in October. On 30 October he was shot down once again, this time during combat and was reported as missing near Sinjewka. He managed to evade capture and returned to his own lines a few days later, again without injury.

In January 1942 most of his Group had moved to Vienna-Aspern where they were rested and re-equipped with Bf 109F-4. From March his Group began to move to the Crimea where he claimed two victories that month and by 1 June had claimed his 30th aerial victory. He was awarded the German Cross in Gold on 2 July in recognition of his success as a fighter pilot over the Balkans and the Soviet Union. From October he served as *Staffelkapitän* of the 4th Squadron of Advanced Training Group East, as an instructor with the rank of *Hauptmann*. On 5 January 1943 he was transferred as *Staffelkapitän* to the 1st Squadron of the 26th Fighter Wing and claimed two victories on 14 February. He claimed two more victories on the 21st and two on the 27th, which included his 40th victory. On 7 March he claimed six victories, to become an 'ace-in-a-day', and celebrated the most successful day of any 1st Group pilot, and he claimed his 50th victory on 5 May, a Petlyakov Pe-2 twin-engined dive-bomber.

On 28 June Hoeckner was appointed *Gruppenkommandeur* of the 2nd Group of the 1st Fighter Wing in Holland. He now flew the Fw 190A-7 and on 12 August he claimed a B-17 Flying Fortress over Liblar, Germany. He claimed three more in October but on the 10th he was hit by return fire from one of the B-17s and was forced to parachute out of his stricken aircraft unharmed, his Fw 190 crashing near Coesfeld. By the end of November Hoeckner had claimed his 55th victory but his Group was facing increased Allied bombings and had lost thirty-two men, which included two *Gruppenkommandeur*s. On 15 February Hoeckner took command of the 1st Group of the 4th Fighter Wing, flying out of Farica di Roma, a small region in Italy. He was now flying the Bf 109G and on 6 April was rewarded for his success and recognition of his 55th victory when he was awarded the Knight's Cross.

On 13 May he claimed two P-40s and four days later claimed a P-47 Thunderbolt, his 59th and last victory. His Group remained in northern Italy until 25 August 1944 when it was moved to Mönchengladbach in Germany where it was deployed in 'Defence of the Reich' missions. That same day Hoeckner crashed during take-off. His aircraft flipped over and burst into flames, killing him.

Max-Hermann 'Anatol' LÜCKE

Oberleutnant

Knight's Cross: Awarded posthumously on 6 April 1944 as *Oberleutnant* and fighter pilot attached to the 9th Squadron of the 51st Fighter Wing '*Mölders*' for operations over the Soviet Union.

Hermann Lücke claimed a total of seventy-eight aerial victories over the Soviet Union during the Second World War. He was born on 2 June 1920 in Scharfoldendorf, Holzminden in southern Lower Saxony and completed his training with a Squadron attached to the 54th Fighter Wing from September 1941.

(Deutsches Wehrkundearchiv)

He transferred into the 8th Squadron of the 51st Fighter Wing as a young *Leutnant* in December 1941, seeing action over the Soviet Union. At the beginning of 1942 he flew the Bf 109F-2 but his Group was in a desperate condition and needed time to build itself up. By April his group had moved to Smolensk and from May flew over the operational area of the 9th Army, where Lücke claimed his first victory on 2 August, an Ilyushin Il-2 ground-attack aircraft. He claimed another Il-2 on the 17th and four days later he claimed his third victory and was shortly after awarded the Iron Cross 2nd Class. On 4 and 5 September he claimed two more victories and from mid-September until February 1943 he served as an instructor with Replacement Fighter Group East.

In May 1943, now with the rank of *Oberleutnant*, Lücke returned to front-line duty with his old Wing and was attached to the 9th Squadron, back in the Soviet Union. He claimed three LaGG-3 aircraft over Dorobusch on 8 May and was awarded the Iron Cross 1st Class. On 1 June he claimed his 10th victory, and he claimed three more the following day, two on the 8th and became an 'ace-in-a-day' on 10 June when he shot down seven Ilyushin Il-4 long-range bombers. He was awarded the *Luftwaffe* Honour Goblet on 1 July in recognition of his success and achievements. Later in July his Group moved to Bryansk where he continued to claim victories at a rapid rate. On 5 July he became an 'ace-in-a-day' once again when he claimed seven aircraft in just a few hours. He claimed four victories on the 6th and three more on the 7th, claiming his 40th aerial victory five days later. He continued to claim victories at a fast rate all through July, claiming four victories on the 17th which included his 50th. On the 17th he claimed three Il-2s, two more the following day and three victories on the 29th, which included his 60th victory. On 1 August his Focke-Wulf Fw 190 was rammed by a Soviet fighter but he managed to parachute from his stricken aircraft and land safely with only minor injuries. He spent the next four weeks resting and on 16 August was awarded the German Cross in Gold in recognition of his 60th victory.

Returning to duty in early September he claimed another six victories that month, and claimed his 70th victory on 6 October. He claimed two victories on 20 and 21 October and two days later he was involved in a mid-air collision with another Fw 190 just after take-off from Krosinskjj airstrip. He was severely wounded and badly burnt and died whilst in hospital on 8 November 1943. He was posthumously awarded the Knight's Cross on 6 April 1944. From May 1943 until his last victory on 21 October he had claimed seventy-three victories in just 167 days, and had he not been wounded and away from the front for four weeks his total could have been over 100.

Paul-Heinrich 'Sarotti' DÄHNE

Hauptmann

Knight's Cross: Awarded on 8 April 1944 as *Oberleutnant* and *Staffelkapitän* of the 2nd Squadron of the 52nd Fighter Wing for claiming his 80th aerial victory whilst flying operations over the Soviet Union.

(Deutsches Wehrkundearchiv)

Paul-Heinrich Dähne claimed over ninety-nine aerial victories during the Second World War, with some researchers crediting him with as many as 128, whilst flying 600 combat missions. Dähne was born in Frankfurt an der Oder, a small town in Brandenburg on the German and Polish border on 7 July 1921.

He trained as a fighter pilot and in late 1940, on completion of his training, was attached to the 2nd Squadron of the 52nd Fighter Wing, operating over the Channel Front. *Leutnant* Dähne claimed his first victory, an RAF Blenheim, on 26 August 1941 over Juist an island in Lower Saxony, Germany and was awarded the Iron Cross 2nd Class soon afterwards. In September his squadron was transferred to the Soviet Union, moving to Orsha and then onto Ponjatowka from October, and later flying in support of the army's advance on Kalinin. On 18 October he claimed his second aerial victory, an Ilyushin DB-3 bomber, and the following day he shot down a Polikarpov R-5 reconnaissance aircraft. By November his squadron had moved to Rusa, about 45 miles west of Moscow, and at the beginning of January 1942 his squadron had moved again and Dähne claimed his fourth victory, a MiG-3 fighter, on 20 January. He claimed two victories on 10 June over Kharkov, both Il-2 ground-attack aircraft, and on the 22nd he claimed his seventh victory and was awarded the Iron Cross 1st Class. He claimed three victories on 22 August over the area of Uljanowo, his 13th to 15th victories.

On 5 July 1943 Dähne was promoted to *Oberleutnant* and the same day he claimed four victories, and his 25th victory the next day. He shot down his 30th victory on 3 August and claimed four victories on the 20th and two on the 21st, which included his 40th victory. On 13 September he was awarded the *Luftwaffe* Honour Goblet and he claimed his 50th victory on 4 October. He claimed two more victories on 16 October, and the following day was awarded the German Cross in Gold after claiming fifty-four victories. He claimed his 60th victory on 21 October and by the end of the month he had achieved sixty-six victories. His success continued into November, he became an 'ace-in-a-day' on the 2nd when he claimed five victories, and was appointed *Staffelkapitän* of the 2nd Squadron of the 52nd Fighter Wing on 13 November.

He claimed three P-39 fighters on 10 March 1944, which included his 75th victory, and on 8 April Dähne was awarded the Knight's Cross in recognition of achieving eighty victories. By the end of the month he had claimed his 85th victory, and on 14 May he claimed his 90th. On 25 May his squadron was selected to be detached from its Group and transferred to 'Defence of the Reich' duties. It was redesignated the 12th Squadron of the 11th Fighter Wing and was re-equipped with the Fw 190A, whilst attached to the 3rd Group under the command of *Hauptmann* Horst-Günther von Fassong. Dähne led his squadron until 2 January 1945 when he was asked to take over as *Gruppenkommandeur* after the death of Fassong.

From March he took over as *Gruppenkommandeur* of the 2nd Group of the 1st Fighter Wing which had just taken delivery of the new He 162 jet fighter, known as the *Volksjäger*. Dähne didn't like this aircraft and had little confidence in its capabilities and design. On 24 April, Dähne took off in a He 162 for the first time, putting off this flight for long enough. He took the aircraft up to a height of about 1,640ft and then put it into a sharp turn, at which point it began to 'skid' through the air before somersaulting with smoke streaming from its engine. Dähne was in trouble, he tried to get the aircraft under control and it then began to lose height, a witness later said '… it looked like a dead leaf falling'. He had forgotten important instructions, such as the *Volksjäger* had twin rudders that could not be used for steep turns because the airflow across them was blanked out by the jets exhaust. Turns had to be made a particular way, which Dähne had forgotten causing him to lose control. He ejected from the aircraft. The seat shot upward perfectly but the canopy did not jettison, something Dähne had also forgotten to do, and his head smashed against the canopy, breaking his neck. His body was later recovered and he is now buried in the military cemetery in Rostock-Warnemünde-Alter, Block I, Grave No. 45. He was posthumously promoted to the rank of *Hauptmann*.

Anton 'Toni' LINDNER

Oberleutnant

Knight's Cross: Awarded on 8 April 1944 as *Leutnant* and fighter pilot with the 1st Group of the 51st Fighter Wing '*Mölders*' for operations over the Soviet Union.

Anton Linder claimed approximately seventy-two aerial victories, all of them on the Eastern Front during the Second World War, and flew more than 650 combat missions. He was born on 12 April 1917 in Hohenkemnath in Amberg just over 30 miles east of Nuremberg and joined the 2nd Squadron of the 51st Fighter Wing as an *Unteroffizier* in December 1939.

(Deutsches Wehrkundearchiv)

He saw action during the Battle of France and on 24 May 1940 he claimed an RAF Spitfire during combat and was shot down himself but managed to bail out over Calais. His claim, however, has never been confirmed. He returned to duty in September, seeing action during the Battle of Britain but failed to score any victories. By June 1941 Lindner had been promoted to *Feldwebel* and his squadron had been transferred to the Eastern Front where he took part in the invasion of the Soviet Union. He claimed his first, confirmed, aerial victory of the campaign on 23 June, a Polikarpov R-5 reconnaissance bomber, and six days later he shot down a SB-3 bomber to claim his second victory. By the end of July he had claimed six victories and had been awarded the Iron Cross 2nd Class and now saw action over Vitebsk, Orsha and the Mogilev area, and by August the operational area had moved to Smolensk. His Group moved often to keep up with the advancing army and by September he had been promoted to *Oberfeldwebel* and flew missions in support of the advance on Moscow. On 6 October he claimed two Petlyakov Pe-2 dive-bombers and from November he had moved to the Staraya Russa area and by the end of the year his deployment in the Moscow area had ended, and he had been awarded the Iron Cross 1st Class and the *Luftwaffe* Honour Goblet.

At the beginning of 1942 he was flying the Bf 109E-7 and his Group had moved to Dno by 8 January due to the Soviet advance. In February he flew near Lake Ilmen, escorting fighter-bombers. He claimed his 10th victory on 7 March, a I-16 fighter, claiming another victory, a MiG-3 on 1 April. On 27 May he was awarded the German Cross in Gold in recognition of his ten aerial victories and for his fighter escort missions. He then started flying missions over the Demyansk area and claimed another victory on 6 July, and by August he was flying missions over Dugino in support of Army Group Centre. His Group then moved to Jesau to be equipped with the Fw 190A, and was by October flying missions over the Leningrad and Dubrovka area, where he claimed another five victories before the end of the year.

On 28 January 1943 he was briefly transferred to Advanced Training Group East as an instructor but soon returned to his squadron a few weeks later. He claimed his 21st and 22nd victories on 24 February and during March he flew combat missions over Bryansk and Orel areas. In July he claimed four victories and on 2 August claimed his 30th victory, a Soviet Boston east of Kromy. He claimed three victories on 5 August, two on the 6th and the 8th, and he claimed his 40th victory on 15 August, an Il-2 ground-attack aircraft. On 1 September he claimed his 50th aerial victory and by the end of October he had scored over sixty victories. He was awarded the Knight's Cross on 8 April 1944 in recognition of his success as a fighter pilot over the Russian Front and for scoring over seventy-five victories although they are unconfirmed because of the lack of witnesses.

On 31 August 1944 he was appointed *Staffelkapitän* of the 1st Squadron of Fighter Replacement Training Wing 1 as a *Leutnant*. He rejoined the 51st Fighter Wing in January 1945 as *Staffelkapitän* of the 2nd Squadron, with the rank of *Oberleutnant*. On 24 April he became the last *Staffelkapitän* of the 15th Squadron of the 51st Fighter Wing and its possible he claimed a further eleven victories during the last weeks of the war, but they have never been confirmed. After the war he served in the *Bundesluftwaffe*, rising to the rank of *Oberstleutnant* before his retirement in March 1972. Lindner died in his home town of Hohenkemnath on 17 February 1994.

Walter 'Sohndel' SCHUCK

Oberleutnant

Knight's Cross: Awarded on 8 April 1944 as *Oberfeldwebel* and fighter pilot with the 9th Squadron of the 5th Fighter Wing in recognition of his 75th aerial victory and for operations over the Soviet Union.

Knight's Cross with Oakleaves: He became the 616th recipient on 30 September 1944 as *Leutnant* and fighter pilot with the 9th Squadron of the 5th Fighter Wing for continued operations over the Soviet Union and for claiming his 169th aerial victory. The Oakleaves were presented personally by *Reichsmarschall* Hermann Göring at the Reich Chancellery in Berlin on 7 November 1944, and also receiving awards that day were twelve other soldiers among them *Generalmajor* Heinz Trettner, *Oberstleutnant* Friedrich August von der Heydte, *Hauptmann* Diether Lukesch and *Hauptmann* Franz Kieslich.

(Deutsches Wehrkundearchiv)

Walter Schuck had a remarkable career as a fighter pilot during the Second World War and he shot down 181 aircraft, including eight victories whilst flying the Me 262 jet fighter. He flew in 500 combat missions and his most notable achievements were eleven Soviet aircraft shot down in a single day. Schuck was born on 30 July 1920 in Frankenholz in the Saarland, at the time the region was governed by Britain and France under a League of Nations mandate. He was one of five children and his father Jacob was a coal miner and upon leaving school the young Walter applied to join his father at the mine but his application was refused and he took a job with a local bricklayer.

In March 1935 Germany introduced compulsory military service and Schuck saw this as a career opportunity. His father, who had experienced trench warfare in the First World War, tried to talk his son out of joining the army or at least to avoid the infantry, so he volunteered to join the *Luftwaffe*. After serving his compulsory six months with the Reich Labour Service he began service with the

Luftwaffe in November 1937. In April 1938 he transferred to the 254th Bomber Wing in Gütersloh, and was assigned to a security unit and after helping a truck driver to deliver material around the air base he learnt to drive a 3-tonne truck. This impressed his commanding officer who transferred him to the glider pilot school just after the Sudeten Crisis.

In February 1939, Schuck attended a training course at Bonn-Hangelar and qualified as a pilot on 14 May 1940. He initially wanted to be a reconnaissance pilot, flying the Dornier Do 17. Due to a few disciplinary problems following unauthorised aerobatics and running the risk of a court martial he decided to transfer to the fighter pilot school at Werneuchen, to avoid further trouble. On 16 June he was assigned to the 3rd Squadron at the school and passed his first flight without problems, and because his disciplinary record was so well known he followed every word of his instructor without deviation and never questioned an instruction. He impressed his course commander *Oberleutnant* Klaus Quaet-Faslem so much that his flying career was saved and he passed. He was then transferred to the 3rd Supplementary Fighter Group in September 1940.

In October he transferred into the 1st Group of the 3rd Fighter Wing and his first assignment was with the aircraft of his Group when they gave cover to Hitler's visit to Belgium. On 25 October his Bf 109E-3 slid off the runway at Saint-Omer-Wizernes and was destroyed, Schuck being lucky to escape serious injury. After coming out of hospital in December he was promoted to *Unteroffizier* and at the same time his unit was detached from the 3rd Fighter Wing and renamed the 7th Squadron of the 5th Fighter Wing. From January 1942 his Squadron was relocated to Norway, at first to Stavanger-Forus and then arriving in February in Bodø. His Squadron then moved to Pechenga, arriving on 24 April, where Schuck claimed his first aerial victory on 15 May 1942, a MiG-3, and four days later he was awarded the Iron Cross 2nd Class. He claimed two victories on 28 May and four on 5 June, but post-war scrutiny has reclassified these last two victories as unconfirmed. He claimed a Hurricane on 13 June and the following day was awarded the Iron Cross 1st Class, presented to him by *Generaloberst* Hans-Jürgen Stumpff who was visiting the 2nd and 3rd Groups at the time. Promoted to *Feldwebel* on 1 December, by the end of the year he had claimed a total of fifteen victories. He claimed three more victories in January 1943, and after claiming his 25th aerial victory was awarded the *Luftwaffe* Honour Goblet on 23 March. On 22 May, Schuck shot down four aircraft, which included three P-39 Airacobras, to claim his 35th victory and as a result was awarded the German Cross in Gold on 24 June 1943.

On 3 September, Schuck, now attached to the 9th Squadron, was scrambled to fend off an air attack on Pechenga airfield. They encountered a flight of five Hurricane fighters near Murmashi and three were shot down, two by Schuck. He claimed three P-40s on 12 September, another four on the 14th and three on the 20th, which included his 50th victory. By the end of the month he had claimed another seven victories and was promoted to *Oberfeldwebel* on 1 October 1943. On 29 January 1944 the 3rd Group flew its first mission in force as all three Squadrons took off and encountered a number of Yakovlev Yak-7 fighters. Schuck claimed two of them. On 17 March he claimed seven aircraft to become an 'ace-in-a-day' and was also made an officer candidate. He claimed his 75th victory on 1 April when he shot down two P-40s, and he claimed three Yak-9s the following day. He claimed six victories to become an 'ace-in-a-day' for the second time on 7 April and the following day was awarded the Knight's Cross in recognition of his 75th victory.

In May parts of the 3rd Group were relocated to Svartres and on the 25th Schuck and members of his Group were scrambled to fend off almost eighty Soviet aircraft attacking a German convoy. The Group claimed thirty-three victories, and Schuck shot down six to become an 'ace-in-a-day' for the third time, which included his 90th victory. On 26 May he claimed four aircraft, and became an 'ace-in-a-day' for the 4th time on 15 June when he shot down six aircraft which included his 100th victory, the 73rd pilot to achieve this number. On the 17th, he had his most successful day as a fighter pilot when he claimed eleven aircraft and apparently he received a case of champagne as a token of appreciation from the Commander-in-Chief of the 5th Air Fleet *General der Flieger* Josef Kammhuber. He continued to claim victories during June, and on the 27th he shot down four aircraft and the following day he became an 'ace-in-a-day' again when he claimed seven aircraft. On 4 July he claimed another four victories and on the 17th he claimed seven victories and on the 22nd he claimed another seven, to become an 'ace-in-a-day' for the seventh time.

In August he was promoted to *Leutnant* and appointed *Staffelkapitän* of the 10th Squadron, and claimed four more victories on the 17th. On the 23rd he claimed five victories and an ace-in-a-day' yet again and he claimed his 150th victory, the 26th fighter pilot to achieve this total. During September he claimed a total of seventeen victories and now had a total of 171. He was wounded on the 19th during combat with an Il-2 aircraft at the Pechenga airfield. His aircraft was hit in the cockpit and glass splinters struck his check and nose. One penetrated his jaw and stuck in his teeth and he needed surgery to remove it. On 30 September, whilst recovering in hospital he received the news that he had been awarded the Knight's Cross with Oakleaves.

On 10 November Schuck was promoted to *Oberleutnant* and on New Year's Day 1945 he was best man at the wedding of his friend and fellow fighter ace, *Hauptmann* Theodor Weissenberger. Schuck returned to his unit on 10 January, and then the following month his squadron was scrambled to intercept twelve American P-51 Mustangs from No. 65 Squadron and ten De Havilland Mosquitoes attacking German shipping in Norangsfjorden. During the encounter Schuck claimed two aircraft, thought to be P-51s, but they were never confirmed victories. On 18 March he took over as *Staffelkapitän* of the 3rd Squadron of the 7th Fighter Wing after the death of *Oberleutnant* Hans Waldmann, and here he flew the new Messerschmitt Me 262 jet fighter. On 20 March he made his maiden flight in the new aircraft, then four days later whilst flying together with another Me 262 on a familiarisation flight they spotted enemy fighters in their vicinity. Schuck immediately set course for the formation and spotted three P-51s about 75 miles south-west of Berlin. At full speed, he and his wingman came up behind the US fighters and opened fire. His wingman claimed the first one and Schuck eventually claimed the other two, as the P-51 pilots were swerving and diving, trying to shake off Schuck. He hit the first one and it blew apart almost immediately, while the wing of the second broke away and it plummeted to earth. Schuck claimed another P-51 near Brunswick on 28 March, and on 7 April he shot down a P-38 reconnaissance aircraft piloted by Captain William T. Heily from the 30th Reconnaissance Squadron of the USAAF 9th Air Force.

On 10 April Schuck claimed four B-17 Flying Fortress bombers in just eight minutes, and just after shooting down the 4th B-17 he was fired upon by a P-51 and his aircraft was struck in the left engine. With his power failing and with low fuel, he headed for Jüterbog airfield with his engine trailing smoke and whilst being chased by two Mustangs. Schuck decided to bail out between Brandenburg-Briest and Jüterbog, and landed safely. He was picked up by a baker on a bicycle and taken to a nearby mill and offered a coffee. He had sprained both ankles and spent a brief time in hospital but before he had fully recovered the war ended. After the war on a visit to the United States in May 2005, Schuck met one of the Mustang pilots that had been chasing him, a Lieutenant Joseph A. Peterburs, and they became good friends. Schuck died on 27 March 2015 in Neunkirchen, Saarland, Germany.

Günther SPECHT

Oberstleutnant

Knight's Cross: Awarded on 8 April 1944 as *Major* and *Gruppenkommandeur* of the 2nd Group of the 11th Fighter Wing for operations over England and the Western Front.

Günther Specht claimed thirty-one aerial victories, of which fifteen were four-engined bombers, whilst flying combat missions over the Western Front during the Second World War. He was born on 13 November 1914 in Frankenstein, Lower Silesia. He joined the *Luftwaffe* in 1935 and trained as a fighter pilot.

At the beginning of the war in September 1939 he was already an *Oberleutnant* attached to the 3rd Squadron of the 26th Destroyer Wing and was supposed to have been equipped with the new Messerschmitt Bf 110 twin-engined fighter but none had been supplied. Instead the entire Wing was equipped with the Bf 109C and D single-engined fighters. He took no part in the Polish campaign, and instead his Wing was based on the North Sea coast near Wilhelmshaven.

On 29 September 1939 he claimed two Hampden twin-engined bombers over south-east Heligoland and was shortly after awarded the Iron Cross 2nd Class. On 3 December he claimed a Wellington bomber north-west of Heligoland and was himself shot down by Corporal Copley, a Wellington tail gunner, and ditched in the sea injured, later being rescued by the German Navy. He had lost an eye during the

(Deutsches Wehrkundearchiv)

engagement with the Wellington and spent the next six months recovering and getting himself back to full operational status, and had been awarded the Iron Cross 1st Class. He returned to his Squadron in May 1940, now equipped with the Bf 110 twin-engined fighter, as Adjutant, flying the occasional combat mission whenever he could. On 23 May he claimed three Spitfires over Calais, but during the course of the air battle with the RAF fighters his Bf 110 had been badly damaged. His rear gunner was wounded and he made a forced landing back at his base. He was badly injured and spent time in hospital, once again away from front-line duty. After he had recovered he served as a staff officer and took up training duties for about a year. He wanted to get back to flying. He was a perfectionist with a high sense of duty, and had put on his aircraft a design of a pencil superimposed on a chevron (a winged pencil) as a comment on being deskbound. On 16 September 1941 he was appointed *Staffelkapitän* of a newly formed night-fighter training unit, and on 31 October he was made *Gruppenkommandeur* of the 3rd Group of the 1st Night Fighter School based at Ingolstadt-Manching.

From February 1943 he was initially assigned to the 10th Squadron of the 1st Fighter Wing and on the 26th he claimed a B-17 Flying Fortress, his first four-engined bomber. This was the beginning of a new war for Specht. The US 8th Air Force had started their bombing offensive on Germany's industrial sites and he was ready for them! On 27 March he was appointed *Staffelkapitän* of the newly-formed 7th Squadron of the 1st Fighter Wing, and by May he had been promoted to *Gruppenkommandeur* of the 2nd Group of the 11th Fighter Wing, based in Jever. His new command was a special Group, issued with Fw 190 and Bf 109G-6 fighters, a strong force in Germany's fight against Allied bombers. Throughout 1943 the *Luftwaffe* took advantage of the large bombers flying over Germany unescorted by fighters, none more so than Specht. He claimed three victories in May, two B-17s and one B-24 Liberator, his 9th and 10th victories. He soon became one of the top fighter aces specializing in shooting down bombers and by mid-August he had claimed sixteen victories, of which ten were four-engined bombers. His skill and bravery was recognised on 23 August when he was awarded the *Luftwaffe* Honour Goblet. He claimed three more bombers during October and claimed a P-38 Lightning over Fürstmann on 13 November, his 20th victory, and on the 25th he was awarded the German Cross in Gold.

He continued to be successful into 1944 and was promoted to *Major* in January and shortly after claimed two victories but both fighters remain unconfirmed victories. On 11 February his group engaged escort fighters returning from a raid on Frankfurt and Specht shot down Second Lieutenant Richard McDonald of the 354th Fighter Group who crashed his P-51 Mustang near Oberalben. Specht claimed a P-47 on 21 February and shot down a P-51 and a B-17 bomber the following day. He had by now claimed twenty-seven aerial victories of which fifteen were four-engined bombers and on 8 April Specht was awarded the Knight's Cross. On 15 April he was appointed *Kommodore* of the 11th Fighter Wing and his orders were to do as much as he could to slow down the Allied bombing offensive. However, this was an impossible task and his units were decimated over Normandy during June and July 1944. Specht himself was wounded in July, suffering head injuries during an emergency landing, but despite being in severe pain he remained on duty. The Allies were now sending huge numbers of bombers by day and night to destroy German industrial and military targets and they were now protected by the P-51 Mustang fighter which could provide fighter cover right into the heart of the Reich.

During Operation Market Garden, the Allied airborne landings in the Netherlands, Specht claimed two RAF Typhoons west of Arnhem, his 29th and 30th victories. On 5 December he claimed his last victory, another P-51, and Hitler ordered his final, desperate attack on the West that month through the Ardennes Forest. However, weather conditions hampered the attack and grounded the *Luftwaffe*, but on New Year's Day the weather improved and Germany launched Operation Bodenplatte – virtually all available fighter groups in the West were allocated to this mission. For this mission Specht wore his full dress uniform with medals, instead of his flight suit. He flew his Fw 190A-9 from Darmstadt-Griesheim towards Aschaffenburg together with a large range of aircraft towards Belgium. Later that day his aircraft disappeared, it was believed to have been shot down by anti-aircraft fire over Brussels. It was later confirmed he had been killed and was posthumously promoted to *Oberstleutnant* and recommended for the Oakleaves, which was never confirmed. Specht, who had been shot down six times during the war was a perfectionist and a highly skilled pilot, even with only one eye! He also wrote detailed mission log reports and wouldn't allow women to visit men at the airfield – even his own wife was turned away, telling her to put herself 'on ice' until after the war!

Hugo FREY

Hauptmann

Knight's Cross: Awarded posthumously on 4 May 1944 as *Hauptmann* and *Staffelkapitän* of the 7th Squadron of the 11th Fighter Wing for operations over Poland, France and the Western Front.

Hugo Frey claimed seventeen aerial victories during the Second World War, all on the Western Front, and all but two were four-engined bombers. He was something of a specialist when it came to shooting down large US bombers which took great skill and courage. Frey was born on 14 April 1925 in Heilbronn, northern Baden-Württemberg and upon leaving school he joined the *Luftwaffe*.

At the outbreak of war in September 1939 he was flying with the 1st Fighter Squadron of the 2nd Training Wing. He claimed his first aerial victory over the area of Poczalkowo, Poland on 4 September and his second victory, a French Potez 630 fighter over south-west Amiens, on 27 May 1940. However, both were later reclassified as unconfirmed

(Deutsches Wehrkundearchiv)

victories, but nevertheless he was awarded the Iron Cross 2nd Class shortly afterwards. In June he remained patrolling the French coastline and later in the year his unit returned to Germany. In December he joined the 2nd Squadron of the 1st Fighter Wing and was for a time stationed in the Normandy area of France. His squadron was later sent to Düsseldorf for refitting and from July 1941 flew from its new air base in Katwijk, a coastal town in the Netherlands. From September he flew from Jever and patrolled the skies over Germany, promoted to *Oberleutnant* and on 26 October was appointed *Staffelkapitän* of the 2nd Squadron.

In early 1943 his group was equipped with the Messerschmitt Bf 109G-1, and on 27 January he claimed his first confirmed aerial victory, a B-17 Flying Fortress four-engined bomber north-west of Tossens. Shortly after this he was awarded the Iron Cross 1st Class. From early April he briefly took command of the 5th Squadron of the 11th Fighter Wing, and from 1 May he commanded the 7th Squadron. By this time he had achieved his fourth victory, another B-17, and on 28 July he claimed one more over Hanover. He claimed three more four-engined bombers during October, and another one on 5 November and claimed three victories on the 26th, two B-17s and a P-47 Thunderbolt, and he was awarded the German Cross in Gold on 25 November. He claimed three victories during December, all B-17s, and on 11 January 1944 he claimed two more, but they would be his last.

On 6 March 1944 it was reported that Frey had shot down four B-17s, each at short range, but return fire from the fifth bomber had sent his Focke-Wulf Fw 190 spiralling down to his death near Emmen, Drente in the Netherlands. However, the authors Mathews and Foreman who have done extensive research in their study *Luftwaffe Aces* do not report these final four victories. It cannot be denied that Frey was something of a four-engined bomber specialist and his loss was a hard blow, coming just four days after the death of the 2nd Fighter Wing's *Kommodore*, *Oberstleutnant* Egon Mayer. Frey was posthumously awarded the Knight's Cross. He now lies at the military cemetery in Ysselsteyn, Netherlands in Block AX, Row 9, Grave No. 20.

Otto WÜRFEL

Leutnant

Knight's Cross: Awarded on 4 May 1944 as *Oberfeldwebel* and fighter pilot attached to the 8th Squadron of the 51st Fighter Wing '*Mölders*' for operations over the Soviet Union.

(Deutsches Wehrkundearchiv)

Otto Würfel claimed seventy-seven victories during the Second World War, all whilst flying 225 combat missions over the Eastern Front. He was born on 3 December 1920 in Uelzen, a town in north-east Lower Saxony, Germany and he joined the *Luftwaffe* in October 1939.

From October 1940, *Gefreiter* Würfel trained as a fighter pilot and was promoted to *Unteroffizier* in October 1941. With the completion of his training in mid-1942 he was assigned to the 9th Squadron of the 51st Fighter Wing. He was flying from Dugino, a village in Rostov in the Soviet Union, flying in support of the 9th Army. In August during Soviet air raids his Group lost seven aircraft and another ten were damaged, and so his chance to score his first victories was delayed for a time. Finally on 2 September he claimed an LaGG-3 fighter, his first victory of the war, and the following day he shot down two more. He claimed a Petlyakov Pe-2 dive-bomber on the 4th and the following day he was awarded the Iron Cross 2nd Class. He claimed an Ilyushin Il-2 ground-attack aircraft on 9 and 10 September, and in November his Group converted to the Focke-Wulf Fw 190A-2 and A-3. In early 1943 he flew over the Rshev area and from 28 January his Group moved to Orel and he claimed his seventh victory the same day. In March his Group relocated to Krasnogvardeysky near Leningrad and on the 18th Würfel claimed his eighth victory and a few days later was awarded the Iron Cross 1st Class. Returning to Orel in May his Group moved to Bryansk in July and from early August until early September he served as a fighter instructor in France.

Würfel returned to his Squadron on 3 September, flying from Poltava in the Ukraine and newly promoted to *Feldwebel*. He claimed two Il-2s on 10 September, another the following day and two more Il-2s on the 12th. He claimed four more victories on the 15th, and on the 20th he claimed another Il-2 aircraft, his 20th aerial victory. From October he flew with his Group from Orsha in Belarus, flying the Fw 190A-5 and he and the Group remained there until the end of the year. He claimed another twenty-two victories during October, which included three on the 14th and the 21st, which included his 40th aerial victory. In November he claimed nine victories, and on the 22nd he claimed his 50th. He was awarded the *Luftwaffe* Honour Goblet on 13 December and received the German Cross in Gold on 26 December.

In January 1944 his Group moved to Polotsk in Belarus and from February he was flying from Bobruisk. He claimed four victories during January and shot down four aircraft on 6 February, which included his 60th victory, and on the 7th he claimed four victories and two more on the 9th and three on the 12th. He became an 'ace-in-a-day' on 21 February when he claimed six victories, which included his 75th. On the 22nd he claimed his last two victories of the war. The following day his luck ran out. He collided with his wingman *Oberfeldwebel* Heinrich Dittlmann who disappeared. He and his Bf 109 where never found. Würfel bailed out and was taken prisoner by the Soviets, and he later died in Prison Camp 280/5 near Stalino on 22 December 1944. He is buried today in Donczk in the Ukraine. He was awarded the Knight's Cross on 4 May, whilst a prisoner and was posthumously promoted to *Leutnant*. Würfel claimed seventy aerial victories in less than 11 months.

Gerhard HOFFMANN

Leutnant

Knight's Cross: Awarded on 14 May 1944 as *Fahnenjunker-Feldwebel* and fighter pilot with the 5th Squadron of the 52nd Fighter Wing in recognition of his 125th aerial victory on the Eastern Front.

Gerhard Hoffmann claimed 130 aerial victories, all on the Eastern Front, and he destroyed 128 vehicles on the ground during the Second World War. He was born on 6 November 1919 in Nieden, Johannisburg in East Prussia, and joined the *Luftwaffe* in early 1940.

Hoffmann trained as a fighter pilot and served as an instructor until June 1942 when he transferred to the 52nd Fighter Wing, joining the 4th Squadron as an *Unteroffizier*. He flew as part of the 2nd Group in Sswoy south of Kursk and during the Soviet summer offensive his unit followed the 6th Army. By September he was flying missions in support of the 1st Army, flying as far as the Caucasus. He claimed his first victory on 26 October, an LaGG-3 fighter, and soon after his squadron

(Deutsches Wehrkundearchiv)

was withdrawn due to the Soviet counter-attack and Hoffmann then flew missions in support of the troops at Stalingrad. On 8 December he claimed two P-40s near Bassargino and was awarded the Iron Cross 2nd Class. At the beginning of 1943 his squadron was in Gigant, west of Ssalsk, where he claimed an La-5 on 25 January 1944. In April his group moved to Anapa on the Black Sea and he claimed a Yak-1 fighter on 19 April and claimed a further two victories the following day, and claimed three more on the 21st. Shortly after he was awarded the Iron Cross 1st Class and by the end of May had achieved twenty-two victories.

At the beginning of June Hoffmann was promoted to *Feldwebel* and claimed his 25th victory over the area of the Black Sea on the 8th. Awarded the *Luftwaffe* Honour Goblet on 9 August in recognition of his 25th aerial victory. He claimed his 30th victory on 29 August over Kharkov, and claimed two more on 5 September and had by the end of the month achieved his 42nd victory. By

November his unit had retreated to Poland because of the Soviet advance and he had been awarded the German Cross in Gold on 12 December for his 40th victory.

In early 1944 his Group was in Bagerowo near Kerch and now equipped with the Bf 109G and deployed to the southern sector of the Eastern Front. He was then appointed a *Fahnenjunker-Feldwebel*, an officer candidate. Hoffmann claimed two victories on 10 February and three two days later. On 2 March he claimed two victories which included his 50th victory, and the Group moved to the Crimea and then into southern Ukraine. Hoffmann now began to claim victories at a fast rate. He claimed four on 11 March, and by 2 April he had achieved his 60th victory. He became an 'ace-in-a-day' on 8 April when he claimed five victories, a Yak-1 and four Il-2 ground-attack aircraft. On 9 April he claimed another five victories which included his 70th victory, to become an 'ace-in-a-day' for the second time. He claimed his 80th victory on 14 April, and on the 17th he became an 'ace-in-a-day' again when he claimed five victories, which included his 90th. The next day he claimed six victories to become an 'ace-in-a-day' yet again, and he claimed four on the 22nd – including his 100th victory. He claimed his 110th victory on 4 May, an Il-2 over the Black Sea near Sevastopol. He continued to claim more victories in May and on the 7th he became an 'ace-in-a-day' for the fifth time when he shot down six aircraft over the area of Sevastopol. He had now claimed 125 victories and on 14 May was awarded the Knight's Cross after achieving so many victories in a short amount of time.

In early June 1944 Hoffmann was promoted to *Leutnant* and was now serving as an instructor with a fighter school – it was the policy of the *Luftwaffe* to remove gifted fighter pilots from front-line duty so they could pass on their skills to younger pilots. From early November he was back on the front line as *Staffelkapitän* of the 4th Squadron of Fighter Replacement Wing 1, and on 8 March 1945 he claimed two Yak-3 fighters. On the 15th he was again transferred as *Staffelkapitän* of the 11th Squadron of the 52nd Fighter Wing and flew from Randnitz in Czechoslovakia. On 10 April he claimed his 130th and last victory, a Soviet P-39. The next day he took off from Görlitz on a supply escort mission to Breslau and it is believed that he crashed on his way due to unknown circumstances and he remains missing.

Peter 'Bonifazius' DÜTTMANN

Leutnant

Knight's Cross: Awarded on 9 June 1944 as *Leutnant* and fighter pilot with the 5th Squadron of the 52nd Fighter Wing for operations over the Soviet Union and for claiming his 90th aerial victory.

Peter Düttmann claimed a total of 147 victories with another forty-five being unconfirmed whilst flying 398 combat missions over the Eastern Front during the Second World War. He was born on 23 May 1923 in Giessen, a historical town in Hesse, Germany and he joined the *Luftwaffe* in late 1942.

Once qualified as a pilot he flew with the Advanced Training Group East until May 1943 when he was transferred to the 52nd Fighter Wing in the Soviet Union. He was attached to the 5th Squadron, part of the 2nd Group, and flew from its base in Anapa on the Black Sea. On 21 May Düttmann claimed his first victory, a Polikarpov U-2 training biplane north-east of Krassnodar, claiming his second victory on 10 June. He claimed his third victory on 10 July, and the following day, shortly after claiming his fourth victory, he had to ditch in the sea south-east of Anapa after damage received from the Boston

(Deutsches Wehrkundearchiv)

bomber he had just shot down. By the end of the month Düttmann had claimed nine victories and on 6 August was awarded the Iron Cross 2nd Class. Three days later he had to make an emergency belly landing in his aircraft after receiving combat damage whilst flying between Kharkov and Belgorod, but he wasn't wounded. He was awarded the Flying Clasp for Fighters in Gold on 17 August and received the Iron Cross 1st Class on the 25th after claiming his 16th victory. During this time he had been shot down twice more and had to make an emergency landing on the 18th in the area of Kharkov and five days later he was wounded when his Bf 109G-6 was struck by anti-aircraft fire.

Düttmann was unhurt when his aircraft was hit by bullets fired by a Soviet Ilyushin Il-2 on 18 September and he had to make an emergency landing at Karlowka airfield. Then seven days later his Bf 109 was struck by anti-aircraft fire and he managed to glide and land his aircraft near Poltava. On 1 October, now a *Feldwebel*, he was once again injured when his aircraft was struck by bullets from an enemy aircraft and he had to make an emergency landing. Then nine days later his aircraft was hit again, this time in the oil tank and the engine cut out. He had to glide for almost 25 minutes and crash-landed at Bevesowk airfield, once again unhurt. By the end of December he had claimed his 25th victory. Although at the time he had claimed forty victories only twenty-five would ever be confirmed victories.

On 23 January 1944 his aircraft was struck again in the engine by a Soviet Il-2 ground-attack aircraft and he managed to land safely. Later that day during anther mission his aircraft was attacked and struck by bullets from three Airacobras and again escaped and landed safely at his base. On 1 February Düttmann was promoted to *Fahnenjunker-Feldwebel*, an officer candidate, and a week later he was awarded the *Luftwaffe* Honour Goblet. He claimed his 43rd victory on 13 March, and that same day his Bf 109 was struck in the engine and oil tank and he had to make yet another emergency landing, and was unhurt. He claimed four victories on 16 and 17 March, which included his 50th aerial victory. The next day he was shot down. His Bf 109G-6 was hit in its engine and he was forced to make a belly landing in the area of Aissul in the Crimea. He claimed three victories on 26 March, all Yak-1 fighters, and in early April he was commissioned as a *Leutnant*.

On 7 April he was unhurt when his aircraft was hit by a Yak-7 during combat and he had to make a forced landing at Karankuta airfield. The following day he shot down his 60th aerial victory and the same day his aircraft was hit by infantry fire and he had to head back to his home airfield for repairs. He claimed two Il-2 aircraft on 9 April and shortly after this was himself shot down after receiving a direct hit in the oil tank and had to glide back to Karankuta airfield. He claimed two victories on 10 April and became an 'ace-in-a-day' the following day when he shot down six aircraft which included his 70th victory. On the 15th Düttmann was rewarded for his bravery and victories scored when he was awarded the German Cross in Gold. By the end of the month he had achieved seventy-six victories and he added more to his score during the following months. On 6 May he claimed three Yak-7 fighters shot down near Bjelbek and on the 7th he became an 'ace-in-a-day' again when he shot down nine aircraft, which included his 90th victory.

On 26 May Düttmann blacked out during an exercise flight and was lucky to have regained consciousness and land his aircraft. It was obvious he was suffering from combat fatigue. He was completely exhausted and put on extended leave for four months. On 9 June he was informed that he had been awarded the Knight's Cross which was presented to him when he returned to duty. He returned to combat in September and by the end of the month he had claimed thirteen victories, including his 100th. He claimed two more on 16 and 18 October, and claimed his 116th victory during the afternoon of 31 October. The next day he claimed four victories in just six minutes over Budapest, which included his 120th victory, but he had been wounded and upon landing collided with another Bf 109. He claimed three more victories on the 13th and was once again wounded when his aircraft was hit by an Il-2 and he had to bail out, landing south-west of Jászbrény, Hungary. He was soon rescued.

On 1 November Düttmann was involved in an accident on the ground at Ferihegy airfield near Budapest, resulting in the death of his wingman *Unteroffizier* Heinrich Wester. Low on fuel Wester had landed his Bf 109G-14 first, but his engine seized due to lack of fuel, leaving him sitting on the runway. Düttmann landed next, but did not see Wester and crashed into his aircraft, killing him instantly and injuring himself. On 23 December, now fully recovered, Düttmann was appointed *Staffelkapitän* of the 5th Squadron of the 52nd Fighter Wing. He was once again wounded on 3 March 1945 when his Bf 109G-10 was hit by anti-aircraft fire and he was forced to land behind enemy lines, about 12 miles east south-east of Gárdony, but he managed to walk to safety. He claimed his 130th victory on 14 March, a Boston bomber, and by 9 April he had claimed his 140th victory. He claimed two victories the next day and on the 13th claimed four victories and he claimed his 147th and last victory on 15 April. On the 24th he was hit by tank fire and had to make an emergency landing with his wheels up, but managed to land safely at Hörsching airfield. He made only two or three more flights before the war ended.

Düttmann was shot down at least twenty-one times and managed to destroy at least two enemy tanks and must be one of the luckiest *Luftwaffe* pilots of the war. He died on 9 January 2001 in Echterdingen in Baden-Württemberg, Germany.

Johann 'Hans' EHLERS

Major

Knight's Cross: Awarded as *Oberleutnant* and *Staffelkapitän* of the 3rd Squadron of the 1st Fighter Wing '*Oesau*' on 9 June 1944 for operations over France, England, the Soviet Union and the Western Front.

(Deutsches Wehrkundearchiv)

Johann 'Hans' Ehlers claimed a total of forty-eight victories, including twenty-two four-engined bombers, of which nineteen were B-17 Flying Fortresses. He was born on 15 July 1914 in Hennestedt near Itzehoe, Holstein in Germany and served with the *Luftwaffe* from 1936. He was a member of the ground crew in Adolf Galland's squadron of the 88th Fighter Group during the Spanish Civil War, where he was awarded the Spanish Cross in Silver with Swords on 14 April 1939.

When he returned to Germany he decided that he wanted to be a fighter pilot and began his training at Salzwedel in August, joining the 2nd Squadron of the 3rd Fighter Wing in December 1939. From May 1940 he participated in the Battle of France as an *Unteroffizier* serving with the 1st Group of the 3rd Fighter Wing. He claimed his first two victories on 18 May, a Spitfire and a Hurricane over Valenciennes, but later that day he was shot down and after making an emergency landing he was taken prisoner by the French. He was later reunited with his unit when he was rescued after Dunkirk. He was awarded the Iron Cross 2nd Class on his return and soon promoted to *Feldwebel* and claimed his third victory on 26 August over Calais. He claimed his fourth victory on 5 September during the Battle of Britain and the same day he collided with a Spitfire over Canterbury and had to nurse his stricken aircraft back to his base in Colembert, France. He was badly wounded and spent several months in hospital before returning to action in January 1941. Soon after claiming his fifth victory on 5 February he was awarded the Iron Cross 1st Class and on 1 March was promoted to *Oberfeldwebel*.

In April he transferred to the 3rd Squadron and from June was deployed to the Soviet Union whilst still attached to the 3rd Fighter Wing. He saw action during the opening day of Operation Barbarossa, the invasion of the Soviet Union, and claimed a Polikarpov I-16 monoplane fighter. Ehlers claimed another victory on the 25th and two more the following day, his 11th and 12th victories. He was injured when his Bf 109F-1 hit an obstruction on the ground on 30 June. He claimed four victories in August, which included the 1,000th victory of the 3rd Fighter Wing. He claimed his last victory over the Soviet Union on 11 October, an Il-2 ground-attack aircraft, whilst flying with the 8th Squadron.

From January 1942 he served with the 6th Squadron of the 1st Fighter Wing in Katwijk, Holland. By mid-May his squadron, part of the 2nd Group had moved to Woensdrecht in the southern Netherlands. On 19 June Ehlers claimed two Spitfires, his 15th and 16th victories. On 6 December he claimed his first four-engined bomber, a B-17, shot down over Ostend. He continued to fly bomber escort missions during January 1943, claiming a Spitfire on the 22nd and another on 11 March. He claimed two more victories on 3 May and one the following day and another on the 14th. He claimed his 24th victory on 10 June and although he claimed another on the 22nd, this remains unconfirmed. He was promoted to *Leutnant* in July and transferred into the 2nd Squadron and from August he was named as Acting *Staffelkapitän*. That same day he claimed two B-17 bombers, his 25th and 26th victories, and he claimed three more during October.

On 8 October after claiming a B-17 he ran out of ammunition and decided to ram the already heavily damaged bomber whilst over Kalle. He quickly had to bail out of his Fw 190 and was badly injured, returning to action a month later. For this act and for claiming thirty victories he was awarded the German Cross in Gold on 24 October, personally presented to him by *Reichsmarschall* Göring at Deelen, Holland. In early November Ehlers was confirmed as *Staffelkapitän* and in December he claimed six B-17 bombers. He claimed another B-17 on 5 January 1944, and two more on the 30th (one was later reclassified as unconfirmed). He claimed his 40th victory on 8 March, a P-47 Thunderbolt fighter over Hannover, and on 13 April he was wounded by return fire from a B-17 and had to make a belly landing near Gütersdorf. Three days later he was named as *Gruppenkommandeur* of the 1st Group of the 1st Fighter Wing, and was promoted to *Hauptmann* a week later. He claimed two further victories in May, a B-17 and a B-24 bomber and was awarded the Knight's Cross, on 9 June, in recognition of his 45th victory, which included at least twenty four-engined bombers. He claimed a B-17 over Gotha-Erfurt on 21 November and on Christmas Day he shot down a B-24.

On 27 December, whilst on a mission to protect ground forces in the area of Dinant-Rochefort during the Battle of the Bulge, his aircraft was shot down by Allied fighters. He had been shot down twelve times but this time his luck ran out. He crashed near Bereborn, Eifel in Germany and was killed. He was posthumously promoted to *Major* and was later submitted for a posthumous Oakleaves but it was never approved.

Otto GAISER

Leutnant

Knight's Cross: Awarded posthumously on 9 June 1944 as *Oberfeldwebel* and fighter pilot with the 10th Squadron of the 51st Fighter Wing '*Mölders*' for operations over the Soviet Union.

Otto Gaiser claimed sixty-six aerial victories in just ten months, all of them on the Eastern Front during the Second World War. He was born on 5 October 1919 in Reutlingen, Baden-Württemberg and he joined the *Luftwaffe* in 1941. With his training complete he was assigned to the 10th Squadron of the 51st Fighter Wing in December 1942. As part of the 4th Group his squadron flew from Vitebsk and was at first equipped with the Messerschmitt Bf 109F-6, and flew combat missions in the area around Velikiye Luki. In February his squadron was equipped with the Focke-Wulf Fw 190A-4 and by August the rest of his Group had been converted.

On 16 March 1943 he claimed his first victory, a Soviet Lavochkin LaGG-3 fighter over north Vazma, and claimed his second victory on 11 April and a further two victories, both Ilyushin Il-2 ground-attack aircraft, on 7 May. He was awarded the Iron Cross 2nd Class shortly after, and just after he achieved his fifth victory on 14 May he was awarded the Iron Cross 1st Class. He claimed his 10th victory on 11 July, and six days later he claimed his 15th victory south-south-east of Maloarkhangelsk. Promoted to *Feldwebel* a few weeks later he claimed three victories on 2 August and claimed another three on 10 August, becoming an 'ace-in-a-day' four days later when he claimed five Il-2s. He claimed his 30th victory on 18 August and continued to claim victories at a rapid pace, claiming two victories on 20 September and six days later he became an 'ace-in-a-day' for the second time, when he shot down five aircraft. On 8 October he claimed his 50th victory, a Yakovlev Yak-9 fighter over Perewolotschnaja.

(Deutsches Wehrkundearchiv)

Promoted to *Oberfeldwebel* on 14 October, that same day he claimed three victories, and claimed his 60th victory, a Lavochkin La-5 fighter south-south-west of Dnepropetrovsk, on 28 November. He claimed a single victory on 12 January 1944, and claimed four more victories three days later. On 22 January he took off in his Focke-Wulf Fw 190 at 10:25, and reported an encounter with four Il-2 aircraft east of Lubyan 20 minutes later but was never seen again. Aircraft were sent out in search of Gaiser and reported heavy ground fire in the area and it was assumed his aircraft had been damaged and he was forced to land, or it had simply blown up. He disappeared and there has never been any trace of him. He was promoted to *Leutnant*, and awarded the German Cross in Gold on 28 January 1944; the *Luftwaffe* Honour Goblet on 3 April and the Knight's Cross on 9 June, all posthumously.

Hans 'Specker' GRÜNBERG

Oberleutnant

Knight's Cross: Awarded on 9 June 1944 as *Leutnant* and fighter pilot with the 5th Squadron of the 3rd Fighter Wing '*Udet*', for operations over the Soviet Union and Western Front.

Hans Grünberg claimed seventy-eight aerial victories during the Second World War, of which sixty-one were gained over the Eastern Front. He was born in Gross-Fahlenwerder in the Soldin area of Pomerania on 8 July 1917. He joined the *Luftwaffe* in early 1942 and was assigned to the 5th Squadron of the 3rd Fighter in May after the completion of his training.

He flew over the Soviet Union as an *Unteroffizier* from June 1942 as part of the 2nd Group, claiming his first aerial victory on 19 August, an Ilyushin DB-3 bomber. He claimed his second victory on 15 October, a Lavochkin LaGG-3 fighter over Sparak. On 16 July he was shot down during combat with a Yakovlev Yak-1 fighter but he parachuted from

(Deutsches Wehrkundearchiv)

his aircraft without injury. By the end of November, Grünberg, now a *Feldwebel*, had claimed six victories and had been awarded the Iron Cross 2nd Class. It wasn't long before he was presented with the Iron Cross 1st Class when towards the end of December he had claimed his 11th victory.

During early 1943 his squadron moved with the rest of the Group to Rostov, due to the Soviet advance. They moved again in February to Makeyevka where they stayed until April when they moved into the Crimea. Grünberg was successful during April, claiming two I-16 fighters on the 11th, two on the 20th and 21st and claimed his 20th victory on 23 April. By the end of the month he had claimed a total of twenty-six victories and later claimed two LaGG-3 fighters on 8 May and claimed his 30th victory on the 31st. He claimed seven aerial victories on 5 July, all Il-2 ground-attack aircraft, to become an 'ace-in-a-day'. The following day he claimed another Il-2, and on the 7th he claimed two more and a Lavochkin La-5 fighter over Kharkov. He claimed his 50th victory on 12 July and four days later he was shot down himself and had to bail out of his aircraft due to engine failure. By 31 July he had recorded his 60th aerial victory, another Il-2, becoming something of an expert in claiming these aircraft. Promoted to *Oberfeldwebel* in August, he was awarded the *Luftwaffe* Honour Goblet on the 6th and the German Cross in Gold on the 31 August.

At the end of August he was transferred with his Group to the Western Front and was now flying against the might of the USAAF. He claimed a B-24 Liberator four-engined bomber on 24 February 1944, and almost four weeks later, on 23 March, he claimed a B-17 Flying Fortress over Soest. He claimed two more B-17s during April and was promoted to *Leutnant* and appointed *Staffelkapitän* of the 5th Squadron on 9 May. On 9 June he was awarded the Knight's Cross after claiming his 65th aerial victory. On 14 August he claimed a P-47 Thunderbolt near Montmirail, France, his 70th aerial victory. The following day his Group was expanded, but on the 22nd the Group was withdrawn from all missions and re-located to Ziegenhain in the Rhineland-Palatinate area, to refresh and await further orders. His Group was then used in operations in 'Defence of the Reich'. However by late November the Group was disbanded and the Staff of the 5th Squadron became the 1st Squadron of the 7th Fighter Wing.

Grünberg was stationed in Königsberg and had been promoted to *Oberleutnant* and appointed *Staffelkapitän* of the 1st Squadron. By early February he was flying the new Messerschmitt Me 262 jet fighter from his base in Kaltenkirchen. On 31 March 1945 Grünberg claimed two Lancaster bombers over the Hamburg area. He went onto claim two B-17s on 10 April over the area of Oranienburg. He was shot down by P-51s the following day and had to bail out, he was only slightly wounded. A week later he was shot down, again, by US fighters whilst he was landing at Žatec, Czechoslovakia, but he was unhurt. He claimed his last aerial victory of the war on 19 April, another B-17 bomber over Prague.

He ended the war as part of Galland's famous *Jagdverband* 44 in Salzburg where he handed himself over to the US Army in early May 1945. He claimed a total of five victories whilst flying the Me 262 jet fighter, of which four were heavy bombers, and was one of only twenty-eight pilots to have claimed an aerial victory whilst flying the world's first jet fighter. He also destroyed twenty-seven trucks, one locomotive and one armoured reconnaissance vehicle during ground-attack missions. Grünberg died on 16 January 1998 in Ellerau, Hamburg.

Josef HAIBÖCK

Hauptmann

Knight's Cross: Awarded as *Hauptmann* and commander of the 1st Group of the 3rd Fighter Wing '*Udet*' on 9 June 1944 for operations over France, England, the Soviet Union and the Western Front.

Josef Haiböck flew a total of 604 combat missions and claimed seventy-three aerial victories, of which all but fourteen were achieved over the Eastern Front during the Second World War. He was born on 28 February 1917 in Linz, Austria-Hungary and joined the Austrian Air Force at the age of 20.

From 1938 the Austrian Air Force (*Luftstreitkräfte*) was absorbed into the *Luftwaffe* and in August 1939 Haiböck was commissioned as a *Leutnant*. He was assigned to the 9th Squadron of the 26th

Fighter Wing from December, flying the Bf 109E-1 out of Essen-Mülheim on security patrols on the western border with Belgium and the Netherlands. In early May 1940 he flew missions over Lille and St. Omer and from the 24th he flew over the Dunkirk area. He saw action during the Battle of France, claiming a Spitfire over western Dunkirk on 29 May, his first victory. Two days later he shot down another Spitfire in the same area and was awarded the Iron Cross 2nd Class. After Dunkirk his squadron moved to La Capelle near Boulogne and he took part in the second phase of the Western campaign. He claimed a Hurricane over Beauvais on 8 June and claimed another one over Folkestone on the 15th, and was shortly after awarded the Iron Cross 1st Class.

In August Haiböck was promoted to *Oberleutnant* and on the 28th he claimed a Defiant over Faversham, Kent and on 3 September he claimed his seventh victory, a Spitfire over Southend. In January 1941 his Group moved to Abbeville-Drucat and then in February went to Düsseldorf where it was refreshed and equipped with the new Bf 109E. In early June his group was moved to Maldegem near Bruges in Belgium and he claimed a Spitfire over the area of St. Omer on 17 June, but it was never confirmed. The following month most of his Group, including his squadron, was converted to the Focke-Wulf Fw 190A-1. He claimed another Spitfire on 7 August over Boulogne and claimed one near Calais on 27 September. On 6 December he was appointed *Staffelkapitän* of the 1st Squadron, succeeding *Hauptmann* Josef 'Pips' Priller. From April 1942 he flew protection missions over the port of Brest and from June his squadron flew from Abbeville in France. On 9 May he claimed a Spitfire over the Channel but he lost his wingman *Unteroffizier* Herbert Hofmann who crashed near Rietveld and was killed. By the end of June he had claimed a total of twenty victories but only thirteen were confirmed.

(Deutsches Wehrkundearchiv)

On 29 October Haiböck transferred to the 52nd Fighter Wing and from 30 December was *Staffelkapitän* of the 1st Squadron. He now saw action over the Eastern Front, flying out of Kursk from late January 1943. On the 29th he claimed two victories over Kursk and from February his squadron was based in Kharkov. On 1 February he was unhurt when his Bf 109G made a forced-landing and later that month he was promoted to *Hauptmann* and went onto claim two victories over East Poltava on 28 February, both Il-2 ground-attack aircraft. He claimed his 20th victory on 17 April, an LaGG-3 fighter, and he claimed three more victories that month. On 5 July he shot down three aircraft south-east of Belgorod and claimed his 30th victory on 20 July. He was wounded during an emergency landing on the 22nd, and claimed three victories on 7 August, and by the end of the month had claimed his 50th victory. On 19 September he claimed his 55th victory, and by 2 October Haiböck had shot down his 60th aerial victory and was awarded the German Cross in Gold on 17 October. By the end of that month he had claimed his 68th victory and on 12 November he shot down two Yak-1 fighters to claim his 70th.

On 8 February 1944 Haiböck was appointed *Gruppenkommandeur* of the 1st Group of the 3rd Fighter Wing. He claimed a P-47 Thunderbolt on 24 February over the area of Cochem and Mosel, Germany, but was later reclassified as an unconfirmed victory. The following day his Bf 109 was damaged by a P-47 and he had to make an emergency belly landing. Whilst successfully landing, as he was trying to get out of the cockpit it was attacked by an Allied fighter and he was seriously wounded. He was hospitalized until September 1945, never returning to combat.

He was presented with the Knight's Cross on 9 June 1944 in recognition of his success as a fighter pilot. In 1956 he joined the *Bundesluftwaffe* in Austria and was appointed commander of an Air Division in 1975. He retired as a *Generalmajor* two years later and settled in Salzburg, Austria where he died on 3 July 2002.

(Deutsches Wehrkundearchiv)

109G-4s and moved to Mönchengladbach
On 17 July he claimed a B-17 Flying Fort
a month later he claimed another B-17
August his Group moved to Bönninghar
Faslem was promoted to *Major*. During t
the Pas de Calais and belly-landed at Lill

From early January 1944 his Group w
he claimed a Mosquito over west Amien
On 30 January, following combat he cras
bad weather and was killed. He was post
buried in the Military Cemetery in Mön

Hans 'Bubi' REMMER

Hauptmann

Knight's Cross: Awarded posthumo
Staffelkapitän of the 1st Squadron of the
1944 for operations over North Africa an

Hans Remmer claimed twenty-one victor
engined bombers, over the Western Fro
War. He was born on 17 August 1920 in
Württemberg, Germany and upon joini
trained as a fighter pilot.

From January 1941 he was assigned to t
Squadron of the 27th Fighter Wing as a
transferred to the 1st Squadron and was p
19th, and his first operation was over the
claimed his first aerial victory, a Buffalo
He later claimed a Hurricane over Sidi
was later reclassified as an unconfirmed v
Class. From late October his Squadron, tc
converted to the new Bf 109F-4. On 10
Libya where he claimed three more victor
victories and had been awarded the Iron

During the first few months of 1942
protection missions for the German *Afrik*
an RAF Hurricane near El Adem, south
10 August. He claimed his 10th victory, a
withdrawn and relocated to Bari for conve
near Sicily where he flew missions over N
and they moved via Athens to Tobruk, a
breakthrough at the beginning of Novem
By mid-December his Group had been m

In early 1943 his Group moved to F
13th victory on 21 April and was promo
Fortress south-west of Doullens, and fro

the 1st Group, flying from San Pietro on the south-west coast of Sardinia. On 25 June he was awarded the *Luftwaffe* Honour Goblet in recognition of claiming his 10th victory. By the end of July he had been appointed *Staffelkapitän* of the 1st Squadron and was now flying from Münster. On 12 August he claimed another B-17 near Bonn, and was awarded the German Cross in Gold on 31 August after claiming fifteen victories and in early September he was promoted to *Hauptmann*. On 2 November he was wounded when his Bf 109G-6 was shot down by return fire from a B-24 Liberator south of Wiener-Neustadt. From early 1944 his Squadron was flying from its base in Fels am Wagram, Austria. Remmer was flying against the might of the US four-engined bombers over Graz, Linz and Salzburg. He claimed a B-24 on 22 February over Graz and the following day he claimed another over south-west Linz. He claimed three victories on 25 February, but later only one, a B-17 bomber, was confirmed. On 19 March he claimed his 20th victory, another B-24 bomber over Marburg, and it was during this time that he flew once again as Acting *Gruppenkommandeur* of the 1st Group.

On 2 April, whilst intercepting a formation of enemy bombers of the US 15th Air Force, he claimed a B-24 bomber before being shot down himself by a US P-38 Lightning west of Graz, Austria. He bailed out of his Bf 109G-6 but fell to his death when his parachute failed to open. He is buried in a war cemetery in Graz.

Heinz 'Heino' SACHSENBERG

Leutnant

Knight's Cross: Awarded on 9 June 1944 as *Fahnenjunker-Feldwebel* attached to the 6th Squadron of the 52nd Fighter Wing for operations over the Soviet Union, and the Western and Eastern Fronts.

Heinz Sachsenberg claimed 104 aerial victories, all but one whilst flying combat missions over the Eastern Front during the Second World War. He was born on 12 July 1922 in Dessau in Saxony-Anhalt, Germany and came from a family of fighter pilots. His father was a pilot during the First World War and winner of the coveted *Pour le Mérite* ('the Blue Max') and his brother Gotthard was a night-fighter pilot.

After flight training he flew with the 52nd Fighter Wing as a *Feldwebel* over the Soviet Union and was assigned to the 6th Squadron in late 1942. He claimed his first victory on 21 April 1943, an Ilyushin Il-2 ground-attack aircraft near Novorossiysk, and on 5 May he made a forced landing north-east of Anapa after combat with Soviet Spitfires, but wasn't wounded. Three days later he claimed his second victory, a

(Deutsches Wehrkundearchiv)

P-39 fighter over west Abinsk, and by the end of May he had achieved eight victories and had been awarded the Iron Cross 1st and 2nd Classes. He continued to claim aerial victories during June and was known for his habit of flying at full throttle, claiming two victories on 5 and 6 June, claiming his 15th victory a week later. He claimed seven more victories during July, which included four on the 26th, most of which were claimed over the Kuban bridgehead. His Squadron was then transferred to the southern Kursk salient to cover the German withdrawal and he claimed four victories on 4 August, which included his 25th, and by the end of the month he had claimed a total of thirty-eight victories.

Sachsenberg was then granted leave due to stress and during this time was awarded the German Cross in Gold on 11 October and the *Luftwaffe* Honour Goblet on 17 October 1943. He returned to the Crimea area in early November to continue the intense air battles over the Kerch Straits. He claimed another six victories during November and claimed his 50th victory on 7 December, another

P-39, and in January 1944 he was made a *Fahnenjunker-Feldwebel*, an officer candidate, He continued to take part in numerous air battles and claimed his 60th victory on 23 January and his 70th victory on 13 March, by the end of the month his tally had increased to seventy-six and he was granted leave. In early May he returned to his unit as a *Leutnant*, flying once again over the Crimea where on 7 May he claimed six aerial victories over Sevastopol to become an 'ace-in-a-day' for the first time. He claimed a single victory on the 8th and three the next day and four victories on 31 May, which included his 90th victory.

Sachsenberg claimed three victories on 2 June and a single on the 6th and two days later he became an 'ace-in-a-day' for the second time when he claimed five victories, which included his 100th. He was now flying over Romania and various Squadrons from his Group, including his, flew in protection of the Ploieşti oilfields in Romania. On 9 June he was awarded the Knight's Cross – well overdue! He continued to fly over Romania and then over Poland and back to Romania and during August his group was expanded by four squadrons. On 23 October 1944 Sachsenberg was seriously wounded during an air battle with US P-51 Mustangs which resulted in him force-landing his Bf 109G-6 near Reni, Romania.

In early 1945 he transferred briefly to the 9th Squadron of the 7th Fighter Wing, flying the Me 262 jet fighter and then in April he joined *Jagdverband* 44 in Munich. His task was to provide air cover for the Me 262 fighters during take-off, flying the Focke-Wulf Fw 190D-9 as *Staffelkapitän*. The aircraft used in this protection squadron were painted red with white stripes on their underbelly to help in their identification by ground forces. Nobody wanted a repeat of the failed Operation Bodenplatte when a number of German aircraft were lost to friendly fire.

After the war Sachsenberg was interviewed and asked why he never flew the jet aircraft and he answered, 'I don't trust anything without a propeller'. He died on 17 June 1951 in Lich, Giessen, Germany following complications from wounds he received on 23 October 1944.

Karl-Heinz 'Charly' WILLIUS

Oberleutnant

Knight's Cross: Awarded posthumously on 9 June 1944 as *Leutnant* and *Staffelführer* of the 2nd Squadron of the 26th Fighter Wing '*Schlageter*' for operations over England, the Soviet Union and the Western Front.

Karl-Heinz Willius claimed forty-nine aerial victories during the Second World War, of which thirty-one were achieved over the Western Front including eleven four-engined bombers. He was born on 5 November 1919 in Kostheim, Mian in Germany and began his pilot training in February 1940 at Fighter Pilot School 3.

On 17 May 1940 *Obergefreiter* Willius was assigned to the 2nd Squadron of the 20th Fighter Wing, equipped with the Bf 109E, seeing action during the Battle of France. Following the Armistice on 22 June 1940 his Group was integrated into the 51st Fighter Wing and Willius, now an *Unteroffizier*, was attached to the 8th Squadron, part of the 3rd Group. From July he took part in the Battle of Britain and flew various escort missions for dive-bombers and other bomber units over targets in southern England. He claimed his first aerial victory on 18 August, a Spitfire over Ramsgate, Kent, and was shortly after awarded the Iron Cross 2nd Class and on the 31st he claimed his second victory, an RAF Hurricane. He claimed two more victories over England during September, both Spitfires, and in early October he was awarded the Iron Cross 1st Class.

(Deutsches Wehrkundearchiv)

From 22 June 1941 he took part in the invasion of the Soviet Union and claimed a Tupolev SB-2 twin-engined bomber on the first day of the campaign. He claimed another victory three days later and claimed two more on the 30th and another on 1 July and he down two Ilyushin DB-3 bombers on 13 July, his 9th and 10th victories. The following day he was transferred to the 1st Group of the 26th Fighter Wing after a request from its *Kommodore Oberstleutnant* Adolf Galland for experienced fighter pilots. Willius was then reassigned to the 3rd Squadron of Galland's Wing which was based in France at St. Omer-Clairmarais in the Pas-de-Calais. He had been promoted to *Feldwebel* and flew missions over the Channel coast. He claimed a Spitfire west of Boulogne on 8 December, whilst flying the Focke-Wulf Fw 190A-2, and from early 1942, with his squadron in Omer-Arques, their orders were to protect the French coast from British fighters.

On 12 February his Group took part in Operation Donnerkeil, the codename for the German operation known as the 'Channel Dash', providing air protection for Germany's three heavy warships, the two battleships *Scharnhorst* and *Gneisenau* and the heavy cruiser *Prinz Eugen*. On 10 April he claimed a Spitfire over north-east Calais and he claimed another one two days later, and before the end of the month he claimed one over Calais and another over Dunkirk. On 17 May he claimed another Spitfire about two miles south of Calais flown by Flight Lieutenant Patrick 'Paddy' Barthropp who bailed out and was taken prisoner. He had been flying as part of the RAF's Operation Ramrod No. 33, attacking the docks at Boulogne, when he was shot down.

Willius was awarded the *Luftwaffe* Honour Goblet on 29 June after gaining eighteen victories and on 18 August took part in the aerial attack on Dieppe to combat the Allied troops that had landed there. He claimed a Spitfire that day, and towards the end of September his group moved to St. Omer-Wizernes where his squadron remained until the end of the year. He was awarded the German Cross in Gold on 15 October and by December he had achieved a total of twenty-two aerial victories. In early 1943 his Group refreshed and prepared for deployment to the Eastern Front while Willius was transferred as an instructor, serving in that capacity until the beginning of March when he returned to his squadron. On the 14th he claimed two victories and was shortly after transferred into the 3rd Squadron. During April and May he saw action over the areas of Orel and Smolensk. He claimed his 25th victory on 21 April and on 13 May claimed four victories that morning in just six minutes! Towards the end of the month he claimed two more victories and on 2 June he shot down two Lavochkin LaGG-3 fighters. Five days later his Group was recalled to Germany and moved at short notice on the 23rd to the Ruhr area after heavy Allied bombing. From July he flew with the 2nd Squadron of the 26th Fighter Wing but now over Belgium and Holland.

On 30 July 1943 Willius led eight Fw 190s from Grimbergen to intercept an Allied formation of B-26 Marauders and Boston bombers from the 386th Bomber Group. Their target was the fighter airfield at Woensdrecht in the Netherlands, and Willius claimed a Boston north-west of Antwerp. Soon after he was commissioned as a *Leutnant* and claimed a Spitfire near Dunkirk on 4 September, his 35th victory. On 25 November he took over as *Staffelkapitän* of the 2nd Squadron, succeeding *Major* Wilhelm Gäth who had been transferred to take command of the 3rd Group. On 1 December Willius claimed his first heavy bomber, a B-17 Flying Fortress, near Koblenz and at the end of the month RAF Bomber Command targeted Ludwigshafen in southern Germany with about 1,300 bombers and escort fighters and defending against the attack were the 1st and 2nd Groups, and Willius claimed another B-17 that day.

On 11 January 1944 the RAF attacked the German aircraft factories at Braunschweig, Oschersleben and Halberstadt, and that day he shot down another B-17, his third four-engined bomber. He claimed a P-38 Lightning on 30 January and on 4 February he claimed his 40th victory, another B-17 over east Cousolre in northern France. Two days later he claimed another B-17 north-east of Brussels, and on the 24th he claimed a B-24 Liberator over Giessen. It was during 'Big Week' or Operation Argument, part of the USAAF and RAF Bomber Command strategic bombing raids against the German aircraft industry. Willius claimed two B-26 Marauder bombers over Zeebrugge on 25 February, but only one was later confirmed. He claimed four more bombers during March, three B-17s and a single B-24 Liberator over the North Sea.

On 8 April he made a head-on attack against a formation of B-24 bombers, downing one of them to claim his 49th aerial victory. Later Willius and other Fw 190s were attacked by P-47 Thunderbolt fighters of the 361st Fighter Group over Zuiderzee near the Netherlands. He was shot down by First Lieutenant Alton B. Snyder, and his Fw 190 was seen to crash into the ground. He had flown 371 combat missions and was posthumously awarded the Knight's Cross on 9 June 1944 which was later presented to his widow. His body was not recovered until 23 October 1967, found in his aircraft near Lake Ijsse in the central Netherlands bordering the provinces of Flevoland, North Holland and Friesland. He now rests in the German War Cemetery in Ysselsteyn, located in Plot TE, Row 6 and Grave No. 67.

Siegfried 'Wumm' LEMKE

Hauptmann

Knight's Cross: Awarded on 11 June 1944 as *Leutnant* and *Staffelführer* of the 1st Group of the 2nd Fighter Wing *'Richthofen'* for operations over the Western Front and Italy.

Siegfried Lemke claimed at least fifty-four aerial victories over the Western Front during the Second World War which included five four-engined bombers. He was born on 7 April 1921 in Schivelbein in Pomerania, now part of Poland, and from October 1942, on completion of his training he was assigned to 1st Squadron of the 2nd Fighter Wing as an *Unteroffizier*.

(Deutsches Wehrkundearchiv)

From the beginning of 1943 he took command of his squadron and saw action over the French Mediterranean coast. He claimed his first victory on 12 March, an RAF Spitfire near Fécamp, and was awarded the Iron Cross 2nd Class. Later that month his Group moved to Brittany and from April he flew out of Évreux near Normandy. On 17 May he claimed a B-17 Flying Fortress south-east of Ile de Croix and claimed another on the 29th, and a third on 4 July. During this time he had been awarded the Iron Cross 1st Class and had been promoted to *Feldwebel*. From September his squadron was relocated to Conches in northern France where he continued to claim victories.

In January 1944 the entire Group moved to southern France where he claimed three Spitfires over Hyéres, Marseilles in southern France. From February they moved again this time to Italy where on the 4th he claimed a B-17 south of Nice and four Spitfires on the 9th, claiming two more on 29 February. Later Lemke flew missions over the Allied beachheads at Anzio and Nettuno and was awarded the *Luftwaffe* Honour Goblet on 31 March after his 30th aerial victory. It was at this time he became an officer candidate and during March claimed fifteen victories of which ten were RAF Spitfires. In April he was commissioned as a *Leutnant* and on the 3rd was awarded the German Cross in Gold after claiming his 35th victory. On 12 May his Group moved to Cormeilles-en-Vexin in north-eastern France, to be used both to protect the French coast and to defend the Reich from air raids. After the Allied invasion of Normandy on 6 June, Lemke's unit relocated to Creil where the following day he claimed three victories, a Spitfire over Tilly and two P-47s over Bayeux and Caen. After heavy fighting over the next few days he was awarded the Knight's Cross on 11 June after claiming his 43rd victory.

Lemke claimed a total of nine victories during June and when his Group was transferred to Husum in Schleswig-Holstein on 13 July they were refreshed and given new aircraft, Focke-Wulf Fw 190A-8s. In June he was promoted to *Oberleutnant* and on the 23rd he was appointed the last *Gruppenkommandeur* of the 3rd Group of the 2nd Fighter Wing, flying from Creil. He had by now claimed a total of forty-eight victories and from August his Group had been relocated from Normandy to Königsberg. On 19 August Lemke claimed a Typhoon over the area of Dreux and from October his Group flew 'Defence of the Reich' missions from Altenstadt. He claimed two victories on 20 October, his 50th and 51st. On 17 December, now flying from Ettinghausen in the Rhineland-Palatinate area of Germany Lemke claimed an RAF Hawker Tempest fighter aircraft, and on the 23rd he shot down two P-47s, his final victories of the war.

During the final months of the war he took part in Operation Bodenplatte, the *Luftwaffe*'s attack on Allied air bases in Belgium and northern France. At this time his Group only had forty operational fighters and twenty-eight pilots. During the mission his Group lost nineteen aircraft with three damaged, and nine pilots killed and four captured. After the failure of the Ardennes Offensive the Group withdrew to central Germany and northern Bohemia from March 1945. It was finally disbanded in Munich where Lemke and his staff surrendered to the Americans. During these final weeks of the war Lemke was promoted to *Major* and recommended for the Oakleaves, but he never received them. He died on 18 December 1995 in Büttelborn, a community in Gross-Gerau district of Hesse, Germany.

Franz-Walter WOIDICH

Oberleutnant

Knight's Cross: Awarded on 11 June 1944 as *Leutnant* and fighter pilot attached to the 3rd Squadron of the 52nd Fighter Wing for operations over North Africa and the Soviet Union.

Franz-Walter Woidich flew almost 1,000 combat missions and claimed eighty-two aerial victories, of which all but three were achieved over the Eastern Front during the Second World War. He was born on 2 January 1921 in Znojmo, a southern region of Moravia in Czechoslovakia, and he joined the *Luftwaffe* in early 1940.

On completion of his training he was assigned as an *Oberfähnrich* to the 5th Squadron of the 27th Fighter Wing from 11 July 1941 whilst stationed at Döberitz, Germany. He flew the Bf 109F-4 fighter and from September his Group flew from Naples and then saw brief action in North Africa from the 22nd. The Allied offensive began on 18 November and Woidich claimed his first victory three days later, a Royal Australian Air Force Curtiss P-40 south of Ain-el-Gazala, but this was later declared an unconfirmed victory. He claimed another P-40 the following day over north-west Bir Hachem, his first confirmed victory. By 7 December his Group began to withdraw and transferred to Gazala and by the 12th they had moved again. In January 1942 he was flying from Libya and on the 21st he flew in a counter-attack on the area of Ajdabiya in north-eastern Libya, a February his Group had relocated to Benina.

(Deutsches Wehrkundearchiv)

From April he flew with the 3rd Squadron of the 52nd Fighter Wing, flying from Artemivsk in the Ukraine. From 22 May Woidich and his squadron were deployed over the Kharkov area, and after the beginning of the summer offensive his Group moved to Novyi-Grinow to follow the German advance. He was awarded the Iron Cross 2nd Class in mid-July shortly after his third victory and by 15 August was flying from Orel-North and had been promoted to *Oberfeldwebel* a few weeks before. He claimed two victories on 2 September and two the following day and was shortly after awarded the Iron Cross 1st Class. On the 22nd his Squadron and Group flew over Orel, Kharkov and Tazinskaja in support of the army and later the Group settled in Pitomnik west of Stalingrad, but by 4 November they had been withdrawn. However, with the beginning of the Soviet counter-offensive in the Stalingrad area his Group rest and refreshment was cancelled and from the 28th Woidich flew the new Bf 109G-2 over the area of Nikolajevka near Stalingrad.

At the beginning of 1943 the 2nd Group was based in Rossosch, and with the commencement of the German offensive his Group flew in support of the advance. On 10 June the *Staffelkapitän* of the 3rd Squadron, *Oberleutnant* Rudolf Miethig had been killed and the following day Woidich took over as *Staffelführer* for a short time. By the beginning of July, Woidich had claimed a total of sixteen victories, he added two more to his score on 5 July and three on the 7th, and by the end of the month he had claimed a total of thirty-one aerial victories. He claimed another four during the first week of August and on the 15th he claimed a single victory whilst flying from Orel-North. On 13 September he was awarded the *Luftwaffe* Honour Goblet after claiming thirty-five victories, and nine days later his Group moved via Orel, Kharkov and Tazinskaya to Pitomnik airfield just west of Stalingrad in support of ground troops. On 17 October Woidich was awarded the German Cross in Gold after claiming his 40th victory, and by the end of that month he had claimed another eight victories and now had a total of fifty-one. On 4 November orders were issued for his Group to be withdrawn, but with the start of the Soviet counter-offensive in the Stalingrad area the Group's refresh was cancelled. Towards the end of the month his Group was assigned the new Bf 109G-2 fighter and he was once again flying over the Stalingrad area.

In early 1944 Woidich was flying from Rossosch near Voronezh where on 11 January he shot down three Yak-9 fighters and a single P-39, which included his 60th victory. On the 17th he claimed five victories to become an 'ace-in-a-day' and from the 25th the Group moved to Kursk and flew escort missions for Stuka dive-bombers. In early February his Group moved to Kharkov-North and from March Woidich was flying with the 1st Squadron of the 52nd Fighter Wing and had been promoted to *Leutnant*. He claimed three victories during March and by mid-April he was flying once again with the 3rd Squadron. He claimed two victories on 14 April and four on the 16th, and two weeks later his Squadron was deployed over Kursk. He claimed his 80th aerial victory on 3 June and eight days later was awarded the Knight's Cross and shortly after was granted some leave to celebrate. During the Soviet counter-offensive of July he flew over the Belgorod area and from 6 August his Group flew from Kharkov-Rogan.

In September his Group left the Eastern Front and was assigned to Germany and soon after arriving Woidich was reassigned to the 6th Squadron of the 400th Fighter Wing. He was flying the new Messerschmitt Me 163B Komet, the only operational rocket-powered fighter aircraft not just of the Second World War but in history. It was also the first piloted aircraft of any type to exceed over 600 miles an hour in level flight. Woidich was appointed *Staffelkapitän* of his Squadron on 17 September and in early 1945 he was promoted to *Oberleutnant*. He flew from Brandis near Leipzig and on 22 April he claimed a four-engined bomber, his 82nd and last official victory. On 19 April his Group was disbanded and in early May together with other squadrons he surrendered to the Allies.

He had flown about 1,000 combat missions and had officially claimed over eighty aerial victories. However, he had also claimed another twenty-nine victories over the Soviet Union but they had never been confirmed for reasons unknown. Woidich settled in the Rhineland-Palatinate area of Germany after the war and in 1953, together with Karl Thress, opened 'The Engineering Office Woidich', an automobile technical engineering bureau in Mainz where his son Gerd joined the business in 1981. Woidich died in Mainz, the capital of the region, on 5 July 2004.

Georg-Peter 'Schorsch' EDER

Major

Knight's Cross: Awarded on 24 June 1944 as *Oberleutnant* and *Staffelkapitän* of the 6th Squadron of the 1st Fighter Wing for operations over England, the Soviet Union and the Western Front, and for claiming his 44th aerial victory.

Knight's Cross with Oakleaves: Awarded on 25 November 1944, to become the 663rd recipient, as *Hauptmann* and still *Staffelkapitän* in the 1st Fighter Wing for claiming his 54th aerial victory (remains unconfirmed), a US P-51 Mustang fighter over France.

Georg-Peter Eder was one of the most colourful characters of the *Jagdwaffe* (Fighter Arm) of the war and although his official victory score is over fifty he had at least another twenty-eight unconfirmed victories to his name. He claimed at least twenty-one victories whilst flying the Me 262 jet fighter, as well as being credited with more than twenty-three four-engined bombers and destroying three Sherman tanks in Normandy. He was shot down seventeen times and wounded fourteen times during his career, and one of Eder's quirks was to have painted on every fighter he flew the number 13, which he considered to be lucky!

(Deutsches Wehrkundearchiv)

Eder was born on 8 March 1921 in Oberdachstetten, Bavaria, and after attending elementary school and secondary school he joined the *Luftwaffe* in October 1938 as a cadet. Posted to the 4th Company of the 62nd Flight Training Regiment in Quedlinburg in the Harz region, he then attended the *Luftwaffe* Air War School in Berlin-Gatow. In April 1940 he was accepted as an officer candidate and in September transferred to the 1st Squadron of the 51st Fighter Wing as a *Fähnrich* or officer cadet. He joined the Wing at the height of the Battle of Britain and flew quite a few sorties but failed to score his first victory. In April 1941, Eder was commissioned as a *Leutnant* and then transferred to the 4th Squadron and in June he flew during the opening phase of the invasion of the Soviet Union. He claimed his first aerial victories on 22 June when he shot down a Polikarpov I-16 single-engined fighter and a Tupolev SB-2 twin-engined bomber, and four days later he was awarded the Iron Cross 2nd Class. On 30 June he claimed his third victory, a DB-3 long-range bomber, and was awarded the Iron Cross 1st Class on 11 July. The following day he claimed a Pe-2 twin-engined dive-bomber and on the 13th he shot down a DB-3 bomber and an I-16 fighter. He claimed his 10th aerial victory on 9 August but on the 22nd he was seriously wounded when his Bf 109F-2 collided with a Junkers Ju 52 transport aircraft on the ground at Ponjatowska. He suffered a fracture at the base of his skull and spent almost two months in hospital. After recovering, Eder served from November as a flight instructor with Fighter Pilot School 2 in Zerbst.

Exactly a year later he was transferred to the 7th Squadron of the 2nd Fighter Wing in Marseille-Marignane, where he took part in the fight against the US 8th Air Force daylight bombing offensive. Together with his Group Commander, *Oberleutnant* Egon Mayer, they devised a method that would bring down heavy bombers and reduce the risk to *Luftwaffe* fighter pilots. They discovered from shot-down aircraft that the weakest area of defensive fire was the front, and early models of the B-17 carried a single rifle-calibre machine gun in the nose, but it was regarded as no more than a 'scare' weapon. Therefore Eder and Mayer concluded that the best solution was to attack from head-on. This had advantages. First, the high closing speed of a head-on attack reduced the time the German fighters were under fire to only a matter of seconds. Secondly, a head-on attack made the cockpit the main target. With no frontal armour or other protection this was very vulnerable. The head-on attack was tried for the first time on 23 November 1942, when the B-17s attacked St. Nazaire.

On 15 February 1943, Eder was appointed *Staffelkapitän* of the 12th Squadron of the 2nd Fighter Wing, still based in France. He claimed a Spitfire on 8 March over Le Petit-Quevilly, his 15th victory. He claimed another Spitfire on 12 March and on the 28th, after shooting down a B-17 bomber he was injured when his Bf 109G-6 was damaged by enemy fire and somersaulted on landing at Beaumont-le-Roger. He soon recovered and by the end of April, his Squadron had received their full complement of sixteen Bf 109G-6 fighters. In early May he led his Squadron against US bombers attacking the Potez aircraft plant at Albert, claiming a P-47 during the attack. On 29 May, the USAAF targeted Rennes, Saint-Nazaire and La Pallice. Eder's Squadron claimed three B-17s, including one by Eder. On 25 June he was awarded the *Luftwaffe* Honour Goblet and the following day he claimed a Spitfire, shot down north of Fécamp. He led his Squadron against US bombers on 29 June and he lost two aircraft and one of his pilots was killed and two were wounded. Eder did however claim another B-17, shot down north of Saint-Valery. On 1 July Eder was promoted to *Oberleutnant* and on the 4th he claimed a another B-17 bomber and six days later claimed two more B-17s and a Spitfire. He claimed two victories on 14 July, both B-17 bombers, and he claimed another Spitfire on the 16th, and two more on 30 July, his 28th and 29th victories.

On 31 August Eder was awarded the German Cross in Gold, in recognition of his success in shooting down at least twelve four-engined bombers. On 5 September, Eder was transferred to the 5th Squadron of the 2nd Fighter Wing where he took over as *Staffelkapitän*, taking over from *Leutnant* Kurt Goltzsch who had been wounded the day before. On 5 November he was slightly wounded when he was forced to bail out of his Bf 109G-6 after it had been damaged during combat over the area of Cambrai. He recovered quickly and returned to his unit and in February 1944 was transferred to the 6th Squadron of the 1st Fighter Wing, based in Wunstorf, Northern Germany. Here he flew missions in what was called in 'Defence of the Reich' – now flying combat missions over Germany. He claimed a B-24 Liberator on 8 April south-west of Salzwebel, his 30th aerial victory and claimed two victories the following day, another B-24 and a P-47 Thunderbolt over Kiel Bay.

By the end of April he had claimed his 37th victory, another seven victories in May and from the 12th he took over as *Gruppenkommandeur* of the 2nd Group of the 1st Fighter Wing. On 29 May 993 heavy bombers of the US 8th Air Force, together with 1,265 fighters targeted the German aircraft factories at Leipzig, Sorau and Posen, and the airfield at Tutow, as well as the hydrogenation factory at Pölitz. At the same time the 15th Air Force attacked similar targets in southern Germany and Austria. The 1st Fighter Wing was scrambled Eder took part in the frontal attacks of the US four-engined bombers, of which nine B-17s were shot down, one by Eder. Later that day he was unhurt when his Fw 190A-8 overturned on landing at Cottbus.

When the Allies launched the invasion of Normandy on 6 June, D-Day, the 2nd Group of the 1st Fighter Wing with strength of thirty-two Fw 190s under the leadership of Eder had been relocated from Störmede to an airfield at Montdidier, France. The following day they flew their first combat mission of the Normandy campaign against the Allied landing fleet near Deauville and Trouville on the southern bank of the Seine. On 24 June he was awarded the Knight's Cross in recognition of his 44th aerial victory, of which seventeen were four-engined bombers.

On 1 July Eder was promoted to *Hauptmann* and in August he took temporary command of the 6th Squadron of the 26th Fighter Wing, replacing *Leutnant* Adolf Glunz. Whilst attacking armour near Dreux on 17 August, Eder shot down an RAF Spitfire at low level over Rambouillet, France, and it crashed between two Sherman tanks, destroying both of them. Shortly after that he shot down another Spitfire in the same area and that also crashed into a tank, setting it on fire. On 4 September he was appointed *Gruppenkommandeur* of the 2nd Group of the 26th Fighter Wing, after the death over St. Trond of *Hauptmann* Emil Lang.

In early October Eder transferred to *Erprobungskommando* (Operational Test Commando) 262, and took command of the 1st Squadron of what would later be called *Kommando Nowotny*. It was a special unit set up with experienced fighter pilots and which from November was redesignated the 7th Fighter Wing. Eder was appointed *Staffelkapitän* of the 9th Squadron, flying the Messerschmitt Me 262 jet fighter. During the Ardennes Offensive, or what became known as the Battle of the Bulge, Eder destroyed forty P-47s on the ground. On 25 November Eder was awarded the Knight's Cross with Oakleaves, records state this was in recognition of his 54th aerial victory but post-war investigations show that at least six were unconfirmed. He claimed five victories whilst flying the Me 262 but these remain unconfirmed. On 22 January 1945, Eder was shot down near Parchim, near Mecklenburg-Vorpommern by P-51s whilst trying to land. He broke both his legs and spent the rest of the war in hospital at Wismar and Bad Wiese, having been promoted to *Major* on 1 February. He was taken prisoner by the US Army in May 1945, and afterwards became a businessman in post war Germany.

Eder became friends after the war with a US fighter pilot, Urban L. Drew, who was the first Allied pilot to shoot down a *Luftwaffe* Me 262 jet fighter in his P-51. It was Eder that confirmed the victory when during interrogation after the war he said he saw a yellow-nosed P-51 dive on a Me 262 and shoot it down. This was enough to confirm Drew's victory. There was also another friendship. Mike Gladych, a Polish pilot who flew for the RAF during the war, remembers Eder's chivalry as a pilot. They encountered each other twice during the war, once in 1943 over Lille, Gladychs' aircraft was shot up and he was desperate to get to his base and says that Eder flew alongside as if to check out the damage, waved at him and then flew off. Gladych later said, 'One burst would have put paid to me'. The two met after the war in a chance encounter in Frankfurt. They only realised they had fought each other during the war when they started to compare notes. They remained good friends. Eder died on in Wiesbaden, Germany on 11 March 1986.

Wilhelm MORITZ

Major

Knight's Cross: Awarded on 18 July 1944 as *Major* and commander of the 4th Group of the 3rd Fighter Wing '*Udet*' for operations over the Soviet Union and the Western Front.

Wilhelm Moritz claimed a total of forty-one aerial victories during the Second World War of which twenty-eight were over the Eastern Front and the rest, which included nine four-engined bombers, over the Western Front. He was born on 29 June 1913 in Altona, Hamburg and Moritz joined the army and in 1933 at the age of 19, transferring into the *Luftwaffe* in September 1939 as a *Leutnant*.

Moritz saw action during the Polish campaign as part of the 2nd Group of the 1st Destroyer Wing mainly flying escort missions and low-level attacks. In mid-September his Group was withdrawn and relocated to Danzig-Langfuhr where his Group took over escort mission for the '*Führer*' Squadron', flying missions to protect Hitler. In

(Deutsches Wehrkundearchiv)

mid-1940, now an *Oberleutnant* he transferred into the 2nd Group of the 77th Fighter Wing and was attached to the 4th Squadron flying from Trondheim in Norway. He claimed his first aerial victory on 6 July, an RAF Blenheim over west Stavanger and was shortly after awarded the Iron Cross 2nd Class. He claimed another Blenheim on 19 August and claimed his third victory over Bergen on 26 October and was awarded the Iron Cross 1st Class.

From January 1941 he served with Fighter School 4 in Fürth-Buchschwabach as a *Staffelkapitän* until March 1942. On 3 April he served as *Staffelkapitän* with the 11th Squadron of the 1st Fighter

Wing where he flew over the Dutch coast, flying the Focke-Wulf Fw 190 from July 1942. He was promoted to *Hauptmann* in August and from October he was transferred as *Staffelkapitän* of the 12th Squadron of the 51st Fighter Wing, flying from Vitebsk in Belarus. Moritz claimed his fourth victory on 30 October, an Il-2 ground-attack aircraft, and in December he claimed another six victories, all of which were Il-2s. In early January 1943 he claimed another Il-2 and by 5 July he had claimed his 15th aerial victory. On 10 July he claimed two more victories and three days later he became an 'ace-in-a-day' when he shot down five Soviet aircraft. On 11 October he was awarded the *Luftwaffe* Honour Goblet in recognition of claiming his 30th aerial victory, a Yak-1 fighter over north-west Kalushino.

On 19 October Moritz was appointed *Staffelkapitän* of the 6th Squadron of the 3rd Fighter Wing and flew in defence of the Reich, flying from Amsterdam-Schiphol. In mid-December their base was devastated by Allied air raids and they had to move to Volkel. By the 25th they were withdrawn and relocated to about 25 miles outside of Bremen. From 18 April 1944 Moritz was made *Gruppenkommandeur* of the 4th Group of the 3rd Fighter Wing and he began to employ ramming tactics in order to bring down the heavy US four-engined bombers. On 22 April he claimed a B-24 Liberator bomber and seven days later he claimed another B-24 over north-west Gardelegen. On 8 May he claimed two more B-24s over north Braunschweig, and he claimed two B-17 Flying Fortress bombers on the 13th over Lake Cummerower, his 36th and 37th victories. After the start of the Allied landings in Normandy on 6 June his Group moved to Dreux about 35 miles west of Paris. On 15 June his Group had moved to Eisenstadt in Austria and from here he took part in the defence operations against the Allied bomber formations from Italy. He claimed a B-24 on 7 July and on the 18th he claimed another and was that same day awarded the Knight's Cross in recognition of his ramming tactics and for claiming thirty-seven victories.

On 1 October Moritz was promoted to *Major* and had by now claimed nine four-engined bombers and on 28 November he claimed his last victory a P-51 Mustang. On 5 December Moritz suffered a complete nervous breakdown. He had been pushing his own tactics in ramming bombers and leading his Group, so he had to be rested and was relieved of his command. He quickly recovered and from early 1945 he flew as *Gruppenkommandeur* of the 4th Group of the 1st Fighter Replacement Wing. On 18 April 1945 he became the last *Kommandeur* of 2nd Group of the 4th Fighter Wing but that same day he was shot down by anti-aircraft fire and wounded, belly-landing his Fw 190 near Thüringen.

He had flown more than 500 combat missions during the war and had been a strong advocate for the ramming of Allied bombers. The pilots that rammed the US bombers were expected to bail out at the last minute and the survival rate was low, and it was at a time when the *Luftwaffe* couldn't afford to lose pilots or aircraft. With the added pressure of this it's no wonder that Moritz had a breakdown, but he had survived the war. In his later years he moved to Ontario, Canada where he died on 28 June 2007, one day before his 94th birthday.

Ernst DÜLLBERG

Major

Knight's Cross: Awarded on 20 July 1944 as *Major* and commander of the 3rd Group of the 27th Fighter Wing for operations over France, England, the Soviet Union, North Africa and the Western Front.

Ernst Düllberg flew about 650 combat missions and claimed a total of forty-three victories of which thirty-four, including nine four-engined bombers, were over the Western Front during the Second World War. He was born on 28 March 1913 in Unna, a town in North-Rhine Westphalia, Germany. He joined the *Luftwaffe* in mid-1936 and as a young *Leutnant* he was at pilots' school in Celle from November 1937.

er served as
nt Training
 Squadron
Hauptmann
ok over as
a Blenheim
was Acting
 Wing and
uadron. He
er he scored
lsey Bill on
iford on 30
ass. By the
 scored five
d.

(Deutsches Wehrkundearchiv)

941 and claimed a Tupolev SB-3 bomber
with the 2nd Group was withdrawn from
irfield at Ain-el-Gazala, west of the port
was attacked by RAF fighters and he was
 his home airfield. He returned to active
h, both US P-40 fighters. On 26 May he
vas appointed *Gruppenkommandeur* of the
month had claimed his 16th aerial victory,

oung pilots and from the 20th it moved to
n Aegean. At the beginning of May most
over Malta as well as fighter missions over
ove south of Athens and by the end of the
e of his squadrons were reorganised. Now
hunting missions over the Aegean Sea. In
Gotzendorf where they were assigned forty
s promoted to *Major*. By mid-September
ported attacks on the Aegean islands. He
and a Walrus biplane over Leros on 30
5 October when he shot down a B-24
14 November and by the end of the year
7 Flying Fortress four-engined bombers.
to Megara in Greece and Düllberg was
the Group had moved to Vienna-Seyring.
, the day the Allies launched the invasion
24 bombers and a Mustang P-51 fighter.
ecognition of his Group's actions in Italy,
ctories, which included nine four-engined
Kommodore of the 76th Fighter Wing and
rial victory a Soviet Yakovlev Yak-9 fighter.
the new Me 262 jet fighter but had little
var. It was said that he shot down another
and have never been confirmed. Düllberg
nd settled in Essen where he died on 27

Herbert BACHNICK

Leutnant

Knight's Cross: Awarded on 27 July 1[...] eight aerial victories over the Soviet Un[...] Squadron of the 52nd Fighter Wing.

Herbert Bachnick claimed a total of sever[...] the Second World War but his last victo[...] all of them over the Eastern Front. He fl[...] He was born on 9 February 1920 in [...] *Luftwaffe* in October 1938 at the age of 1[...] and was eventually assigned to the 52nd [...] 9th Squadron as an *Unteroffizier* whilst [...] Ssoldatskaja in the Soviet Union from D[...]

Bachnick claimed his first three victori[...] bomber, a Polikarpov I-5 biplane and an [...] he was awarded the Iron Cross 2nd Clas[...] He claimed two more victories on 4 Augu[...] fighter pilot. He began to score victories [...] and shot down three more the following [...] awarded the Iron Cross 1st Class on 7 Se[...] his 30th aerial victory, an Il-2 over East Z[...] Honour Goblet and claimed four victorie[...] achieved forty-six victories and had been [...]

On 7 January 1944 he claimed five [...] German Cross in Gold on 5 February [...] on 12 March and became an 'ace-in-a-[...] just 25 minutes. By the end of March B[...] was transferred to Fighter Group East [...] commissioned as a *Leutnant* and on 7 J[...] bombers and fighters and had to make a[...] his old Squadron and on the 27th was a[...] with a formation of USAAF P-51 Mus[...] been confirmed officially. However, durin[...] badly damaged, more than he thought. H[...] embankment near Birkental, Upper Siles[...]

Hans-Joachim BIRKNER

Leutnant

Knight's Cross: Awarded as *Fahnenjunke*[...] Fighter Wing on 27 July 1944 for opera[...] claiming his 98th aerial victory.

Hans-Joachim Birkner claimed 117 ae[...] World War of which all but one were ov[...] Schönwalde, East Prussia and after compl[...]

to the 9th Squadron of the 52nd Fighter Wing in Dnepropetrowsk in the Soviet Union.

Birkner flew his first mission in August 1943, but it wasn't until his 54th mission on 1 October that he claimed his first victory, a P-39 south-south-west of Bolkschoj Tokmak. It could be said he was a bit of a late starter, but once started there seemed to be no stopping the young fighter pilot. He claimed his second victory on 4 October, and his third came the following day, with his next coming on 9 October when he was awarded the Iron Cross 2nd Class. By the end of the month he had achieved thirteen victories and had been awarded the Iron Cross 1st Class in late September. He saw action during the Battle of the Caucasus and from mid-October flew combat missions over the right flank of the 1st Army and over the Dnieper and left flank of the 6th Army.

(Deutsches Wehrkundearchiv)

In 1944 he continued to be successful when on 3 January he claimed two victories, 25th and 26th. He was promoted to the rank of *Fahnenjunker-Feldwebel*, an officer candidate, and claimed five P-39 fighters to become an 'ace-in-a-day' on 15 January. He was awarded the German Cross in Gold on 20 March after claiming his 30th aerial victory. On 15 April he claimed three victories and on the 16th claimed another two, and claimed four more on the 18th and then became an 'ace-in-a-day' for second time on 19 April when he shot down six aircraft. The following day Birkner was awarded the *Luftwaffe* Honour Goblet in recognition of his 40th aerial victory (it was unusual to receive the Honour Goblet after the German Cross in Gold). He claimed his 50th aerial victory on 23 April and by the 27th he had claimed his 60th victory, and claimed five victories on 30 May to become an 'ace-in-a-day' yet again and to claim his 70th victory. On 27 July he was awarded the Knight's Cross in recognition of his 98th victory and his skill as a fighter pilot. It must also be noted that Birkner flew as wingman to fighter aces who would later become living legends and he must have learnt something from them. He flew first with Günther Rall (275 victories) and later with Erich Hartmann (352 victories), the top *Luftwaffe* fighter ace of the war.

From October Birkner was commissioned as a *Leutnant*, and flew as *Staffelkapitän* of the 9th Squadron of the 52nd Fighter Wing. He became an 'ace-in-a-day' for the fourth time on 16 October. He claimed his 110th victory on 25 October and claimed his 113th and final victory two days later. On 14 December his Bf 109G-14 suffered engine failure, crashed near Cracow, Poland and he was killed.

Ernst BÖRNGEN

Major

Knight's Cross: Awarded as *Hauptmann* and commander of the 1st Group of the 27th Fighter Wing on 27 July 1944 for operations over England, the Balkans, the Soviet Union, North Africa, Italy and the Western Front.

Ernst Börngen claimed thirty-five aerial victories from 450 combat missions during the Second World War, of which thirty-three were over the Western Front and which included fourteen four-engined bombers. He was born on 7 February 1916 in Meusekwitz, a small town in the Altenburger Land district of Thuringia, Germany.

Börngen joined the *Luftwaffe* in November 1937 as a *Fähnrich* or Officer Candidate and attended officer training school. In August 1938 he was commissioned as a *Leutnant* and from early 1939 he began his training as a fighter pilot, serving briefly in the Air Ministry in December 1939 as an *Oberleutnant*. From June 1940 he served as Technical Officer attached to the 4th Squadron of the 27th

Fighter Wing in Wunsdorf, Germany. On 18 August he claimed two Spitfires over Selsey Bill in the English Channel during the Battle of Britain. Shortly after this he was awarded the Iron Cross 2nd Class, and later took part in the Balkan campaign and claimed a Greek Gladiator biplane fighter near Kalambaka on 15 April 1941. From June he saw action during the invasion of the Soviet Union, claiming his fourth victory on 25 June, and claimed a Blenheim bomber on 21 December when shortly after he was awarded the Iron Cross 1st Class.

In late September his Group was moved down to North Africa where on 20 May 1942 he was appointed *Staffelkapitän* of the 5th Squadron of the 27th Fighter Wing, replacing *Hauptmann* Ernst Düllberg who had been wounded. On 30 May he claimed a P-40 ground-attack aircraft, and claimed another three between June and early July. He claimed an RAF Spitfire over El Alamein on 11 July, his 10th aerial victory. On 20 July he shot down a P-40 and on 20 September he was wounded when

(Deutsches Wehrkundearchiv)

his Bf 109 was hit in the cockpit during combat with Allied aircraft. He wasn't seriously injured and landed his aircraft safely, and by the end of October he had claimed his 16th aerial victory.

He was awarded the *Luftwaffe* Honour Goblet on 25 January 1943 and during the spring when the Germans were forced out of North Africa Börngen's command moved to Italy where he was promoted to *Hauptmann* on 29 April, and the same day he claimed his 18th victory, a P-38 Lightning. He shot down another P-38 on 22 May and three days later he claimed a B-17 Flying Fortress over the area of Marettimo in the Mediterranean and six days later he shot down a B-24 Liberator and a B-25 Mitchell twin-engined bomber in the same area. Börngen claimed two B-24s on 2 July, a Spitfire on the 10th and he claimed another B-24 on 16 July, his 26th victory. However, during the attack his Bf 109G-5 was hit by defensive fire from the bomber and he was severely wounded, but despite this he managed to crash-land his aircraft at San Vito dei Normanni in Italy. As a result of his wounds he didn't participate in combat duties for almost eight months, returning to duty in April 1944. He had been awarded the German Cross in Gold on 31 August in recognition for achieving twenty-six victories.

During April 1944 he claimed five B-17 bombers and one B-24 but post-war investigations now discount one of the B-17s and the B-24. In May the Allies initiated the 'Oil Campaign', targeting various facilities supplying Germany with oil. On 12 May, the US 8th Air Force sent a force of 886 heavy bombers, protected by 980 escort fighters, against the oil refineries in central Germany. Börngen and the 1st Group engaged a formation of B-17s just east of Eschborn, and during the attack Börngen claimed two B-17s, but the *Gruppenkommandeur*, *Major* Ludwig Franzisket, was severely wounded. The following day Börngen took over as *Gruppenkommandeur* and handed his own command over to *Leutnant* Karl Wünsch. On 13 May Börgen claimed a B-24 and six days later the Allies targeted Berlin and Braunschweig and sent over 888 heavy bombers protected by 964 escort fighters. Börngen was ordered to lead his Group and meet up with the 3rd and 4th Groups and engage these aircraft. While the 3rd and 4th Groups formed up near Magdeburg ready to engage the fighters, Börngen's 1st Group attacked the B-24 bombers, and claimed seventeen victories, with Börngen claiming two himself. He rammed the second bomber and although severely injured managed to bail out and land safely where he was immediately taken to the *Luftwaffe* hospital at Helmstedt where his right arm had to be amputated. He spent several months recovering but he never returned to combat. He was awarded the Knight's Cross on 27 July 1944 in recognition of achieving thirty-five victories and for flying operations over England, the Balkans, the Soviet Union, North Africa and Italy, he was also awarded the Wound Badge in Silver. He was promoted to *Major* in October and spent the rest of the war in an administrative post. He died in Mering, Bavaria on 30 June 1989.

Horst-Günther von FASSONG

Hauptmann

Knight's Cross: Awarded on 27 July 1944 as *Hauptmann* and commander of the 3rd Group of the 11th Fighter Wing for operations over the Soviet Union and the Western Front.

(Deutsches Wehrkundearchiv)

Horst-Günther von Fassong claimed sixty-three aerial victories during the Second World War, all of them over the Eastern Front. He was born on 27 April 1919 in Kassel, central Germany and joined the Army at the age of 19 and was assigned to Reconnaissance Battalion 7, part of the 4th Panzer Division. As a *Gefreiter* he took part in the occupation of Austria and later the Sudetenland, and in 1939 he participated in the occupation of Czechoslovakia and the invasion of Poland.

In May 1940 Fassong transferred as a *Leutnant* to the *Luftwaffe* and on completion of his training was attached to the 3rd Squadron of the 51st Fighter Wing from June 1941. He saw action during the opening stages of Operation Barbarossa, the invasion of the Soviet Union claiming two Polikarpov I-16 fighters on 3 July. Awarded the Iron Cross 2nd Class on 18 July, Fassong was seriously injured when his aircraft caught fire during take-off near Stara-Bykhov ten days later, and he spent almost nine months recovering.

He returned to his old squadron in late April 1942 as an *Oberleutnant* and claimed a MiG-3 on 3 May and another on 13 July. He was awarded the Iron Cross 1st Class on 23 November and on 12 February 1943 he was appointed *Staffelkapitän* of the 10th Squadron of the 51st Fighter Wing stationed in Orel. Fassong claimed his fifth victory on 8 March, and his sixth on 9 May, then claimed two on 2 June and three more eight days later. From July his success rate began to increase. He claimed four victories on the 5th and five the next day, to become an 'ace-in-a-day'. He claimed three more on 9 July, three on the 13th, two on the 17th and the 22nd. He claimed a total of thirteen victories during the month of August, which included five on the 14th, to become an 'ace-in-a-day' for the second time! On 17 October Fassong was awarded the German Cross in Gold in recognition of scoring forty victories. He claimed a further five victories towards the end of October and shot down his 50th victory on 29 November over south-east Annovojevka. He continued to add to his score in January 1944, claiming his 60th victory on the 25th, an Il-2 ground-attack aircraft.

From April he took command of the 7th Squadron of the 11th Fighter Wing and the following month was promoted to *Hauptmann*. During May he flew from Reinsehlen, Lower Saxony and during this time he claimed two B-17 bombers, and towards the end of the month he was appointed *Gruppenkommandeur* of the 3rd Group. From June his group moved back to the Eastern Front near Minsk and from there the Group flew fighter-bomber missions over Bobruisk and Vitebsk. On 27 July Fassong was awarded the Knight's Cross in recognition of gaining sixty-three aerial victories. During the second half of 1944 his Group moved a number of times due to the Soviet advance and by August had settled in East Prussia and had been reinforced with four squadrons. From late 1944 the 3rd Group had moved again and was involved in the Ardennes Offensive and on 1 January 1945 Fassong was shot down by two P-47 Thunderbolts during a low-level attack. His wingman *Unteroffizier* Armin Mehling later reported that they had been pounced upon by six P-47s, and two had chased Fassong. His Fw 190A-8 was hit at a height of 70–100ft, cartwheeling in a ball of flames upon impact. Fassong had no chance: his body was never found.

Hans KOLBOW

Oberleutnant

Knight's Cross: Awarded posthumously on 27 July 1944 as *Oberleutnant* and *Staffelkapitän* of the 6th Squadron of the 51st Fighter Wing for operations over France, England and the Soviet Union.

Hans Kolbow claimed twenty-three aerial victories during the Second World War, of which fourteen were over the Western Front and nine over the Eastern Front. He was born on 8 January 1914 in Hamburg and flew during the Spanish Civil War as part of the Condor Legion and was awarded the Spanish Cross in Gold with Swords on 14 April 1939.

He was commissioned as a *Leutnant* in 1939 and joined the 3rd Squadron of the 20th Fighter Wing, seeing action during the French campaign in 1940. He claimed his first victory, a French Potez 630 twin-engined fighter, on 12 May over south-east Antwerp On 29 May he claimed his first confirmed victory, a Spitfire over Calais, and two days later he claimed a Fleet Air Arm Skua aircraft over Dunkirk but

(Deutsches Wehrkundearchiv)

this was later reclassified as unconfirmed. That same day, whilst attacking a formation of RAF Defiant fighters, his aircraft was hit by return fire and he had to make a belly-landing south of Calais, but wasn't wounded. He had been awarded the Iron Cross 1st and 2nd Classes by this time he claimed two more victories on 30 June, a Blenheim over St. Omer and a Spitfire over west Etaples.

On 4 July 1940 his unit was upgraded and changed its name to the 3rd Group of the 51st Fighter Wing. Kolbow saw action over the Channel and the coastal areas and from the 10th he took part in the Battle of Britain. He now flew as part of the 9th Squadron and claimed a Spitfire over Dover on the first day, and claimed two more Spitfires, one on 19 July and the other on 8 August. However, both of these claims have since been reclassified as unconfirmed. Four days later his Group was taken out of action and moved to Jever in Germany to be refreshed and during September took over air protection duties over the western Danish area. At the beginning of October his Group moved back to France, and Kolbow was told that his Squadron would be converted and fly fighter-bomber missions over England with 250kg bombs fitted to each aircraft. He claimed a Hurricane over London on 15 October and two weeks later he shot down a Spitfire, his eighth victory. From December his Squadron, together with the entire 2nd Group, was withdrawn and relocated to Mannheim-Sandhofen for refitting and conversion to the Bf 109F fighter. By February 1941 his Squadron had returned to France and he was based in Dunkirk, and flew coastal protection missions over the Channel. He claimed his ninth victory, a Spitfire, over Sheerness on 8 April.

Promoted to *Oberleutnant* in late April his Group was again relocated in early June to Dortmund and converted to the Bf 109F-2 and made ready for the invasion of the Soviet Union. At the beginning of the campaign he flew low-level attacks on Soviet airfields, and he claimed five Ilyushin DB-3 bombers over Lake Wygonowski on 25 June to become an 'ace-in-a-day'. By the end of the month he had claimed another four victories, and had now claimed eighteen victories. He claimed an Il-2 ground-attack aircraft on 3 July and two Petlyakov Pe-2 dive-bombers on 11 July and a DB-3 on the 12th and 13 July. Three days later Kolbow was shot down by Soviet anti-aircraft fire during a low-level attack on Stara Bycow and he attempted to bail out from a height of only 65ft. It was too low, his parachute failed to fully open and he was killed. He was posthumously awarded the Knight's Cross on 27 July 1941. His remains were never found but his name has been added to the memorial book at the German War Cemetery in Telushy, Belarus.

Franz RUHL

Oberleutnant

Knight's Cross: Awarded as *Leutnant* and *Staffelführer* of the 4th Squadron of the 3rd Fighter Wing '*Udet*' on 27 July 1944 for operations over the Soviet Union and the Western Front.

Franz Ruhl claimed thirty-five aerial victories in 200 missions during the Second World War, of which sixteen were achieved over the Western Front including thirteen four-engined bombers. He was born on 12 December 1922 in Regensburg in eastern Bavaria and was the cousin of Heinrich Setz, a fighter ace and holder of the Knight's Cross with Oakleaves.

On completion of his training Ruhl was assigned to the 2nd Group of the 3rd Fighter Wing from October 1942 with the rank of *Leutnant*. He flew from Soltsy about 25 miles from Lake Ilmen and from late November his Group moved to Smolensk. After the 6th Army had been encircled at Stalingrad his Squadron was relocated there where he

(Deutsches Wehrkundearchiv)

flew escort missions for transport aircraft leaving the area. At the beginning of 1943, because of the Soviet advance his Group moved to Tatsinskaya Airfield, and from early February moved to Makiivka in the Ukraine. On 10 March Ruhl claimed his first victory, an Ilyushin Il-2 ground-attack aircraft, and in early April his Group moved again, to Kerch in the Crimea. He claimed his second victory on 12 April and a third over the Black Sea on 20 April and was shortly after awarded the Iron Cross 2nd Class. He claimed his fourth victory on 28 April and the following day he claimed four victories and was awarded the Iron Cross 1st Class a few days later. He claimed another four victories during May and was flying from Kharkiv in the Ukraine from early July, claiming his 19th victory on the 31st.

In August his Group's mission over the Eastern Front ended and they were relocated to Uetersen in Schleswig-Holstein, Germany and were refreshed and converted to the Bf 109G-5 and G-6. From September his Group moved to Amsterdam-Schiphol and Ruhl claimed a Bristol Beaufighter over west Den Helder on 16 September, his 20th victory. He then claimed a B-17 four-engined bomber over the North Sea on the 24th and another on the 27th. He was now flying in 'Defence of the Reich' over the Ruhr area and claimed two more B-17s on 8 October and shortly after he made a belly landing at Groningen with a damaged aircraft but wasn't injured. On the 24th he was appointed *Staffelkapitän* of his Squadron but he wasn't a well man, his health keeping him away from his command occasionally. On 23 November he claimed two more Beaufighters over north Texel in the Netherlands and was awarded the *Luftwaffe* Honour Goblet on the 26th and during December he claimed three P-47 Thunderbolts but these were later reclassified as unconfirmed.

At the beginning of 1944 the entire Group was posted to Bad Wörishofen in Germany and on 5 February, Ruhl was awarded the German Cross in Gold for recognition of his success as a fighter pilot. He claimed a B-17 four-engined bomber over Braunschweig on 10 February and another on the 21st but this was unconfirmed, on the 24th he claimed two B-24 Liberator four-engined bombers over Eschwege but only one was confirmed. On 8 March he claimed two B-17s and another over Aachen on 8 May, and the Group was relocated to Ansbach on the 20th. In June he was struck by a severe illness resulting in temporary paralysis and he was hospitalized – missing the Allied invasion of Normandy, where his Squadron was deployed. Whilst recovering he was awarded the Knight's Cross on 27 July 1944.

Ruhl returned to his squadron in late November and claimed two RAF Lancaster bombers over Bottrop-Recklinghausen in the Ruhr area. On the 24th his Bf 109 was shot down by US fighters near Liège, Belgium, his aircraft hitting the ground and exploding. His body has never been recovered.

Gerhard SOMMER

Hauptmann

Knight's Cross: Awarded posthumously on 27 July 1944 as *Hauptmann* and *Staffelkapitän* of the 4th Squadron of the 11th Fighter Wing for operations over the Western Front.

Gerhard Sommer claimed twenty aerial victories over the Western Front and all but six were four-engined bombers claimed in just 14 months before being shot down himself. He was born on 14 September 1919 in Steinpleis near Zwickau in Saxony, Germany and after completing his pilot training in December 1941, *Leutnant* Sommer joined the 2nd Squadron of the 1st Fighter Wing. At this time he flew over Germany in 'Defence of the Reich' duties, covering the quiet north-western approaches across the North Sea.

(Deutsches Wehrkundearchiv)

He claimed his first aerial victory, a Mosquito, north-east of Scharmbeck on 19 August 1942 and was awarded the Iron Cross 2nd Class. In the autumn he was transferred as *Staffelkapitän* of the 1st Squadron of the 1st Fighter Wing and by the beginning of 1943 the 1st Group was equipped with the Bf 109G-1 fighter. On 26 February Sommer claimed his second victory, a B-17 Flying Fortress near Sengwarden just north of Wilhelmshaven. It was his first large bomber and he would soon become something of an expert in shooting them down. The daylight attacks by US four-engined bombers would become constant and steadily increase in size. On 22 March Sommer claimed B-24 Liberator bomber and was shortly after awarded the Iron Cross 1st Class. The German commanders now decided to improve their tactics against these large formations and a new fighter wing was authorised to be set up in 'Defence of the Reich'.

On 1 April 1943 the 2nd Group of the 11th Fighter Wing was created and Sommer, now an *Oberleutnant* was appointed *Staffelkapitän* of the 4th Squadron, flying the Bf 109G-1 from his base in Jever. On 14 May he claimed another B-24 during an Allied raid on the U-boat pens at Kiel and a week later he claimed a B-17 bomber in the same area. Sommer also claimed two four-engined bombers and a P-38 Lightning during June. During the last week of July the Allies pounded the Reich, the Americans by day and the British by night, including the devastating Hamburg fire-raid on 27 July which claimed the life of almost 37,000 people (some reports state more). During that time Sommer's Group became the first aircraft to carry the new BR21 rocket system under the wings of their aircraft and during that time Sommer a B-17 on 26 July and two more on the 28th. He claimed a B-24 on 4 October and a B-17 five days later and from early November his Group moved to Plantlünne, Wesel in order to fly escort missions for the aircraft of the 26th Destroyer Wing.

During December 1943 Sommer claimed three P-47 Thunderbolts and in January 1944 he claimed a B-17 bomber even though due to bad weather the Allies were flying limited operations. From February the P-51 Mustang was a fighter capable of escorting the large bombers the full distance to their target, tipping the scales further in the Allies' favour in the bombing campaign against Germany. On 20 February the Allies began Operation Avalanche, their coordinated assault on the *Luftwaffe*, its airfields and factories and from March they turned their attention to Hitler's capital – Berlin.

Sommer was awarded the German Cross in Gold on 20 March in recognition of his sixteen victories. He claimed a B-24 on 29 April and his 20th and last victory was claimed on 8 May 1944, a P-47 Thunderbolt over Hannover.

On 12 May *Hauptmann* Sommer was shot down by US P-47 fighters south of Paderborn and crashed at Salzkotten and is buried today at the Military Cemetery in Salzkotten. At the time of his death he was one of the *Luftwaffe*'s highest scoring four-engined bomber aces and in recognition of his victories he was posthumously awarded the Knight's Cross on 27 July 1944.

Bernhard VECHTEL

Oberleutnant

Knight's Cross: Awarded on 27 July 1944 as *Fahnenjunker-Oberfeldwebel* and fighter pilot with the 10th Squadron of the 51st Fighter Wing 'Mölders' for operations over the Soviet Union and in recognition of his 79th aerial victory.

Bernhard Vechtel claimed 108 aerial victories whilst flying a total of 860 combat missions over the Eastern Front during the Second World War. He was born on 31 July 1920 in Vohren, Warendorf, North Rhine-Westphalia and upon entering the *Luftwaffe* in the summer of 1940 he trained as a fighter pilot.

(Deutsches Wehrkundearchiv)

In May 1942 he qualified as a fighter pilot and was assigned to the 10th Squadron of the 51st Fighter Wing as an *Unteroffizier*. He flew as part of the 4th Group over the Soviet Union, remaining there with this unit until the end of the war. During May the Group was briefly withdrawn from combat for a period of maintenance and equipment update in Smolensk. Then Vechtel and his Group were sent to Dugino where he flew cover missions over the left flank of Army Group Centre in the area of the 9th Army. In July his Group moved south and on the 30th, the Soviets launched the First Rzhev-Sychyovka Offensive Operation. Their plan was to crush the Rzhev salient held by the 9th Army. On 2 August Vechtel claimed his first victory, an Il-2 ground-attack aircraft near Rzhev, with his second victory being achieved on 3 September, a MiG-3 fighter. From early October his Group moved to Vitebsk to be deployed over the area between Army Group North and Army Group Centre. He remained there with his Group until the end of the year and took part in many defensive battles during the Soviet winter offensive. He claimed four more victories during December and was awarded the Iron Cross 2nd Class.

In early February 1943 his Group went back to Germany briefly and then returned to Orel on the Eastern Front. In early May Vechtel was promoted to *Feldwebel* and he claimed two victories on both 7 and 8 June and was awarded the Iron Cross 1st Class. On 2 August his Group moved to Bryansk and then later to Poltava and during August he claimed ten victories and on 20 September he claimed his 25th victory. He claimed two victories on 24 September, another on the 26th, three on the 27th and two on the 29th, including his 33rd victory. During October he claimed ten more victories and was promoted to *Oberfeldwebel*. He claimed his 50th on 28 November, an Il-2 ground-attack aircraft over Pretrovka, and from December he flew from Zhitomir.

On 3 January 1944 he was awarded the *Luftwaffe* Honour Goblet in recognition of claiming thirty victories and he was awarded the German Cross in Gold on 28 January by which time he had claimed over fifty victories. From February 1944 his Group was relocated to Orsha. Over the last few months he had moved from the 10th Squadron to the 12th and was now back with the 10th again.

He claimed his 60th victory on 22 April and by the end of the month he had claimed his 65th. On 1 May he claimed a Yak-9 fighter, his 66th victory and the 51st Fighter Wing's 8,000th victory of the war. By the end of May Vechtel had achieved a total of seventy-nine victories and on the 28th he had been promoted to *Leutnant* and granted leave. On 27 July he was awarded the Knight's Cross and he claimed even more victories during August. He claimed three on the 13th, two on the 15th, three on the 17th and he claimed three more on the 24th, which included his 90th victory.

He was shot down on 1 September by ground fire and was seriously wounded and was away from combat duties for some time. From November he flew from Modlin in Poland, and on 11 December he was appointed *Staffelkapitän* of the 14th Squadron, replacing *Oberleutnant* Horst Walther who had been transferred. On 12 January 1945 the Soviets launched the Vistula-Oder Offensive and two days later their forces reached Modlin, forcing his Group to move to Danzig-Langfuhr. On 25 March Vechtel claimed his 100th victory and a few days later he was promoted to *Oberleutnant* and on 1 May he received orders to relocate to Flensburg in northern Germany. The following day he decided with other pilots to desert and refused to fly to Flensburg and he led four aircraft to his home town of Warendorf near Münster. He arrived with two other pilots, a third having been shot down and captured by British forces, and later Vechtel and his two comrades also surrendered to the British. He died on 21 August 1975 in Speyer, a city in Rhineland-Palatinate.

Hans WEIK

Hauptmann

Knight's Cross: Awarded on 27 July 1944 as *Leutnant* and *Staffelführer* of the 10th Squadron of the 3rd Fighter Wing '*Udet*' for operations over the Soviet Union and the Western Front.

Hans Weik claimed thirty-four aerial victories during the Second World War and twenty-three were achieved over the Western Front of which twenty-two were four-engined bombers. He was born on 6 July 1922 in Heilbronn northern Baden-Württemberg in Germany and joined the *Luftwaffe* in October 1941.

In February 1943, with his training complete, *Leutnant* Weik was assigned to the Staff Squadron of the 3rd Fighter Wing, seeing action over the Soviet Union. From March he flew as part of the 1st Group, flying the Bf 109G-4, and claimed his first victory on 9 March, a Yak-1 fighter over south-west Marjewka. By the end of March he had claimed four victories and in early April was awarded the Iron Cross 2nd Class.

(Deutsches Wehrkundearchiv)

He claimed two more victories on 11 April, and by the 21st he had claimed a total of eleven victories and had been awarded the Iron Cross 1st Class. From May he was assigned to the Advanced Fighter and Training Group East as an instructor. On 16 September Weik claimed a B-17 Flying Fortress south of La Rochelle in France, having been assigned to the Western Front. This was his only victory with this unit and he returned to the 3rd Fighter Wing in November, serving with the 9th Squadron in 'Defence of the Reich' duties. He claimed another B-17 on 19 December, 10 miles south-east of Innsbruck.

On 11 February 1944 Weik, now an *Oberleutnant*, was appointed *Staffelkapitän* of the 10th Squadron of the 3rd Fighter Wing, part of the 3rd Group based in Bad Wörishofen, Germany. He claimed two victories in February, both B-17s, and during the first eight days of March he claimed another four B-17s. On 23 March after claiming a B-17 south-west of Dissen he was shot down and belly-landed his Bf 109G-6 at Klottingen but was unharmed. By the end of the month he had claimed a total of twenty-one victories and on 24 April he claimed three more Flying Fortresses and that same day he was shot down and bailed out near Giessen, but was unhurt. He claimed two more bombers five days later and had become something of a four-engined bomber specialist. On 8 May he claimed two B-24 Liberators over Germany as well as a B-17 over south-western Hoya in Lower Saxony. On his way back to base he was attacked and forced to make another belly landing due to damage, this time at Nieuwburg in the Netherlands. but again he wasn't hurt. He was awarded the German Cross in Gold on 10 May 1944 in recognition of his twenty-five victories and on the 12th he claimed two more B-17 bombers. He claimed two more the next day and on the 15th he was awarded the *Luftwaffe* Honour Goblet.

With the start of the Allied invasion of Normandy on 6 June his Group moved to St. André de l'Eure the following day so they could be deployed over the Allied landing area. His Group had to move airfields a number of times in June due to air raids. On 7 July Weik claimed another B-24, this time over Aschersleben, and on the 18th, shortly after claiming a B-17 bomber, he was himself shot down. His Focke-Wulf Fw 190 crashed at Kempten. He was seriously injured, and it was his 85th and last combat mission of the war. He spent several weeks in hospital and was awarded the Knight's Cross on 27 July and on 1 September he was promoted to *Hauptmann*. Once he had recovered he was assigned to the 3rd Group of the 2nd Advanced Fighter and Replacement Group from April 1945 but saw no active service, remaining on the ground, helping with the conversation of the Group to the Messerschmitt Me 262 jet fighter.

After the war he studied agriculture and then became an architect and built sports facilities, including school sport auditoriums and other buildings. In retirement he indulged his passion for building model ships. Weik died on 6 June 2001 in Heidenheim an der Brenz in Baden-Württemberg, southern Germany.

Walter WOLFRUM

Oberleutnant

Knight's Cross: Awarded on 27 July 1944 as *Leutnant* and pilot with the 1st Group of the 52nd Fighter Wing for operations over the Soviet Union and for claiming his 123rd aerial victory.

Walter Wolfrum claimed 134 aerial victories, all achieved whilst flying 424 combat missions over the Eastern Front during the Second World War. He was born on 23 May 1923 in Schmölz in Upper Franconia and joined the *Luftwaffe* in late 1941. He trained as a fighter pilot with Air Combat School 2 and later served with Fighter Replacement and Training Group East.

He was promoted to *Leutnant* in February 1942 and was assigned to the 5th Squadron of the 52nd Fighter Wing in January 1943. From mid-January he was flying the Bf 109G from Rostov on the Eastern Front and in February his Group moved to Nikolayev in the Ukraine. On the 27th his Group moved to Anapa on the Black Sea and on

(*Author's collection*)

10 March he crashed his Bf 109G-4 but wasn't injured. He claimed his first victory on 28 May, a Yak-1 fighter near Kijewskoje, and on 18 July he was shot down and wounded when he crashed at Gostagajewska airstrip. Then on 21 July he claimed an LaGG-1 fighter and claimed his third victory the following day, and he claimed two Yak-1 fighters on the 25th and was awarded the Iron Cross 2nd

Class three days later. He claimed three victories during August and his Group relocated twice during that time. He claimed his 11th victory on 9 September and on the 22nd he was awarded the Iron Cross 1st Class. From 2 October his Squadron flew from Kerch and he claimed three more victories on the 22nd, and by 6 November his Group had moved to Rzeszow in Poland, and by the end of the year Wolfrum had claimed a total of twenty victories.

At the beginning of 1944 his Group was in Bagerovo near Kerch in the Crimea, and between 7 and 15 February he claimed another ten victories and had now claimed a total of thirty combat victories. He remained in the southern sector of the Eastern Front claiming six victories on 19 March to become an 'ace-in-a-day' and which included his 40th aerial victory. He claimed three victories on the 22nd and four on the 26th, which included his 50th victory, and he achieved his 60th victory two weeks later. He was awarded the *Luftwaffe* Honour Goblet on 20 April and had by this time claimed his 69th victory. He claimed his 70th victory on 16 May and that same day he was appointed *Staffelkapitän* of the 1st Squadron of the 52nd Fighter Wing. On 18 May he was awarded the German Cross in Gold in recognition of gaining over sixty victories, but by the time it was presented he had achieved seventy-five victories. By late May he was flying from a base in Romania and on the 20th he claimed six aerial victories to become an 'ace-in-a-day' for the second time, all over Grigoriopol. On 30 May he claimed eleven victories to become a double 'ace-in-a-day' yet again and had by this time claimed his 89th victory. The following day he achieved six victories, becoming an 'ace-in-a-day' and the next day he repeated the achievement when he claimed five victories to become an 'ace-in-a-day' for the fifth time!

He claimed his 100th victory on 4 June and from the 16th his Squadron converted to the Focke-Wulf Fw 190 fighter. Throughout July he claimed even more victories, and he claimed four on the 7th, three on the 14th and four on the 15th. He became an 'ace-in-a-day' for the sixth time and a double ace in a day for the second time when he claimed ten victories the next day and shortly after shooting down the 10th aircraft near Zoloecev he was himself shot down and severely wounded by shrapnel in his hip. He was away from combat for six months, during which time he was awarded the Knight's Cross on 27 July and was promoted to *Oberleutnant* on 1 September 1944.

He returned as *Staffelkapitän* of the 1st Squadron of the 52nd Fighter Wing, flying from Breslau-Schöngarten, Germany from 10 February 1945. That same day he claimed a Yak-9 fighter, his 125th aerial victory, and shortly after he was himself shot down and had to make a belly landing south-west of Steinau but wasn't wounded. On 15 March he claimed four more victories and the following day he claimed another two, all P-39 fighters. On 17 April he claimed two victories, his 133rd and 134th and last. Two days later his Group moved to Deutsch-Brod in Czechoslovakia. Here he and his men surrendered to the US 90th Infantry Division and a few days later were handed over to the Soviets. However, Wolfrum was released after only two months due to his many wounds. In the 1960s he became a successful aerobatics pilot, winning the German Championships in 1962 and taking second place in 1961, 1963, 1964 and 1966. He died on 26 August 2010, in Schwabach, Bavaria.

Franz DÖRR

Hauptmann

Knight's Cross: Awarded on 19 August 1944 as *Oberleutnant* and *Staffelkapitän* of the 7th Squadron of the 5th Fighter Wing for operations over England and the Soviet Union and for achieving his 90th aerial victory.

Franz Dörr claimed a total of 122 aerial victories whilst flying 437 combat missions over the Eastern Front during the Second World War. Born in Mannheim on 10 February 1913, he flew as a reconnaissance pilot during both the Polish and French campaigns. He joined the Fighter Replacement

Group of the 3rd Fighter Wing based in the Netherlands where as a *Feldwebel* he trained as a fighter pilot. On 1 January 1942 his unit was renamed the 7th Squadron of the 5th Fighter Wing and transferred to the Eastern Front. From March Dörr flew combat missions from the airfield at Pechenga, an urban area near Murmansk, and was shortly afterwards promoted to *Oberfeldwebel*.

Dörr claimed his first aerial victory on 9 May 1942, a Soviet Hurricane over Pechenga, and he claimed his second victory on the 15th, another Hurricane. On 28 May he claimed a third Hurricane but on 12 July he was shot down and had to bail out of his Bf 109 but was unhurt. A few days before he had been awarded the Iron Cross 2nd Class and shortly after claiming his eighth victory on 23 January 1943 Dörr was awarded the Iron Cross 1st Class. He was promoted to *Leutnant* in June and appointed *Staffelkapitän* of his squadron later that month. He had by this time achieved his 24th aerial victory, and he

(Deutsches Wehrkundearchiv)

claimed his 30th and 31st on 25 November. In Late 1943 he was promoted to *Oberleutnant* and was awarded the *Luftwaffe* Honour Goblet on 28 February 1944 and the German Cross in Gold on 20 March after claiming thirty-one victories.

In May he was appointed *Gruppenkommandeur* of the 3rd Group of the 5th Fighter Wing and claimed seven victories on the 16th he claimed seven victories, to become an 'ace-in-a-day'. On 25 May he claimed four victories, which included his 50th, and on 26 May he became an 'ace-in-a-day' for the second time when he shot down five aircraft. Dörr claimed four more victories on 15 June and became an 'ace-in-a-day' again when he claimed eight aircraft on the 17th. He claimed six aircraft on both 27 and 28 June, to become an 'ace-in-a-day' for the fourth and fifth time – he had now claimed his 78th victory. On 4 July he claimed five more victories, his sixth 'ace-in-a-day', and on 19 August he was awarded the Knight's Cross and on the 23rd he claimed seven victories, which included his 100th, and became an 'ace-in-a-day' for the seventh time. He was promoted to *Hauptmann* in early October he claimed six victories on the 9th, his eighth 'ace-in-a-day', and by 21 October had claimed his 122nd and last victory.

He was taken prisoner by the Americans in May 1945 and was lucky not to have been handed over the Soviets, being released in August that year. He settled in southern Germany where he died in Konstanz on 13 October 1972.

Heinrich 'Heinz' HACKLER

Leutnant

Knight's Cross: Awarded on 19 August 1944 as *Fahnenjunker-Oberfeldwebel* and whilst attached to the 3rd Group of the 77th Fighter Wing for operations over the Balkans, Crete, the Soviet Union, North Africa, Italy and the Western Front.

Heinrich Hackler claimed thirty-seven aerial victories during the Second World War of which thirteen were achieved over the Western Front. He was born on 14 December 1918 in Siegen, part of North Rhine-Westphalia and he joined the *Luftwaffe* in 1939 and trained as a fighter pilot.

In February 1941, with his training complete, *Feldwebel* Hackler was assigned to the 3rd Group of the 77th Fighter Wing and was attached to the 8th Squadron based in Saint-Brieuc, France. From 21 June he saw action over the Soviet Union as part of Operation Barbarossa, and he claimed his first victory the next day, a Polikarpov I-16 fighter. He claimed his second victory, an Ilyushin DB-3 bomber, on 8 July and on 26 September he shot down four aircraft to claim his sixth victory. Soon after he was awarded the Iron Cross 2nd Class and claimed a Petlyakov Pe-2 dive-bomber on 15 October whilst flying mission in support of the 11th Army. On 27 October he claimed two more victories and a few days later he was finally awarded the Iron Cross 1st Class.

From late October he flew over the Crimea where in December the 3rd Group moved to the eastern part of the Crimean Peninsula and continued to be successful – since the beginning of the campaign his Group had claimed almost 500 aerial victories. At the beginning of 1942 the Group was equipped with Messerschmitt Bf 109F-4 fighters and flew missions over Sevastopol. On 5 January Hackler claimed an I-153 fighter, and he claimed three DB-3 bombers on the 10th, however three of these victories remain unconfirmed. At the end of February he was promoted to *Oberfeldwebel* and just before his Group was withdrawn from the front he claimed his 15th victory and Hackler was awarded the *Luftwaffe* Honour Goblet on 16 March.

(Deutsches Wehrkundearchiv)

His Group returned to the Soviet Union at the end of May, and he claimed an Il-2 ground-attack aircraft over Kharkov on 11 June. Hackler was then attached to the Staff of the 3rd Group and claimed two victories, both Il-2s, on 2 July, and he claimed his 20th aerial victory two weeks later. In late October the 3rd Group was completely withdrawn from the Soviet Union and was rested and then equipped with the new Bf 109G fighter. Hackler then moved to North Africa and began flying missions over El Alamein, but the Group suffered from lack of spare parts and had problems with some of its technical equipment. During November they moved several times due to the British ground offensive and as a result Hackler only claimed two victories in a month.

At the beginning of 1943 Hackler returned to the 8th Squadron, flying combat missions over Libya. He took part in the defensive battles for Tunisia and claimed his 27th victory on 29 March, a P-40 fighter over Maknassy. In May his Group moved to Sciacca in Sicily and flew evacuation flights between Tunisia and Sicily, during which time they transferred ground crew in the hulls of bombers. He claimed his 30th victory on 18 June, a B-25 Mitchell bomber, and six days later he shot down a P-38 Lightning, which remains an unconfirmed victory.

After the surrender of the Italians in Africa the Group moved various times and by the end of September they settled on the east coast of Corsica. At the beginning of 1944 his Squadron became part of the 2nd Group and Hackler claimed a B-24 near Pitesti, Romania on 5 April and a B-17 Flying Fortress on the 24th. He claimed two B-24s and one B-17 in May and from 1 June Hackler flew as *Staffelkapitän* of the 8th Squadron of the 77th Fighter Wing and was promoted to *Leutnant* in early July. He claimed a P-51 Mustang on 3 July over Silistra, Romania and in August he was transferred to the 11th Squadron, claiming a Yak-9, his 37th and last victory, on 23 August. He was awarded the Knight's Cross on 19 August in recognition of his victories and success as a fighter pilot.

In December his Group took part in the Ardennes Offensive in Belgium and he was awarded the German Cross in Gold on 12 December. On 1 January Hackler was shot down by anti-aircraft fire in the area of Antwerp and was killed. He is buried today in the military cemetery at Ysselsteyn, Netherlands, Block X, Row 11 and Grave No. 260.

Hans-Heinrich 'Kira' KOENIG

Hauptmann

Knight's Cross: Awarded posthumously on 19 August 1944 as *Oberleutnant* and *Staffelkapitän* of the 3rd Squadron of the 11th Fighter Wing for operations over the Western Front.

Hans-Heinrich Koenig claimed twenty-four aerial victories of which nineteen were four-engined bombers, all of them over the Western Front during the Second World War. He was born on 23 July 1921 in Halle a city in central Germany and he joined the *Luftwaffe* as a *Leutnant* in 1940.

(Deutsches Wehrkundearchiv)

With his pilot training complete he was assigned to the 5th Squadron of the 76th Destroyer Wing in the spring of 1941. He flew the Messerschmitt Bf 110 twin-engined fighter-bomber and saw action over Greece from May and later Crete. He claimed an RAF Blenheim over Blankenberge in the Netherlands on 18 September but this remains an unconfirmed victory. On 15 October he claimed another Blenheim over the Western Front and this was a confirmed victory, his first official one, and he was awarded the Iron Cross 2nd Class. From November his unit was renamed as the 8th Squadron of the 3rd Night Fighter Wing and he claimed an RAF Lancaster bomber over Bad Zwischenahn and was later awarded the Iron Cross 1st Class. He converted to the Fw 190 in March 1943 when he was transferred from night-fighter duty to day fighters, when he was assigned to the 3rd Squadron of the 11th Fighter Wing

Koenig claimed his fourth victory on 26 June over Fehmarn, an island in Germany and this was an RAF Wellington twin-engined bomber. During the attack his Fw 190A-4 was hit by return fire and Koenig was seriously wounded, losing an eye. Once recovered he joined the 2nd Group of the 11th Fighter Wing as an *Oberleutnant* in April 1943 and on 4 October he claimed another B-24 bomber. Later he flew as part of the 3rd Squadron and flew defensive missions over the German Bight, part of the North Sea bounded by the Netherlands and Germany to the south, and Denmark and Germany to the east. By June his Group was flying the Fw 190A-6 and continued to fly protection missions over the German coast. On 11 December he claimed a B-17 Flying Fortress over north-east Spijk in the Netherlands and shortly after was shot down but was only slightly wounded.

During February 1944 he claimed two B-17s and on the 11th he was again shot down during combat and parachuted uninjured from his aircraft south of Saarbrücken. On 6 March he claimed two more B-17s and two days later claimed a B-17 and a P-47 Thunderbolt over the area of Hoya in the Netherlands. Before the end of March he claimed two more B-17s and during April he claimed a total of nine victories, all but one being four-engined bombers. In early May Koenig was appointed *Gruppenkommandeur* of the 1st Group of the 11th Fighter Wing and was flying the Bf 109G. He claimed a B-17 over east Limburg on the 12th and on the 24th he shot down another B-17 but this had fatal consequences for the ace pilot. The weather conditions were terrible south-west of Kiel and he led his Group during a frontal attack on the Flying Fortresses, all heading for Berlin. The one-eyed Koenig must have misjudged his distance in the terrible conditions and when the bomber exploded he collided head-on. His Fw 190 minus a wing was seen to fall into the cloud below. Koenig did not bail out, obviously wounded, and he was killed.

Koenig was one of the most experienced pilots in his Group with nineteen confirmed four-engined bomber victories. He was also one of the most successful formation leaders in the day fighter force. It was later said that because of his bad eyesight in such poor weather conditions may have accounted for the collision, but other witnesses said that the B-17 exploded and Koenig's aircraft was hit by the debris. He was posthumously awarded the Knight's Cross on 19 August 1944 and the German Cross in Gold on 1 October 1944.

Johann PICHLER

Leutnant

Knight's Cross: Awarded on 19 August 1944 as *Oberfeldwebel* and fighter pilot with the 3rd Group of the 77th Fighter Wing for operations over Crete, the Soviet Union, North Africa, Italy and the Eastern Front.

Johann Pichler claimed twenty-three victories over the Eastern Front and sixteen over the Western Front during the Second World War, of which ten were four-engined bombers. He was born on 15 December 1912 in Oberschweinbach, Fürstenfeldbruck in Bavaria and he joined the *Wehrmacht* in November 1934, initially with the army.

(Deutsches Wehrkundearchiv)

Pichler transferred into the *Luftwaffe* in 1938 and began training as a fighter pilot the following year and was assigned to the 77th Fighter Wing in August 1940. He flew his Messerschmitt Bf 109 from Trondheim where he flew protection missions for the battleship *Gneisenau* lying in the harbour and later flew similar missions over Berlin. At the beginning of 1941 *Feldwebel* Pichler flew as part of the 3rd Group out of action and from March his group was taken out of action and relocated to Münchendorf near Vienna in preparation for the Balkans campaign. On 16 May he claimed his first aerial victory, an RAF Hurricane over Crete, and was shortly after awarded the Iron Cross 2nd Class. Then six days later he was injured when he crash-landed his aircraft at Molaoi, Greece. Operating from rough landing grounds was hazardous and even the best pilots could be caught out, especially if their aircraft had suffered battle damage.

On 22 June his Group was transferred to the Soviet Union and he flew as part of Operation Barbarossa and he claimed two victories on 22 July, both Polikarpov I-16 fighters. He claimed two more victories on 31 July and was awarded the Iron Cross 1st Class shortly afterwards. Pichler claimed two more victories in August, during which time he was flying missions in support of the 11th Army. He claimed three MiG-3 fighters on 5 September and by the end of the month he had claimed twelve victories. From October until early 1942 he flew missions over the Crimea, equipped now with the Bf 109F-4, and during that time he was promoted to *Oberfeldwebel* and claimed his 21st victory on 19 March. After some rest and refitting back in Germany Pichler and his Group returned to the Eastern Front until his unit was withdrawn from the Soviet Union in mid-October and transferred to North Africa.

From late October Pichler flew over the El Alamein area and claimed two more victories before they had to abandon that area due to the British ground offensive in November. In December he was flying from Libya and by the end of the month his Group had to be withdrawn again. From early 1943 he took part in the defensive fighting around Tunisia in January and February. His Group moved several times in March a April and Pichler was awarded the German Cross in Gold on the 18 March. By May his Group had moved to Sicily and then on to Sardinia and during this time he claimed his 30th victory, and on 25 June he was awarded the *Luftwaffe* Honour Goblet. After the Italian surrender his Group moved to Corsica on 20 September and two days later they flew from the Italian mainland.

Towards the end of October he flew protection missions over the oil fields in Ploiești, Romania and continued to fly combat missions in this area into 1944. His Group moved several times but remained in Romania where between April and July 1944 he claimed nine victories, all of which were four-engined bombers, including three in one day on 3 July.

On 28 July 1944 his Bf 109G was shot down by USAAF fighters and he bailed out, severely wounded near Titu, Romania and upon reaching the ground he was hospitalized. Pichler was captured by advancing Soviet forces on 30 August whilst still in hospital and did not return to Germany until January 1950. On his return he learnt that he had been awarded the Knight's Cross on 19 August 1944, and this was later presented to him. He had flown over 700 combat missions during the war and had claimed thirty-nine victories. He died in his home town of Oberschweinbach in Bavaria on 16 February 1995.

Alfred 'Fred' TEUMER

Hauptmann

Knight's Cross: Awarded as *Oberleutnant* and *Staffelkapitän* with the 3rd Group of the 54th Fighter Wing on 19 August 1944 for operations over the Soviet Union and the Western Front.

Alfred Teumer claimed a total of seventy-four aerial victories during the Second World War, most over the Eastern Front, and he also claimed seven victories over the Western Front, which included three four-engined bombers. He was born on 1 February 1918 in Neustadt am Rübenberge, a town in the district of Hannover, Lower Saxony and in December 1941 after he had completed his pilot training he was assigned to the 3rd Squadron of the 54th Fighter Wing.

Whilst piloting his Bf 109F-2, *Leutnant* Teumer claimed his first victory on 28 December, a Petlyakov Pe-2 dive-bomber, but for the next three weeks he was grounded due to bad weather. At the beginning of 1942 he was flying from Krasnogvardeysky south-west of Leningrad and he claimed his second victory, a Yak-1 fighter, on 9 January and

(Deutsches Wehrkundearchiv)

claimed two MiG-1 fighters two days later. In mid-January his Group was again affected by the weather and he only claimed one more victory that month and was awarded the Iron Cross 2nd Class a few weeks later. He managed to claim three victories during March but again in April his Group was grounded due to the weather. By the end of the month his Group had converted to the Bf 109F-4 and from July he was flying from a base in Finland but was back in Krasnogvardeysky in mid-August. He made two forced landings in September, one on the 9th and the other on the 14th when his aircraft was hit by anti-aircraft fire and he was wounded and made an emergency landing. He was away from combat for three months.

In January 1943 he was promoted to *Oberleutnant* and the weather improved and he claimed four victories on the 12th and became an 'ace-in-a-day' on the 14th when he claimed five victories. He was awarded the Iron Cross 1st Class soon afterwards and he claimed his 20th victory on 27 January. From February his Group converted to the Focke-Wulf Fw 190A, and he returned to combat in the Soviet Union in March, and on 12 April he was awarded the *Luftwaffe* Honour Goblet after claiming twenty-five victories. In May he transferred to the 5th Squadron and claimed five victories that month and shortly after claiming another victory on 7 July he transferred to the 10th Squadron. Teumer shot down eight Soviet aircraft during August and was awarded the German Cross in Gold on 17 October after claiming his 46th victory.

From December he was appointed *Staffelkapitän* of the 2nd Squadron of the 54th Fighter Wing and claimed his 50th victory, an Ilyushin Il-2 ground-attack aircraft, on the 16th and from January he was flying from Wesenberg in Estonia. He claimed four victories on 8 January and claimed his 60th, a Yak-9, on 25 February and over the Baltic Sea during combat patrols in early April he claimed four more victories. At the end of April he transferred to the 7th Squadron, part of the 3rd Group, and claimed a B-24 Liberator on 19 May. He claimed his 70th victory on 27 May, a B-17 Flying Fortress, and on 8 June he claimed a P-51 Mustang over Dives-sur-Mer in France. On 10 June he was shot down during combat with US fighters of the 365th Fighter Group. He bailed out and landed with only minor injuries near the Orne estuary in France. He was awarded the Knight's Cross on 19 August after claiming seventy aerial victories and then later he transferred as *Staffelkapitän* to the 2nd Squadron of the *Kommando Nowotny*, flying the Messerschmitt Me 262 jet fighter.

On 4 October whilst landing at Achmer near Osnabrück his aircraft suffered engine failure and crashed, and he was killed. He was posthumously promoted to *Hauptmann*. He had flown over 300 combat missions, and is buried today in the German Evangelical Cemetery in Osnabrück in Row 9, Grave No. 3.

Paul BRANDT

Leutnant

Knight's Cross: Awarded as *Oberfeldwebel* and fighter pilot with the 4th Group of the 54th Fighter Wing on 5 September 1944 for operations over the Soviet Union and the Western Front.

Paul Brandt claimed twenty-five aerial victories over the Eastern Front and five over the Western Front and flew a total of 500 missions during the Second World War. He was born on 29 April 1915 at Rehhof in Stuhn, West Prussia and joined the 1st Group of the 54th Fighter Wing in October 1941 as an *Unteroffizier*. Attached to the 3rd Squadron from December, flying from Krasnogvardeysky near Leningrad he claimed his first aerial victory on 3 December, a Polikarpov I-16 fighter. He claimed his second victory on 9 January 1942, an Il-2 ground-attack aircraft, and shortly after was awarded the Iron Cross 2nd Class. Brandt was promoted to *Feldwebel* in August and by the beginning of September he had achieved his eighth victory and had been awarded the Iron Cross 1st Class.

(Deutsches Wehrkundearchiv)

Brandt was presented with the *Luftwaffe* Honour Goblet on 26 June 1943 after his ninth victory and from July he was attached to the 4th Squadron, part of the 2nd Group based in Schwerin. He claimed eight victories during July, and on 20 September he claimed his 20th victory and was promoted to *Oberfeldwebel*. He claimed a Pe-2 twin-engined dive-bomber south-east of Velikiye Luki on 12 October and five days later he was awarded the German Cross in Gold. He claimed two more victories before being transferred in March 1944 to the Advanced Training Group East as an instructor. On his return to front-line duty in August he was attached to the 15th Squadron of the 54th Fighter Wing and had been commissioned as a *Leutnant*. On 4 September he was awarded the Knight's Cross in recognition of his 25th aerial victory and for his success as a ground-attack pilot. In fact, during his time on the Eastern Front, Brandt had flown numerous ground-attack missions and was one of a number of pilots who had been adept at disabling and destroying Soviet tanks, making something of a name for himself in what was far from an easy task.

On 27 November Brandt was appointed *Staffelkapitän* of the 16th Squadron, part of the 4th Group of the 54th Fighter Wing operating from Münster-Handorf and then Vorden in Lower Saxony. He claimed a P-38 Lightning on 17 December and the following day he claimed two more victories, one over Malmédy. On 24 December after returning from a mission his Fw 190 aircraft caught fire due to a technical problem and he crashed north of Coerde about three miles north-north-east of Münster and was killed. He is buried today in the War Cemetery in Münster-Lauheide, Field A and Grave No. 179.

Rudolf 'Rudi' RADEMACHER

Leutnant

Knight's Cross: Awarded on 30 September 1944 as *Leutnant* and pilot attached to the 1st Group of the 54th Fighter Wing for operations over the Soviet Union and the Western Front.

Rudolf Rademacher flew 500 combat missions and claimed a total of ninety-three aerial victories during the Second World War, of which seventy-seven were over the Eastern Front. He claimed sixteen over the Western Front whilst flying the Messerschmitt Me 262 jet fighter, and this included eleven four-engined bombers. He was born on 19 June 1913 in Lüneburg in northern Germany and joined the Army in November 1934 and left in October 1935 to resume his civilian career as a butcher.

(Deutsches Wehrkundearchiv)

In August 1939 Rademacher joined the *Luftwaffe* and attended flight school between June 1940 and May 1941, and he was then assigned from December to the 3rd Squadron of the 54th Fighter Wing as an *Unteroffizier*. From January 1942 he flew as part of the 1st Group based in Krasnogvardeysky in the Soviet Union and flew the Messerschmitt Bf 109F-2. He claimed his first victory on 9 January, an Ilyushin Il-2 ground-attack aircraft over north-east Ostkaja. He claimed his second victory on 25 February, a P-40, and by the end of April he had claimed a total of ten victories and had been awarded both the Iron Cross 1st and 2nd Classes and had been promoted to *Oberfeldwebel*. He claimed three victories during July and by the end of August Rademacher had claimed nineteen. On 19 October he was awarded the *Luftwaffe* Honour Goblet in recognition of achieving twenty-one victories.

In January 1943 he claimed ten victories, which included four on the 15th, giving him a total of thirty-two of which two were later reclassified as unconfirmed. From March he flew with the 1st Squadron of the 54th Fighter Wing and claimed two victories on the 7th, which included his 35th. On 25th he was awarded the German Cross in Gold after claiming his 35th victory and on 5 July he became an 'ace-in-a-day' when he shot down seven aircraft. He claimed two victories on the 6th and 7th and on 8 July he claimed an LaGG-3 fighter, his 50th aerial victory. By the end of the month he had claimed a further eight victories and then he fell ill and was away from combat duty for three months.

He returned to duty at the beginning of October 1943, claiming his 60th victory on 11 November. By the beginning of 1944 his Group had moved to Orscha and in February Rademacher was commissioned as a *Leutnant*. His Group moved several times during June a July and by the end of that time he had claimed his 75th victory, a Yak-9 fighter. He then was assigned to the 1st Squadron of the Supplementary Group North as an instructor. On 18 September during a training mission he was shot down during combat with American heavy bombers and bailed out of his Focke-Wulf Fw 190 and was wounded upon landing. On the 30th he was awarded the Knight's Cross for his skill as a pilot and for claiming seventy-seven victories.

From January 1945 Rademacher flew with the 11th Squadron of the 7th Fighter Wing where he trained and later flew in combat with the Messerschmitt Me 262 jet fighter and became one of its best pilots. He flew this aircraft for the first time 'in anger' on 30 January over his homeland where he was based and claimed his first victory with this new aircraft on 1 February, a Tempest near Brunswick. On the 3rd he claimed two four-engined bombers, a B-17 Flying Fortress and a B-24 Liberator, over Magdeburg, his 79th and 80th victories. He claimed two B-17s on the 9th, and by the end of February Rademacher had achieved eight-six aerial victories – claiming his last victory on 10 April, a P-51 Mustang.

During the last few months of the war he had claimed sixteen four-engined bombers and claimed a further twenty-three victories on top of his official figure of ninety-three but had no witnesses and so they were never confirmed and this was probably why he was never considered for the Oakleaves. Rademacher continued to fly gliders after the war and died in a glider accident near Lüneburg on 13 June 1953.

Heinz 'Piepl' WERNICKE

Leutnant

Knight's Cross: Awarded on 30 September 1944 as *Leutnant* and pilot attached to the 2nd Group of the 54th Fighter Wing for operations over the Soviet Union and the Eastern Front and for claiming his 110th aerial victory.

Heinz Wernicke claimed a total of 118 aerial victories in just 18 months, all achieved whilst flying combat missions over the Eastern Front during the Second World War. He was born on 17 October 1920 in Berlin and was assigned to the 3rd Squadron of the 54th Fighter Wing on completion of his training in April 1942.

From the autumn of 1942 *Unteroffizier* Werneicke served as an instructor with Advanced Fighter Group East and from early 1943 was attached to the 6th Squadron of the 54th Fighter Wing on the Eastern Front. He claimed his first victory on 7 March, an Ilyushin Il-2 ground-attack aircraft, and was during this time a *Feldwebel* serving as part of the 2nd Group based in Rjelbitzi, an airfield south of Leningrad.

(Deutsches Wehrkundearchiv)

From 11 March his Squadron was commanded by *Hauptmann* Heinrich Jung and later saw combat during the Siege of Leningrad. He claimed his second victory on 19 March, an LaGG-3 fighter over Pushkin-Mag, and he claimed a Yak-4 the following day. He claimed two more victories on 27 May and was awarded the Iron Cross 2nd Class, and following five more victories during June Wernicke was awarded the Iron Cross 1st Class and became an instructor and underwent officer training.

Wernicke returned to the 6th Squadron in October 1943, claiming two more victories. On 5 November he claimed five victories to become an 'ace-in-a-day', and he claimed another victory on the 22nd, and three more on the 28th – which included his 20th victory. He claimed his 30th victory on 13 January 1944 and between the 14th and 15th he claimed five Il-2 ground-attack aircraft. By 4 February Wernicke had claimed his 40th victory, and five days later he claimed two more, and became an 'ace-in-a-day' again on the 16th when he shot down six aircraft. He achieved his 50th victory on 21 February and on 20 March he was awarded the German Cross in Gold, followed by the *Luftwaffe* Honour Goblet, presented on 24 April. In May his group was briefly withdrawn whilst being converted to the Focke-Wulf Fw 190A and the following month Wernicke was promoted to *Leutnant* and transferred to the 5th Squadron.

Wernicke now flew from Immola in Finland and saw action during the Soviet summer offensive from 9 June. He claimed a total of fourteen victories in June, which included his 60th victory. He claimed his 70th victory on 9 July, and claimed three victories on the 23rd, one on the 24th, four on 26 and 27 July – having by now reached a total of eighty-five victories. He claimed his 90th victory on 20 August and six days later he was appointed *Staffelkapitän* of the 1st Squadron, still with the 54th Fighter Wing. He continued to claim victories at a fast rate, claiming three near Malpils and over Riga on 14 September, which included his 100th victory. Between the 15th and 20th he claimed ten more victories and on 30 September after claiming 112 victories he was finally awarded the Knight's Cross, presented to him by *General der Flieger* and Commander-in-Chief of the 1st Air Fleet Curt Pflugbeil.

On 12 October he claimed his 117th victory and on 27 December shortly after claiming a Yak-9 near Doblen Wernicke collided with his wingman *Unteroffizier* Horst Wollin just west of Dobele, Latvia and both pilots were killed.

Helmut GROLLMUS

Leutnant

Knight's Cross: Awarded posthumously on 6 October 1944 as *Leutnant* serving with the 4th Squadron of the 54th Fighter Wing for operations over the Soviet Union.

Helmut Grollmus claimed sixty-eight aerial victories, all of them over the Eastern Front, during the Second World War. He was born on 8 January 1918 in Lissa in Posen, Prussia and he joined the *Luftwaffe* in the early 1940s.

From late 1941 he served as a *Gefreiter* with the Supplementary Fighter Group attached to the 54th Fighter Wing based in the Soviet Union. From March 1942 he served in the 2nd Squadron in Krasnogvardeysky as an *Unteroffizier* and saw brief action over the Soviet Union before his unit was converted to the Messerschmitt Bf 109F-4. From July he flew escort and the occasional combat mission over Finland, returning to Krasnogvardeysky in August. In January

(Deutsches Wehrkundearchiv)

1943 whilst attached to the 1st Group Grollmus claimed his first aerial victory, a Ilyushin Il-2 ground-attack aircraft over south-west Wischera. He claimed his second victory on 28 January, a MiG-1 single-engined fighter, and towards the end of February he was awarded the Iron Cross 2nd Class and on the 28th he claimed his fourth victory, a Petlyakov Pe-2 dive-bomber over south-east Schlüsselburg.

From about June he served in the 12th Squadron of the 54th Fighter Wing and on the 12th he claimed his fifth victory and the following day he claimed three victories and was shortly after awarded the Iron Cross 1st Class. From mid-1943 he flew in the 12th Squadron as part of the 3rd Group from his base in Jesau and during August he claimed a total of fourteen aerial victories. Promoted to *Feldwebel* at the end of August he claimed his 25th victory on 1 September, a MiG-3 interceptor near Jelnja. He claimed a total of eight victories during October, claiming his 30th victory on the 21st over the River Dnieper, one of three victories that day. He claimed two victories on 5 November, two on the 22nd and three on the 29th, which included his 40th victory. On 12 December he was awarded the German Cross in Gold in recognition of his success over the Soviet Union.

In early February 1944 Grollmus was promoted to *Oberfeldwebel* and continued to claim victories over the Soviet Union whilst serving in the 4th Squadron of the 54th Fighter Wing once again in Finland. He claimed three victories on 19 March which included his 50th aerial victory. On 15 April he claimed his 60th victory. Soon afterwards he was promoted to the rank of *Leutnant* and on 19 June he claimed six victories to become an 'ace-in-a-day'. That same day his Focke-Wulf Fw 190 was shot down by Soviet ground fire, He managed to bail out and parachuted from his stricken aircraft but he was killed by soldiers on the ground. Some reports state they were Soviet soldiers, while others say he was shot by Finnish troops near Vyborg north-west of Leningrad. He had managed to shoot down sixty-eight aircraft in 17 months and on 6 October he was posthumously awarded the Knight's Cross in recognition of his success. Grollmus is buried in the military cemetery in Helsinki in Row 4, Grave No. 52.

Franz EISENACH

Major

Knight's Cross: Awarded on 10 October 1944 as *Hauptmann* and fighter pilot with the 2nd Group of the 54th Fighter Wing for operations over the Soviet Union and the Eastern Front and for claiming his 107th aerial victory.

(Deutsches Wehrkundearchiv)

Franz Eisenach claimed 129 aerial victories, of which forty-seven were Ilyushin Il-2 ground-attack aircraft, whilst flying 317 combat missions on the Eastern Front. He was born in Reetz in the Arnswalde region of Neumark, Germany on 11 August 1918, and joined the *Luftwaffe* in 1937 as an officer cadet.

Commissioned as a *Leutnant* in September 1939 he flew with the 2nd Group of the 76th Destroyer Wing in mid-1940. He took part in the Western campaign flying fighter-bomber missions out of Le Mans in France in the twin-engined Bf 110. From early 1941 his Group flew from Jever and from May he moved to Greece, flying combat missions over Crete. In November Eisenach transferred to the 1st Supplementary Squadron of the 51st Fighter Wing where he flew the single-seater Messerschmitt Bf 109. From January 1942 he served in the 4th Group of the 1st Fighter Wing, taking part in Operation Donnerkiel, known as the 'Channel Dash', to protect the battleships *Gneisenau* and *Scharnhorst* and the heavy cruiser *Prinz Eugen* from Allied air attacks.

In June 1942, now an *Oberleutnant*, Eisenach was appointed *Staffelkapitän* of the 12th Squadron of the 51st Fighter Wing, stationed in Germany. In July his squadron, together with the entire Group was converted to the Fw 190 fighter. He saw very little action at this time and in October he transferred as *Staffelkapitän* to the 7th Squadron of the 54th Fighter Wing in Smolensk on the Eastern Front. On 8 November, flying his 21st combat mission, he claimed his first victory, south-west of Schlüsselburg, a P-40 fighter. A month later he transferred to the 9th Squadron and during December he claimed three more victories. He had already been awarded the Iron Cross 2nd Class and was soon awarded the Iron Cross 1st Class after claiming victory number seven on 12 January 1943.

On 17 April he transferred to the 3rd Squadron of the 54th Fighter Wing, and claimed two Il-2 ground-attack aircraft on 24 May. He claimed two more victories on 17 June and on 5 July, and the following day he claimed three victories and on the 7th he claimed his 20th victory. The next day he claimed a Boston twin-engined bomber over south-west Maloarkhangelsk, but during the attack his aircraft was hit by return fire and he had to make an emergency landing, sustaining minor injuries and was briefly hospitalized. Eisenach was awarded the *Luftwaffe* Honour Goblet on 31 August and returned to duty a few weeks late, claiming two victories on 30 September, and claimed his 25th victory on 9 October. By the end of the month he had claimed thirty-five victories, and claimed three more on 5 and 10 November. He claimed four victories on 15 December and two on the 18th, his 48th and 49th victories. Shortly after claiming these he was shot down by anti-aircraft fire and managed to bail out, but he was seriously wounded and spent almost six months recovering.

Eisenach was awarded the German Cross in Gold on 16 January 1944 in recognition of the amount of combat missions flown and for achieving forty-nine aerial victories. He returned to duty in June, serving with the Staff Squadron of the 54th Fighter Wing, still on the Eastern Front. He claimed three victories on 26 June over Pskov and north-east Ostrov, which included his 50th victory. On 24 July he transferred to the 4th Squadron and by the end of the month had achieved seventy-one victories, including becoming an 'ace-in-a-day' on 30 July when he shot down five aircraft. He continued to claim many more victories in August and by the 15th had achieved his 80th victory. Meanwhile he had been promoted to *Hauptmann* and on 9 August took over as *Gruppenkommandeur* of the 1st Group of the 54th Fighter Wing. He had replaced *Hauptmann* Horst Ademeit who was reported as missing when his aircraft was shot down. Eisenach became an 'ace-in-a-day' for the second time on 14 September when he claimed nine victories, which included four Pe-2 twin-engine dive-bombers and five Il-2 ground-attack aircraft, shot down near Riga. By the end of October he had claimed his 107th victory and on the 10th was awarded the Knight's Cross and granted some extended leave.

On 14 December he claimed two victories and the next day he shot down another four and by the end of the month had claimed his 117th victory. On 1 January 1945 he was promoted to *Major*, and five days later he claimed his 120th victory over north Doblin. In March his Group moved to Neuhausen and Eisenach claimed three victories on the 5th, one on the 6th and claimed his final two victories on the 19th. At the end of April his Group moved to Flensburg where in early May they surrendered to the Allies. Eisenach spent a few months in a prisoner-of-war camp before being released and returning home. In 1956 he joined the *Bundeswehr* and served as an instructor at the officer's school until 1970, retiring four years later as an *Oberstleutnant*. He lived in Ottobrunn near Munich until his death on 21 August 1998.

Gerhard 'Knall' KOALL

Hauptmann

Knight's Cross: Awarded as *Hauptmann* and *Staffelkapitän* with the 4th Group of the 54th Fighter Wing on 10 October 1944 for operations over the Balkans, the Soviet Union and the Eastern Front.

Gerard Koall claimed thirty-five aerial victories over the Eastern Front and another two whilst flying combat missions over Yugoslavia during the Second World War. He was born on 7 June 1912 in Berlin and joined the *Luftwaffe* in 1935, initially serving as a reconnaissance pilot.

In August 1939 he was promoted to *Oberleutnant* and joined the air combat school in Fürstenfeldbruck, Bavaria and trained as a fighter pilot. From January 941 he served with the 54th Fighter Wing and was attached to the 7th Squadron of the 3rd Group in Dortmund. His Group moved to St. Dizier in north-eastern France at the end of March and then to Graz-Thalerhof in Austria and made ready for the Balkan

(Deutsches Wehrkundearchiv)

campaign. On 6 April Koall claimed his first victory, a Bf 109 of the Yugoslavian air force, a rare event as they only had forty-six serviceable aircraft of that type. The following day he claimed a PZL 11, a Polish-built aircraft, and soon after he was awarded the Iron Cross 2nd Class.

In mid-June, with the Balkan campaign finished, Koall's Group moved to East Prussia and converted to the Bf 109F-2 fighter aircraft. He saw action on 22 June, the first day of the invasion of the Soviet Union, but was forced to make a belly landing at Litzmannstadt in central Poland, although he wasn't injured, and the following day he claimed his third victory, a P-40 fighter. From July he flew from Ostrow Wielkopolski in west-central Poland and claimed three more victories that month and was awarded the Iron Cross 1st Class. His Group moved numerous times over the next few months and by the end of September he was flying combat missions over the Leningrad area, where he claimed two more victories.

On 23 February 1942 Koall was appointed *Staffelkapitän* of the 3rd Squadron of the 54th Fighter Wing, taking over from *Hauptmann* Hans Schmoller-Haldy who had been seriously wounded. He flew missions over Lake Ladoga and claimed his ninth victory, a P-40, on 27 February and in March he claimed his 10th and 11th victories. At the end of April his squadron left the front to be refreshed and converted to the Bf 109F-4 and Koall had been promoted to *Hauptmann*. He claimed a Yak-7 and an LaGG-3 on 20 July, and claimed two more victories on 2 August over Leningrad. However, the following day he was himself shot down by Soviet anti-aircraft fire and bailed out but was only slightly wounded. On 24 and 25 August he claimed one aerial victory and on 15 January 1943 he claimed three more, which included his 20th. By 19 February he had claimed twenty-six victories and his squadron began to convert to the Fw 190A. He was awarded the *Luftwaffe* Honour Goblet on 1 March and two weeks later on the 16th he claimed two more victories. In April he was appointed *Staffelkapitän* of the 4th Squadron and he claimed four victories between July and September, a combination of enemy ground attacks and the weather kept him from for flying as much as he would have liked. On 17 October he was awarded the German Cross in Gold in recognition of achieving his 30th aerial victory.

In March 1944 he was appointed Acting *Gruppenkommandeur* of the 4th Group and continued to fly over the Eastern Front. He claimed a Yak-4 light bomber on 25 March and he shot down three more aircraft in April, which included his 36th victory over south-west Selo near Leningrad. On 20 May he claimed an Ilyushin Il-2 ground-attack aircraft south-west of Ostrov but this would be his last victory. In late May Koall was appointed *Gruppenkommandeur* of the 1st Group of the 101st Fighter Wing stationed at Pau-East in France. By October his Group had moved to Bad Wörishofen in Bavaria and he was flying over Germany in 'Defence of the Reich' missions. On 10 October Koall was finally awarded the Knight's Cross in recognition of his leadership and for achieving thirty-seven aerial victories.

In January 1945 he took command of the 2nd Group of the 1st Fighter Replacement Squadron, flying from Strausberg in Brandenburg, Germany. His Group later moved to Berlin-Gatow and was disbanded in April. On the 25th he took command of the 4th Group of the 3rd Fighter Wing, flying from Tutow, but two days later during a ground-attack mission he was killed when his Fw 190 was shot down by Soviet anti-aircraft fire over Anklama, a town in the Western Pomeranian region of Mecklenburg, Germany.

Helmut MISSNER

Oberfeldwebel

Knight's Cross: Awarded posthumously on 10 October 1944 as *Oberfeldwebel* and fighter pilot in the 3rd Squadron of the 54th Fighter Wing in recognition of his skill as a fighter pilot over the Eastern Front.

(Deutsches Wehrkundearchiv)

Helmut Missner claimed eighty-three aerial victories over the Eastern Front during the Second World War. He was born on 19 May 1921 in Stuttgart-Zuffenhausen, part of the German state of Baden-Württemberg, and entered the *Luftwaffe* in November 1938. He trained as a fighter pilot from October 1939 and was assigned to the 1st Group of the 54th Fighter Wing as an *Unteroffizier* in the summer of 1942.

From August he flew the Bf 109F-4 from Krasnogvardeysky near St. Petersburg in the Soviet Union as part of the 2nd Squadron of the 54th Fighter Wing, claiming his first aerial victory, a Petlyakov Pe-2 twin-engined bomber, over north-east Gatchina on 15 September 1942. From early 1942 his squadron had been converted to the Fw 190A fighter and on 14 February 1943 Missner claimed two victories and was awarded the Iron Cross 2nd Class. The following day he claimed four more victories over Luban and by the 23rd he had claimed a total of nine victories and had been awarded the Iron Cross 1st Class. He claimed his 20th victory on 7 July and he claimed two more victories on the 8th, another on the 9th and on the 17th he claimed his 30th and 31st victories and the 5,000th victory of his Wing. In recognition for his success rate Missner was awarded the German Cross in Gold on 17 October 1943.

In early 1944 Missner moved to the 3rd Squadron and was now flying from Orsha in Belarus, and later moved to Wesenberg in Estonia. On 25 February he claimed two Il-2 ground-attack aircraft, on 6 March he claimed three La-5 fighters over Narva, his 39th to 41st victories. By the end of March he had achieved forty-eight victories and had been promoted to *Oberfeldwebel* and that same day he claimed three more victories which included his 50th victory. He claimed a total of thirteen victories during April and by the end of the month he had claimed his 60th victory, and by 29 May he claimed his 70th victory. In June his squadron moved around quite a lot, from Turku in Finland then onto Polotsk in Belarus in July, and at this time he had achieved eighty-three victories. In July Missner was transferred to the 1st Squadron of Advanced Training Group North as an instructor, and here experienced pilots like Missner, with such a high score record were rotated back to the Reich's training centres for temporary tours to share their front-line skills and knowledge with the young pilots who had just come out of training school. However, on 12 September whilst flying at almost 21,400ft he suffered altitude sickness and crashed his Fw 190A-8 at Sagan in Germany (now part of Poland), and was killed. He is today buried at Poznan-Milostowo in Poland in a mass grave. He was posthumously awarded the Knight's Cross on 10 October 1944 and just before his death he was recommended for promotion to *Leutnant*.

Franz SCHALL

Hauptmann

Knight's Cross: Awarded on 10 October 1944 as *Leutnant* and *Staffelführer* of the 3rd Squadron of the 52nd Fighter Wing for operations over the Soviet Union.

Franz Schall claimed 133 aerial victories during the Second World War of which 117 were achieved over the Eastern Front and sixteen over the Western Front whilst flying the Me 262 jet fighter, which included five four-engined bombers. He was born on 1 June 1918 in Graz, Austria-Hungary and saw action as a gunner with an anti-aircraft unit of the *Luftwaffe* from 1939.

From October 1940 Schall served with the 38th Anti-Aircraft Regiment before training as a fighter pilot from September 1941. He was promoted to *Leutnant* in September 1942 and with his training complete he joined the 3rd Squadron of the 52nd Fighter Wing and saw action over the Soviet Union. He claimed his first victory on 6 May

(*Author's collection*)

1943, a Lavochkin LaGG-3 fighter over north-eastern Belograd, and he claimed his second a week later but it was never confirmed. On 30 May he claimed one of many Ilyushin Il-2 ground-attack aircraft, his second confirmed victory, over north Krymsk. On 11 June he claimed another Il-2 and was shortly after awarded the Iron Cross 2nd Class. He claimed four more victories during July and on the 31st he was unhurt when had to make a forced-landing in his Bf 109 after being shot down by return fire near Kerch. Shortly after he was awarded the Iron Cross 1st Class and he claimed his 15th victory on 20 October and the end of the year he had claimed a total of twenty-six victories.

At the beginning of 1944 his Squadron, as part of the 1st Group, was in Mala-Wyska west of Kirovograd in the Ukraine. His Group moved several times in early January and even had to vacate at very short notice due to an advancing Soviet troop column. He claimed ten victories during January and the Group moved again a number of times during February and March and he claimed only three victories during this time. However, on 20 March he was rewarded for his dedication and skill as a pilot in claiming thirty victories and was awarded both the *Luftwaffe* Honour Goblet and the German Cross in Gold. On 5 April his Group moved to Leipzig, in Romania (not the one in Germany) and he claimed a Boston medium bomber on 19 April, his 40th victory, and claimed three more victories on the 24th over Leipzig. Schall claimed another victory before the end of April and claimed three more victories on 2 May and claimed his 50th victory on 17 May, a P-39 over south Grigoriopol. During the last two days of May he claimed five victories, and claimed his 60th victory on 4 June.

On 16 June his Squadron retrained with the Focke-Wulf Fw 190 fighter and they transferred back to the Eastern Front. Schall claimed two victories on 26 June in his new fighter, another on 7 July, four on the 14th, two more the following day and four on the 16th to claim his 73rd aerial victory. He claimed four victories over north-west Brody on the 16th and continued to claim regular victories throughout August. On 11 August he was appointed *Staffelkapitän* of his Squadron and he claimed his 80th victory on 24 August and on the 26th he claimed eleven victories to achieve a double 'ace-in-a-day', and had now claimed his 94th victory. On the 28th he claimed three victories and on the last day of August he claimed an amazing thirteen victories, almost a triple 'ace-in-a-day' and all over Opatów, Poland. He claimed five victories on 1 September, to become an 'ace-in-a-day' yet again and the following day he claimed another three victories.

On 24 September he transferred to the 2nd Squadron of *Erprobungskommando* (Testing Commando) *Nowotny*, flying the Messerschmitt Me 262 jet fighter. The unit was headed by *Major*

Walter Nowotny who just a few weeks later would be awarded the Knight's Cross with Oakleaves, Swords and Diamonds personally by Hitler. Schall claimed his first victory in a Me 262 on 7 October but this was not confirmed. His first confirmed victory, a P-51 over Coesfeld in North Rhine-Westphalia, was achieved on 28 October. Now with the rank of *Oberleutnant* he shot down a P-51 Mustang on 6 November and three more on the 8th, to record his 122nd aerial victory.

On 19 November Nowotny's unit was disbanded and became the 3rd Group of the 7th Fighter Wing and Schall was appointed *Staffelkapitän* of the 10th Squadron. By January the Group had reached the strength of nineteen aircraft but aerial combat was restricted due to pilot training and the Group only recorded two aerial victories in January as part of the 'Defence of the Reich'. On 18 March Schall claimed his first victory in his new appointment, a B-17 Flying Fortress over Brandenburg, his 123rd victory. He claimed another seven victories during March and his Group moved from Bavaria to Prague in April 1945 where they stayed until the end of the war. Bad weather made combat difficult but Schall managed to claim a Lancaster four-engined bomber on 4 April and another on the 9th. The following day shortly after combat with a P-51 which he claimed as his last victory, his aircraft was damaged by return fire and he had to make a forced landing at his base in Parchim, Mecklenburg. Upon landing his aircraft hit a bomb crater and exploded, Schall being killed instantly. He now lies in the Military Cemetery in Parchim in Field 8, Grave No. 44.

He had flown approximately 550 combat missions and had destroyed many ground vehicles, which included three tanks and a locomotive, and he had destroyed twenty-one bridges. He had been recommended for the Oakleaves before the end of the war but it was never confirmed. Of his 133 victories, sixty were Il-2 ground-attack aircraft shot down between May 1943 and September 1944.

Franz HRDLICKA

Hauptmann

Knight's Cross: Awarded on 18 October 1944 as *Hauptmann* and *Staffelkapitän* with the 2nd Group of the 77th Fighter Wing for operations over the Balkans, Crete, the Soviet Union, North Africa, Italy and the Western Front.

Franz Hrdlicka claimed over forty-four victories whilst flying more than 500 combat missions over the Eastern and Western Fronts during the Second World War. He was born on 15 October 1920 in Maxdorf, Bunn in Czechoslovakia and he joined the *Luftwaffe* in November 1939 at the age of 19.

From early 1940 he was assigned to the Supplementary Fighter Group of the 77th Fighter Wing based at Götzendorf, and after attending an advanced fighter pilot training course he was assigned to the 1st Squadron of the Supplementary Fighter Group in Merseburg. From May 1941 he flew with the 5th Squadron of the 77th Fighter Wing during the Balkan campaign and the invasion of Crete. On 22 June he flew during the invasion of the Soviet Union where he claimed his first aerial victory, a Polikarpov I-16 monoplane fighter, on 6 July. After the German attack over the Dniester on 17 July he flew in support of the XI Army Corps on the Dniester bridgehead in the Black Sea area in the Ukraine. On 6 August he claimed his second victory a MiG-3 fighter and four days later he claimed a Tupolev SB-2 and was awarded the Iron Cross 2nd Class. On 22 September he crashed his Bf 109E-7 upon landing at Tschaplinka in the Ukraine but wasn't injured. A few days later his Group moved to

(Deutsches Wehrkundearchiv)

Berislav and by September they had moved again to Chaplinka. In early October he flew in support of the German advance on Rostov and from the 12th his Group moved to the area near Taganrog and claimed two more victories. He claimed another in mid-November and then at the beginning of December his Group, which had been decimated by Soviet attacks, was relocated to Vienna-Aspern for rest and refitting.

By February 1942 most of the Group had been equipped with the Bf 109F-4, and from March he moved with his Squadron to the Crimea. He claimed his eighth and ninth victories in early March and on the 24th he claimed an I-16, his 10th aerial victory, and was awarded the Iron Cross 1st Class. The group was relocated to Kastoronje on 5 July and he claimed ten victories during July which included three on the 21st and 24th. On 13 September Hrdlicka was awarded the *Luftwaffe* Honour Goblet after claiming his 24th aerial victory. His Group moved various times during September and October and in early November their time on the Eastern Front had ended and Hrdlicka moved via Mizil, Sofia, Salonika, Bari and Naples to Comiso in Sicily.

In early January his Group moved to Africa during the course of the retreat of German troops. On 1 April he claimed his 30th victory, a Spitfire east of El Guettar and by May his Group was rested. They were back in June and Hrdlicka had been promoted to *Oberleutnant* and claimed another victory on 20 June and claimed three more the following month and was awarded the German Cross in Gold on 12 July. Just four days later the Group was badly hit by an Allied air raid and had to be taken out of action until 1 August when it flew missions over the Strait of Messina. After the Italian surrender the Group moved again and by the beginning of January 1944 they were based about 30 miles from Turin. Hrdlicka claimed his 40th victory on 29 May, a B-24 bomber over Zagreb, and he claimed a Spitfire on 4 June and another B-24 at the end of June.

From August he was attached to the 1st Group of the 2nd Fighter Wing based in St. Trond, Belgium and flew missions in 'Defence of the Reich'. On 18 October he was awarded the Knight's Cross for achieving more than forty victories. He was appointed *Gruppenkommandeur* of the 1st Group on 18 December and five days later he claimed a B-26 Marauder over Roetgen, his 44th victory. During January 1945 his Group took part in Operation Bodenplatte, the *Luftwaffe*'s attack on Allied air bases in Belgium and northern France. The operation failed to achieve air superiority even temporarily, and was the last large-scale strategic offensive operation mounted by the *Luftwaffe* during the war. On 25 March Hrdlicka was shot down near Betzenrod in Büdingen, a town in Hesse, and his body was not discovered until 8 September 1951. He had been recommended for the Oakleaves but it was never awarded.

Anton-Rudolf 'Toni' PIFFER

Leutnant

Knight's Cross: Awarded posthumously on 20 October 1944 as *Leutnant* and *Staffelführer* of the 1st Squadron of the 1st Fighter Wing '*Oesau*' for operations over the Western Front.

Anton-Rudolf Piffer claimed twenty-nine aerial victories, of which twenty-one were four-engined bombers whilst flying combat missions over the Western Front during the Second World War. He was born on 16 May 1918 in Zirl, Innsbruck in Austria-Hungary. He joined the *Luftwaffe* in 1938 and began training as a fighter pilot.

Assigned to the 11th Squadron of the 1st Fighter Wing in April 1942, he claimed his first aerial victory, a highly-prized RAF Mosquito, a high-speed fighter bomber, on 19 September and was awarded the Iron Cross 2nd Class soon afterwards. He soon became one of the most successful fighter pilots operating over Germany, flying the Focke-Wulf Fw 190 from July in 'Defence of the

Reich' missions. A year later in April 1943 his Squadron became the 2nd Squadron and he was flying from Deelen in the Netherlands, against enemy bomber formations. By the end of May his Group had moved to Schiphol and on 22 June he claimed a B-17 Flying Fortress south of Dinkslaken and was awarded the Iron Cross 1st Class. He was promoted to *Oberfeldwebel* in August and claimed another B-17 that month and four more during October. By December when his Group had been relocated to Dortmund-Brakel in Germany he had claimed four more B-17s.

From early 1944 he was flying the Fw 190A from Dortmund in 'Defence of the Reich' duties over northern Germany and the Netherlands. During January he claimed two B-17s and a P-38 Lightning and claimed another B-17 in February. He was awarded the German Cross in Gold on 29 March and shortly after claiming two more four-engined bombers he was awarded the *Luftwaffe* Honour Goblet on 24 April. Piffer claimed his 20th victory, another B-17, on 29 April west of Magdeburg, and in early May was commissioned as a *Leutnant* and was appointed *Staffelführer* of the 1st Squadron of the 1st Fighter Wing. He claimed a P-51 Mustang on 8 May and a B-24 Liberator on the 12th. The following day he was rammed by a P-47 Thunderbolt and had to make an emergency belly-landing near Hamburg but was unhurt.

(Deutsches Wehrkundearchiv)

By the end of May he had claimed twenty-six victories and on 6 June his Squadron was alerted to the Allied landings at Normandy and moved to France. He claimed an Auster, a small two-seater liaison aircraft, very much like the German Storch, just north of St. Lô in France. The following day he claimed two RAF Spitfires over the Flers area near Normandy, to claim his 28th and 29th and last victories. On the 17th he was shot down and killed during combat with P-51s, his Fw 190 crashed at Le Cordonniere. He was posthumously awarded the Knight's Cross on 20 October 1944. *Leutnant* Piffer lies in the Military Cemetery in La Cambe, France, Block 22, Row 4, Grave No. 66.

Willy UNGER

Leutnant

Knight's Cross: Awarded on 23 October 1944 as *Fahnenjunker-Feldwebel* and fighter pilot with the 15th Squadron of the 3rd Fighter Wing '*Udet*' for operations over the Western Front.

Willy Unger claimed a total of twenty-one victories, which included eighteen four-engined bombers, all over the Western Front during the Second World War. He was born on 27 March 1920 in Warstein, Arnsberg in North Rhine-Westphalia, Germany and joined the *Luftwaffe* in August 1939, spending several years as a technical instructor.

(Deutsches Wehrkundearchiv)

Despite the fact he had an engineering degree and a pilot's licence he did not start to train as a fighter pilot until 1942.

In December 1943 he transferred as an *Unteroffizier* into the 11th Squadron of the 3rd Fighter Wing and rapidly became something of a four-engined bomber specialist. He claimed his first victory, a B-24 Liberator, on 9 April 1944, but without witnesses it remains unconfirmed. Two days later he claimed a B-17 Flying Fortress, his first official victory, and on 13 April he claimed another. He was soon awarded the Iron Cross 2nd Class and on the 18th he claimed two more B-17s and the following day he claimed another and was awarded the Iron Cross 1st Class. On 24 April he claimed another B-17 and on 8 May just after he had claimed a B-24, his seventh victory, he was forced to make a belly-landing in his Bf 109 at Oebidfelde airfield but was unhurt.

He was awarded the *Luftwaffe* Honour Goblet on 21 June and in early July was promoted to *Feldwebel*. Unger claimed two B-24s near Aschersleben on 7 July, and on the 18th, shortly after claiming a B-17, he was shot down by a P-51 Mustang. He bailed out of his Fw 190A-8 from an altitude of only 820ft, but landed safely south-west of Memmingen, Bavaria with only minor injuries. On 3 August he claimed two more B-24s and was again shot down by return fire from one of the bombers and he bailed out just south of Reutte, Austria and landed safely. On 29 August he claimed two B-17s over Brünn and was awarded the German Cross in Gold. He claimed two more in September and in early October was promoted to *Oberfeldwebel* and nominated as an officer candidate. On 7 October he claimed another B-17 and on the 23rd was awarded the Knight's Cross after claiming a total of twenty four-engined bombers. In December he was promoted to *Leutnant* and on 22 January 1945 he was appointed *Staffelkapitän* of the 14th Squadron of the 3rd Fighter Wing. He claimed three more victories whilst leading his Squadron, claiming his 20th and 21st and last victory on 15 March. He then transferred to the 7th Fighter Wing in April, where he flew the Messerschmitt Me 262 jet fighter.

Unger surrendered to US forces in May 1945 and was released about a month later. He had flown fifty-nine combat missions and claimed twenty-one victories, of which eighteen were four-engined bombers, a great achievement and in less than 12 months. He died on 23 June 2005 in his home town of Warstein in North Rhine-Westphalia.

Franz BARTEN

Hauptmann

Knight's Cross: Awarded posthumously on 24 October 1944, as *Oberleutnant* and *Staffelkapitän* in the 3rd Group of the 53rd Fighter Wing for operations over Poland, France, England and the Soviet Union.

Franz Barten claimed fifty-two victories in 895 combat missions during the Second World War, and all but thirteen were achieved over the Eastern Front. He was born on 26 January 1912 in Saarbrücken and joined the *Luftwaffe* as a fighter pilot. After the completion of his training in July 1939, he was assigned to the 1st Group of the 77th Fighter Wing as a *Feldwebel*. Barten took part in the invasion of Poland and then from May 1940 he flew during the French campaign without scoring a victory. He was awarded the Iron Cross 2nd Class in December 1939 for the support missions he flew over Poland.

(Deutsches Wehrkundearchiv)

Barten claimed his first victory on 14 September 1940, an RAF Hurricane shot down during the Battle of Britain. He was presented with the Iron Cross 1st Class on 29 September and on 17 October he shot down a Hurricane and a Spitfire over Tunbridge Wells. On 21 November the 4th Group of the 51st Fighter Wing was formed from the 77th Fighter Wing and Barten moved into this new unit. He now flew missions from his new base in Marquise, north-east of Boulogne, France, flying combat missions over England. On 14 April 1941 he claimed his fourth victory, a Spitfire, over Boulogne, and had been promoted to *Oberfeldwebel*.

In June his Group moved to the Eastern Front and took part in Operation Barbarossa, the invasion of the Soviet Union. He claimed his first victory over Russia on 22 June, the first day of the invasion. His victory tally was steady, and by 13 July he had claimed his 10th victory, and by 6 October he had claimed his 20th, a MiG-1 fighter. Awarded the *Luftwaffe* Honour Goblet on 20 October, Barten shot down two Tupolev SB-3 twin-engined bombers on 12 November and claimed his 30th victory on 21 March 1942. He was awarded the German Cross in Gold on 22 May in recognition of his 33rd victory. He claimed his 35th victory on 13 July and during August he claimed six victories before being seriously wounded on 10 November when his Bf 109F-2 was damaged during a dogfight and he had crash-landed. It took him some time to get back to his own lines but he made it and spent a considerable time in hospital.

He returned to combat in the spring of 1943, and in April was commissioned as a *Leutnant*, and claimed two victories on the 8th, both Il-2 ground-attack aircraft, and these would be his last victories on the Eastern Front. On 1 June Barten was transferred as *Staffelführer* of the 7th Squadron of the 53rd Fighter Wing, based in Torrazzo, Italy. He claimed a Spitfire on 12 July over south-east Ramacca, and then three days later he was appointed *Staffelkapitän* of the 9th Squadron, replacing *Oberleutnant* Hans Roehrig who had been killed. He was promoted to *Oberleutnant* in early August and on the 19th he claimed his 45th victory, a US B-17 Flying Fortress east of Salerno. On 1 December he shot down a B-24 Liberator near Della Pecara to score his 50th victory. He claimed a Spitfire on 6 February 1944 and on 13 June he claimed his 52nd aerial victory, a P-47 Thunderbolt. His squadron was then transferred to Germany for 'Defence of the Reich' duties, based at Bad Lippspringe. On 4 August Barten was shot down during aerial combat with a P-47 near Reinshlen. He bailed out of his aircraft only to be shot and killed whilst hanging from his parachute. He was posthumously awarded the Knight's Cross and promoted to *Hauptmann*. He is buried today at the Lippstadt Cemetery, Grave No. 63.

Heinz GOSSOW

Oberfeldwebel

Knight's Cross: Awarded on 24 October 1944 as *Oberfeldwebel* and pilot with the 1st Group of the 302nd Fighter Wing for operations over the Soviet Union and the Western Front.

Heinz Gossow was initially a bomber pilot who served in France and later the Soviet campaign, flying about 340 missions before training to become a fighter pilot in 1943. He flew 409 combat missions with the 302st Fighter Wing from 1944 and claimed only eight victories but they were all bombers. He was born on 23 November 1917 in Piesteritz, Wittenberg, joined the *Luftwaffe* in 1941 and trained as a pilot.

During the winter of 1941 he was assigned to the 6th Squadron of the 53rd Bomber Wing as a *Feldwebel*, and flew from northern France. In June his Group moved to Lübbe in Silesia and later took part in the invasion of the Soviet Union. At the beginning of 1942 he flew missions over the central sector of the Eastern Front, and from the

(Deutsches Wehrkundearchiv)

autumn he flew in support of the army in its advance towards Stalingrad. During September his Group moved to Korowje-Selo to support the German army in the fighting for Demyansk, and on 5 November he was awarded the German Cross in Gold.

In the summer of 1943 Gossow transferred to fighters and began his retraining before being assigned to the 302nd Fighter Wing '*Wilde Sau*', flying 'Defence of the Reich' missions. On the night of 31 August and 1 September he flew his first combat mission as a fighter pilot, flying the Bf 109G, as part of the 1st Squadron of the 1st Group. Now an *Oberfeldwebel*, Gossow claimed his first victory on 22 September, again at night, an RAF Lancaster bomber, and then 45 minutes later, at 22:30, he shot down a second Lancaster. At the beginning of 1944 his Squadron moved to Jüterbog airfield and on 11 January Goosow was shot down and bailed out of his aircraft near Nordweide. He sustained minor injuries while abandoning his aircraft and was taken to the first-aid station. On 13 February his Squadron moved to Malmi near Helsinki, and by May they had moved again to Vienna-Seyring.

On 16 April he claimed a B-24 Liberator over south Kamaron, Hungary, then in August he became very successful. He claimed a B-17 Flying Fortress over Magdeburg on 5 August and claimed another on the 16th over Kassel. On 20 August he claimed another B-17 over Budapest and on the 21st and 22nd he claimed a B-24 over Hungary. On 24 October he was awarded the Knight's Cross by *Oberstleutnant* Fritz Auffhammer, the *Kommodore* of the 301st Fighter Wing. It was a proud day for the entire Wing and Gossow had truly earned this high decoration.

Gossow continued to fly and in 1945 was transferred to the 7th Fighter Wing where he flew jet aircraft but failed to add to his victories. He survived the war and retired to Wittenberg in Saxony-Anhalt, where he died on 1 January 1988.

Horst HAASE

Major

Knight's Cross: Awarded on 24 October 1944 as *Hauptmann* and *Staffelkapitän* of the 16th Squadron of the 3rd Fighter Wing '*Udet*' for operations over the Soviet Union and the Western Front.

Horst Haase flew over 500 combat missions and claimed fifty-four aerial victories of which ten were four-engined bombers over the Western and Eastern Fronts. He was born on 22 May 1921 in Danzig and on completion of his fighter pilot training he was assigned to the 10th Squadron of the 51st Fighter Wing.

Leutnant Haase first saw action during Operation Barbarossa, the invasion of the Soviet Union in June 1941. He claimed his first victory, a Polikarpov R-5 reconnaissance aircraft, on 29 June, and claimed his second on 2 July, an Ilyushin DB-3 long-range bomber. After claiming two more victories, both Tupolev SB-2 bombers, on 3 July, Haase was awarded the Iron Cross 2nd Class. By the end of the year he had claimed ten aerial victories and had been awarded the Iron Cross 1st Class.

(Deutsches Wehrkundearchiv)

On 10 April 1942 he was appointed *Staffelkapitän* of the 10th Squadron and he claimed another victory on 10 July. On 2 August his Bf 109F-2 was shot down during combat near Rschew. He managed to bail out and was slightly wounded. From October he served on the Staff of the 51st Fighter Wing and whilst still recovering from his injuries, he returned to front-line duty in February 1943. He claimed three Il-2 ground-attack aircraft that month and in April was appointed Acting *Staffelkapitän* of the 1st Squadron. He claimed his 20th aerial victory on 6 May, was promoted to

Oberleutnant the following month and took over as *Staffelkapitän* of the 2nd Squadron soon after. He was awarded the *Luftwaffe* Honour Goblet on 9 August and he claimed his 30th and 31st victories three days later and by the end of the month had claimed his 35th victory. On 11 October he claimed another Il-2, his 40th victory, and then moved to Bobruisk from December when the entire Group converted from the Focke-Wulf Fw 190 to the Messerschmitt Bf 109G.

He claimed his 17th Il-2 on 22 February and was awarded the German Cross in Gold on 20 March. On 25 June his Squadron relocated to Germany where on 7 July Haase claimed two B-24 Liberators over the area of Aschersleben. He claimed a B-17 Flying Fortress over south-east Kempten on 18 July, and he claimed another on the 29th over the Herrsching area. On 10 August his unit was renamed the 16th Squadron of the 3rd Fighter Wing and he remained as *Staffelkapitän*. During this time he claimed another three B-17s to record his 50th victory on 22 August, and he claimed a B-24 on the 24th. On 1 September Haase was promoted to *Hauptmann* and ten days later he claimed another B-17 over Riesa in Saxony. On the 27th he shot down a B-24 over Eisenach and the following day he claimed another B-17 over west Halberstadt, his 54th and last victory.

On 24 October Haase was awarded the Knight's Cross in recognition of his success as a fighter pilot and for downing ten four-engined bombers in just eight weeks. Shortly after that he was appointed *Gruppenkommandeur* of the 3rd Fighter Wing now stationed in Erfurt, Germany. From 24 November his group flew from Paderborn to support the Army during the beginning of the Ardennes Offensive. Two days later during one of these support missions Haase collided with his wingman near Erkelenz, western Germany and was killed. He was posthumously promoted to the rank of *Major* and is buried today in Elsdorf-Abgelsdorf War Cemetery.

Ernst-Erich HIRSCHFELD

Oberleutnant

Knight's Cross: Awarded posthumously on 24 October 1944 as *Oberleutnant* and fighter pilot attached to the 6th Squadron of the 300th Fighter Wing for operations over the Western Front.

Ernst-Erich Hirschfeld flew approximately 100 combat missions during the Second World War, claiming eighteen aerial victories, which included nine four-engined bombers, all but one over the Western Front. He was born in Breslau on 25 August 1918 and at the outbreak of war in September 1939 he was attached to an army anti-aircraft regiment. In 1940 he transferred to the *Luftwaffe* and began his training as a fighter pilot.

Hirschfeld completed his training in 1941 and became a flight instructor, serving in this role until early 1943. On 1 February he was commissioned as a *Leutnant* and in March transferred to the 5th Squadron of the 54th Fighter Wing, based in Kalinin on the Baltic

(Deutsches Wehrkundearchiv)

coast. He claimed his first aerial victory on the Eastern Front on 26 May, an La-5 fighter – his only Eastern Front victory. On 3 August Hirschfeld transferred to the 5th Squadron of the 300th Fighter Wing, flying over Germany in 'Defence of the Reich' missions. From mid-August he flew what were called '*Wilde Sau*' or 'Wild Sow' operations, attacking British bombers over Germany, mainly at night but some by day. He claimed his first four-engined bomber on 22 September, an RAF Stirling over Hanover. Then five days later he shot down two more bombers again over Hanover, a Lancaster and another Stirling, and a few days later he was awarded both the Iron Cross 1st and 2nd Class.

On the night of 17/18 November he claimed two four-engined bombers but these remain unconfirmed victories. He shot down a Lancaster bomber over the Leipzig area on 20 February 1944 and claimed a B-24 Liberator over Achmer the following day. On 8 March he claimed a USAAF P-38 twin-engined fighter near Twente in the Netherlands, and was then shot down himself near Weersleo but he successfully managed to bail out of his Fw 190A-5 with slight burns to his legs. On 15 May he was awarded the *Luftwaffe* Honour Goblet and in early June he was named *Staffelkapitän* of the 6th Squadron of the 300th Fighter Wing. He claimed two B-24 Liberators over the Weilhaim area on 13 June, but again after post-war scrutiny these remain unconfirmed victories. He claimed three more B-24s on 21 June near Berlin, which included his 10th victory, and five days later he claimed another B-24. Promoted to *Oberleutnant* at the end of June he claimed yet another B-24 on 7 July over Magdeburg. He shot down his 15th victory on 19 July, a P-51 Mustang over Immenstadt, Bavaria and he claimed a B-24 on the 25th and another P-51 and a B-17 Flying Fortress over Austria the following day, his last victories.

On 27 July 1944 he was shot in the elbow whilst flying and as a result couldn't control his aircraft and had no choice but to bail out. Unfortunately his parachute failed to open and he plunged to his death near Gering, Erfurt. He was posthumously awarded the German Cross in Gold on 10 September and the Knight's Cross on 24 October. His body now lies in a war grave in Sokołowiec, a small village in Poland.

Karl-Wilhelm HOFMANN

Oberleutnant

Knight's Cross: Awarded as *Leutnant* and *Staffelkapitän* with the 2nd Group of the 26th Fighter Wing on 24 October 1944 for operations over the Western Front and for claiming his 40th aerial victory, an RAF Spitfire over Nijmegen.

(Deutsches Wehrkundearchiv)

Karl-Wilhelm Hofmann claimed forty-four aerial victories, of which all but one were scored over the Western Front and which included six four-engined bombers. He was born on 24 March 1921 in Reichelsheim, Germany and joined the *Luftwaffe* and trained as a fighter pilot, later joining the 2nd Squadron of the Advanced Training Group West in 1942.

In June he transferred to the 1st Squadron of the 26th Fighter Wing as an *Unteroffizier*, flying the Focke-Wulf Fw 190 from his base in Saint Omer, France. He claimed his first victory, an RAF Spitfire, on 11 October over Cassel and was awarded the Iron Cross 2nd Class. During August he flew missions over the Dieppe area in support of German ground forces. On 26 September he was severely wounded just north of Watten when his Fw 190A-4 crashed and he spent several months in hospital, not returning to duty until 31 March 1943. By May he had been promoted to *Feldwebel* and flying over the Soviet Union and on 14 May he claimed his second and only victory on the Eastern Front, a Lavochkin La-5 fighter. His time on the Eastern Front was brief, returning to Germany on 23 June, flying out of Rheine and, from August, flew over Belgium and Holland.

From October he served as *Staffelkapitän* of the 8th Squadron, still with the 26th Fighter Wing, flying from Cambrai-Epinoy in France. On 18 October he claimed his third victory, a Spitfire over the area of Ardes in northern France, and in January 1944 he was promoted to *Leutnant*. He claimed his fourth victory on 4 January, another Spitfire, and that same day he also claimed a B-17 Flying Fortress just east of Boulogne and was a few days later awarded the Iron Cross 1st Class. He claimed another B-17 on 11 January and he shot down a P-51 on the 28th and a B-17 the following day to claim his eighth victory. On 30 January his wingman was killed. *Unteroffizier* Karl Bierkamp's Fw 190A-6 was attacked by a P-47 Thunderbolt, hitting its drop-tank which exploded.

With the start of the Allied invasion on 6 June, his group moved to Guyancourt where they were deployed against the Allied landings. On 8th he claimed three victories, two P-47 Thunderbolts and a P-51 Mustang, his 14th to 16th victories, and a few days later he was awarded the *Luftwaffe* Honour Goblet. By the end of June Hofmann had achieved his 25th victory and he was awarded the German Cross in Gold on 23 July. During August he claimed another ten victories which included his 30th on 20 August a P-47 near Paris. On 16 September he lost another wingman, *Leutnant* Josef Grimmer, who was shot down by enemy anti-aircraft fire, bailed out at low altitude and broke both of his legs, but he survived the war. On the 21st Hofmann claimed two more victories, a Dakota transport aircraft over Deelan and a P-47, and then on 2 October he claimed his 40th victory, a Spitfire, and was promoted to *Oberleutnant*.

On 22 October he was injured in a freak accident. Whilst closely examining a dismounted aircraft machine gun, the bolt closed suddenly injuring his eye. He retained his sight but lost the ability to focus the eye. He refused to go to hospital and returned to his unit wearing a patch over his eye, and insisted on flying combat missions but the job of leading was temporarily given to *Leutnant* Wilhelm Meyer. On 24 October he was awarded the Knight's Cross in recognition of claiming twenty-six victories of which twelve were achieved over the invasion front.

On 15 January 1945 Hofmann took over from *Oberleutnant* Gerhard Vogt as *Staffelführer* of the 5th Squadron after Vogt had been shot down and killed. He served as deputy to various squadron commanders and from 15 February he took over as *Staffelkapitän*. On 28 February he claimed a P-47 over the Mönchengladbach area and on 1 March he claimed two more victories over the same area. On 19 March he lost another wingman. *Oberfähnrich* Johann Spahn was hit during combat and he had to bail out but unfortunately his parachute didn't open and he was killed. Hofmann had flown with Spahn since before his eye accident and he had served as Hofmann's eyes during numerous take-offs.

On 26 March, shortly after shooting down a Tempest over Munster, Hofmann, who was flying his 260th mission, was shot down. It seemed at first that he had been shot down by one of his own pilots. As a result *Oberfähnrich* Erich Schneider was arrested and the next day he stood trial at the headquarters of the 14th Air Division, but was acquitted. Apparently Schneider, upon landing had stormed jubilantly into the mess hall and announced he had shot down his first victory, only to be told, 'Do you know whom you have shot down? Our *Staffelkkapitan*!'. It seems that Hofmann had been fired on when his aircraft loomed up suddenly through the haze. His body was not found until 2 April, in a forest half a mile from the wreckage of his aircraft. He had bailed out, but at very low altitude and his parachute had failed to open. Hofmann was buried in a forest, but his body was later exhumed after the war and buried in a military cemetery, but in the post-war chaos its identity has been lost. Not until 1988 was his identity officially confirmed and his name could then be removed from the list of pilots missing in action. It is also highly likely that he wasn't shot down by Schneider but by an RAF Tempest of 33 Squadron near Bissel.

Julius 'Jule' MEIMBERG

Major

Knight's Cross: Awarded on 24 October 1944 as *Hauptmann* and *Gruppenkommandeur* of the 2nd Group of the 53rd Fighter Wing for actions over France, England, North Africa and the Western Front, and it was presented by *Oberst* Karl Hentschel, the commander of the 5th Fighter Division.

Julius Meimberg claimed forty-five aerial victories over the Western Front during the Second World War of which four were four-engined bombers. He was born on 11 January 1917 in Münster, North Rhine-Westphalia and he joined the *Luftwaffe* in October 1937 and trained as a fighter pilot in Schleissheim.

(Deutsches Wehrkundearchiv)

After the completion of his training, in March 1940 he was transferred to the 4th Squadron of the 2nd Fighter Wing as a *Leutnant* and saw action over France and during the Battle of Britain. On 11 May he was unhurt when his Bf 109E overturned on landing after combat with British aircraft, and he claimed his first aerial victory eight days later, an RAF Hurricane near Tournai, and in early June was awarded the Iron Cross 2nd Class. His second victory was a Curtiss Hawk over Paris on 3 June and he claimed his third victory on 4 September, a Spitfire over Ashford in Kent, during the Battle of Britain. On 6 September he claimed two more Spitfires over Ashford, and on the 26th he was wounded when his Bf 109 crashed at Hamminkeln and he was in hospital until 2 October. On the 10th he claimed his sixth victory, a Hurricane near Portland, and that same day he was awarded the Iron Cross 1st Class. Before the end of October he claimed another two victories, a Spitfire over the Isle of Wight and a Blenheim over the Channel, his eighth and ninth victories.

On 15 April 1941 he was appointed *Staffelkapitän* of the 3rd Squadron of the 2nd Fighter Wing and saw action over the Channel. He flew mainly reconnaissance missions at this time, and claimed a Spitfire on 3 July and another on the 17th, his 11th victory. On 24th he claimed three victories, two Handley Page Hampden twin-engined bombers and a Wellington bomber over Brest. However, after taking return fire from the Wellington he was seriously wounded and his aircraft crash-landed near Brélès about eight miles from St. Renan, France. Promoted to *Oberleutnant* in late 1941 whilst recovering in hospital, he did not return to combat until May 1942 when he was appointed *Staffelkapitän* of 3rd Squadron of the 2nd Fighter Wing. He claimed a Spitfire on 17 and 19 May, and claimed his 20th victory on 28 July, another Spitfire.

On 1 August he transferred as *Staffelkapitän* to the 11th Squadron of the 2nd Fighter Wing and from November saw action over North Africa. He was awarded the German Cross in Gold on 29 October after achieving over twenty victories, and he claimed three more victories in December over Mateur, Tunisia but they were all unconfirmed, then on the 5th he claimed three Spitfires which were confirmed as his 22nd to 24th victories whilst attached to the 53rd Fighter Wing. He claimed his 25th victory on 6 December whilst attached to the 7th Squadron of the 53rd Fighter Wing. On 1 February 1943 he claimed a B-17 four-engined bomber near Pont du Fahs, Tunisia but was hit by return fire and his cockpit burst into flames. He managed to bail out but his hands were badly burnt. He spent six months recovering in hospital in Munich and during that time was promoted to *Hauptmann*. On his return in August he was awarded the *Luftwaffe* Honour Goblet and assigned as a staff officer with the 53rd Fighter Wing in Italy but in April 1944 he returned to hospital for further treatment.

In early May Meimberg was back in action as *Gruppenkommandeur* of the 3rd Group of the 53rd Fighter Wing and claimed a B-24 bomber north of Braunschweig on 8 May and later that month claimed a B-17 Flying Fortress four-engined bomber, his 30th victory. He claimed his 35th victory on 24 September and on 24 October he was awarded the Knight's Cross after achieving over forty aerial victories, although at least ten would later be classified as unconfirmed. In early December he was promoted to *Major* and on the 16th he claimed a P-47 over Stuttgart and on the 26th he claimed three more P-47s and it was during this time he had to bail out of his aircraft over Stuttgart after his Bf 109 had been damaged during a dogfight, and was hospitalized for a few weeks. He claimed another P-47 on 10 April 1945 and on the 13th he claimed his last official victory of the war, a Spitfire over Biberach, Germany. Meimberg was shot down again on 17 April by ground fire near Nuremberg but was unhurt. He flew a total of 250 combat missions during the war, all of them over the Western Front. He died on 17 January 2012 at his home in Münster, in North Rhine-Westphalia.

August MORS

Leutnant

Knight's Cross: Awarded on 24 October 1944 as *Leutnant* and fighter pilot attached to the 1st Squadron of the 5th Fighter Wing for operations over the Soviet Union and the Western Front.

August Mors flew about 600 combat missions and claimed forty-eight victories whilst flying combat missions over the Eastern Front and another ten over the Western Front during the Second World War. He was born on 20 June 1921 in Sigmaringen, a town in southern Germany in Baden-Württemberg, and after the completion of his training was assigned to the 5th Fighter Wing in July 1942.

(Deutsches Wehrkundearchiv)

Unteroffizier Mors was assigned to the 6th Squadron and saw action on the Polar front, flying from Petsamo in Finland and achieving his first victory, a Hurricane, on 27 September. In October his Squadron moved to Alakuritti in Sweden where the Group stayed for a number of months due to the weather conditions. He didn't return to full deployment until early 1943 when on 9 January he claimed two victories, a Hurricane and an LaGG-3 fighter, and soon after he was awarded the Iron Cross 2nd Class. He claimed his fourth victory on 13 April and another on the 29th, and then on 8 June he claimed three Typhoon fighter-bombers and was awarded the Iron Cross 1st Class. A week later he was shot down in combat with Soviet fighters and bailed out of his Bf 109 and was listed as missing, last seen about 10 miles north-west of Murmansk but he managed to get back to his own lines a day later unharmed. On 9 August he claimed two more aircraft which included his 10th victory, and he claimed four more victories during September and at the beginning of November his Group was withdrawn from operations in the north and moved to south of Pskov.

In January 1944 his Group had moved to the central sector of the Eastern Front and later flew in support of the army in Lapland. Mors claimed three victories during January and by 27 February had claimed his 24th aerial victory, an La-5 fighter near Pustoschka. On 17 and 18 March he shot down two Yak-9 fighters and on the 20th he claimed eight victories to become an 'ace-in-a-day'. On 25 March he claimed another three victories which included his 40th, and during April he claimed another eight victories, and was awarded the German Cross in Gold on 14 April after claiming forty-two victories. By 31 May his Group had moved to Gardelegen in Germany and was now deployed in 'Defence of the Reich' duties. From 15 June his group moved to Evreux to be deployed against the Allied landings in Normandy.

Towards the end of June he was promoted to *Leutnant* and was transferred to the 1st Squadron of the 5th Fighter Wing and continued to fly over France. At the beginning of July his Squadron moved to Frières-Faillouël in northern France and he claimed his 50th victory, a Typhoon over Tricqueville. He claimed eight more victories during July and on 5 August Mors took over as *Staffelkapitän* of the 1st Squadron, and the following day he was shot down over Beaumont-sur-Oise, about 18 miles north of Paris. He bailed out of his Bf 109G-6 and landed in a tree, dying from his wounds two days later in a *Luftwaffe* hospital at Clichy. He is buried today in the German War Cemetery in Champigny-St. Andre and is located in Plot 3, Row 9, Grave No. 756. He flew a total of 600 combat missions during the Second World and was posthumously awarded the Knight's Cross on 24 October 1944.

Karl RAMMELT

Major

Knight's Cross: Awarded on 24 October 1944 as *Major* and commander of the 2nd Group of the 51st Fighter Wing '*Mölders*' for operations over Soviet Union, North Africa, the Balkans and the Eastern Front.

Karl Rammelt claimed forty-one aerial victories in about 450 missions during the Second World War, claiming nineteen over the Eastern Front and the remainder over the Western Front, including eight four-engined bombers. He was born on 10 June 1914 in Nebra, Querfurt in southern Saxony-Anhalt and he joined the *Luftwaffe* as ground staff in 1934.

In 1940 he retrained as a fighter pilot, and from May 1942, with the rank of *Oberleutnant*, he flew with the 2nd Group of the 51st Fighter Wing. He was attached to the 4th Squadron and flew over the Eastern Front, claiming his first victory a Yak-1 fighter on 12 June, south-west of Bolkhov. On 5 July he claimed seven aerial victories to become an 'ace-in-a-day', but later one was reclassified as unconfirmed. Shortly

(Deutsches Wehrkundearchiv)

afterwards he was awarded the Iron Cross 2nd Class. He claimed two more victories on 4 and 5 August and was awarded the Iron Cross 1st Class. By the end of the month he had claimed another nine victories, but four were later reclassified as unconfirmed. On 3 September he made a forced landing in his Bf 109F-2 but wasn't hurt, claiming two more confirmed victories later that month.

His Group converted to the Focke-Wulf Fw 190 in October 1941 but it soon became apparent that they would soon be transferred to the Mediterranean and switched back to the Messerschmitt Bf 109F-2. On 15 November his Group moved to Tunisia and then to Trapni in Sicily and by the end of the month they were back in Tunisia. He claimed a Spitfire south-west of Bizerta on 27 November and claimed two more the following day. At the beginning of 1943, whilst still in Tunisia his Group flew escort missions for transport units flying in from Italy. Rammelt then took part in low-level attacks against Allied airfields and supply columns. He claimed a P-40 Warhawk on 20 March and the next day he claimed a Spitfire and a B-17, but only the British fighter was ever confirmed. He claimed his 20th victory on 29 March and around the same time his group moved to La Frauconnerie as part of the German withdrawal to France. During this time he had also been appointed *Staffelkapitän* of the 4th Squadron, and by 19 June he had claimed a total of twenty-two victories and was presented with the *Luftwaffe* Honour Goblet six days later.

On 7 June he took over as *Gruppenkommandeur* of the 2nd Group, still with the 51st Fighter Wing and led his Group against the Allied landings in Italy. He claimed his 25th victory on 18 June and within a few weeks Sicily had been evacuated and by August his group was flying from Neubiberg in Germany and Rammelt was now flying defensive missions as part of the 'Defence of the Reich' campaign. He claimed a B-17 Flying Fortress on 14 October and another north-east of Graz on 2 November and had by now been promoted to *Hauptmann*. During combat with a B-24 on 28 December his aircraft was hit by return fire south of Rovigo and he managed to jettison his canopy and bailed out, but was wounded in the process. As a result of his injuries he didn't return to combat until early 1944. Shortly after being awarded the German Cross in Gold he was appointed Area Fighter Commander in Bulgaria, stationed in Sofia-Bojania until August 1944, now with the rank of *Major*.

Rammelt claimed his 30th victory, another B-24 on 5 April 1944, and ten days later he claimed a P-38 Lightning over Rashka, Serbia. On 13 October he claimed his 35th victory, an Il-2 Ilyushin ground-attack aircraft. On 24 October he was awarded the Knight's Cross in recognition of his 35th victory and his success against four-engined bombers – he had by this time claimed seven. He claimed two more victories on 8 December and claimed three more, which included his last victory of the war. On the 23rd his Bf 109G-14 was attacked by Soviet fighters and he was wounded and had to bail out. His wounds were serious enough to prevent him from returning to duty. After the war he joined the *Bundeswehr*, and retired on 30 September 1969 with the rank of *Oberstleutnant*. Rammelt died at the age of 94 on 13 May 2009 in Fürstenfeldbruck, a town near Munich.

Oskar ZIMMERMANN

Leutnant

Knight's Cross: Awarded on 24 October 1944 as *Leutnant* and *Staffelführer* with the 3rd Group of the 3rd Fighter Wing '*Udet*' for operations over the Soviet Union and the Western Front.

Oskar Zimmermann claimed at least twenty-eight victories, of which over twenty-two were claimed over the Western Front and at least eleven of these were four-engined bombers. He was born on 6 December 1917 in Wiesenthal, Löwenberg in Germany and entered the *Luftwaffe* in 1939 at the age of 21, and with the completion of his fighter-pilot training was assigned to the 8th Squadron of the 51st Fighter Wing in early 1942.

From February *Feldwebel* Zimmermann flew the Bf 109F-2 fighter mainly over the Rzhev area of the Soviet front and in early April his Group moved to Smolensk. By May he was flying once again over Rzhev in support of the 9th Army. He claimed his first aerial victory on

(Deutsches Wehrkundearchiv)

4 August, an Ilyushin Il-2 ground-attack aircraft, but in the middle of August his Group suffered the loss of seven aircraft with another ten damaged. In late November during the Soviet winter offensive his Group was in Dugino where they converted to the Focke-Wulf Fw 190A-2 and A-3. From early January 1943 he was deployed in the Rzhev area once again and from the 28th his Group moved to Orel and from March flew from Krasnogvardeysky near Leningrad and he was promoted to *Leutnant*. He claimed his second victory on 18 March 1943, and from May he was flying from Orel once again.

In July he moved to the Staff Squadron of the 3rd Group, still with the 51st Fighter Wing, and claimed three more victories during July and was awarded the Iron Cross 2nd Class. He claimed an LaGG-3 fighter on 18 August and shortly after was flying from Poltava until October when he was based at Orsha in Belarus. He remained here until the end of the year and from January until March 1944 he flew as a fighter instructor with Fighter Replacement Group East, based in St. Jean-d'Angély in France under the command of *Major* Viktor Bauer. From March he flew from Leipheim in Bavaria as part of the 11th Squadron of the 3rd Fighter Wing and took part in 'Defence of the Reich' missions. He claimed a B-17 Flying Fortress four-engined bomber on 8 April near Braunschweig and was shortly after awarded the Iron Cross 1st Class. On 11 April he claimed three victories, two B-17s and a P-38 Lightning west of Haldensleben, Germany, his 10th aerial victory. By 24 April Zimmermann had claimed a total of fourteen victories, which included eight four-engined bombers, with another two unconfirmed.

On 29 April he transferred to the 6th Squadron of the 3rd Fighter Wing and was appointed *Staffelkapitän*, and on that day he claimed another B-17 over Magdeburg. He claimed another five victories during May, of which two were B-24 Liberators and one was a B-17. On 19 May he collided with his wingman, but managed to bail out without injury south-east of Wittenberge, and on the 30th he claimed his 20th victory. After the beginning of the Allied invasion of Normandy in June his Group moved to Evreux and from the 7th were deployed over the Allied landing areas. They moved a few times due to persistent air raids, and he claimed two P-51 Mustangs in July and was now flying from his new base in north-eastern France. On 25 July he was shot down by a US P-51 flown by Lieutenant T.D. Schank of the 55th Fighter Group. He was injured but managed to bail out over Nogent-le-Roi in the Loire region of France and soon recovered.

From mid-August he flew as part of the 9th Squadron of the 3rd Fighter Wing, flying from France where he claimed three more victories. The Group's mission in France ended in Senon near Verdun at the end of August and from 1 September his group had moved to Limburg in the Netherlands to be refreshed. From the 11th he flew from Wittenweier in Baden-Württemberg on 'Defence of the Reich' missions. Zimmermann was awarded the German Cross in Gold on 1 October after claiming more than twenty-five victories, and on the 24th he was awarded the Knight's Cross. By December his Group had relocated to Bad Lippspringe in North Rhine-Westphalia where they stayed until late January 1945. He claimed his 28th victory on 1 January and his Group moved again on the 28th to Märkisch Friedland in Poland. During the course of the next few weeks the constantly-shifting front lines and the German withdrawals meant they moved many times. On 15 March Zimmermann fell ill and spent the rest of the war recovering on light duties. He had flown almost 600 combat missions during the war and he died on 12 February 1976 in Bad Hersfeld in north-eastern Hesse, Germany.

Werner GERTH

Hauptmann

Knight's Cross: Awarded on 29 October 1944 as *Oberleutnant* and *Staffelkapitän* of the 14th Squadron of the 3rd Fighter Wing '*Udet*' for operations over the Western Front.

Werner claimed twenty-three aerial victories during the Second World War and was something of a four-engined bomber expert, as they made up twenty of his victories. He was born on 10 May 1923 in Pforzheim, south-west Germany and joined the 7th Squadron of the 53rd Fighter Wing in mid-1943, seeing action in the Mediterranean.

Gerth was promoted to *Leutnant* in June 1943 and from July he saw action during the Allied landings in Sicily. Then shortly after the German withdrawal from Sicily parts of the Group were distributed to different areas and Gerth and his squadron moved to Grazzzanise in the Italian region of Campania. On 22 August he claimed his first victory, a twin-engined B-26 Marauder south-west of Capri, and was awarded the Iron Cross 2nd Class shortly afterwards. On 17 September Gerth was wounded during an attack on the airfield at Rom-Caimpino and was away from duty for a number of weeks. In January 1944 he joined the *Sturmgruppe* of the 3rd Fighter Wing and took part in 'Defence of the Reich' duties until February. He transferred to the 4th Group on 22 February and later claimed a B-17 Flying Fortress over the Bieefeld area but this was never confirmed. Nevertheless, he was shortly afterwards awarded the Iron Cross 1st Class. On 6 March he claimed two B-17s in just three minutes near Hannover, and on 11 April he claimed two B-24 Liberators also in less than three minutes. Two days later he claimed his sixth victory, a B-17 over Mannheim, and on 29 April he claimed two more B-17s. Towards the end of the month the 4th Group was dissolved its pilots and ground crew formed the 11th Squadron with Gerth named as the *Staffelkapitän*, and now part of the 3rd Fighter Wing.

(Deutsches Wehrkundearchiv)

After the Allied invasion of Europe in June 1944 his Group moved to St. André de l'Eure near Normandy to take part in the attack on the Allied landing area. In the days and weeks that followed his squadron moved airfields several times as attacks by Allied bombers threatened their bases. On 7 July Gerth claimed two B-24 bombers in just two minutes over the area of Aschersleben, and on the 18th he shot down two B-17 bombers. He claimed another B-17 on the 19th and shot down a Lightning P-38 fighter on 30 July. In late August the 11th Squadron was renamed the 14th Squadron and on 11 September he claimed his 20th and 21st victories. He claimed his 22nd victory on 7 October another B-17 bomber over Atern-Naumburg and then on 2 November he claimed yet another B-17, his last aerial victory of the war. During this encounter his aircraft was struck by return fire, and some sources state that he rammed the aircraft, but this seems very unlikely. His own wingman, *Feldwebel* Oscar Bösch, couldn't confirm the story and could only watch as Gerth fell to his death as his parachute had failed to open. His body landed near Eislben in Saxony-Anhalt and Gerth is buried today at the military cemetery at Pforzheim in Field 90, Grave No. 115. He was posthumously promoted to *Hauptmann* and awarded the German Cross in Gold.

Ulrich 'Pipifax' WERNITZ

Leutnant

Knight's Cross: Awarded on 29 October 1944 as *Feldwebel* and fighter pilot attached to the 1st Group of the 54th Fighter Wing for operations over the Soviet Union and the Eastern Front.

Ulrich Wernitz claimed 101 aerial victories whilst flying just over 240 combat missions over the Eastern Front during the Second World War. He was born on 23 January 1921 in Schweinitz, Herzberg in Saxony-Anhlat, Germany and he joined the *Luftwaffe* in late 1941. On completion of his fighter-pilot training in April 1943, he was posted to the 3rd Squadron of the 54th Fighter Wing.

Unteroffizier Wernitz claimed his first victory on 2 May 1943, a Lavochkin La-5 fighter near Pushkin during the Siege of Leningrad, flying from Staraja-Russa on the northern sector of the Eastern Front. He claimed his second victory on 21 May and his third three days later, a P-40 east of Mga. From June he flew from Orel and transferred to

(Deutsches Wehrkundearchiv)

the Staff Squadron and claimed two more victories that month. He was awarded the Iron Cross 2nd Class and claimed two more victories on 16 July, claiming his 10th victory over Mga on 1 August. By October he had been awarded the Iron Cross 1st Class and was flying from Vitebsk back with the 3rd Squadron and claiming three more victories on 9 October.

By the end of the year, now with the rank of *Feldwebel,* he had claimed eighteen victories, and was flying from Orsha where his Group remained until the New Year. He claimed his 20th victory on 6 January 1944 and on 22 February Wernitz was hospitalized with carbon-monoxide poisoning due to a faulty heater in his barracks at Vinnitsa. He returned to combat in mid-March, claiming two victories on the 30th, which included his 25th. He was awarded the *Luftwaffe* Honour Goblet on 17 April after achieving twenty-five victories. He claimed three more victories during April, and claimed his 30th victory on 8 May. On the 29th he claimed three victories over Finland and the Baltic Sea, and on 15 June he shot down four aircraft, which included two Yak-9 fighters and an Il-2 ground-attack aircraft. A few days after his Group moved to Polotsk in Belarus, he claimed two victories on 28 June and became an 'ace-in-a-day' on the 30th when he claimed five victories.

Wernitz claimed two victories on 3 July, both P-39s, and on the 16th he claimed his 50th victory, another P-39. He claimed four victories on the 21 July and three on the 27th and from August his Squadron flew from Riga. He claimed four more victories on 1 August which included his 60th victory and by the 25th he had achieved his 75th aerial victory. He claimed four more victories on 28 August and shortly after he was shot down. He wasn't hurt but fell ill soon after and was briefly hospitalized. Whilst resting he was awarded the Knight's Cross on 29 October and on 1 January 1945 he was presented with the German Cross in Gold.

Wernitz had during his time with the 54th Fighter Wing frequently flown as wingman to aces Hermann Schlenhege, Günther Scheel and Swords recipient Otto Kittel. He returned to fighter duties in early February and was promoted to *Leutnant* and appointed *Staffelführer* of his Squadron. He flew from Sabile in Latvia and on 5 March he became an 'ace-in-a-day' for the second time when he claimed eight victories over the Courland Pocket. At the end of the war the 1st Group moved to Flensburg where Wernitz and the rest of the Group were taken prisoner. He later joined the *Bundesluftwaffe* and rose to the rank of *Oberstleutnant* before retiring in March 1978, and he died on 23 December 1980 in Fürstenfeldbruck, Bavaria.

Konrad 'Pitt' BAUER

Oberleutnant

Knight's Cross: Awarded as *Feldwebel* on 31 October 1944 as fighter pilot with the 5th Squadron of the 300th Fighter Wing for operations over the Soviet Union and the Western Front.

Konrad Bauer claimed about thirty-eight aerial victories, which included thirteen four-engined bombers, after flying 416 combat missions during the Second World War. He was born on 9 February 1919 in Gelsenkirchen in North Rhine-Westphalia, Germany.

Bauer joined the *Luftwaffe* in 1939, trained as a fighter pilot and was posted to the 51st Fighter Wing on the Eastern Front in March 1943 with the rank of *Unteroffizier*. He was assigned to the 10th Squadron and claimed his first victory on 20 March, a Petlyakov Pe-2 twin-engined bomber and he claimed his second victory on 17 July, an Ilyushin Il-2 ground-attack aircraft. He was awarded the Iron Cross 2nd Class soon after and from September was assigned to the Staff

(Deutsches Wehrkundearchiv)

Squadron of the 1st Group of the 51st Fighter Wing flying from Poltava in the Ukraine. He claimed three victories during September and claimed his sixth on 29 November. He became an 'ace-in-a-day' on 15 December when he claimed six aircraft in 10 minutes!

Promoted to *Feldwebel* in January 1944, he claimed four victories that month and in March was transferred to the 2nd Squadron of the 3rd Fighter Wing. He was awarded the *Luftwaffe* Honour Goblet on 31 March and claimed a B-17 Flying Fortress over Zehdenick, Brandenburg on 18 April. In June he transferred to the 300th Fighter Wing being attached to the 5th Squadron flying from Frankfurt am Main, equipped with the Focke-Wulf Fw 190A. According to some sources he shot down three B-17s and five B-24s between 13 and 29 June, but these remain unconfirmed after post-war scrutiny. On 7 July he claimed two B-24s and a single P-38 to score his 20th aerial victory, and by the end of the month he had claimed his 27th victory. He claimed five victories during August and on 11 September shot down three P-51 Mustangs in six minutes. He was described by fellow pilots as one of the more ferocious attack pilots of the *Luftwaffe*. During his short battle with the P-51s a bullet hit his right hand and he lost two fingers.

Whilst recovering he was awarded the Knight's Cross on 31 October 1944 in recognition of his 36th victory. He returned to his squadron as an *Oberfeldwebel* in late January 1945, as part of the 2nd Group flying from Löbnitz, taking part in 'Defence of the Reich' duties. He claimed a B-24 Liberator over the Magdeburg area on 9 February and a P-51 on 2 April. He flew briefly as *Staffelkapitän* of the 5th Squadron and was commissioned as a *Leutnant* at the same time and within a few weeks was promoted to *Oberleutnant*. It was thought he was one of the best marksmen in his Group, a typical fighter pilot. He drank more than was good for him, both before and after missions, but this didn't seem to affect him. His Focke-Wulf fighter had Red 3 painted on the side and the inscription '*Kornjark*', a reference to his favourite alcoholic drink. During his career he was shot down seven times and considering this and his drinking it's a surprise that he survived. He states he was recommended for the Oakleaves but there is no proof of this. He joined the *Bundeswehr* after the war, retiring in December 1960 as a *Hauptmann*. He died in his home town of Gelsenkirchen on 26 October 1990.

Johannes (Hans) 'Focke' NAUMANN

Major

Knight's Cross: Awarded on 9 November 1944 as *Hauptmann* and commander of the 2nd Group of the 6th Fighter Wing for operations over France, England and the Western Front.

Johannes Naumann claimed thirty-four aerial victories, of which seven were four-engined bombers, all whilst flying combat missions over the Western Front during the Second World War. He was born on 11 October 1917 in Dresden and joined the *Luftwaffe* in 1938. He trained as a fighter pilot and was assigned to the 26th Fighter Wing as a *Leutnant* in August 1939.

From November 1939 Naumann flew from Essen-Mülheim and received orders to secure the Western borders against Belgium and the Netherlands. In July 1940 his Group moved to Döberitz where he flew fighter protection missions over Berlin and later when the air war over France intensified he flew missions over the Channel and the British coast. On 12 August Naumann claimed his first victory but this was later unconfirmed and he had to wait until 3 September for his first confirmed victory, an RAF Spitfire over Southend, and he was

(Deutsches Wehrkundearchiv)

awarded the Iron Cross 2nd Class. From October his Squadron was converted to fighter-bombers and deployed over south-east England, and from November he flew from Abbeville, France. From January 1941 he flew from Dieppe, equipped with the Bf 109E, and from February he flew protection missions over the Reich. In April his Squadron moved back to France and Naumann claimed his second victory a Hurricane over Boulogne on 21 June and he claimed a Spitfire on 3 July and after claimed his fourth victory, another Spitfire, on 21 August he was awarded the Iron Cross 1st Class. From October his Group was converted to the Focke-Wulf Fw 190F-4 and his Group flew over the Channel coast until the end of the year.

At the beginning of 1942 his Group was being converted to the Fw 190A-1 and *A-2* and was flying against Allied bombers over the coastal areas. Naumann, now an *Oberleutnant,* took part in securing the skies during the breakout of the battleships *Scharnhorst, Gneisenau* and the heavy cruiser *Prinz Eugen* through the English Channel on 12 February in which Naumann claimed two Swordfish torpedo bombers over north Gravelines, France. On 19 August he flew fighter protection missions over the Dieppe area and although he failed to score a victory his Group claimed nine aerial victories. Promoted to *Hauptmann* in early September, he was appointed *Staffelkapitän* of the 6th Squadron of the 26th Fighter Wing on the 21st and flew defensive missions over Abbeville until the end of the year. In early 1943 his Group moved to Vitry-en-Artois on the Pas-de-Calais and stayed there until he summer, during this time Naumann claimed a further seven victories. By now he had claimed sixteen victories. On 22 June during a fight with a US four-engined bomber over Antwerp he was shot down by a P-47 over Antwerp, but managed to claim the bomber before he bailed out. Three days later he was awarded the *Luftwaffe* Honour Goblet in recognition of his fifteen aerial victories. He soon returned to action and on 26 July he claimed a Boston medium bomber over Vendeville, and four days later he claimed a B-17 Flying Fortress. He claimed his 20th victory on 17 August, another B-17, and two days later he took over as Acting *Gruppenkommandeur* of the 2nd Group of the 26th Fighter Wing, replacing Wilhelm-Ferdinand Galland who had been killed. On 31 August he was awarded the German Cross in Gold in recognition of achieving twenty-two aerial victories, and he added to his score on 2 September when he claimed a P-47 near Merville.

On 9 September 1943 Naumann returned as *Staffelkapitän* of the 6th Squadron once again, flying from Beauvais-Tille in France. He claimed a Typhoon near Forges on 11 September and on the 21st he shot down a B-25 Mitchell twin-engined bomber. On 1 October the 2nd Group expanded to four squadrons and the 4th became the 6th and his squadron became the 7th Squadron and it was relocated to Cambrai-Epinov on the 3rd, where it remained until the end of the year. On 14 October he claimed a B-17 Flying Fortress near Maastricht on 11 November, claimed another north-west of Breda and on 21 December he shot down a Spitfire near Douai. In early March he took over as *Gruppenkommandeur* of his Group once again, and with the start of the Allied invasion of Normandy on 6 June his Group was relocated to Guyancourt in northern France that same day.

On 22 June shortly after noon Naumann took off with seven Fw 190s from his Group to Caen to hunt for Allied fighter-bombers. They soon encountered two 414 Squadron Mustangs from the Canadian Air Force, which were scouting the battle lines and they were attacked. One Canadian pilot bailed out and wasn't hurt and the second crash-landed with injuries, but during the chase Naumann's Fw 190 was hit by British anti-aircraft fire. He was able to re-cross the German lines before bailing out from an altitude of 650fe, but he then hit both legs on the tail of his aircraft, injuring them severely. He was hospitalized and the 2nd Group was taken over by *Hauptmann* Emil Lang.

Naumann returned to action in September, taking over as *Gruppenkommandeur* of the 2nd Group of the 6th Fighter Wing, flying from Eudenbach, Germany. He claimed an Auster monoplane over Huy on 8 September and four days later he claimed two P-38s, his 30th and 31st victories. From October his group flew from Hagenau and on the 14th he claimed a P-38 over Cologne, his last aerial victory of the war. In November his Group received its first Fw 190A-9s and from 16 December he flew during the Ardennes Offensive. On 9 November he was awarded the Knight's Cross after claiming a total of thirty-four aerial victories of which seven were four-engined bombers.

At the beginning of 1945 his Group was located in Bissel near Oldenburg and in early January took part in Operation Bodenplatte, the German offensive against Allied air bases in northern France, Holland and Belgium. His Group targeted the Volkel air base in Holland but only minor damage was caused and shortly after the Group moved to Gross-Stein near Oppeln. On 1 March Naumann was promoted to *Major* and in early April he was transferred as *Gruppenkommandeur* of the 3rd Group of the 7th Fighter Wing, but during this time the Group's base was bombed by the Allies and a large number of buildings and aircraft was destroyed. A decision was made to move the Group to north-eastern Bavaria but this took longer than planned due to bad weather and Allied attacks. On 8 May most remaining aircraft left were destroyed by the Germans while some pilots flew their machines close to their home towns and surrendered.

Naumann had flown over 350 combat missions and after the war he joined the Bundesluftwaffe, retiring with the rank of *Oberst*. He died on 22 March 2010 in Fürstenfeldbruck, Bavaria at the age of 92.

<u>Klaus</u> Karl Theobald BRETSCHNEIDER

Oberleutnant

Knight's Cross: Awarded on 18 November 1944 as *Leutnant* and fighter pilot with the 5th Squadron of the 300th Fighter Wing for operations over the Western Front.

Klaus Bretschneider claimed twenty-two aerial victories, which included nineteen four-engined bombers, all over the Western Front. He was born on 4 May 1920 in Berlin-Stieglitz and upon completion of his fighter-pilot training he was posted to the 5th Squadron of the 300th Fighter Wing in July 1943, commanded by *Oberstleutnant* Hajo Hermann. Bretschneider claimed his first aerial victory at night, a Stirling four-engined bomber over Nuremberg, on 28 August 1943. Between 6 September and 18 March 1944, he claimed ten victories, all four-engined bombers, but after post-war investigations they remain unconfirmed. Nevertheless at the time the victories counted and Bretschneider had been awarded the Iron Cross 1st and 2nd Classes.

(Deutsches Wehrkundearchiv)

He claimed two confirmed four-engined bombers on 25 March, and claimed another at night on the 31st, then on 26 June he claimed two B-24 Liberators and a third on 7 July.

On 19 July Bretschneider was appointed *Staffelkapitän* of the 5th Squadron of the 300th Fighter Wing, and continued to claim four-engined bombers. By 27 July he had officially achieved twenty-one aerial victories, although at the time he had claimed a total of thirty-six. He claimed two victories in August and on 12 September claimed two B-17 bombers and one P-51 Mustang fighter, which remains an unconfirmed victory. His best day came on 7 October when he shot down three B-17s, one of which he rammed. His aircraft was severely damaged after this and he had to parachute to safety, and was found hanging in his parachute from a tree on the edge of a deep ravine. He was rescued successfully and returned to his Squadron the following day.

He was awarded the Knight's Cross on 18 November and had a few days before being presented with the German Cross in Gold. On 24 December Bretschneider was killed whilst attacking a group of four-engined bombers near Kassel. His Focke-Wulf Fw 190A-8 was struck by gunfire from a P-51 Mustang from 357 Fighter Group, and he crashed over the Knüll Mountains in the Kassel area. He is today buried in the military cemetery in Berlin-Nikolassee, Zehlendorf, located in Block H, Grave No. 58.

Rudolf KLEMM

Major

Knight's Cross: Awarded on 18 November 1944 as *Hauptmann* and *Staffelkapitän* with the 4th Group of the 54th Fighter Wing for operations over the Soviet Union, the Western and Eastern Fronts.

(Deutsches Wehrkundearchiv)

Rudolf Klemm claimed forty-three aerial victories during the Second World War of which ten were four-engined bombers shot down over the Western Front, achieved whilst flying 293 combat missions. He was born on 10 February 1918 in Haltingen in the district of Lörrach in Baden-Württemberg, Germany.

Klemm joined the *Luftwaffe* in 1937 and served for several years as a flight instructor before being assigned to the 8th Squadron of the 54th Fighter Wing in the Soviet Union from December 1941. At the beginning of 1942 *Oberfeldwebel* Klemm saw action over Leningrad and on 7 February whilst flying the Bf 109F-2 he claimed his first victory, a Polikarpov R-5 bomber. Later that month his unit was converted to the Bf 109F-4 fighter and on 4 April Klemm claimed his second aerial victory, and the 2,000th victory of his wing, a Pe-2 biplane over the Leningrad area, and later saw action over the area of Demyansk. He claimed his third victory on 11 August and on 1 September he shot down an LaGG-3 fighter over the area of Schüsselburg and was awarded the Iron Cross 2nd Class. He claimed another three victories in mid-September and on the 19th he shot down five aircraft, which included four Polikarpov I-16 fighters, to become an 'ace-in-a-day'. The following day he claimed his 13th victory and was awarded the Iron Cross 1st Class.

From late December he flew over the Smolensk area as part of the 9th Squadron and in January 1943 he claimed seven victories and from February his squadron was relocated to the Vendeville airfield in France and he was promoted to *Leutnant*. He had now claimed twenty-three aerial victories and on 22 February he was awarded the *Luftwaffe* Honour Goblet. On 17 April he claimed a B-17 Flying Fortress, his first four-engined bomber of the war, over south-west Ahlhorn, Lower Saxony. He claimed his 25th victory on 14 May, a B-24 Liberator over Rieseby near Schleswig-Holstein, Germany, and shortly after his Bf 109 was struck by anti-aircraft fire. He was blinded in one eye but managed to land safely. Despite this obvious handicap he returned to combat duty after only a few weeks. From July his Group flew escort missions for coastal shipping to the East Frisian Islands, and from late August they moved to the area near Schwerin and he and his fellow pilots were given the opportunity to relax. Later his Squadron was deployed in defensive duties protecting the Reich and on 9 October, *Oberleutnant* Klemm claimed two more B-17 bombers, this time over Neubrandenburg.

On 1 February 1944 he was appointed *Staffelkapitän* of the 7th Squadron of the 54th Fighter Wing and was awarded the German Cross in Gold for achieving his 25th victory on 24 February. He claimed his 30th and 31st victories on 6 March, a B-17 and a B-24 Liberator, and two days later he bailed out of his Bf 109 after combat with P-38s and was slightly injured. On 8 April he claimed two more B-24 bombers, one over Celle and the other over south-west Twistringen, Lower Saxony. The next day he was himself shot down by a P-47 of the 56th Fighter Group, flown by Captain T. Anderz on secondment from 315 Polish Squadron of the Royal Air Force. Klemm's Bf 109 crashed near Kiel and his wounds were such that he had to have two toes amputated.

In July Klemm took command of the 12th Squadron of the 54th Fighter Wing, now flying the Focke-Wulf Fw 190A and back on the Eastern Front. He claimed his 40th victory on 26 September and was promoted to *Hauptmann* around the same time. After claiming his 48th aerial victory he was awarded the Knight's Cross on 18 November and in early December he took over as *Gruppenkommandeur* of the 4th Group of the 54th Fighter Wing, claiming his last victory on 19 March 1945, a P-51 Mustang over north-west Nordhorn. Later his command was redesignated the 4th Group of the 16th Fighter Wing and was now based in Varrelbusch, Germany. On 5 April he was flying a reconnaissance mission when his aircraft was hit by anti-aircraft fire and damaged and he had to return to base. On the 17th he relinquished his command and was ordered to the 7th Fighter Wing in Prague to take over as *Gruppenkommandeur* of the 2nd Group but he never arrived, surrendering to the Allies in early May 1945.

He was said to have a reputation of being aloof on the ground towards his fellow pilots and seemed overly concerned for his own personal safety when flying and concentrating on his own advancement. Klemm died in an air crash on 5 July 1989 near Basel, Switzerland.

Heinz LANGE

Major

Knight's Cross: Awarded on 18 November 1944 as *Hauptmann* and Acting commander of the 4th Group of the 51st Fighter Wing '*Mölders*' for operations over the Eastern Front.

Heinz Lange claimed seventy-three aerial victories, all but one whilst flying combat missions over the Eastern Front during the Second World War whilst flying 628 combat missions. He was born on 2 October 1917 in Cologne and entered the Air School Wildpark-West in Potsdam in 1937. He transferred into the 4th Squadron of the 234th Fighter Wing as a young *Leutnant* at the beginning of 1939, and from July he flew with the 1st Squadron of the 132nd Fighter Wing. On 16 September he was unhurt when he crash-landed his Bf 109D-1 between Klein-Zechen and Sokoly-Rostken due to weather conditions.

On 30 October 1939 now an *Oberleutnant* he claimed his first aerial victory, an RAF Blenheim of 18 Squadron on a reconnaissance mission over Germany. He was awarded the Iron Cross 2nd Class and in 1940

(Deutsches Wehrkundearchiv)

he flew during the Battle of France, mainly on escort missions, flying over Eben-Emael and the Maastricht area. From 1 to 4 June he flew in support of army operations over the Lower Somme area. On the 8th he joined the Staff of the 54th Fighter Wing and in August he moved to the 8th Squadron seeing action over England. In April 1941 his squadron moved to the Balkans and from 29 June he was stationed in Dünaburg on the Russian Front and where the following day he claimed two DB-3 bombers over Dünaburg. On 5 July he claimed two more and by 23 September he had claimed his eighth victory and had been awarded the Iron Cross 1st Class. On 1 October he replaced *Leutnant* Walter Nowotny, a future Knight's Cross with Oakleaves, Swords and Diamonds winner, as *Staffelkapitän* of the 1st Squadron of the 54th Fighter Wing. During his time with the 1st Squadron he claimed a total of eleven aerial victories and late October was appointed *Staffelkapitän* of the

3rd Squadron of the 51st Fighter Wing. With twenty aerial victories now to his name, although one would later be reclassified as unconfirmed, he was awarded the *Luftwaffe* Honour Goblet on 27 October.

At the beginning of 1943 he was flying from Vyazma-South and in January he claimed his 25th aerial victory. In February his Group moved from the frontline to refresh and converted to the Focke-Wulf Fw 190A, and he flew the new aircraft in March at Vyazma for the first time and loved it. He thought the visibility from the cockpit was better than the Bf 109 and he found it more manoeuvrable. The radial engine of the Fw 190A was also more resistant to enemy fire. The central cannon of the Bf 109 was more accurate, but only a real advantage in fighter-to-fighter combat. The Fw 190A's 30mm cannon often jammed and Lange lost at least six victories that way! In March his Group moved to Orel-West and then onto Bryansk and towards the end of the month Lange was promoted to *Hauptmann* and after claiming two more victories he was awarded the German Cross in Gold on 17 May. In July he claimed four victories, which included two Il-2 ground-attack aircraft, and his 30th victory over north-east Maloarkhangelsk. His Squadron returned to Bryansk on 2 August during which time Lange claimed his 40thaerial victory and by the end of October he had achieved fifty aerial victories, and during the last two months of the year his Group left the front line to be converted to the Messerschmitt Bf 109G.

At the beginning of 1944 Lange was flying from Orscha in Belarus and on 1 and 4 January he claimed three victories over south Vitebsk, all Il-2s. On 9 May he was appointed *Gruppenkommandeur* of the 4th Group of the 51st Fighter Wing, flying from Zhytomyr in the Ukraine. Lange claimed his 60th aerial victory on 29 June, a P-39 fighter north-north-east of Beresino. During the gradual withdrawal from the area he claimed two victories in July and another in August. On 7 October he claimed three Soviet Boston bombers and he claimed five victories over Poland which included his last on 16 October, a Yak-9 about 15 miles north-east of Nasielsk. On 18 November 1944 Lange was awarded the Knight's Cross in recognition of his 70th aerial victory.

On 12 April 1945, now with the rank of *Major*, Lange managed to fly into the base of the 51st Fighter Wing at Littansdorf which had been under constant attack. He had flown across 250 miles of enemy-held territory to take over from *Major* Fritz Losigkeit as the final *Kommodore* of the 51st Fighter Wing. But there was little left to fly or command and his only duty was to organize the dissolution of the Wing. He then returned to command the 4th Group once again and on 29 April he was involved in his last dogfight with four La-7 aircraft over Neubrandenburg together with his wingman *Oberfeldwebel* Alfred Rauch, but it was Rauch who claimed the 51st Fighter Wing's last victory of the war. After the war Lange received a doctorate in law from the University of Kiel and then worked for an insurance company. Once he had retired Lange settled in Bergisch Gladbach, a city in the Cologne and Bonn Region of North Rhine-Westphalia where he died on 26 February 2006.

Fritz 'Paulo' LÜDDECKE

Oberfeldwebel

Knight's Cross: Awarded posthumously on 18 November 1944 as *Oberfeldwebel* and fighter pilot with the Staff Squadron of the 51st Fighter Wing 'Mölders' for operations over the Eastern Front.

Fritz Lüddecke claimed fifty-one aerial victories over the Eastern Front whilst flying a total of just over 600 combat missions during the Second World War. He was born on 23 February 1920 in Brakel, Höxter in North Rhine-Westphalia, and joined the *Luftwaffe* as a fighter pilot and was assigned to Fighter Replacement Group East from November 1941.

In May 1942 he transferred to the 6th Squadron of the 51st Fighter Wing flying the Messerschmitt Bf 109F-2 as an *Unteroffizier*. From July he flew from Orel and in August his Group moved to

Dugino and on the 24th Lüddecke claimed his first victory, a MiG-3 fighter near Kozelsk. In early October his Group was withdrawn and from November his 6th Squadron became the Staff Squadron and was relocated to Tunisia. Here he flew mainly escort missions for transport aircraft flying in from Sicily, remaining in the Mediterranean area until the end of the year.

From the beginning of 1943 he returned to the Eastern Front and was flying the Focke-Wulf Fw 190A, and claimed his second victory on 9 March and his third six days later. Promoted to *Feldwebel* he claimed two more victories in July and was awarded the Iron Cross 2nd Class, and in August he claimed eight victories which included four Il-2 ground-attack aircraft on the 20th and he was awarded the Iron Cross 1st Class. By the end of 1943 he had claimed a total of eighteen victories and had been awarded the *Luftwaffe* Honour Goblet on 13 December, and was promoted to *Oberfeldwebel*. He claimed his 20th

(Deutsches Wehrkundearchiv)

victory on 5 February 1944 over north-west Paritschi and claimed two victories on the 22nd, and claimed his 25th victory on 23 June. He claimed a total of twelve victories in June, and the following month he claimed another seven victories which included his 40th on 2 July. He claimed two victories on and 4 August and went on to claim two more on the 7th and another on the 8th and his last victories were claimed on the 9th.

The following day he was shot down by Soviet anti-aircraft guns. He managed to belly-land his Fw 190A-8 near Wilkowischken, Lithuania but it exploded and he was killed. He was posthumously awarded the German Cross in Gold on 1 October and the Knight's Cross on 18 November 1944.

Heinz 'Negus' MARQUARDT

Fähnenjunker-Oberfeldwebel

Knight's Cross: Awarded on 18 November 1944 as *Oberfeldwebel* and pilot with the 13th Squadron of the 51st Fighter Wing '*Mölders*' for operations over the Eastern Front and for claiming his 88th aerial victory.

Heinz Marquardt claimed a total of 121 aerial victories in just 18 months, whilst flying approximately 320 combat missions over the Eastern Front during the Second World War. He was born on 29 December 1922 in Braunsberg, East Prussia and joined the *Luftwaffe* in March 1940 at just 17 years old.

In July 1940 he joined the 31st Flight Training Regiment and from June he served as an instructor with the 1st Fighter Pilot School and from September with the 5th Fighter Pilot School. In August 1943, with the rank of *Unteroffizier*, Marquardt served with the 11th Squadron of the 51st Fighter Wing in the Soviet Union. He claimed

(Deutsches Wehrkundearchiv)

his first aerial victory on 17 October, a Yakovlev Yak-1 fighter over south-west St. Budniza, and he claimed his second victory, another Yak-1, on the 28th. He claimed an Il-2 ground-attack aircraft on 21 and 22 November and soon after he was awarded the Iron Cross 2nd Class.

In 1944 his Squadron moved around, from Zhitomar at the beginning of the year and then to Orscha, and by April he was flying missions from Lysyatchi in the Ukraine. Now a *Feldwebel*,

Marquardt claimed three victories on 29 April, which included his 10th and soon after was awarded the Iron Cross 1st Class. During May he claimed seven victories, and on 8 June he claimed three victories which included his 20th victory. By the end of June he was flying from Minsk and on 4 July he claimed four victories over Molodeczno, and he claimed two more on the 6th and the 9th, which included his 30th victory. Promoted to *Oberfeldwebel* in mid-July he was awarded the *Luftwaffe* Honour Goblet on the 26th and by 2 August he had claimed his 40th victory. By mid-August he was flying with the 13th Squadron of the 51st Fighter Wing and by the end of the month had claimed a total of fifty-six aircraft. During September he shot down seven aircraft and was awarded the German Cross in Gold on the 10th after claiming his 60th victory. He became an 'ace-in-a-day' on 7 October, when he shot down eight aircraft over south-west Modlin and east Nasielsk. He claimed two more victories on 13, 15 and 17 October, which included his 75th, and he claimed three victories on the 19th. By the end of October he had shot down a total of ninety aircraft and he claimed five victories on 24 October to become an 'ace-in-a-day' for the second time.

On 18 November he was awarded the Knight's Cross in recognition of his success over the Eastern Front. In March he was made a *Fahnenjunker-Oberfeldwebel*, an officer candidate, and his Squadron moved to Danzig. On 14 April he claimed his 100th victory and on the 15th he claimed three victories, two on the 16th, and four on 18 and 24 April.

On 1 May 1945 he claimed his 121st aerial victory, and his last of the war, because shortly after this he was shot down by a Spitfire from 41 Squadron, flown by Flight Lieutenant Peter Cowell. During the attack Marquardt smashed his head on his gun sight, managed to bail out and fell unconscious. He awoke to find his parachute hooked on the turret of a castle near Lake Schwerin as some nuns were pulling him to safety. He did not return to combat as the war was almost over. In August 1956 he joined the *Bundesluftwaffe* serving with the 73rd and 74th Fighter Wings and he reached the rank of *Oberstleutnant* before retiring in 1973. It was during his retirement that he made contact with Peter Cowell and they remained good friends until his death on 19 December 2003 in Hemmersbach in Hessen, Germany.

Karl BORRIS

Major

Knight's Cross: Awarded on 25 November 1944 as *Major* and commander of the 1st Group of the 26th Fighter Wing '*Schlageter*' for operations over France, England and the Western Front. It was presented to him by the Inspector of Day Fighters, *Oberst* Hannes Trautloft at Fürstenau on 5 December 1944.

Karl Borris claimed forty-three aerial victories (including five four-engined bombers), all of them over the Western Front. He was described as dour and humourless by his colleagues, but a good pilot. He was born on 3 March 1916 in Heinsdorf, Jüterbog and he joined the *Luftwaffe* in November 1935. From November 1937 he attended the *Luftwaffe* War School in Dresden and from 1 December 1938 he was attached to the 1st Group of the 130th Fighter Wing in Jesau.

(Deutsches Wehrkundearchiv)

On 1 September 1939, the day Germany invaded Poland, Borris was commissioned as a *Leutnant* and transferred to the 1st Fighter Pilot School in Schleissheim. From December he was attached to the 2nd Group of the 26th Fighter Wing '*Schlageter*', under the command of *Hauptmann* Herwig Knüppel. He was based at Werl, Germany and Borris patrolled the German borders during the 'Phoney War', without contact with the enemy. From January 1940 his Group was stationed in Dortmund, and on 13 May, during the Battle of France, his Bf 109E-3 was shot down by a Defiant fighter near Dordrecht. He managed to bail out and was slightly wounded, and returned to his squadron four days later. Borris claimed his first victory on 1 June, an RAF Hurricane over Dunkirk, and the following day he claimed a Spitfire in the same area. On 13 August the Germans launched *Adlertag* or Eagle Day, the name given to the operation to destroy the RAF, and on that day Borris claimed two Hurricanes over the Maidstone area. On 6 September he claimed another Hurricane north-west of Folkestone and the next day he was awarded the Iron Cross 2nd Class. On 28 September he was appointed Technical Officer of the 2nd Group of the 26th Fighter Wing and claimed his final victory during the Battle of Britain on 25 October, a Spitfire over Maidstone.

On 5 March 1941 he was sent to the *Luftwaffe* main testing ground at Rechlin and took part in operational testing of the new Focke-Wulf Fw 190. In August he was ordered to the Le Bourget airfield near Paris and there he began training the 2nd Group of the 26th Fighter Wing on the new Fw 190A-1. On 9 August he claimed a Spitfire over Campagne, flying the new fighter. He was awarded the Iron Cross 1st Class on 5 September and five days later he claimed another Spitfire. On 21 September twelve Bristol Blenheim bombers escorted by fourteen squadrons of Spitfires and Hurricanes targeted Béthune and Gosnay. In combat over Étaples, Borris managed to shoot down a Spitfire of 315 Polish Squadron. On 6 November, *Hauptmann* Johann Schmid, the *Staffelkapitän* of the 8th Squadron was killed, and Borris was named as his successor. He claimed his 10th victory on 13 March and on 4 April he claimed two Spitfires. On 25 May Borris was awarded the *Luftwaffe* Honour Goblet and by on 8 September he was awarded the German Cross in Gold in recognition of his 21st aerial victory.

On 14 May 1943, the USAAF targeted four separate targets in Germany, Belgium and The Netherlands. Borris was shot down in his Fw 190A-5 by defensive fire from a B-17 Flying Fortress over Wevelgem. He bailed out at 23,000ft but opened his parachute too soon, causing it to partially collapse and he sustained multiple injuries, requiring a lengthy stay in hospital. On 23 June, the *Kommodore* of the 26th Fighter Wing, *Oberst* Josef Priller appointed Borris his new *Gruppenkommandeur* of the 1st Group, he telephoned him in hospital with the good news. On 25 July, still not completely fit, Borris led the 1st Group against US B-26s attacking the Ghent coke furnaces. The group engaged the escorting fighters and shot down four Spitfires without loss, Borris claiming two. On 17 August the USAAF targeted the German aircraft industry when they attacked the factories at Schweinfurt-Regensburg. It was carried out by sixty B-17 bombers of which one was claimed by Borris.

In April 1944 Borris was promoted to *Major*, and had by this time claimed a total of thirty-seven victories. On 16 September he claimed his 40th victory and the following day the Allies launched Operation Market Garden to secure a bridgehead over the Rhine. The Allies flew supplies to the combat area around Arnhem on 23 September and German fighters were dispatched. Borris led the 1st Group to the Goch-Wesel area where he claimed a P-51 Mustang, his 51st aerial victory. On 24 November Priller the Staff of the 26th Fighter Wing and Borris with the 1st Group moved to an airfield near Fürstenau where Borris was awarded the Knight's Cross. The presentation was made on 5 December by *Oberst* Hannes Trautloft, Inspector of Day Fighters. Later Borris led five new Fw 190s against a formation of B-17 bombers, managing to shoot one down, and later flew twelve combat missions in support of the Ardennes Offensive.

In late December 1944 aircraft from the 3rd Group of the 54th Fighter Wing under the command of *Oberleutnant* Hans Dortenman arrived at Fürstenau. There they were briefed by Borris who was to lead a mission together with Priller. This was Operation Bodenplatte, an attempt at gaining air superiority during the slow stage of the Battle of the Bulge. The German force took off on 1 January 1945, and they sustained losses during the approach to the target, mainly due to anti-aircraft fire.

The airfield at Gimbergen which they were targeting was almost deserted and the damage inflicted was minimal, but the losses sustained to the 3rd Group were significant. They lost five pilots killed or listed as missing and another four were taken prisoner. Borris lost six of his pilots. There were further missions and Borris claimed his last victory on 14 January during the German retreat in the Ardennes. He led thirty-one Fw 190D-9s from Fürstenfeld airfield during a mission to protect the jet-bomber airfields near Rhine-Hopsten. Borris and his aircraft encountered RAF Spitfires, and during this engagement Borris claimed a Spitfire over Ibbenbüren.

During early May 1945 Borris and his Group were stationed in Flensburg where on 6 May he surrendered his Group to British forces. Had he not been the tough disciplinarian, unapproachable by nature, enforcing the slightest of regulations on his men, then he may have achieved more victories and the respect of his men. However he impressed his commanders and was the only pilot to serve continuously with the 26th Fighter Wing through the entire war. Borris lived a quiet life after the war and died on 18 August 1981 in Bornum, Wolfenbittel in Lower Saxony.

Klaus NEUMANN

Leutnant

Knight's Cross: Awarded on 25 November 1944 as *Feldwebel* and fighter pilot with the 16th Squadron of the 3rd Fighter Wing '*Udet*' for operations over the Soviet Union and the Western Front.

Klaus Neumann claimed at least nineteen aerial victories during the Second World War, of which seventeen were four-engined bombers. He was born on 5 October 1923 in Wettin-Löbejün, a small town in the Salle District of Saxony-Anhalt, Germany, and joined the *Luftwaffe* in early 1943. After the completion of his training he was assigned to the 2nd Squadron of the 51st Fighter Wing.

(Deutsches Wehrkundearchiv)

He first saw action over the Soviet Union, flying from Orel in May and then later moving to Bryansk and to Poltava at the end of August. From October to December his Group was converted to the Bf 109G. At the beginning of 1944 *Unteroffizier* Neumann was flying from Bobruisk and from 25 June his Group moved to Germany to fly 'Defence of the Reich' missions, where on 7 July he claimed his first victory, a B-24 Liberator four-engined bomber near Aschersleben, and was awarded the Iron Cross 2nd Class. On 20 July he claimed two B-17 Flying Fortresses over the Chemnitz area, and nine days later he claimed another and was awarded the Iron Cross 1st Class. On 3 August he claimed a B-17 and a B-24 over France and a week later his Group and moved to Germany where it was renamed the 16th Squadron of the 3rd Fighter Wing. He claimed a B-17 on 15 and 16 August and he claimed a B-24 on 22 and 23 August, his 10th aerial victory. He claimed a P-51 Mustang and another B-17 during August and claimed five more four-engined bombers during September. On 25 October about two weeks after claiming another B-17 bomber Neumann was awarded the German Cross in Gold in recognition of his success as a bomber ace. On 2 November he claimed two more B-17s but that same day he was shot down and wounded during combat with Allied fighters and he bailed out of his Fw 190 near Halle, Germany. On 25 November he was awarded the Knight's Cross which was personally presented to him by Hitler on 9 December at the Reich Chancellery in Berlin.

In January 1945 he joined the 7th Fighter Wing but within a few short weeks he clashed with the *Kommodore Major* Theodor Weissenberger and in March he transferred to *Jagdverband* 44, where he flew the new Me 262 jet fighter whilst under the command of *Generalmajor* Adolf Galland. He flew many practice flights and soon learnt how to control this new fighter and on 20 March 1945 he flew together with *Oberstleutnant* Johannes Steinhoff and *Leutnant* Blomert in what is believed to be the first combat operation by fighters from *Jagdverband* 44. Whilst flying in formation around the Plauer See just south of Briest shortly after take-off, the three jets flew towards Berlin, and then to the east, towards Frankfurt an der Oder. They flew into light flak and then turned for home when they suddenly encountered a formation of Soviet fighters over the river. They came upon some Il-2s attacking a German transport column and Steinhoff shot one down. They had to leave as they were running short of fuel and reached their base at Brandenburg on the very last of their reserve fuel. Neumann claimed three more victories in April 1945 whilst flying the Me 262 fighter but these have always been unconfirmed victories. He ended the war as one of the youngest Knight's Cross holders of *Jagdverband* 44, and one of their highest scorers.

Neumann survived the war and joined the *Bundesluftwaffe* in January 1956 where he continued to fly jets until his retirement in September 1974 with the rank of *Oberst*. He died on 10 December 2000 in Mittelhof, a district of Altenkirchen, in Rhineland-Palatinate.

Heinz-Gerhard VOGT

Oberleutnant

Knight's Cross: Awarded on 25 November 1944 as *Leutnant* and *Staffelführer* of the 5th Squadron of the 26th Fighter Wing '*Schlageter*' for operations over the Western Front.

Heinz-Gerhard Vogt claimed forty-seven aerial victories, which included eight four-engined bombers, all achieved over the Western Front during the Second World. He was born on 29 November 1919 in Raudna, Lüben in Lower Silesia and after completing his training as a fighter pilot he was attached to a Fighter Wing on the Channel Front as an *Obergefreiter* in September 1941.

Vogt was assigned to the 6th Squadron of the 26th Fighter Wing and flew the Focke-Wulf Fw 190A-1. His Squadron was part of the 2nd Group under the command of *Hauptmann* Walter Adolph, but he was killed just two days after Vogt had arrived and his successor was *Hauptmann* Joachim Müncheberg. Vogt claimed his first victory

(Deutsches Wehrkundearchiv)

on 6 November 1941, a Spitfire over Calais, flown by a pilot attached to 452 Squadron of the Royal Australian Air Force. On 23 November he claimed his second victory, a Spitfire from 315 Polish Squadron just west of Dunkirk, and shortly after he was awarded the Iron Cross 2nd Class.

At the beginning of 1942 Vogt flew protection missions along the coast of France and on 12 February flew over the battleships *Scharnhorst* and *Gneisenau* as well as the heavy cruiser *Prinz Eugen*. Vogt was shot down on 24 March by a Spitfire of 412 Squadron flown by Warrant Officer L.N. Powell, who only claimed it as damaged, and he managed to land his Fw 190 at Abbeville airfield and was only slightly wounded. He was promoted to *Unteroffizier* and claimed another Spitfire on 4 April and by 17 August he had claimed his seventh victory, all Spitfires, and was awarded the Iron Cross 1st Class. On 27 August he claimed a Spitfire from 111 Squadron whilst on fighter escort missions for bombers targeting the *Luftwaffe* airfield at Abbeville-Drucat, Vogt's home airfield. By the end of the year Vogt had claimed a total of eleven victories and all of them Spitfires.

From early 1943 Vogt flew combat missions against Allied bomber formations and on 8 January his Group moved to Vitry-en-Artois in the Pas-de-Calais and remained there until the summer. On 2

February he was shot down by Spitfires of 331 Squadron, flown by Flight Lieutenant H.G.E. Grundt-Spang, Lieutenant S. Heglund and Sergeant E. Berg-Olsen. He was severely wounded in his shoulder and foot and bailed out west of Ypres and spent four months in hospital. After heavy defensive battles, in which Vogt, now a *Feldwebel*, claimed a B-17 Flying Fortress on 22 June, his Group was withdrawn and relocated to Deelan on 28 July. Two days later Vogt was again shot down and wounded by return fire from a B-17, bailing out of his Fw 190A-4 north-east of Duisburg. The Group moved to the Netherlands and from there returned to France on 15 August and on 3 September he was once again shot down by return fire from a B-17 and was slightly wounded when he crash-landed his Fw 190A-4 at Romilly-sur-Seine, and the next day he claimed two Spitfires near Berck-sur-Mer, his 14th and 15th victories. Later that day Vogt was shot down yet again, this time by a Spitfire flown by Australian Flight Lieutenant Tony Gaze of 66 Squadron near Le Tréport.

At the beginning of 1944 his Group was in Cambrai-Epiony in France and on 8 March Vogt claimed two B-17 bombers which included his 20th victory. On 17 March his Group moved to Cambrai-South and three days later Vogt was awarded the German Cross in Gold. He claimed five more victories during April and was promoted to *Oberfeldwebel*. With the start of the Allied invasion on 6 June his group moved to Guyancourt from where he was deployed over the Allied landing area. During the course of heavy dogfights he claimed five victories during June and was promoted to *Leutnant*, and from 20 June he took over as *Staffelführer* of the 7th Squadron after *Oberleutnant* Waldemar Radener had been seriously wounded. On 5 July he was once more shot down, again during combat with Spitfires, and he crashed at Bure-Mele sur Sarthe and was injured.

On 15 August he handed over command of the 7th Squadron to *Leutnant* Hans Prager and was appointed *Staffelkapitän* of the 5th Squadron, and later that day he claimed a P-47 Thunderbolt over Versailles, his 31st victory. On 21 September he claimed a Douglas C-47 Dakota transport aircraft over Nijmegen during the Battle of Arnhem. He claimed his 40th victory on 23 September and on 28 October he shot down a Typhoon from 182 Squadron, but was then himself hit by another Typhoon and had to make a forced landing near Venlo and was slightly wounded. He returned to duty in early November and on the 19th he claimed a Spitfire and later that month his Group relocated to an airfield at Reinsehlen, south of Hamburg where they received the Fw 190D-9. On 25 November he was awarded the Knight's Cross in recognition of scoring forty-four aerial victories, and he claimed his 47th and last victory on 26 December during the Battle of the Bulge.

On 1 January 1945, Vogt led his Squadron during Operation Bodenplatte, an attempt at gaining air superiority during the Battle of the Bulge. The 2nd and 3rd Groups of the 26th Fighter Wing attacked the Allied airbase at Nordhorn. The 2nd Group lost thirteen Fw 190s, with nine pilots missing, five killed and four captured and the 3rd Group lost six Bf 109s and four pilots. On 14 January, on his 174th mission during the retreat of German forces in the Ardennes, Vogt was shot down and killed by USAAF P-51 fighters of the 78th Fighter Group south-west of Porz-Eil, Cologne. He was either promoted just before he was killed or posthumously to the rank of *Oberleutnant*. He was shot down seven times during his career. He is today buried at the Military Cemetery in Cologne-Wahn.

Peter KALDEN

Oberleutnant

Knight's Cross: Awarded on 6 December 1944 as *Leutnant* whilst serving in the 13th Squadron of the 51st Fighter Wing *'Mölders'* for operations over the Soviet Union and the Eastern Front and for claiming his 65th aerial victory.

Peter Kalden claimed sixty-nine aerial victories in just 18 months during the Second World War, and all of them whilst flying combat missions over the Eastern Front. He was born on 17 August 1923 in Wittenberg, Saxony-Anhalt situated on the River Elbe in Germany.

On completion of his training he was assigned as a fighter pilot to the 11th Squadron of the 51st Fighter Wing as a *Leutnant* in early 1943. From February his squadron was equipped with the Focke-Wulf Fw 190A-4 and towards the end of July they converted to the Messerschmitt Bf 109G. Kalden claimed his first victory on 13 July, a Yak-1 fighter over the Soviet Union, and he claimed his second victory the following day. His Group moved to Bryansk in August and by mid-September he had claimed his sixth victory and on 3 October he shot down two La-5 fighters over Arlik. By the time he had achieved his 10th victory on 30 November he had already been awarded the Iron Cross 1st and 2nd Class.

(Deutsches Wehrkundearchiv)

At the beginning of 1944 Kalden was again involved in much aerial activity, claiming an La-5 fighter on 5 January and he claimed three victories over Vinnica five days later. He claimed his 20th victory on 1 February and claimed two more during April. On 2 May he claimed a further three victories, two Il-2 ground-attack aircraft and a single Yak-9 over Brody, Poland. That same day he was himself shot down near Kurowice, near Lodz in central Poland, and was slightly wounded but managed to get back to his own lines and land safely. He was awarded the *Luftwaffe* Honour Goblet on 8 May after claiming his 22nd aerial victory. During July he claimed another nine aerial victories, including his 30th on the 19 July, a Polikarpov R-5 reconnaissance aircraft over Zolochiv in the Ukraine.

On 17 July he was appointed *Staffelkapitän* of his Squadron, the 11th Squadron and he claimed his 34th victory on 23 July. By mid-August his 10th Squadron had been renamed the 13th Squadron after some Group changes and he claimed his 40th and 41st victories on 17 August. He claimed three more on 1 September north-east of Warsaw and claimed his 45th victory eight days later. He shot down three aircraft on 7 October and claimed his 50th victory, another Il-2, over Warsaw on 10 October. In fact during October he claimed a total of twenty aerial victories which included four on the 13th and 14th, and two on the 15th and 19th, for a total of sixty-five. This was thought to be the magic number at the time to be awarded the Knight's Cross. When he landed on 24 October after claiming his 65th victory he was greeted by shouts and cheers and lifted out of his cockpit and a large wooden cross was put around his neck to symbolize the Knight's Cross. However, *Luftwaffe* bureaucracy worked slowly and his award wasn't announced until 6 December 1944.

He claimed another four victories in January 1945, which included three on the 24th. Then his luck ran out. On 11 March he was shot down in his Bf 109G-14 by Soviet anti-aircraft fire whilst attacking tanks near Neustadt. He made an emergency landing and was captured, and held until 1950. During his wartime career he claimed a total of eighty-four aerial victories over the Eastern Front of which fifteen were unconfirmed. It was reported that he was awarded the German Cross in Gold in January 1945 but this has never been confirmed. He died on 11 June 1996 in Friedrichsdorf, about 12 miles from Frankfurt-am-Main in Germany.

Gerhard 'Gerd' THYBEN

Oberleutnant

Knight's Cross: Awarded on 6 December 1944 as *Leutnant* and fighter pilot in the 7th Squadron of the 54th Fighter Wing for operations over the Soviet Union, the Western Front and the Eastern Front.

Knight's Cross with Oakleaves: He became the 822nd recipient on 8 April 1945 as *Oberleutnant* and *Staffelkapitän* of the 7th Squadron of the 54th Fighter Wing for operations over the Eastern Front and for claiming his 151st aerial victory. The award was personally presented by Hitler at the Reich Chancellery in Berlin in April 1945.

Gerhard Thyben flew 385 combat missions mainly over the Eastern Front and claimed 157 aerial victories during the Second World War. He also flew twenty-two fighter-bomber missions that resulted in the destruction of seven vehicles and two enemy aircraft on the ground. Thyben was born on 24 February 1922 in Kiel, at the time the capital of the Province of Schleswig-Holstein. He left school in July 1940 and joined the *Luftwaffe*, and on completion of his basic training in Vienna was assigned, in October, to the 3rd Company of the 32nd Air Training Regiment in Rochfort-en-Terre for flight training. From mid-1941 he was assigned to the 2nd Fighter Pilot School and was transferred to the 5th Fighter Pilot School. From there he was posted to the 3rd Squadron of the Fighter Replacement Group East, a specialized training unit for new fighter pilots, and in November he trained in the 1st Squadron of the Fighter Replacement Group South.

On 13 December 1942 he was posted to the 2nd Group of the 3rd Fighter Wing and was attached to the 6th Squadron on the southern sector of the Eastern Front. During January and early February his squadron had moved several times and on 26 February he claimed his first aerial victory, a Boston medium bomber. In April he moved again with his squadron, to the Crimea and on 6 May claimed his second victory, another Boston over Balakleya in the Ukraine. He claimed two more victories on the 8th and one on the 11th and the 14th, before being awarded the Iron Cross 2nd Class. Thyben claimed ten victories during June, and was awarded the Iron Cross 1st Class on 19 June, after claiming his 19th aerial victory. By the end of July he had achieved his 32nd victory, and in early August his Group moved to Uetersen

Gerhard Thyben shortly after receiving the Knight's Cross. (Deutsches Wehrkundearchiv)

where it was rested and where the Group's aircraft were upgraded to the Bf 109G-5 and G-6. He was awarded the *Luftwaffe* Honour Goblet after his 32nd victory on 30 August 1943. In September the Group moved to Schiphol south of Amsterdam and Thyben flew defensive missions over Holland and the Ruhr. On 24 October he was awarded the German Cross in Gold and was shortly afterwards promoted to *Feldwebel*. On 11 February he claimed three P-38 Lightnings over St. Vith in Liège, Belgium, his 35th to 37th victories.

Commissioned as a *Leutnant*, Thyben transferred to the 2nd Group of the 54th Fighter Wing in April and was attached to the 5th Squadron based in Immola, Finland. He claimed five victories during May, and claimed his 50th victory on 23 June, and by the end of the month he had achieved his 54th victory. He was transferred to the 7th Squadron of the 3rd Group in August and by the end of the month had claimed his 69th aerial victory. He gained another thirty-one victories during September which included four on the 6th, four on the 15th and six on the 16th, to become an 'ace-in-a-day', and four on the 25th. He claimed three victories on the 29 September which included his 100th victory, becoming the 84th fighter pilot to achieve his century. During October the 6th and 7th Squadrons together with the 3rd Group were moved to Oldenburg and equipped with the Focke-Wulf Fw 190A. Thyben claimed a further fifteen victories during October and on 6 December was awarded the Knight's Cross in recognition of his 116th victory. He claimed two victories on 14 December, three on the 15th and four on the 21st, and became an 'ace-in-a-day' again when he claimed five victories on the 22nd. Promoted to *Oberleutnant* in December, he claimed three more victories on the 23rd and four on the 19th and that day his unit was moved to Handrup, Lower Saxony.

In early January 1945 the 7th Squadron became part of the 3rd Group, flying out of Libau and from the 5th they had again moved to Varrelbusch in Germany. Thyben claimed two victories on 20 January and on the 26th claimed his 140th victory, and just three days later he became the 30th fighter pilot to achieve 150 aerial victories. He claimed his 152nd victory on 5 March and on 8 April he was awarded the Knight's Cross with Oakleaves. On the morning of 8 May Thyben took off in his Fw 190, with his chief mechanic Albert Mayes crammed into the radio compartment behind him trying hard not to disturb the tail control rods and cables running the length of the fuselage. As Thyben headed out over open water, the smoke and ruins of Libau began to slip away behind him. Suddenly just in front of him he spotted a Petlyakov Pe-2 dive-bomber flying across his path, almost certainly looking for German refugee ships escaping from the besieged Courland Pocket. In seconds he dived out of the sun and fired at the bomber, sending it into the waters of the Baltic Sea. It was probably the last aerial victory of a Fw 190 during the Second World War. He then flew on and surrendered to British troops that afternoon. He was released from captivity in 1946 and went to live in Spain and then Argentina. He later settled in Colombia where he served for a time as a flight instructor with the Air Force before retiring some years later. Thyben died in Santiago de Cali, Colombia on 4 September 2006.

Ulrich 'Seppl' WÖHNERT

Leutnant

Knight's Cross: Awarded on 6 December 1944 as *Leutnant* and pilot with the 5th Squadron of the 54th Fighter Wing '*Grünherz*' for operations over the Soviet Union and the Eastern Front.

Ulrich Wöhnert claimed a total of at least eighty-three aerial victories all achieved whilst flying combat missions over the Soviet Union during the Second World War. He was born on 24 October 1914 in Wolfshagen, Brandenburg west of Berlin, joined the *Luftwaffe* in 1940 and trained as a fighter pilot.

(Deutsches Wehrkundearchiv)

He was assigned to the 2nd Squadron of the 54th Fighter Wing in April 1942 with the rank of *Unteroffizier*, and flew the Bf 109F-4 over the Soviet Union from his base in Krasnogvardeysky, unable to fly much due to the thaw. Promoted to *Oberfeldwebel* in July he claimed his first aerial victory on the 21st, an Ilyushin Il-2 ground-attack aircraft. He claimed a MiG-3 fighter on 15 August and a Yak-1 on 29 September and was awarded the Iron Cross 2nd Class towards the end of the year. From February 1943 his Group moved to Heiligenbeil where they were converted to the Focke-Wulf Fw 190A, returning to the front in early March. His Group moved to Nikolskoye in May and to Orel in June and by the end of July he had claimed a total of twelve victories and had been awarded the Iron Cross 1st Class. On 14 August he claimed his 15th and 16th victories and claimed two more on the 19th and three on the 20th, and by the end of the month he had claimed a total of twenty-seven victories whilst flying from Poltava. He claimed his 30th victory on 5 September, an Il-2, and on the 7th he claimed four victories over Kirov, all Lavochkin LaGG-3 fighters and shot down in less than 10 minutes. He claimed his 40th victory on 10 October whilst flying from Vitebsk and by 15 October he had claimed another five victories, which included four Il-2 aircraft. On 8 November he was awarded the *Luftwaffe* Honour Goblet and on the 14th he was awarded the German Cross in Gold.

In early December his Group moved to Orscha where they stayed until late January 1944 when his Group moved to Wesenberg in Estonia and Wöhnert claimed his 50th victory over the Baltic Sea on

21 March. He was promoted to *Leutnant* in April and from 19 June he flew with the 1st Squadron from Turku in Finland. On 27 June his Group moved to Polotsk and from 1 July he was flying from Daugavpils in south-east Latvia. He claimed three victories on 27 July, which included his 60th victory, a Petlyakov Pe-2 twin-engined dive-bomber. In mid-August he was appointed *Staffelkapitän* of the 5th Squadron of the 54th Fighter Wing and claimed his 70th victory on 26 August. He claimed two victories on 3 and 17 September and claimed three on the 19th and claimed his 80th victory on 28 September, an Il-2 over north Malpils. After claiming more than eighty victories he was finally awarded the Knight's Cross on 6 December 1944.

In January 1945 Wöhnert was removed from his command on health grounds, although it is believed he returned to combat just before the end of the war and probably made further claims against Soviet aircraft. He was captured by the Soviets in May 1945 and some reports state he died in captivity of pneumonia but most say that he committed suicide on 14 August 1947.

Walter MATONI

Major

Knight's Cross: Awarded on 16 December 1944 as *Hauptmann* and commander of the 1st Group of the 2nd Fighter Wing '*Richthofen*' for operations over France, England, the Soviet Union and the Western Front.

Walter Matoni claimed twenty-nine aerial victories, all but three achieved over the Western Front, of which ten were four-engined bombers. He was born on 27 June 1917 in Duisberg, Germany and joined the *Luftwaffe* from college in October 1936.

In the summer of 1940 *Unteroffizier* Matoni was posted to 9th Squadron of the 27th Fighter Wing and he recorded his first victory on 30 September, an RAF Hurricane over Tunbridge Wells during the Battle of Britain. He was awarded the Iron Cross 2nd Class on 12 September 1940 and was promoted to *Feldwebel* in October, and was awarded the Iron Cross 1st Class in November. From June 1941 he flew

(Deutsches Wehrkundearchiv)

over the Soviet Union and claimed his second victory on 17 July and before the end of the month he claimed two more victories. From August he flew with the 7th Squadron of the 2nd Fighter Wing and on 21 September he was removed from operations due to illness. He flew with Replacement Fighter Group West from October and later served as an instructor with the rank of *Leutnant* until early 1943.

On 13 February Matoni was assigned to the 6th Squadron of the 26th Fighter Wing, based in France. He claimed an RAF Spitfire on 17 June over Zeebrugge and claimed another on 15 July, his sixth aerial victory. On 27 August *Oberleutnant* Matoni, newly promoted, shot down a B-17 Flying Fortress over Merville but his own aircraft was hit by return fire and he was wounded. He had to make an emergency landing at Montider, but was back in action by December. He claimed a Spitfire on 21 December and a B-24 Liberator nine days later.

In January 1944 he claimed two four engine-bombers, but only one was ever confirmed and he also shot down a Spitfire over Doullens in northern France. He claimed his 12th victory on 24 February, a B-24 bomber, and the following day he was appointed *Staffelkapitän* of the 5th Squadron. In March he claimed three B-17 Flying Fortresses, which included his 15th victory, and on the 31st he was awarded the *Luftwaffe* Honour Goblet. In April he claimed four more victories and on 15 May he was awarded the German Cross in Gold in recognition of his success as a fighter pilot in shooting down ten four-engined bombers. He claimed four more victories during June and from 15 August he served as *Gruppenkommandeur* of the 1st Group of the 11th Fighter Wing, based in Wiesbaden. In August he claimed a P-47 near Paris and in September he shot down a Spitfire near Nijmegen, and then in late September he was transferred and took over as *Gruppenkommandeur* of the 1st Group of the 2nd Fighter Wing based in Merzhausen near the town of Freiburg im Breisgau. He claimed two P-38 Lightnings during October and he shot down a P-47 Thunderbolt over Düren on 19 November, his last aerial victory of the war.

On 6 December 1944 he was severely injured during a take-off accident at Merzhausen base and would never fly again. He was awarded the Knight's Cross on 16 December in recognition of his courage and success as a fighter pilot. He was promoted to *Major* in early 1945 and took command of the 2nd Group of the 2nd Fighter Wing but in a non-flying capacity. He held this position until 28 February, when he finally retired and entered a fighter pilot's rest-home at Bad Wiesse, Bavaria. He had flown over 400 combat missions during his career and had claimed at least twelve four-engined bombers (only ten were ever confirmed). He died on 26 June 1988 in Frankfurt am Main.

Johann-Hermann MEIER

Leutnant

Knight's Cross: Awarded posthumously on 16 December 1944 as *Leutnant* and *Staffelführer* in the 1st Group of the 52nd Fighter Wing for operations over the Soviet Union and the Western Front.

(Deutsches Wehrkundearchiv)

Johann-Hermann Meier claimed seventy-six aerial victories during the Second World War, all of them over the Soviet Union. He was born on 10 June 1921 in Kronprinzenkoog, Heide in Schleswig-Holstein and he joined the 1st Squadron of the 52nd Fighter Wing in October 1942.

He first saw action in the Soviet Union in late 1942 and for a time served as an instructor with Fighter Replacement Group East. From early 1943 he was back flying with the 1st Squadron of the 52nd Fighter Wing flying from Kharkov. He claimed his first aerial victory on 1 February, an Ilyushin Il-7, near Kursk and he claimed his second on 28 April, a Yak-1 fighter over Smolenskaja, and after claiming his third on 14 May east of Prochorowka he was awarded the Iron Cross 2nd Class. By the end of May he had claimed a total of seven victories, and he claimed his 10th victory on 5 June and shortly after claiming eleven victories on the 8th he was awarded the Iron Cross 1st Class. On 11 June he took over as *Staffelkapitän* of his Squadron he claimed a single victory on the 14th and three on 16 June, and on 5 July he became an 'ace-in-a-day' when he shot down six victories which included his 20th victory.

By mid-June 1943 he was no longer *Staffelkapitän* as it had only been a temporary position while a replacement was found as Meier was only a 22-year-old *Leutnant* at the time. On 13 September Meier was awarded the *Luftwaffe* Honour Goblet after achieving his 25th aerial victory, and by the end of the month his total had increased to forty-four victories. In mid-October he transferred from the 1st Squadron to the 3rd Squadron, and on 20 October he claimed two victories which included his 50th and a few days later he was awarded the German Cross in Gold. He claimed another nine victories during October and on 5 November he shot down an Il-2 ground-attack aircraft over south-western Perekop to claim his 60th victory.

From early 1944 his Squadron flew from its airfield in Mala Wyska, in the Ukraine and Meier claimed two victories on 6 January, one on the 7th and two on the 11th, all Yakovlev Yak-9 fighters over Kirovgrad, which included his 70th victory. With seventy-six victories to his name he transferred as *Staffelkapitän* to the 1st Squadron of the 26th Fighter Wing on 29 February. He flew his Focke-Wulf Fw 190A from Florennes, south-west of Dinant in the Walloon region of Belgium and his squadron was used in 'Defence of the Reich' missions. On 15 March whilst taxing across the airstrip in his Fw 190 – according to witnesses he was very drunk – he veered across into his wingman, *Unteroffizier* Hans Ruppert. Both aircraft burst into flames and Meier burned to death but Ruppert survived but was severely traumatised and never fully recovered.

After an inquiry Meier, who had flown 305 combat missions, was posthumously awarded the Knight's Cross on 16 December 1944, but wasn't promoted. He lies today in the Military Cemetery at Lommel, Block 5, Grave No. 427.

Hermann WISCHNEWSKI

Leutnant

Knight's Cross: Awarded on 16 December 1944 as *Fahnenjunker-Oberfeldwebel* and pilot attached to the 2nd Squadron of the 300th Fighter Wing for operations over the Western Front.

Hermann Wischnewski claimed at least twenty-four aerial victories during the Second World War but only eight, which included at least four four-engined bombers, were ever confirmed. He was born on 9 February 1917 in Tensefeld in the northern German state of Schleswig-Holstein and joined the *Luftwaffe* as a pilot in early 1940.

From December 1941 he served as a transport pilot with the rank of *Gefreiter* with the 1st Group of Special Combat Group 700, flying the Junkers Ju 52 transport aircraft. His Group was under the command of *Major* Ferdinand Muggenthaler and he flew many difficult supply missions over the Eastern Front, including missions in the Demyansk battle areas in the spring of 1942. In October, now with the rank of *Obergefreiter* he had transferred to the Special Bomber Group Frankfurt based in the Mediterranean theatre of operations.

(Deutsches Wehrkundearchiv)

On 26 May 1943 he was awarded the *Luftwaffe* Honour Goblet mainly for his efforts as a bomber pilot and from July, now with the rank of *Feldwebel*, he underwent conversion training to single-engined night fighters. He was posted to Fighter Group Herrmann, under the command of *Oberstleutnant* Hajo Herrmann, flying the Focke-Wulf Fw 190 out of Deelen in the Netherlands, intercepting Allied bombers. He claimed a four-engined bomber on 26 July but this was never confirmed, then five days later he claimed his first confirmed victory, an RAF Stirling heavy bomber over west Remscheid, and was awarded the Iron Cross 2nd Class. In late August his unit was redesignated the 3rd Squadron of the 300th Fighter Wing and by the end of September Wischnewski had achieved another victory, although he had also claimed another which was later unconfirmed, and had been awarded the Iron Cross 1st Class. On 17 October he was awarded the German Cross in Gold in recognition of his time as a transport pilot during very difficult circumstances.

At the beginning of November Wischnewski, now with the rank of *Oberfeldwebel* and still attached to the 300th Fighter Wing, claimed two four-engined bombers over Mannheim on the 18th but these were never confirmed. During January 1944 still flying over Germany he claimed ten more aerial victories, all four-engined bombers, but only one claimed over Düsseldorf on 23 April was ever confirmed. He had another claim confirmed on 23 May and during June he claimed another two victories and these were also confirmed victories. In June he switched to a day fighter serving with the 2nd Squadron of the 300th Fighter Wing and recorded his first day victory on 21 June, a USAAF B-24 Liberator over Rangsford, his fifth confirmed victory.

On 29 July, now with the rank of *Fahnenjunker-Oberfeldwebel* (officer candidate), he shot down two B-17 four-engined bombers but was shot down himself. He was wounded in the left leg and foot. He bailed out of his Bf 109G-6 near Gelbstadt at low level, and the force of his parachute opening wrenched his arms out of their sockets. Because of the low altitude his landing was heavy and resulted in further injuries. He was hospitalized at Apolda for six months and never returned to combat. He had flown a total of 500 missions, mainly as a transport pilot, and was awarded the Knight's Cross on 16 December 1944. Wischnewski died on 28 November 1993 in Lübeck, northern Germany.

1945

Eduard ISKEN

Leutnant

Knight's Cross: Awarded on 14 January 1945 as *Oberfeldwebel* whilst attached to the 13th Squadron of the 53rd Fighter Wing for operations over North Africa, Italy and the Western Front.

Eduard Isken claimed over forty-four aerial victories including twenty-five over the Eastern Front and at least another nineteen over the Western Front. He was born on 15 April 1918 in Hagendingen in Metz and after the completion of his training he joined the 7th Squadron of the 77th Fighter Wing in late 1940.

He flew operations over the Balkans and the Soviet Union during 1941 as a *Feldwebel*, claiming his first two victories on 25 July, both Polikarpov I-153 fighters. He claimed his third on 29 August, a Ilyushin DB-3 long-range bomber, and he claimed two more DB-3s on 4 September and was awarded the Iron Cross 2nd Class. He claimed another four victories during September and shortly after claiming his 10th victory on 5 October Isken was awarded the Iron Cross 1st Class.

(*Author's collection*)

Shortly after shooting down another DB-3 on 6 November he was himself shot down by Soviet anti-aircraft fire and was forced to make an emergency landing in his Bf 109 near Belograd Tal, but he wasn't injured.

At the beginning of 1942 his squadron was equipped with the Bf 109F-4 and flew protection missions over the Crimea and Sevastopol. In March his Group was withdrawn to Germany to be refreshed, returning to the Soviet Union in May where Isken achieved another three victories which included his 17th. By late July he was flying from Kharkov and claimed another five victories in July, which included his 25th. By the end of October his Group had been withdrawn from the Soviet Union and was transferred to El Alamein in Egypt where his squadron suffered due to lack of spare parts and from November because of the British ground offensive and they had to move. He did, however, claim two Hurricanes over Quotafiya on 4 November and in early 1943 he was promoted to *Oberfeldwebel* and his Group had moved to Bir Dufan in Libya. After the beginning of the British winter offensive his group moved again to El Asabaa and later Isken took part in the defensive battles for Tunisia and later saw action over Sicily. He claimed his 30th victory on 4 April and was awarded the German Cross in Gold on 28 April 1943 and unusually he was awarded the *Luftwaffe* Honour Goblet on 26 July – it was received before the German Cross. On 25 September he was shot down during combat with US heavy bombers, and had to bail out of his aircraft, landing successfully near Modena but was slightly injured upon landing.

He spent a few months recovering from his wounds and was posted to Training Fighter Group South as an instructor towards the end of 1943. On 1 June 1944 he moved to France with the 200th

Fighter Wing and fought against the invasion of southern France during August, where he was estimated to have shot down at least twelve aircraft although only seven have been confirmed. He then moved to a special squadron, *Sonderstaffel Klaatsch*, but only briefly and by October he had joined the 13th Squadron of the 53rd Fighter Wing. He was awarded the Knight's Cross on 14 January in recognition of his achievements as a fighter pilot. It is believed that he claimed several victories during the last few months of the war, including a B-17 bomber in April 1945. It is unclear exactly how many aerial victories he had achieved but he flew 946 combat missions and was shot down nine times! Isken died in Wolfsburg, Lower Saxony on 7 January 1997.

Ekkehard TICHY

Hauptmann

Knight's Cross: Awarded posthumously on 14 January 1945 as *Oberleutnant* whilst attached to the 4th Group of the 3rd Fighter Wing 'Udet' for operations over the Soviet Union and the Western Front.

Ekkehard Tichy claimed thirteen victories over the Eastern Front and six victories over the Western Front, which included five four-engined bombers, during the Second World War. He was born on 26 August 1922 in Mährisch Neustadt in Czechoslovakia. His family moved to Germany, and he joined the *Luftwaffe* in 1940.

(Deutsches Wehrkundearchiv)

With his pilot training complete he was assigned to the 1st Group of the 53rd Fighter Wing in July 1942 as an officer candidate. He saw action over the Soviet Union during the summer offensive and from September his Group was transferred to Pitomnik to be deployed over the Stalingrad area. In October he moved to the 9th Squadron of the 3rd Fighter Wing and was commissioned as a *Leutnant*, still flying in support of the 6th Army at Stalingrad. From November with the start of the winter offensive which led to the encirclement of the 6th Army his Group moved to Morozovskaya-West. He then flew fighter missions and escort missions for transport aircraft flying in and out of the Stalingrad area. In early January 1943 his Group had to move due to the Soviet advance and the entire Wing relocated several times during the first three months and by April he had moved to Kerch on the Crimean Peninsula. He claimed his first victory on 20 April south of Novorossiysk and he claimed three victories during May. On 21 July he claimed three more victories and by the 31st he had claimed a total of thirteen victories and had been awarded the Iron Cross 1st and 2nd Classes.

In early August his Group was sent to Germany to be refreshed and Tichy was given some leave. On the 26th his Group had moved to their new base in Bad Wörishofen in Bavaria and after converting to the Bf 109G-6 they flew air defence missions over the Reich. On 6 September Tichy claimed a B-17 Flying Fortress south of Stuttgart and claimed another on 14 October but this one was never confirmed. He was appointed *Staffelkapitän* of his Squadron in November and continued to fly from Bad Wörishofen into 1944, flying over the Reich. He claimed his 16th victory, another B-17, on 25 February and on 18 March he claimed a P-51 Mustang over north-east Stuttgart but during the air battle his own aircraft had been damaged and he had to bail out severely wounded, landing near Ursberg, Bavaria. He was awarded the *Luftwaffe* Honour Goblet on 15 April and the following day he was awarded the German Cross in Gold, having now claimed seventeen aerial victories.

He was promoted to *Oberleutnant* in May and, fully recovered from his injuries, he transferred to the 10th Squadron of the 3rd Fighter Wing the following month. He flew as part of the 4th

Group and from early July was appointed *Staffelkapitän* of his squadron, and he claimed a B-17 over Bouzonville, France on 3 August. A few days later he was transferred to the 2nd Group of the 300th Fighter Wing and was now flying from Erfurt-Bindersleben airbase in Germany, and on 9 August he claimed another B-17, his 19th victory. On the 16th, whilst engaged in heavy fighting with B-17s he was killed when he either collided with or rammed one of the four-engined bombers over the Albshausen area of Germany. He was posthumously promoted to *Hauptmann* and awarded the Knight's Cross on 14 January 1945, after claiming at least nineteen victories. He is today buried at the German Military Cemetery in Göttingen, Stadfriedhof.

Fritz GROMOTKA

Leutnant der Reserve

Knight's Cross: Awarded on 28 January 1945 as *Leutnant der Reserve* and *Staffelführer* of the 9th Squadron of the 27th Fighter Wing for operations over the Balkans, the Soviet Union, North Africa, the Mediterranean and the Western Front.

Fritz Gromotka flew 438 combat missions, bailed out of his aircraft five times and shot down twenty-two aircraft, all but two over the Western Front during the Second World War. He was born on 2 June 1915 in Kronschlow, Kempen in Posen, at the time part of Poland.

(*Author's collection*)

He joined the *Luftwaffe* in early 1940 and with the completion of his flight training he flew with the 6th Squadron of the 27th Fighter Wing in November. *Unteroffizier* Gromotka first saw action during the Balkan campaign and he shot down two RAF Blenheims over south-west Bitolj-Kenalo, Macedonia on 13 April 1941. The next day he claimed his third victory, a Gladiator. This victory remains unconfirmed, but he was still awarded the Iron Cross 2nd Class. He also flew low-level attacks on Greek and British positions as well as escort and fighter missions. From 22 June he took part in the invasion of the Soviet Union, claiming two DB-3 bombers over Vilna on 25 June. The following day he had to make a forced landing when his Bf 109E-8 ran out of fuel west of Minsk. He was listed as missing but returned to his squadron two days later, dirty and exhausted, and soon after Gromotka was officially awarded the Iron Cross 1st Class.

In September his Group relocated to North Africa where on 29 November he claimed a Hurricane south-west of El Adem. By the beginning of 1942 he had been promoted to *Feldwebel* and on 23 February claimed his sixth aerial victory, an RAF Blenheim. On 21 May, during combat with RAF Kittyhawks he was shot down by Flight Lieutenant Hinde of 260 Squadron east of Timini in Libya. Gromotka managed to land safely but ten days later he was shot down again, this time by a Tomahawk of 5 Squadron of the South African Air Force. He was listed as missing near Acroma, Libya but he returned to his base the following day. From July 1942 he took time out from the front line when he was appointed as an instructor with Fighter School 4 at Fürth-Buchschwabach, where he remained until September 1943. Now with the rank of *Oberfeldwebel* Gromotka transferred to the 9th Squadron as part of the 3rd Group flying combat missions over Greece and the Balkans. He claimed two RAF Spitfires over Kos on 27 September, and the following day he claimed another Spitfire. On 5 October he shot down a B-24 Liberator west of Eratini, and claimed another three days later. He claimed a Beaufighter on 10 November and claimed two B-24 bombers on 6 December, but only one was ever confirmed.

In February 1944 his Group moved from Greece to Vienna-Seyring via Serbia and Bulgaria. With the beginning of the Allied invasion of Europe in June his Group began to take losses, and after heavy bombing raids his Group began to reinforce their squadrons. From March he flew on the Invasion Front and flew 'Defence of the Reich' missions. On 6 March he was awarded the *Luftwaffe* Honour Goblet and claimed another B-24 south-east of Marburg on 19 March. On 12 April he claimed a B-17 Flying Fortress north-west of Wiener Neustadt. He claimed three more B-17s on 12 May, one later reclassified as unconfirmed, and he was awarded the German Cross in Gold in recognition of his success as a fighter pilot on 25 May. He claimed two more victories in June, both P-47 Thunderbolts, and he claimed his last victory of the war on 19 August 1944, another P-47. In September his group left France and moved to Cologne-Wahn where it was refreshed and deployed in the defence of the Reich.

At the beginning of 1945 his Group was equipped with the Bf 109K, and he took part in Operation Bodenplatte, an attempt to cripple the Allied air forces in the Low Countries, but it was a failure. On 1 February Gromotka took over as *Staffelkapitän* of the 9th Squadron, having to move airfields in March because of the Allied advance. On 28 February he was awarded the Knight's Cross and promoted to *Leutnant der Reserve*. Most of his missions were directed against Allied ground troops. Finally on 2 May his Group reached Salzburg where they surrendered to the Americans. Gromotka lived in Germany after the war, settling in Remscheid, North Rhine-Westphalia, where he died on 2 November 1979.

Reinhold HOFFMANN

Leutnant der Reserve

Knight's Cross: Awarded posthumously on 28 January 1945 as *Leutnant der Reserve* whilst attached to the 3rd Group of the 54th Fighter Wing for operations over the Soviet Union and the Western Front.

Reinhold Hoffmann claimed sixty-seven aerial victories on the Eastern Front, and three four-engined bombers on the Western Front. He was born on 9 August 1921 in Petersdorf, Hirschberg and he joined the *Luftwaffe* in 1941 and on completion of his training he was assigned to the 54th Fighter Wing as a fighter pilot.

In February 1942 he was assigned to the 5th Squadron and flew the Bf 109F-4 on the Eastern Front, and from March he flew over the Demyansk area in support of ground forces. From June he was flying the Fw 190A, and on 27 July Hoffmann claimed his first victory, a Yakovlev Yak-1 fighter over south-east Pola, and he claimed his second victory on 22 August, an Il-2 ground-attack aircraft. From December he was flying out of Kalinin but failed to claim another victory until 21 March 1943 when he shot down another Yak-1. In May his squadron moved to Orel and Hoffmann claimed a P-40 east of Schusselburg on 30 May, being awarded the Iron Cross 2nd Class a few days later. The rate of aerial victories had so far been slow for Hoffmann but from July things began to change.

(Deutsches Wehrkundearchiv)

On 12 July he claimed his fifth victory and on the 13th he shot down three Boston twin-engined bombers. Three days later he claimed three Il-2s over south-east Mzensk and soon after was awarded the Iron Cross 1st Class. By the end of August he had claimed twenty-four victories and been promoted to *Feldwebel*. He claimed his 30th victory on 8 September and was awarded the *Luftwaffe* Honour Goblet on the 23rd. Hoffmann now began to make up for his slow start. Between 20 October and 6 November he claimed twenty-seven victories, which included becoming an 'ace-in-a-day' three times. He shot down seven aircraft on 21 October, eight on the 22nd and eight on 3 November. On 14 November he was awarded the German Cross in Gold after achieving his 58th victory and for claiming so many victories in only four weeks. Hoffmann claimed his 60th victory on 8 April, and claimed three victories on the 17th, all Il-2s. On 8 May he transferred to the 9th Squadron and flew from Illesheim near Neustadt-Bad in Bavaria to take part in 'Defence of the Reich' duties, quickly adding three B-24 Liberator four-engined bombers to his score on 19 May. Five days later whilst attempting to make an emergency landing at Friesack, a town in the Havelland district near Brandenburg, following battle damage he lost control, crashed and was killed. He was posthumously awarded the Knight's Cross on 28 January 1945 and was promoted to *Leutnant*, and lies today in a grave in Piechowie, Poland.

Hermann SCHLEINHEGE

Leutnant der Reserve

Knight's Cross: Awarded on 28 January 1945 as *Leutnant der Reserve* and pilot with the 8th Squadron of the 54th Fighter Wing for operations over the Soviet Union and the Eastern Front.

Hermann Schleinhege claimed ninety-four aerial victories whilst flying 484 combat missions over the Eastern Front and his total included thirty-eight Soviet Ilyushin Il-2 ground-attack aircraft. He was born on 21 February 1916 in Essen, the second largest city in the Ruhr district of Germany.

(*Author's collection*)

Schleinhege joined the *Luftwaffe* before the war and upon completion of his training in February 1941 he served as a flight instructor. On 13 April 1942, now an *Unteroffizier*, he was assigned to the 6th Squadron of the 54th Fighter Wing, stationed near Leningrad. On 15 May Schleinhege damaged his Bf 109F-4 during take-off at Lyubau but he wasn't injured. He took some time before he recorded his first victory which he achieved on 9 August, a Polikarpov R-5 light reconnaissance bomber over west Chrenowaja.

At the beginning of 1943 his Group had converted to the Focke-Wulf Fw 190A and he claimed his second victory on 7 January, an LaGG-3 fighter. He claimed another two victories during February and his fifth victory on 7 March, a Petlyakov Pe-2 dive-bomber, and was awarded the Iron Cross 2nd Class. From the spring he was assigned to the headquarters flight or the *Geschwaderstab* of the 54th Fighter Wing, and he began flying as wingman to *Oberstleutnant* Hannes Trautloft and from July with *Major* Hubertus von Bonin and *Major* Anton Mader. He claimed his 10th victory on 23 June and had been promoted to *Oberfeldwebel* and awarded the Iron Cross 1st Class. On 9 July he crashed his Fw 190 near Oryol but again wasn't hurt and went on to claim six victories that month and three during August and was now based in Orsha flying fighter support missions for Army Group Centre. He was awarded the *Luftwaffe* Honour Goblet on 11 October after claiming nineteen victories and by the end of the year he had added ten more to that total.

Schleinhege claimed his 30th victory on 26 February 1944, and was awarded the German Cross in Gold on 20 March. In August, on the completion of his officers training, *Leutnant* Schleinhege transferred into the 7th Squadron of the 54th Fighter Wing. He claimed his 40th victory on 5 September and claimed three victories on the 15th, a single Il-2 on the 17th, two more victories on the 18th and the 19th, and one on the 23rd and he claimed his 50th victory the next day. On 9 October, now based at Riga, he claimed two P-39 Airacobras and two Il-2s, and claimed his 60th victory on 14 October. By the end of the month his score had risen to sixty-seven victories and in November he was appointed *Staffelkapitän* of the 8th Squadron, a position he kept until the end of the war. He claimed his 80th victory on 26 January 1945 whilst flying missions based in Libau supporting troops isolated in the Courland Pocket, and two days later he was awarded the Knight's Cross after claiming seventy-five victories.

Schleinhege claimed six victories in February and during this period he covered the naval evacuation of the Courland. He was based in Labau until March and then his Group moved to Heiligenbeil near Königsberg where they stayed until the end of the war. He claimed his last victory, a Yak-3, over the Courland area on 9 April. His last flight was on 8 May when he squeezed his two mechanics into his small single-seat Fw 190 and flew to Kiel to surrender to the British. After the war he settled in Soest, Germany where he died at the age of 98 on 11 March 2014.

Peter WERFFT

Major der Reserve

Knight's Cross: Awarded on 28 January 1945 as *Oberleutnant der Reserve* and commander of the 3rd Group of the 27th Fighter Wing for operations over England, North Africa and the Western Front.

(Deutsches Wehrkundearchiv)

Peter Werfft claimed nineteen aerial victories, which included nine four-engined bombers, all over the Western Front during the Second World War. He was born on 8 October 1904 in Vienna, Austria-Hungary and after the completion of his flight training he was assigned as a *Gefreiter* to the 1st Group of the 27th Fighter Wing.

From July 1940 Werfft flew with the 1st Squadron from the beginning of the Battle of Britain. He claimed his first victory over Sevenoaks in Kent, a Hurricane on 27 September. That same day he claimed a second Hurricane over Brighton but this was never confirmed. Nevertheless, shortly after he was awarded the Iron Cross 2nd Class. From October he flew from Brittany in France and then flew from Cherbourg, flying protection missions over the French and British coast. In early December his Squadron was moved to Döberitz in Germany where it was refreshed. Werfft was then promoted to *Feldwebel* and served as an instructor before rejoining his Squadron in North Africa in mid-1941.

On 19 July he claimed his second confirmed victory, a P-40 over Sollum Bight, and on 9 September he claimed a Hurricane over the same area. In October his Group relocated to Germany to convert to the Bf 109F-4, returning to North Africa with the 7th Squadron in November. At the beginning of 1942, still in North Africa he took part in the attack on Tobruk and flew over El Alamein from June. Werfft claimed his 4th victory on 26 October, a Boston twin-engined bomber over north-east Moschee El Daba and shortly after was promoted to *Leutnant*, and was awarded the Iron Cross 1st Class. On 31 October he was shot down during combat with Kittyhawks, his Bf 109F-4 coming down south-west of El Alamein. He was listed as missing in action, but returned to his Squadron a day later. On 2 November he transferred to the 9th Squadron and claimed a Spitfire south-east of El Alamein. From 20 August 1943 Werfft flew as *Staffelkapitän* of the 9th Squadron of the 27th Fighter Wing, and continued to fly combat missions during the El Alamein offensive. After the start of the British counter-attack in late October there were many heavy aerial attacks. On 8 October Werfft claimed a B-24 Liberator but this was never confirmed. During the German retreat his Group withdrew to

Tobruk on 2 November and then to Benghazi a few days later. On 12 November his Group received orders to move to Crete and Werfft claimed a B-17 Flying Fortress on 6 December west of Milos Island, and on the 20th he claimed another B-17 and a P-38, both over north-west Mcgra.

From January 1944 he was flying over Greece and by February his Group had moved to Hungary and by the following month he was flying from Vienna. On 19 March he claimed two B-24s over Marburg, Germany, but both were unconfirmed victories. He claimed two more over north-west Wolfsberg on 2 April, his 9th and 10th victories, and on the 6th he claimed a B-17 over Nuremberg. He claimed two more B-24s a few days later but again these were never confirmed, then on 23 April he claimed a B-24 and on 12 May he claimed a B-17 north-north-east of Hanau and both were confirmed victories. On the 19th he claimed two B-24s over East Helmstedt, but shortly after he was seriously wounded when his aircraft was shot down by US fighters near Gardelegen, and he was away from active service until October. During his time away he was presented with the *Luftwaffe* Honour Goblet on 15 July and on the 23rd he was awarded the German Cross in Gold in recognition of his nine four-engined bomber victories.

In late November 1944 he flew his Bf 109K from Groisenheim, Saxony and from there was deployed as part of the 'Defence of the Reich' and he flew during the Battle of the Bulge. He was promoted to *Oberleutnant* in December and claimed another four victories, which included two P-38 Lightnings on the 27th. In January Werfft flew during Operation Bodenplatte, an attempt by the *Luftwaffe* to cripple Allied air forces in the Low Countries, to gain air superiority during the Battle of the Bulge, but it failed, due to fuel shortages and lack of planning. On 28 January Werfft was awarded the Knight's Cross, in recognition of his skill as a four-engined bomber ace. On 2 May, with the end of the war in Europe only days away, Werfft and his Group, together with the 1st Group under the command of *Oberleutnant* Emil Clade, decided to act on their own initiative. They led their Groups to Dalzburg, Austria, a collecting point for *Luftwaffe* units in the southern half of the Reich, now divided in two by the link-up of American and Soviet forces along the River Elbe. There they simply left their fighters standing among the general confusion and, without any higher authority, instructed the two groups combined personnel, pilots and ground staff – some 1,000 men in all – to form a column and march to the American lines.

After the war Werfft returned to Austria and established a pharmaceutical and chemical company in 1948, and became very successful, converting to veterinary medicine in 1983. In fact the company survived until January 2020 when its business assets were acquired by another veterinary company. Werfft died on 23 July 1970 in Vienna, he had been one of the oldest operational fighter pilots of the *Luftwaffe* during the war, being 40 in 1945, and he had been wounded six times.

Walther WEVER

Oberleutnant

Knight's Cross: Awarded on 28 January 1945 as *Leutnant* and fighter pilot with the 3rd Squadron of the 51st Fighter Wing '*Mölders*' for operations over the Soviet Union and the Eastern Front.

Walther Wever claimed forty-four aerial victories during the Second World War, of which all but one were achieved over the Eastern Front. He was born on 16 January 1923 in Munich, the son of *Generalleutnant* Walther Wever, former Chief of the General Staff of the *Luftwaffe* from March 1935 until his death in an air crash near Dresden on 3 June 1936.

Wever joined the *Luftwaffe* in 1942 and with the completion of his fighter training was assigned as a *Leutnant* to the 3rd Squadron of the 51st Fighter Wing in the summer of 1943. From May his squadron, which was attached to the 1st Group flew from Bryansk in the Soviet Union. Wever flew the Fw 190A, claiming his first victory on 19 June, a Boston southwest of Tschaikovka. He claimed an Il-2 ground-attack aircraft near Zamenskoje on 1 August and the following day his Group moved to Bryansk and the same day he claimed two more Il-2s and was awarded the Iron Cross 2nd Class. He claimed two more victories on the 3rd and shortly after he was appointed *Staffelführer* of the 3rd Squadron, and claiming his 10th victory on 30 August and was awarded the Iron Cross 1st Class.

On 5 September Wever claimed three victories in five minutes, all Ilyushin Il-2s, and he claimed two more victories on the 14th and two on the 30th. From October until the end of the year his Group was converted to the Messerschmitt Bf 109G fighter. By the end of 1943 Wever had claimed a total of twenty-three aircraft, of which seventeen had been Il-2s. At the beginning of 1944 his Group was flying from Bobruisk in the Soviet Union and he claimed a Yak-9 fighter on 4

(Deutsches Wehrkundearchiv)

January. He claimed two more victories on the 6th, and on the 14th he claimed three more, which included his 30th victory. On 20 March he was awarded both the *Luftwaffe* Honour Goblet and the German Cross in Gold in recognition of his victories and his skill as a fighter pilot especially against Ilyushin Il-2s. On 29 March his Group moved to Orsha and Wever claimed five victories that day to become an 'ace-in-a-day'.

He was appointed *Staffelkapitän* of the 3rd Squadron on 9 May, a time when the fighting became even more intense and his Group moved a number of times due to the Soviet advance. Wever claimed a single victory on 28 May, and his 40th victory on 25 June. He claimed his 44th and last aerial victory on 30 June, a Lavochkin La-5 aircraft, south-south of Beresino. On 10 July his Bf 109G-6 was shot down by ground fire and he was hit in the foot and leg. Wever managed to land in German-occupied territory and was taken to hospital where his foot was amputated. He spent months in hospital and recuperating at home and on 28 January 1945 he was awarded the Knight's Cross.

He returned to combat on 12 February and was promoted to *Oberleutnant* and appointed *Staffelkapitän* of the 7th Squadron of the 7th Fighter Wing. He flew the new Me 262 jet fighter over Germany against US bombers, and on 10 April he was shot down near Neuruppin, Brandenburg and was killed. He had flown at least 250 combat missions during the war. His victor was either Captain J.K. Brown of the 20th Fighter Group or Lieutenant J.W. Pritchard and Second Lieutenant C.A. Ricci of the 352nd Fighter Group. In fact 10 April went down in American aviation history as 'the day of the great jet massacre', as P-47 and P-51 pilots had claimed no fewer than twenty Me 262s, with bomber crews claiming at least another five. It had been known for the Allied pilots to claim many times the actual losses suffered by the *Luftwaffe*, but on 10 April they tallied exactly. A document compiled by the *Wehrmacht* Operations Staff stated the losses: five pilots killed, fourteen missing, thirteen aircraft lost, fourteen missing and eight damaged.

Peter JENNE

Hauptmann

Knight's Cross: Awarded as *Hauptmann* and *Staffelkapitän* of the 12th Squadron of the 300th Fighter Wing on 2 February 1945 for operations over the Soviet Union and the Western Front.

Peter Jenne claimed over twelve victories, which included seven four-engined bombers, over the Eastern and Western Fronts and took part in numerous ground-attack missions during the Second

World War. He was born on 5 June 1920 in Wittenberg, Sachsen and entered the *Luftwaffe* in November 1939 and was assigned to the 42nd Air Training Regiment at Salzwedel. He continued with his training for the next year or so and was commissioned as a *Leutnant* in April 1941.

In July 1942 Jenne served with the 1st Squadron of the 1st Destroyer Wing on the Eastern Front, flying the Messerschmitt Bf 110 twin-engined fighter. He took part in various ground-attack missions and achieved considerable success, destroying twelve tanks, ten artillery guns and eight rocket launchers. His success was recognized when on 20 June he was awarded the Iron Cross 2nd Class and on 4 August he was awarded the Iron Cross 1st Class. He claimed an LaGG-3 fighter on 19 September 1942 and was awarded the *Luftwaffe* Honour Goblet on 20 November 1942. Jenne flew ground-support missions during December and January 1943 in support of the 6th Army and claimed a MiG-3 fighter on 13 December. On 20 January he crashed his Bf 110 at a snow-covered airfield in the Stalingrad area. His aircraft was almost completely destroyed and Jenne was slightly injured but the incident claimed the life of his radio operator.

(Deutsches Wehrkundearchiv)

On 1 April 1943 he was promoted to *Oberleutnant* and was awarded the German Cross in Gold and his unit was redesignated the 1st Squadron of the 26th Destroyer Wing and continued to fly over the Eastern Front. On 9 October Jenne was appointed *Staffelkapitän* of the 1st Squadron and the Group moved to Germany and flew 'Defence of the Reich' missions. He shot down a B-17 Flying Fortress on 20 December and two days later he claimed two B-24 Liberators in just five minutes over the Netherlands.

Promoted to *Hauptmann* in April 1944 his unit was again redesignated, this time to the 1st Squadron of the 6th Fighter Wing and he now flew the Focke-Wulf Fw 190, a single-engined fighter. On 12 September he was named as *Staffelkapitän* of the 12th Squadron of the 300th Fighter Wing, and he claimed a P-51 that same day and on the 25th he claimed an RAF Spitfire. He claimed a further two B-24s on 17 December and another one on the 31st over Hannover. On 1 January 1945 he was appointed *Gruppenkommandeur* of the 3rd Group of the 300th Fighter Wing and shortly after achieving his last victory he was awarded the Knight's Cross on 2 February. During an encounter with P-51s of the 39th Fighter Group over Schmerwitz, near Bad Belzig, Jenne was shot down and killed.

Armin KÖHLER

Major

Knight's Cross: Awarded on 7 February 1945 as *Hauptmann* and commander of the 3rd Group of the 77th Fighter Wing for operations over the Soviet Union, the Mediterranean and the Eastern Front.

Armin Köhler claimed at least thirty aerial victories during the Second World War, of which nineteen were over the Western Front. He was born on 31 March 1912 in Thalheim, Stollberg in Lower Austria to a circus family and in his youth it was rumoured he performed with the Rivels, a famous trapeze act. He joined the *Luftwaffe* in early 1939 and trained as a *Feldwebel* with the Fighter Air School in Jever, staying for a time as an instructor.

From 1942, now a *Leutnant*, Köhler was attached to the 3rd Squadron of the 77th Fighter Wing and from the spring he briefly

(*Author's collection*)

flew over the Soviet Union and claimed his first victory on 21 April, a Polikarpov R-5 reconnaissance bomber over the Ukraine. The next day he shot down an LaGG-3 fighter and on the 24th he claimed three Polikarpov I-15 biplanes and was awarded the Iron Cross 2nd Class. He continued to fly with his Squadron over the Crimea and claimed six victories during May, which included three on the 16th and two on the 18th, and was awarded the Iron Cross 1st Class after being credited with ten aerial victories. In late June his Group was withdrawn from the Eastern Front and moved to Sicily, and from July, now with the 2nd Squadron he flew combat missions over most of Sicily and later over Malta. He claimed two RAF Spitfires during July and claimed a third on 13 October over north-west La Valetta. On 25th his Group moved to North Africa after the start of the Allied offensive at El Alamein and he claimed two P-40s on 4 November and another the next day over the area of Fuka. On 24 November he was awarded the *Luftwaffe* Honour Goblet in recognition of his 12th aerial victory.

On 1 February 1943 Köhler was appointed *Staffelkapitän* of the 2nd Squadron and took part in the defensive battles near Fatnassa in Tunisia and on the 8th he claimed a B-25 Mitchell bomber south-west of Fatnassa. He claimed another B-24 and a P-40 on 24 March and on 3 April he claimed his 20th victory, a Spitfire. Towards the end of April he flew sorties during the final stages of the battle for the Tunisian bridgehead. From May his Group moved back towards Sicily and the updated Bf 109G-6 was now available to Köhler and his Squadron. His Squadron moved again in June and deployed in the air defence of Sicily and later moved to San Peitro against Allied bomber formations. Due to the numerous heavy defensive missions and losses the number of operational fighters fell during July and his Group struggled to supply the full number of aircraft, but Köhler managed to claim a B-25 on 2 July and the next day he shot down a P-40. After the Allied landings in Sicily on 10 July his Group moved again to the Apulia region of Italy as Sicily was evacuated. By mid-July his Group had moved to Botricello after a heavy air raid and a large number of personnel had fallen ill with malaria and stomach problems, including Köhler. He was diagnosed with malaria but he refused home leave and pumped himself full of Atebrin and continued to fly. During this time he was made Acting *Gruppenkommandeur* of the 1st Group and with the loss of Sicily his Group moved to San Severs in mid-August. Later he saw action during the Allied landings near Salerno and by the end of September his Group moved again to Cecina and were used as air cover during the army's evacuation of Corsica. On 16 October Köhler was awarded the German Cross in Gold in recognition of achieving twenty-three aerial victories.

At the beginning of 1944 his Squadron moved to Centocelle near Rome and then to Lagnasco south of Turin. Köhler who had been promoted to *Oberleutnant* a few weeks before claimed a B-17 Flying Fortress on 30 January, and he claimed another on 18 March, his 25th victory. The next day he shot down a B-24 over west Gurkfeld, and by the end of the month he had been promoted to *Hauptmann*. In April he claimed three more B-24s and from May he served once again as Acting *Gruppenkommandeur* of the 1st Group, whilst still *Staffelkapitän* of the 2nd Squadron. From June his Group was based in Romania and in August he took over as *Gruppenkommandeur* of the 3rd Group now based in Beneschau, Czechoslovakia and he claimed what would be his last victory on 3 February, a Petlyakov Pe-2 dive-bomber. Then from 4 April he took over as *Gruppenkommandeur* of the 2nd Group, flying from Germany and where he was taken prisoner in May by the Soviets. He was sent to Siberia. He managed to escape en route but was recaptured and wasn't released from captivity until 1953: not reaching Siberia probably saved his life. He ended the war as a *Major* and was described as one of the unsung heroes of the *Luftwaffe* fighter force and his strong Saxon accent was instantly recognizable over the radio as he railed his men during aerial attacks. He died on 28 March 1999 in Giessen, central Germany.

Wilhelm HÜBNER

Leutnant

Knight's Cross: Awarded on 28 February 1945 as *Leutnant* and pilot attached to the Staff Squadron of the 51st Fighter Wing '*Mölders*' for operations over the Soviet Union.

Wilhelm Hübner claimed about sixty-two aerial victories over the Eastern Front during the Second World War. He was born on 20 February 1919 in Waldau near Liegnitz in Silesia and joined the Staff Squadron of the 51st Fighter Wing in early 1943.

(Deutsches Wehrkundearchiv)

From March 1943 *Unteroffizier* Hübner's Staff Squadron was based in Bryansk on the Eastern Front and where on the 17th he claimed his first victory, a Lavochkin La-5 fighter over north-west Moschna, and he claimed his second victory over Bryansk on 5 April. By May he was based in Orel and he scored two more victories during July and was awarded the Iron Cross 2nd Class. In August his Squadron moved to Poltava, and by the end of the month he had claimed his 10th victory and had been awarded the Iron Cross 1st Class. He claimed four more victories during September and in early October he was promoted to *Feldwebel* and by 28 March had claimed his 20th aerial victory.

In June 1944 he was promoted to *Leutnant* and claimed eight victories on 23 June to become an 'ace-in-a-day', and by the end of the month he had claimed his 35th victory. He claimed two victories on 16 July over Pruzhany in Belarus and he claimed three over Lubomi on the 18th, a Yak-9 over Cholm the next day and two more on 20 July. Hübner claimed his 45th aerial victory over Minsk on 30 July and he flew during the summer offensive protecting Army Group Centre. He was awarded the German Cross in Gold on 1 October, probably for gaining his 50th victory.

From 8 January 1945 he was *Staffelkapitän* of the Staff Squadron and continued to claim aerial victories but the actual dates for these victories are not known. Some records show that he claimed over sixty aerial victories and was awarded the Knight's Cross on 28 February 1945 which gives credibility to him gaining more victories in 1945. On 7 April his Focke-Wulf Fw 190A-8 was hit by Soviet anti-aircraft fire and crashed near Nekuhren in East Prussia and he was killed.

Leo SCHUHMACHER

Leutnant

Knight's Cross: Awarded on 1 March 1945 as *Leutnant* and pilot attached to the 2nd Group of the 1st Fighter Wing for operations over Norway and the Western Front.

Leo Schuhmacher claimed at least eight victories, which included three four-engined bombers, whilst flying combat missions over Norway and during the Battle of Britain during the Second World War. He was born on 13 November 1914 in Wiesental, located in the Rhine valley in the south-western state of Baden-Württemberg. He joined the *Luftwaffe* in 1934, and trained as a pilot

From April 1940 he flew during the campaign against Norway with the 2nd Squadron of the 76th Destroyer Wing, flying from its base in Aalborg in Denmark. He claimed his first victory, a Wellington bomber, near Stavanger, south-western Norway and was awarded the Iron Cross 2nd Class. He claimed two Blenheim twin-engined bombers again over Stavanger on 9 July and was shortly afterwards awarded the Iron Cross 1st Class. He claimed his fourth victory on 15 August, an RAF Spitfire over East Blythe, London during the Battle of Britain. Then from September 1940 he transferred to instruction duties, training new fighter pilots, and didn't return to combat duty until late 1943.

He returned to combat duty with the 6th Squadron of the 1st Fighter Wing based in Rheine, in the district of Steinfurt in Westphalia, flying the Focke-Wulf Fw 190 as wingman to Heinz Bär. He claimed a B-17 Flying Fortress four-engined bomber on 14 October but it was never confirmed and he claimed a Thunderbolt P-47 on 11 November but again this was not a confirmed victory. He claimed two more victories in early 1944 and again both were unconfirmed. Then on 6 March he claimed a B-17, his fifth victory, and he shot down another B-17 on 6 March to claim another. Whilst still flying combat missions over the Reich he claimed his seventh victory on 8 May, a B-24 bomber and on the 19th he claimed a P-47 fighter near Osnabrück. After the start of the Allied landings in Normandy on 6 June his Squadron, part of the 2nd Group, moved to Le Mans in France where it was employed as a fighter-bomber unit. On 10 June Le Mans was attacked by Allied bombers and put out of action for the next few days and his Group moved to Semallé in north-western France from 18 June.

(Deutsches Wehrkundearchiv)

In late 1944 he transferred to the Staff Squadron of the 3rd Fighter Wing, flying again as wingman to Heinz Bär and his adjutant for a time. In early 1945 he joined Bär when he transferred to *Jagdverband* 44, equipped with the Me 262 jet fighter, flying from Munich and later from April 1945 from Salzburg. On 1 March Schuhmacher was awarded the Knight's Cross in recognition of claiming twenty three victories but the lack of witnesses and microfilm confirmation does mean that his total is probably too high. He flew a total of 250 combat missions and was promoted to *Leutnant* before the end of the war before surrendering to US forces in May 1945.

He died on 13 February 1997 in Waghäusel, a city in the Rhine valley in the south-western state of Baden-Württemberg.

Hugo BROCH

Leutnant

Knight's Cross: Awarded as *Feldwebel* and fighter pilot with the 8th Squadron of the 54th Fighter Wing on 12 March 1945 for operations over the Soviet Union and the Eastern Front.

Hugo Broch claimed eighty-one aerial victories and flew 324 missions, all of them over the Eastern Front during the Second World War. He was born on 6 January 1922 in Leichlingen in the Rheinisch-Bergischer District of North Rhine-Westphalia. He joined the *Luftwaffe* in late 1939, at the age of just 17 and from January 1940 he was attached to Construction Company 42 of Air Region XII in Giessen. Promoted to *Gefreiter* in October he requested a transfer to flying school as he wanted to be a fighter pilot. On 10 November he began his flight training and a year later he was accepted at the Fighter Pilot School in Kamenz. From November 1942 he was at the Fighter Pilot School in Zerbst and from there he was transferred to the Advanced Training Group East as an instructor.

(Deutsches Wehrkundearchiv)

In January 1943 he transferred to the 2nd Group of the 54th Fighter Wing, and was attached to the 6th Squadron in Kalinin, the Soviet Union. He claimed his first victory on 13 March, a Il-2 ground-attack aircraft west of Volchov, and six days later he claimed another one. By 16 July he had claimed his fifth victory and was awarded the Iron Cross 2nd Class, and he claimed his eighth victory at the beginning of August. By 11 August he had claimed his 11th victory and was awarded the Iron Cross 1st Class. He claimed a further two victories on the 19th, another on the 21st and two on 22 and 24 August. He claimed his 20th victory on the 28th, claiming two more on the 31st. On 7 September he claimed his 25th victory and on 17 October he was awarded the German Cross in Gold in recognition of his 30th victory. Between 25 and 29 October he claimed six more victories and on 2 November he claimed three victories. He was awarded the *Luftwaffe* Honour Goblet on 8 November after claiming his 40th victory, unusually presented after the German Cross in Gold!

Hugo Broch flew in a Spitfire at Biggin Hill in Kent in June 2017. He was asked if he wanted to take the controls but politely declined. (*Private source*)

From 9 December 1943 until the end of June 1944 he served as an instructor with the 1st Squadron of the Supplementary Fighter Group East in Liegnitz, commanded at the time by *Major* Viktor Bauer. Broch returned to his unit in July which was now flying from its base in Finland and then later from Riga. He claimed two victories on 21 August, both Lavochkin La-5 fighters, and he claimed another two victories on the 25th, which included his 50th. He claimed nine victories during September and claimed his 60th, a Petlyakov Pe-2 dive-bomber, on 10 October. He continued to score victories: on 28 October he claimed three Il-2s, and claimed two more on 14 and 15 December. In January 1945 Broch was promoted to *Feldwebel* and claimed three victories on the 20th and on 12 March he was awarded the Knight's Cross in recognition of his 79th victory – shortly afterwards being commissioned as a *Leutnant*. He claimed his last two victories of the war on 26 March, and by May his Group was in Flensburg, Germany, where they surrendered to the Allies. Broch was kept in captivity until 26 July 1945, when he returned home.

He visited the United Kingdom in June 2017 and flew in an RAF Spitfire as a special guest at the Chalke Valley History Festival in Wiltshire. He was still alive as of 12 April 2023, and has celebrated his 100th birthday.

Rudolf 'Rudi' LINZ

Leutnant

Knight's Cross: Awarded posthumously on 12 March 1945 as *Leutnant* whilst attached to the 12th Squadron of the 5th Fighter Wing for operations over Norway.

Rudolf Linz claimed fifty-three aerial victories during the Second World War, with all but two being over the Eastern Front. He was born on 14 February 1917 in Ilmenau, Arnstadt and after pilot training joined the 8th Squadron of the 5th Fighter Wing as a *Feldwebel* on 10 March 1942 in the Soviet Union.

He claimed a Hurricane on 13 June 1942, his first aerial victory, over the region of Murmaschi and ten days later he claimed another Hurricane. He claimed his third victory, another Hurricane, on 7 July and was awarded the Iron Cross shortly afterwards. From early 1943 he

(*Author's collection*)

served as an instructor and was promoted to *Oberfeldwebel* before returning to front-line duty with his old unit in September, and claimed three P-40 ground-attack aircraft that month and was awarded the Iron Cross 1st Class. He claimed his 10th victory on 7 April 1944 and claimed a further four victories on the 23rd, all P-39s. He now started to become very successful, claiming three victories on 10 May and two on the 11th, and he claimed his 20th victory two days later. On the 16th he claimed five victories to become an 'ace-in-a-day' and he became an 'ace-in-a-day' on the 25th and the 26th – now with a total of thirty-five victories.

By the middle of June 1944 he had been made an *Oberfähnrich*, an officer candidate, and on the 17th he claimed nine aerial victories to become an 'ace-in-a-day' for the fourth time. Linz was promoted to *Leutnant* in July and on 5 August he became *Staffelkapitän* of the 11th Squadron of the 5th Fighter Wing, part of the 3rd Group and he moved south to Norway. On 17 August he claimed two Yak-9 fighters and a single Pe-2 twin-engined dive-bomber and these included his 50th victory. Towards the end of 1944 he was appointed *Staffelkapitän* of the 12th Squadron, part of the 3rd Group flying the Fw 190A-8 from Herdla, in Norway.

On 9 February he claimed a Beaufighter over north Sagnefjord and a P-51 over the Horstad area and shortly after he was shot down and killed. It was reported after the war that he was probably shot down by either Flying Officer J. Butler or Flying Officer W.L. Black, flying Mustangs of 65 Squadron. His Fw 190 crashed near Meistadt and he was posthumously awarded the Knight's Cross on 12 March 1945. It was reported that he was also awarded the German Cross in Gold shortly after his death. He is buried in the Military Cemetery in Bergen-Solheim, Block 1, Row 17, Grave No. 10.

It has often been said that he shot down more victories over the Soviet Union during the summer of 1942 and has even been associated with as many as seventy! However, there are only two claims from his squadron during that time, and so a total of seventy or more victories are far too much of an exaggeration.

Wilhelm MAYER

Leutnant

Knight's Cross: Awarded posthumously on 12 March 1945 as *Leutnant* and *Staffelführer* of the 5th Squadron of the 26th Fighter Wing '*Schlageter*' for actions over the Western Front which included shooting down seven four-engined bombers.

Wilhelm Mayer claimed a total of twenty-seven aerial victories, which included seven four-engined bombers, after flying 124 combat missions over the Western Front during the Second World War. He was born on 5 December 1917 in Fürth, northern Bavaria and joined the *Luftwaffe* in November 1938.

From November 1940 he flew with the 3rd Squadron of Fighter Pilot School 5 in Vienna, and as part of his basic training he was posted to the 2nd Squadron of the Supplemental Group of the 26th Fighter Wing based in Abbeville in August 1941 with the rank of *Unteroffizier*. In January 1942, now a *Feldwebel*, he transferred to 6th Squadron and flew his first major combat missions in support of Operation Thunderbolt, the *Luftwaffe*'s aerial protection of the *Kriegmarine*'s battleships *Scharnhorst* and *Gneisenau* and the heavy cruiser *Prinz Eugen* as they made their 'Channel Dash' from Brest in France to Wilhelmshaven in Germany on 12 February. On 17 July he was forced to make an emergency landing at Abbeville when his Fw 190A-2 developed engine

(Deutsches Wehrkundearchiv)

problems. He claimed a Spitfire over the Channel on 31 July but this was an unconfirmed victory. Later on 19 August he took part in the aerial action over the Allied amphibious landings at Dieppe, without scoring a victory. He claimed two more Spitfires in August but both were unconfirmed, and it wasn't until 14 March 1943 that he finally claimed his first confirmed aerial victory, a Spitfire over the Somme Estuary. He claimed another Spitfire on 4 April but this was later reclassified as unconfirmed, then on 13 June he claimed his second confirmed victory, a P-47 over Ostend. By now he had been awarded both the Iron Cross 1st and 2nd Classes and had been promoted to *Feldwebel*.

On 30 July Mayer was shot down by return fire from a B-17 bomber near Apeldorn in the Netherlands but suffered only slight injuries in a successful forced-landing of his Fw 190A-5 at Netterden. On 3 September he claimed his third confirmed victory, another B-17, and three days later he claimed another B-17. In early September Mayer transferred to the 7th Squadron, and by the end of the year had claimed another Spitfire and two more heavy bombers. In January 1944 he claimed his 11th aerial victory as well as two more which remain unconfirmed, and on 11 February he claimed his 12th victory, a P-38 Lightning over Vitry-en-Artois. On 18th his Squadron was ordered to scramble from Grevillers, France to intercept a British formation of fifteen RAF De Havilland Mosquito twin-engined bombers, escorted by eight Typhoon fighters, in the attack on the Amiens prison to aid the escape of French Resistance fighters held there. During the attack Mayers claimed one Mosquito, his 13th confirmed aerial victory. He claimed a B-17 on the 24 February and shortly after he was promoted to *Oberfeldwebel*.

On 31 March he was awarded the *Luftwaffe* Honour Goblet for achieving over twenty aerial victories but at least ten were later reclassified as unconfirmed, and on 16 April he was awarded the German Cross in Gold. On 5 April he transferred to Fighter Group West to undertake instructing duties and remained there until 27 July when he returned to the 26th Fighter Wing. He was now attached to the 5th Squadron, and during August he claimed another three victories, before taking part in attacking the Allied airborne landings at Arnhem, during Operation Market Garden on 19 September when he claimed two P-51 Mustangs over Nijmegen. He claimed another P-51 on the 23rd over Goch, and an RAF Spitfire four days later over Kirchhellen, Germany.

In October Mayer was appointed *Staffelkapitän* of the 8th Squadron of the 26th Fighter Wing, and on 19 November he claimed two Spitfires over north Kirchhellen, then in mid-December he was promoted to *Leutnant*. On 14 January 1945, his 124th combat mission, he was shot down and killed over Lohner Bach, near the Dutch border with Germany, by a RAF Spitfire from 56 Squadron. He was posthumously awarded the Knight's Cross on 12 March and is buried today in the military section of the New Cemetery in Lingen, Germany, Row R, Grave No. 31.

Helmut NEUMANN

Leutnant

Knight's Cross: Awarded on 12 March 1945 as *Leutnant* and *Staffelführer* of the 14th Squadron of the 5th Fighter Wing for operations over the Eastern Front.

Helmut Neumann claimed sixty-two victories, all but two over the Eastern Front during the Second World War. He was born on 21 November 1921 in Frankfurt-am-Main and was assigned to the 7th Squadron of the 5th Fighter Wing in August 1942 on completion of his training.

On 13 August, his second full day as a qualified fighter pilot, he was shot down by anti-aircraft fire over Finland and had to bail out of his stricken Bf 109E-7, but he wasn't hurt. At the beginning of 1943, *Unteroffizier* Neumann was attached to the 3rd Group of the 54th Fighter Wing and was flying the Bf 109 from his base in Petsamo, Finland. His Squadron was later deployed to the Arctic Ocean front where he flew over the Murmansk area and the Fischer Peninsula in the Soviet Union. He claimed his first victory on 22 July, a Hurricane, and on the 25th he claimed two P-39 fighters and on 18 August he claimed two more south-east of Eina-Guba, near Murmansk and was awarded the Iron Cross 2nd Class. He claimed another victory on 23 August and three more during September, which included two on the 14th, his eighth and ninth victories. On 26 September his Bf 109G-6 was hit by anti-aircraft fire and he was seriously wounded and absent from combat for the next seven months.

On his return to front-line duties he was promoted to *Fahnenjunker-Feldwebel* and was appointed Adjutant of the 3rd Group of the 5th Fighter Wing. He now started to claim victories at a faster rate than before. He claimed his 10th victory on 11 May, and claimed two on the 16th, three on the 25th and four on the 26 May. On 16 June he claimed his 20th and 21st victories and on the 17th he became an 'ace-in-a-day' when he claimed eight victories, and was shortly after promoted to *Leutnant*. On 27 June he claimed three more victories and the next day he became an 'ace-in-a-day' for the second time when he shot down six aerial victories in four hours. On 1 July his Group was withdrawn to Salzwedel to refresh, and three days later he claimed three victories over Norway, which included his 40th victory.

(Deutsches Wehrkundearchiv)

In August he took over as *Staffelkapitän* of the 14th Squadron, still flying with the 5th Fighter Wing, and claimed his 50th victory on 26 September. The following day he claimed four more victories in Finland over the areas of Kiberg and Eckero, and claimed a single victory on 29 September. On 8 October he claimed a P-39 over Eckero and the following day he claimed four victories south-east of Pechenga, two P-39s and two Boston medium bombers, which included his 60th. By now he was flying fewer missions as the Soviets were advancing and at the beginning of November his group moved to Stavanger in Norway.

At the beginning of 1945 the 4th Group was spread over Stavanger, Lister and Kjevik and Neumann managed to claim his last two victories west of Lister in mid-January and his last on 16 February. On 12 March Naumann finally received the Knight's Cross in recognition of his leadership and for achieving thirty-eight aerial victories, and there is evidence to suggest that he may have also been awarded the German Cross in Gold in early 1945. The war ended for him in Norway and he was credited with 162 combat missions during his career. Neumann died on 21 April 1992 in his home town of Frankfurt-am-Main.

Waldemar 'Waldi' RADENER

Oberleutnant

Knight's Cross: Awarded on 12 March 1945 as *Oberleutnant* and acting commander of the 2nd Group of the 26th Fighter Wing *'Schlageter'* for operations over the Western Front.

Waldemar Radener claimed twenty-three victories, which included twelve four-engined bombers, all of them over the Western Front during the Second World War. He was born on 24 January 1921 in Lüchtringen, Höxter in eastern North Rhine-Westphalia, Germany.

Radener joined the *Luftwaffe* and trained as a fighter pilot, and on the completion of his training he was assigned as a *Leutnant* to the 4th Squadron of the 26th Fighter Wing in February 1943. He flew the Focke-Wulf Fw 190A-4 as part of the 2nd Group, based in northern France whilst under the command of *Major* Wilhelm-Ferdinand Galland. On 13 March he claimed his first aerial victory, an RAF Spitfire east of Étaples, France but this was an unconfirmed victory. He claimed his first confirmed victory on 3 May, when he attacked a pair of Spitfires and claimed one off Dieppe and was awarded the Iron Cross 2nd Class. On 14 May he claimed a B-17 Flying Fortress north-west of Antwerp. The bomber was badly damaged and was forced to separate from its combat box, which normally counted as an aerial victory. On this occasion, however, Radener was not credited with the victory. His second confirmed victory was a US P-47 Thunderbolt, shot down north-west of Domburg, and just four days later he claimed another P-47. Shortly afterwards he claimed two more victories and these were also later reclassified as unconfirmed, but he was soon awarded the Iron Cross 1st Class.

(Deutsches Wehrkundearchiv)

On 30 July, now with the 6th Squadron of the 26th Fighter Wing, he claimed two more P-47s, his fourth and fifth victories. From 18 August Radener was given temporary command of the 6th Squadron. During a mission over Schweinfurt-Regensburg on 17 August, *Gruppenkommandeur* Galland was killed and *Hauptmann* Johannes Naumann was given temporary command. He had led the 6th Squadron until then and Radener was chosen to replace him temporarily as *Staffelkapitän*. From September Naumann returned as *Staffelkapitän* and Radener transferred into the 7th Squadron, and claimed two more victories on 30 December, a P-47 and a B-17.

In early January 1944 Radener claimed two more victories, and he claimed his 11th victory, a B-24 Liberator four-engined bomber, on 4 February. Five days later he was named as the new *Staffelkapitän* of the 7th Squadron. On 18 February the RAF flew a low-level attack on the prison at Amiens in German-occupied France to free French Resistance fighters. As a result of the 832 prisoners, 102 were killed by the bombing, 74 were wounded and 258 escaped, but two-thirds were later recaptured. During the attack Radener claimed one of the Typhoons, shot down north of Amiens. On the 24th and 25th he claimed a total of five aerial victories, but only three were ever confirmed. On 31 March he was awarded the *Luftwaffe* Honour Goblet. Shortly after claiming his 16th victory he was awarded the German Cross in Gold on 16 April 1944 and a few days later Radener was promoted to the rank of *Oberleutnant*. He claimed his 19th victory on 29 April, a B-17 over south-east Roubaix in northern France. On 8 May he claimed another P-47 and on the 11th he downed a B-24 from the 487th Bombardment Group but accidentally rammed another B-24 and he had to bail out of his Fw 190A-8, slightly injured. He soon returned to flying. On 15 June he was shot down by a P-51 Mustang east of Bonneval and bailed out but his parachute was entangled on his aircraft and he suffered injuries on landing and didn't return to flying until mid-September, retaining his command of the 7th Squadron. He claimed two more victories on 23 December and both were Lancaster bombers over Cologne, his 22nd and 23rd and last victories.

On 1 January 1945 he led his Squadron during Operation Bodenplatte, the attempt to gain air superiority during the Battle of the Bulge in the Ardennes. On the 30th Radener was appointed *Gruppenkommandeur* of the 2nd Group of the 26th Fighter Wing, but this was a brief command as he was transferred on 26 February as *Gruppenkommandeur* of the 2nd Group of the 300th Fighter Wing. He was awarded the Knight's Cross on 12 March for his success as a fighter pilot as he claimed a total of twelve four-engined bombers and for his service to the 26th Fighter Wing.

After the war he joined the *Bundesluftwaffe* and was promoted to *Hauptmann* before being killed in a flying accident. He was at the time flying a Canadian Car and Foundry-manufactured variant of the North American T-6 Texan near Peissenberg, in the Weilheim-Schongau area of Bavaria on 8 February 1957. During a practice spin during a training lesson he crashed, the first *Bundesluftwaffe* pilot to die in a flying accident.

Rudolf (Rudi) 'Bulle' ZWESKEN

Oberfeldwebel

Knight's Cross: Awarded on 21 March 1945 as *Oberfeldwebel* and fighter pilot attached to the 6th Squadron of the 300th Fighter Wing for operations over the Soviet Union and the Western Front.

Rudi Zwesken claimed over twenty-three aerial victories during the Second World War, which included fourteen four-engined bombers over the Western Front. He was born on 13 August 1919 in Marschendorf, Mährisch-Schönberg in Czechoslovakia and later his family moved to Germany. He joined the *Luftwaffe* in 1941 and trained as a fighter pilot. Once his training was complete he was assigned to the 1st Squadron of the 52nd Fighter Wing in early 1943.

Feldwebel Zwesken saw action over Belgorod on the Eastern Front from April 1943 and from there he was deployed over Kursk. In May he flew mainly hunting and escort missions and in July his Group moved to Melitopol in south-eastern Ukraine and then to Bessonovka in the Soviet Union.

(Deutsches Wehrkundearchiv)

After the Soviet counteroffensive the 1st Group moved further south to the Donetsk region and from August began to retreat and eventually settled in Kharkov. By the end of September Zwesken was flying protection missions for bombers during the Kuban withdrawal. He later flew during the defensive battles east of Zaporozhye and from the end of October flew over the Crimea, and his group moved to Mala-Wyska west of Kirovograd in the Ukraine in December.

In early January 1944 his Group kept on the move due to the Soviet advance. In March he was flying from the small village of Kanta Kusenka near the Bug River, but within a few days the Group was under Soviet artillery fire and had to move again. From April to June he flew as a bomber pilot over the Ukraine whilst attached to the 6th Squadron of the 51st Bomber Wing. He then joined the 300th Fighter Wing, flying from Frankfurt am Main, as part of the 2nd Group whilst attached to the 6th Squadron. On 21 June he claimed his first victory, a B-17 Flying Fortress over Oranienburg, Germany, and was awarded the Iron Cross 2nd Class, and four days later he claimed his second victory, a B-24 Liberator bomber near Tullen. He claimed another Liberator on 7 July and on the 19th he shot down a P-38 Lightning south of Munich. On 22 July he was awarded the Iron Cross 1st Class and in August his Group was reclassified and strengthened and moved to Erfurt-Bindersleben. On 22 August he claimed three P-38s and a B-24 and before the end of the month he claimed another two four-engined bombers. In October his Group moved to Löbnitz in Saxony, and on 17 December he claimed two more B-24s. He was awarded the *Luftwaffe* Honour Goblet on 18 November after gaining ten victories, of which seven were four-engined bombers. On Christmas Eve he shot down a P-51 Mustang over West Schwalmstadt, and on New Year's Eve he claimed two B-17s over the Rotenburg area. He had become something of a four-engined bomber specialist and was promoted to the rank of *Oberfeldwebel*.

He was still flying from Löbnitz during the first months of 1945 and claimed at least five more victories, of which three were four-engined bombers, before the end of April. He had also been awarded the German Cross in Gold and on 21 March he was awarded the Knight's Cross after claiming his 14th four-engined bomber. In May his Group merged with the 3rd Group and became Fighter Group 300, commanded by *Major* Günther Rall.

Zwesken survived the war and was taken prisoner by the Americans in May 1945, and upon his release he committed suicide on 22 February 1946 in the Bitterfeld district of Saxony-Anhalt, Germany. However, it has been said that on his release from Allied captivity he headed straight for a bar which was full of British and American soldiers and when they learnt that Zwesken was a German there was a scuffle, and Zwesken was shot. To avoid a scandal it was covered up and reported that he committed suicide. However, the circumstances are unclear and it's only a rumour.

Karl 'Quaz' SCHNÖRRER

Leutnant der Reserve

Knight's Cross: Awarded on 22 March 1945 as *Leutnant der Reserve* and *Staffelführer* of the 11th Squadron of the 7th Fighter Wing for operations over the Soviet Union and the Western Front.

Karl Schnörrer claimed forty-five aerial victories during the Second World War of which eleven were achieved over the Western Front, nine of these whilst flying the Me 262 jet fighter. He was born on 22 March 1919 in Nuremberg and he trained as a fighter pilot with Fighter Pilot School 5 in Vienna where he became friends with Walter Nowotny.

(Deutsches Wehrkundearchiv)

In early 1941 he flew with the Supplementary Group of the 54th Fighter Wing and from July he was attached to the 1st Squadron during the invasion of the Soviet Union as wingman to his friend Nowotny. *Gefreiter* Schnörrer claimed his first aerial victory on 13 December, but it was never confirmed. From early 1942 his Squadron, attached to the 1st Group operated from the Krasnogvardeysky district south-west of Leningrad, flying the Bf 109F-2. At the beginning of the year few mission were flown due to the extreme weather conditions, then from April operations suffered again due to the thaw. On 12 May Schnörrer claimed his first confirmed victory, a Yak-1 near Luban. In July his Group moved to Finland briefly, returning to the Soviet Union in August where on the 13th he claimed his second victory, a Petlyakov Pe-2 dive-bomber.

In February 1943 his Squadron moved to Heilogenbeil and they were converted to the Fw 190A, and during this time he and his friend Nowotny together with Anton Döbele and Rudolf Rademacher formed a team known as the 'Chain of Devils' or the 'Nowotny *Schwarm*'. During the course of the war in the Soviet Union they were credited with almost 500 aerial victories, making them the most successful team in the *Luftwaffe*. On 23 February the Soviets launched an attached which was repelled by the LIV Army Corps under the command of *Generalleutnant* Carl Hilpert. That day all available aircraft of the 1st Group flew defensive missions and by nightfall thirty-two Soviet aircraft had been destroyed – Schnörrer claiming one himself. It wasn't until 15 March that he claimed his fourth victory, another Il-2 aircraft, and a few days later he was awarded the Iron Cross 2nd Class. From June he flew from Orel and claimed another three victories that month and on 7 July he claimed two more victories which included his 10th and 11th and was awarded the Iron Cross 1st Class. He was promoted to *Feldwebel* at the beginning of August and claimed a total of eight victories that month. Schnörrer had learnt a great deal from being wingman to Nowotny and they had become very good friends. After claiming his 30th aerial victory on 13 October, six days later he accompanied Nowotny to Hitler's headquarters in East Prussia where his friend received the Knight's Cross with Oakleaves, Swords and Diamonds personally from Hitler. Later Nowotny even introduced Schnörrer to Hitler and praised him as an invaluable wingman! Two days later Schnörrer was awarded the German Cross in Gold in recognition of his 30th victory and the following day he was awarded the *Luftwaffe* Honour Goblet.

On 12 November, shortly after claiming a Yak-9 over Lake Ordovo, Belarus, Schnörrer was shot down at close range and was seriously wounded. He had bailed out far too low and his parachute failed to open. He fell 230ft and came down in some trees. He suffered concussion and broken ribs, together with both knees and arms. German infantrymen rescued him from no man's land. He was taken to the nearest airbase and *Generaloberst* Robert Ritter von Greim, the commander of the 6th Air Fleet, ordered that Schnörrer be flown back to Germany in his own private aircraft to receive the best treatment. He spent seven months in hospital and Nowotny visited him once every three months to take him food, drink and cigarettes. It was whilst in hospital that his friend told him he could join a new unit where he could fly the new Me 262 jet fighter.

Seven months later in June 1944 Schnörrer left hospital having fully recovered and was commissioned as a *Leutnant* and transferred to Lechfeld air base where he trained to fly the new Me 262 jet fighter. In September the new aircraft was ready to fly in combat and his friend Nowotny was brought in to lead the project, but progress was slow due to bad weather conditions. On 8 November Nowotny led five Me 262 aircraft from the 7th Fighter Wing in one of its first group combat missions against a US bomber formation and was shot down and killed. All those associated with the project were shocked, especially Schnörrer, who together with other aces formed an honour guard at his funeral.

The Fighter Wing now known as the 7th Fighter Wing '*Nowotny*' was led by *Oberst* Johannes Steinhoff and on 19 November remnants of the command were redesignated Brandenburg-Briest. From February 1945 Schnörrer was attached to the 9th Squadron and claimed a B-17 Flying Fortress on the 3rd near Berlin. On the 9th he shot down a P-51 Mustang over the same area and during March he claimed nine aircraft, which included eight B-17s. On 18 March he was appointed *Staffelführer* of the 9th Squadron and on the 22nd he was awarded the Knight's Cross. On the 30th he flew against a USAAF raid of more than 1,300 heavy bombers, escorted by 852 fighter aircraft, that were attacking the U-boat pens and oil storage facilities at Hamburg, Bremen, Wilhelmshaven and Farge. Me 262 fighters were sent to intercept this huge force. Schnörrer claimed two B-17s over Hamburg before his aircraft was struck by crossfire from a US bomber and pursued by P-51 fighters. With only one engine operating at full power he saw no chance of escape and rolled his aircraft onto its back and dropped clear from the cockpit. However, in bailing out he struck the aircraft's tail, sustained serious leg injuries and had to have his leg amputated. It was the end of his combat career.

After the war Schnörrer worked for the German Press Association as a photographer. During his career he had flown a total of 536 combat missions and was the seventh most successful jet-fighter ace of the war. He died in his home town of Nuremberg on 25 September 1979.

Wilhelm STEINMANN

Major der Reserve

Knight's Cross: Awarded on 28 March 1945 as *Major der Reserve* and commander of the 1st Group of the 4th Fighter Wing for operations over the Western Front, the Soviet Union and Italy.

Wilhelm Steinmann first flew as a bomber pilot and didn't transfer to fighters until May 1943, claiming thirty-three victories of which five were four-engined bombers over the Western Front. He was born on 15 January 1912 in Nuremberg and joined the *Luftwaffe* in 1936, training as a bomber pilot.

In May 1939 *Leutnant* Steinmann flew with the 3rd Squadron of the 53rd Bomber Wing, flying the Heinkel He 111 bomber. He took part in the Polish campaign from September 1939 and later flew reconnaissance missions during the French campaign and the Battle of Britain. From June 1941, *Oberleutnant* Steinmann saw action during

(Deutsches Wehrkundearchiv)

the invasion of the Soviet Union, flying in support of Germany's ground troops. Later he transferred as a Technical Officer with the 2nd Air Corps, serving under *Generaloberst* Bruno Loerzer.

Promoted to *Hauptmann* in October 1942 he transferred to the 3rd Squadron of the 27th Fighter Wing in May 1943. He claimed his first victory, a Typhoon over the Strait of Dover, on 18 May and' his second victory was a Spitfire claimed over Le Touquet near Boulogne but it was never confirmed. On 1 June he mistakenly shot down *Hauptmann* Erich Hohagen, a Group Commander with the 27th Fighter Wing, who crashed-landed his Messerschmitt Bf 109E north of Marquise, France with skull fractures. He later recovered fully and flew again. As a punishment Steinmann was taken off flying duties and transferred to the ground staff of Fighter Leader Romania. However, he soon returned to the 4th Fighter Wing as *Staffelkapitän* in mid-June, as the *Luftwaffe* needed experienced fighter pilots.

He flew his first defence operation over Romania on 1 August against US bombers attacking the oil refineries near Ploiești. On that day his Group had reported that they had achieved twelve aerial victories, two being B-24s claimed by Steinmann. In mid-November his squadron relocated to Udine in Italy, flying against Allied bomber units. He claimed two victories in January 1944, and on the 23rd he was made temporary *Gruppenkommandeur* of the 1st Group of the 4th Fighter Wing until 14 February. His Group moved a number of times but remained in northern Italy until August from where Steinmann was deployed once again against Allied bomber units. He was awarded the *Luftwaffe* Honour Goblet on 1 May 1944 after claiming fourteen victories and on the 14th he claimed his 15th victory, and by the end of the month he had claimed another four. On 26 August he returned as *Gruppenkommandeur* of the 1st Group during the 'Defence of the Reich' campaign having moved to Mönchengladbach the day before. By the end of the year his Group had moved to Darmstadt-Griesham by which time Steinmann had claimed his 25th aerial victory, an RAF Mosquito.

In early January 1945 Steinmann was awarded the German Cross in Gold and in March he was promoted to *Major* and assigned to the 3rd Group of the 2nd Fighter Replacement and Training Wing in Husum-Schauendahl in Germany, flying the Fw 190A. He claimed a B-17 Flying Fortress on 12 and 15 March and three days later he shot down two P-51 Mustangs. He was awarded the Knight's Cross on 28 March in recognition of achieving thirty-three victories. From April he transferred to Munich to join Adolf Galland's *Jagdverband* 44, flying the Me 262 jet fighter, but he failed to score any victories. During the war Steinmann had flown 234 combat missions of which 180 were as a fighter pilot. He died on 1 August 1966 in Ansbach, Bavaria.

Helmut SCHÖNFELDER

Oberfeldwebel

Knight's Cross: Awarded on 31 March 1945 as *Oberfeldwebel* and fighter pilot with the Staff Squadron of the 51st Fighter Wing '*Mölders*' for operations over the Soviet Union and the Eastern Front.

Helmut Schönfelder claimed fifty-six aerial victories during the Second World War, all of them over the Eastern Front. He was born on 30 April 1914 in Nienburg, Lower Saxony in Germany and after his pilot training was completed he was attached to the 6th Squadron of the 51st Fighter Wing as an *Oberfeldwebel* from October 1941.

In October he flew with his Squadron over the area of Orel-West on the Eastern Front in support of German units south-east of Moscow and on the 27th he scored his first victory, an Ilyushin DB-3 north-east of Mtsensk. He claimed his second victory, a MiG-3 interceptor, just over a mile south-east of Kashira on 28 November and from December

(Deutsches Wehrkundearchiv)

his group faced intensified aerial battles because of the strong Soviet advance. From early 1942 his Group flew from Bryansk in support of the 4th Army and 2nd Panzer Army west of Moscow. He claimed two victories on 13 January, both I-16 fighters, and was shortly after awarded the Iron Cross 2nd Class. On 7 March he claimed two more victories and was awarded the Iron Cross 1st Class after claiming his eighth victory on 1 May. His Group moved to Orel-North in mid-July and he claimed his 10th victory, an LaGG-3, on 26 September. On 4 October his Group was withdrawn and moved to Jesau to be re-equipped and converted to the Fw 190A, and his Squadron left the Group and became the Staff Squadron while the remainder of the Group transferred to the Mediterranean.

At the beginning of 1943 his Group flew from Vyazma-South and then moved via Smolensk and Vitebsk to the frozen Ivan Lake about 30 miles west of Velikiye Luki. From April until August he served with Fighter Replacement and Training Group East and after helping to train new fighter pilots he rejoined the Staff Squadron with the 51st Fighter Wing back on the Soviet front. He claimed three victories during October and by the beginning of 1944 his Group had moved to Bobruisk. In late March they were flying from Orsha. He was awarded the *Luftwaffe* Honour Goblet on 19 June and claimed two victories on 23rd and 24 June, claiming his 20th victory on 8 July. By 30 July he had claimed a total of twenty-seven victories and claimed his 30th victory, a Yak-9 on 4 August. In October his Group had moved to Zichenau in East Prussia and then to Latvia and by this time Schönfelder had claimed a total of forty-one victories.

From early 1945 his Group flew from Austria and he claimed another six victories and was awarded the Knight's Cross on 31 March. It was also reported that he was awarded the German Cross in Gold and some records state he was presented it in early 1945 but this has not been confirmed. On 2 May, whilst flying his 540th combat mission, he was shot down by Spitfires near Schwerin in Germany. He managed to bail out safely but was captured by British troops. Schönfelder died on 23 September 2003 in Taunusstein, Darmstadt in Germany.

Anton 'Toni' RESCH

Oberleutnant

Knight's Cross: Awarded on 7 April 1945 as *Oberleutnant* and *Staffelkapitän* of the 3rd Squadron of the 52nd Fighter Wing for operations over the Soviet Union and the Eastern Front.

Anton Resch claimed ninety-two aerial victories, whilst flying over 210 combat missions over the Eastern Front during the Second World War. He was born on 26 November 1921 in Stolberg, Aachen and on completion of his training was assigned to the 1st Group of the 52nd Fighter Wing.

From October 1943 he served as a *Gefreiter* in the 3rd Squadron of the 52nd Fighter Wing, seeing action over the Soviet Union. He claimed his first victory, an Ilyushin Il-2 ground-attack aircraft over west Bolschoj Tokmak on 21 October, and two days later he claimed two Yakovlev Yak-1 fighters near Kalinowka. By the end of the month Resch had claimed six aerial victories and had been awarded the Iron Cross 2nd Class, and was flying combat missions over the Crimea. On 9 November he claimed two more victories over south Gromowka, both Polikarpov U-2 training biplanes. On the 19th he claimed two more victories and was shortly after awarded the Iron Cross 1st Class.

(Deutsches Wehrkundearchiv)

On 26 January 1944 Resch, now an *Unteroffizier*, claimed his 11th victory, a P-39 fighter near Grammatikovo, and the following day his Bf 109 was shot down during combat with Soviet Airacobras near Kerch and as a result Resch was severely wounded. He returned to combat in late May and claimed two P-39s on the 31st and shortly after claiming three more victories he was commissioned as a *Leutnant*. He claimed his 20th and 21st victories on 22 July, and by 4 August he had claimed his 25th and 26th victories. He claimed three more on 12 August, claimed his 30th victory on 24 August, and became an 'ace-in-a-day' the following day when he shot down five aircraft. On the 25th he claimed seven victories to become an 'ace-in-a-day' again, and he didn't stop there – on the 27th he claimed four more victories over Opatów, Poland, three being Il-2 ground-attack aircraft. He claimed his 50th victory on the 28th, another Il-2, and on the 31st he became an 'ace-in-a-day' again when he claimed seven more victories. He claimed two more victories on 1 September, which included his 60th victory and he shot down three more aircraft the next day. Nine days later he was shot down by Soviet anti-aircraft fire and managed to bail out of his Bf 109 near Altsoh, but was seriously wounded and didn't return to combat for a few months.

During the last few weeks of 1944 and the first weeks of January 1945 Resch flew from Cracow in Poland. He claimed his 50th victory on 1 January and his Squadron moved a number of times during January a February and Resch claimed four victories on 20 February and by early March his Squadron had moved into Germany where on 5 March he claimed a Yak-9 fighter. He claimed his 80th victory on 11 March, another Il-2, and he claimed another victory on 23 March, two on the 24th, and he claimed his last four victories on 25 March. On 7 April he was finally awarded the Knight's Cross and just before Germany surrendered he was promoted to *Oberleutnant*. On 8 May 1945 his Group surrendered to US forces in Deutsch-Brod, but due the 'Yalta Agreement' made between the four major powers (the Soviet Union, America, Britain and France) at the end of the war because he had flown against Soviet aircraft over their country he was handed over to the Soviets and spent the next few years in prison. He was released in the mid-1950s and returned to Germany where he died on 16 July 1975 in his home town of Stolberg, he was only 53 years old.

Anton Hermann BENNING

Leutnant

Knight's Cross: Awarded as *Leutnant* and *Staffelkapitän* of the 1st Squadron of the 301st Fighter Wing on 13 April 1945 for operations over the Western Front and for claiming thirteen aerial victories, which included ten four-engined bombers.

Anton Benning was an ex-transport pilot who became a fighter pilot in 1943, claiming thirteen aerial victories, of which ten were four-engined bombers, from 100 combat missions. He was born on 15 May 1918 in Hakenberg Büreu, North Rhine Westphalia and joined the *Luftwaffe* in 1938 at the age of 20. He served first as an instructor and in 1942 he became a transport pilot, and flew supplies in and soldiers out of the Stalingrad Pocket in January and February 1943. He won the Iron Cross 2nd Class in September 1940 and in January 1942 was awarded the Iron Cross 1st Class.

(Deutsches Wehrkundearchiv)

In the spring of 1943 he started to train as a fighter pilot and from July served with the 8th Squadron of the 300th Fighter Wing as a *Feldwebel*. From July he flew from Oldenburg and 22 September claimed his first two aerial victories, both RAF Lancaster bombers over Bremen. From early 1944 he was flying with the 1st Squadron of the 302nd Fighter Wing from its base in Bonn-Hargelar. He claimed his third victory, another Lancaster, on 24 March, over Berlin and on 10 May he shot down two B-24 Liberators and on 29 May he claimed his sixth victory, another B-24. He claimed two more victories on 9 June and a few weeks later his squadron had moved to Herzogenaurach, Bavaria, from where he flew out to claim two more B-24s on the 9th, with another being shot down four days later. He claimed his 10th victory on 26 June when he shot down a USAAF P-51 Mustang. By October he had moved again to Borkheide and claimed a P-51 and B-24 the following month, his 11th and 12th victories. On 5 December Benning claimed his last victory of the war, a Mustang over the Reich.

At the end of the year he was promoted to *Oberfeldwebel* and in early January 1945 was awarded the German Cross in Gold. In February he was appointed *Staffelführer* of the 1st Squadron of the 301st Fighter Wing and had been commissioned as a *Leutnant*. He was awarded the Knight's Cross on 13 April, and by this time his squadron was flying out of Salzburg. Benning survived the war and died at the age of 95 in Recklinghausen in the Ruhr district of Germany on 29 September 2013.

Friedrich 'Fritz' KARCH

Hauptmann

Knight's Cross: Awarded as *Hauptmann* and commander of the 2nd Group of the 2nd Fighter Wing '*Richthofen*' on 17 April 1945 for operations over North Africa and the Western Front.

Friedrich Karch claimed over twenty-three aerial victories, which included six four-engined bombers, all of them over the Western Front, and flew more than 270 missions during the Second World War. He was born on 17 January 1920 in Munich and joined the *Luftwaffe* in 1940 and trained as a fighter pilot, becoming a very good instructor.

He joined the 6th Squadron of the 2nd Fighter Wing on the Channel front from September 1942 and was commissioned as a *Leutnant* a few months later. He later flew as part of the 2nd Group over Sicily where he took part in protection missions for convoys in the Mediterranean that were sailing to and from Tunisia. By the beginning of 1943 he was flying from Tunis, flying the Fw 190A, and on 17 January he claimed

(Deutsches Wehrkundearchiv)

his first aerial victory, a Spitfire west of Kiro. The very next day he claimed another Spitfire west of Djebel Abiod, Tunis, and on the 26th he was awarded the Iron Cross 2nd Class. He claimed a third victory, a P-38, on 15 February and by mid-March his Group had relocated to France. By May they were equipped with the Messerschmitt Bf 109G-3 and were flying out of Beaumont-le-Roger and on 29 May Karch was awarded the Iron Cross 1st Class.

He claimed two victories on 26 June, a Spitfire and a B-17 four-engined bomber, and was now flying from Poix near the Somme in France. Karch claimed another three B-17s during July and claimed another on 12 August (unconfirmed victory) shortly before his Group moved to Vitry-en-Artois. His Group was now mainly used against four-engined bombers and suffered considerable losses during intense aerial battles. He claimed a Spitfire on 19 August and another a month later over north-west Wissant, his 12th victory. On 9 October, in recognition of claiming six four-engined bombers and five Spitfires and two P-38s he was awarded the German Cross in Gold.

Karch claimed another B-17 over the Paris area on 26 November and claiming two more in December. At the beginning of 1944 his Group flew from Creil and during this time he claimed a P-38 over south Rouen on 14 January and he claimed a B-24 Liberator on 6 March. Now with the rank of *Oberleutnant* and *Staffelführer* of the 6th Squadron Karch flew missions during the beginning of the Allied invasion in June 1944, and his Group moved to St. Trond in August. By September he was flying from Frankfurt-Eschborn, and during October claimed two more victories, both P-47 Thunderbolts, which included his 20th aerial victory.

During the last few days of 1944, now a *Hauptmann*, Karch claimed at least two aerial victories, both P-47 Thunderbolts. When *Hauptmann* Walter Matoni was seriously wounded during a crash in February 1945 Karch took over as *Gruppenkommandeur* of the 2nd Group, holding this position until the end of the war. During the last months of the war his Group was based in Nidda, a town northeast of Frankfurt, and he claimed what is probably his last victory of the war on 28 March, a P-51 Mustang. On 17 April Karch led the remains of his Wing back into Bavaria and it was here, as the armoured spearheads of General Patton's US 3rd Army approached the small fields outside Straubing, on the banks of the Danube, that his last few Bf 109s were set on fire and destroyed. On that same day he learnt that he had, at last, been awarded the Knight's Cross. He surrendered his group to the US forces a few days later. It is highly likely that he received his Knight's Cross after the war and he lived in Germany until his death in Bayreuth on 30 December 2001.

Hans-Joachim KROSCHINSKI

Leutnant

Knight's Cross: Awarded as *Oberfeldwebel* whilst attached to the 3rd Squadron of the 54th Fighter Wing on 17 April 1945 for operations over the Soviet Union and the Eastern Front.

Hans-Joachim Kroschinski claimed at least seventy-four aerial victories whilst flying almost 360 combat missions over the Eastern Front during the Second World War. He was born on 11 May 1920, in Saafel, Möhringen, part of East Prussia, and on completion of his fighter pilot training he joined the 2nd Squadron of the 54th Fighter Wing.

As an *Unteroffizier* in August 1942 he was attached to the 1st Group and flew from Krasnoyarsk in Siberia. He flew the Bf 109F and on 5 August he claimed his first victory, a MiG-3 interceptor over north-east Malaya Vishera, and six days later he claimed an Il-2 ground-attack aircraft. Towards the end of the year he was promoted to *Feldwebel* and claimed four more victories in January 1943. In February his Group

(Deutsches Wehrkundearchiv)

was converted to the Fw 190A, and moved to Heiligenbeil airfield, and he was soon awarded the Iron Cross 1st and 2nd Classes and during that month claimed his 12th victory. In May the 1st Group moved to Nikolskoye and from June flew from Orel, and by this time Kroschinski had achieved sixteen victories. On 21 July he was shot down by a Soviet Lavochkin La-5 fighter and managed to parachute to safety without injury. He claimed another six victories that month and nine more in August, which included his 30th victory.

He claimed his 35th victory on 14 September and shortly after transferred into the 11th Squadron where he stayed until October. It was a only brief assignment but he claimed three more victories during that time and was awarded the *Luftwaffe* Honour Goblet on 11 October. He returned to his former Squadron in late October and his Squadron moved to Orsha, Belarus in December where he claimed two victories and was awarded the German Cross in Gold on 24 October after achieving thirty-five victories.

Between April and September 1944 he served as an instructor with Fighter Replacement and Training Group East and claimed two four-engined bombers, but three remain unconfirmed. During this time he was promoted to *Oberfähnrich* – senior officer candidate. In September he returned to the 54th Fighter Wing, being assigned to the 3rd Squadron in Latvia. He claimed a P-39 on 29 October and the next day he claimed three more victories. On 7 November he was promoted to *Oberfeldwebel* and that same day he claimed three victories, all Il-2s. On 15 December he claimed three victories and on the 21st he became an 'ace-in-a-day' when he shot down five Petlyakov Pe-2 twin-engined bombers. That same day he was himself shot down by a rear gunner from a Pe-2. He parachuted to safety, but was severely wounded, losing his eyesight and his right leg. Unsurprisingly, after a long stay in hospital, he retired from the *Luftwaffe* on medical grounds. He was commissioned as a *Leutnant* in early 1945 and awarded the Knight's Cross on 17 April. He died on 7 January 1995 in Eutin, a district in the northern German state of Schleswig-Holstein.

Hans DORTENMANN

Oberleutnant

Knight's Cross: Awarded as *Oberleutnant* and *Staffelkapitän* of the 3rd Squadron of the 26th Fighter Wing '*Schlageter*' on 20 April 1945 for operations over the Soviet Union and the Western Front.

Hans Dortenmann flew 150 combat missions and flew twenty-eight ground-attack missions, claiming thirty-nine aerial victories, of which twenty-two were over the Western Front, including one four-engined bomber. He was born on 11 December 1921 in Weingarten in the Württemberg region of Germany and served in the army before transferring into the *Luftwaffe* in January 1943 as a *Feldwebel*.

He trained as a fighter pilot with the 103rd Fighter Wing and then with the Supplementary Group East, seeing action in the Soviet Union. From October he was assigned to the 3rd Squadron of the 54th Fighter Wing and in February 1944 he was transferred to the 2nd Squadron.

(Deutsches Wehrkundearchiv)

He scored his first victory on 6 February, when he rammed a Lavochkin La-5 fighter, damaging his own aircraft, and had to make an emergency landing at Orscha-South airfield. Three weeks later he shot down another La-5 over south-west Narva and the following day he claimed two Ilyushin Il-2 ground-attack aircraft and was shortly afterwards awarded the Iron Cross 2nd Class. Dortenmann claimed two victories on 8 March, claimed another victory over the Gulf of Finland on 26 March. By the end of the month had scored ten victories and had been awarded the Iron Cross 1st Class.

On 10 June his squadron was withdrawn from the Eastern Front and relocated to the Western Front where he joined the 3rd Group and had by this time accumulated a total of fifteen victories. On 20 June he was appointed *Staffelkapitän* of the 2nd Squadron of the 54th Fighter Wing, which in August became the 12th Squadron after reorganization of the fighter forces on the Western Front. On 26 June he was shot down over the area near Paris and was hurt when he managed to bail out of his Focke-Wulf Fw 190A-8. Whilst flying combat missions over the Invasion Front he claimed six more victories and in mid-August his Group was withdrawn to Germany to be refitted. In late September the Group received its first new aircraft, the Fw 190D-9, and his squadron was renamed the 13th Squadron. He was promoted to *Oberleutnant* a few weeks later and was awarded the German Cross in Gold in recognition of achieving twenty-one victories.

On 2 November 1944 he claimed his only four-engined bomber, a B-17 Flying Fortress over Engelbertswald south-west of Lingen, and later that month his squadron was assigned to Achmer where he flew protection missions for the new Me 262 jet fighters of *Kommando Nowotny*. On 29 December Dortenmann claimed his 25th victory, an RAF Tempest shot down over Münster-Handorf, but it was also a terrible day for the Group when they lost their *Gruppenkommandeur Hauptmann* Robert Weiss, and twelve other pilots. The following day Dortenmann was named as Acting *Gruppenkommandeur* of the 3rd Group, taking over from Weiss, position he held until January 1945. From February he was *Staffelkapitän* of the 11th Squadron and claimed two P-47 Thunderbolts over Nassau. On 13 February he claimed a P-51 Mustang on 21 and 22 February and two more on 19 March to claim his 30th and 31st victories. On 28 March he took over as *Staffelkapitän* of the 3rd Squadron of the 26th Fighter Wing, part of the 1st Group under *Gruppenkommandeur Major* Karl Borris. He claimed his 32nd victory that same day, an RAF Tempest near Münster, and three days later he claimed an RAF Auster observation aircraft near Ludwighausen. On 12 April he claimed two Tempests over North Uelsen, and five days later he claimed another one over Lubeck. On 20 April he was awarded the Knight's Cross in recognition of his 30-plus victories and this was presented to him a few weeks later, becoming the last member of the 26th Fighter Wing to receive the award.

He claimed a Spitfire over Buchholz on 21 April and during the last few days of April he shot down two Soviet aircraft near Berlin. Germany's armed-forces infrastructure was rapidly falling apart and the *Luftwaffe* no longer made a distinction between the Western and Eastern Fronts. On 5 May he decided together with some other pilots to surrender to Allied forces near Flensburg and upon landing they destroyed their aircraft and surrendered to British troops. He wasn't handed over to the Soviets like many of his comrades and was soon released from captivity and settled in Heidelberg, Germany where he died on 1 April 1973.

Heinz 'Esau' EWALD

Leutnant

Knight's Cross: Awarded on 20 April 1945 as *Leutnant* and fighter pilot with the 5th Squadron of the 52nd Fighter Wing for operations over the Soviet Union and the Eastern Front.

Heinz Ewald claimed eighty-three aerial victories and flew almost 400 missions over the Eastern Front during the Second World War. He was born in Zoppot, a town on the Baltic coast near Danzig, now part of Poland, on 1 September 1922. He joined the *Luftwaffe* in early 1943 and trained as a fighter pilot whilst attached to Air Training Regiment 23 in Kaufbeuren, Bavaria. From September he served with the 52nd Fighter Wing in Anapa, Russia where he completed his training whilst attached to the 2nd Group as a *Gefreiter*. He transferred to the 6th Squadron in November claiming his first victory six days later in only his fourth mission! During this time he was wingman to *Hauptmann* Gerhard Barkhorn for a while, flying more than 100 combat missions with this future ace.

(Deutsches Wehrkundearchiv)

Promoted to *Unteroffizier* he had by the end of December scored eight victories which included three in just 18 minutes on the 31st. On 8 January 1944 Ewald was awarded the Iron Cross 2nd Class, and during that month claimed another seven victories, although four would be later reclassified as unconfirmed. By the end of February he had claimed a total of seventeen aerial victories, and shortly after claiming his 19th victory on 2 March he was awarded the Iron Cross 1st Class. After claiming just over twenty victories Ewald was awarded the Flying Clasp for Fighters in Gold on 22 March and on 25 May he was awarded the *Luftwaffe* Honour Goblet. He claimed his 25th victory on 3 June, and shortly after claiming his 28th victory on the 12th he was promoted to *Leutnant*. On the 24 June the 2nd and 3rd Groups, which included Ewald's squadron, took on the US 15th Air Force, about 300 four-engined bombers heading for the Romanian oilfields. During the engagement Ewald claimed a B-24 bomber (unconfirmed), and five *Luftwaffe* fighters were shot down. Two of the pilots were killed, a third was shot while hanging in his parachute and a fourth escaped without injury. Ewald managed to bail out of his burning aircraft at the last minute, but was badly burnt and spent some time recovering. The fifth pilot escaped unharmed.

In October he returned to active duty with the 7th Squadron, part of the 2nd Group, flying from Tiakta-Kanez and later Ferihegy in Hungary. He had by this time achieved his 31st victory and claimed two more on 1 November, and had by the end of the month claimed his 41st victory and was awarded the German Cross in Gold on the 30th. By the end of 1944 he had claimed forty-eight victories, and in January 1945 transferred back to the 6th Squadron, still based in Hungary. He claimed two victories on the 2nd, which included his 50th, and claimed five on the 3rd to become an 'ace-in-a-day', and by the end of January he had claimed his 66th victory. On 15 February he was appointed acting *Staffelkapitän* of his squadron, and five days later he crash-landed at Raab after his Bf 109 was struck by return fire.

On 1 March Ewald together with three other fighters from his squadron spotted eight US P-51 Mustangs north of Lake Balaton, Hungary, and they attacked without properly assessing the situation. Ewald hit one of the Mustangs, which left trailing smoke, but within a few minutes twenty to thirty more P-51s appeared. Ewald and his three comrades were outnumbered nearly ten to one. His comrades were soon shot down or were so badly damaged they had to leave Ewald to face the pack of P-51s alone. He was chased for some time, and was hit at least twice. He had to twist and turn to try and escape being hit again, trying to work his way back towards his base. At the controls of his damaged Bf 109 Ewald had to drop down to a lower altitude hoping that the P-51s would be scared off by the anti-aircraft fire. However, as he approached his base his own aircraft came under fire from the airfield defences, took a hit and the controls began to feel heavy, Ewald knew he had to bail out. With just enough height he jumped over the side of the cockpit, immediately tugging on the ripcord. Even his parachute came under fire from the German troops below as they disembarked from a train and firing upwards at what they thought was a Soviet pilot. Ewald came down about two miles from his airfield with a hard landing, as he lay on the ground he was approached by Hungarian workers shouting '*Ruski … kaput … kaput!*'. It took all his skill to convince them he was German. It was later said that he drove across to the anti-aircraft gunners and told them what he thought of them. However Ewald stated that he was driven to the gun emplacement by another pilot and it was him who was so enraged by the incident that he shouted at the gunners and even threw a live hand-grenade at them. They quickly disappeared into their foxholes and nobody was hurt. The battery commander later telephoned *Gruppenkommandeur* Wilhelm Batz and apologised for shooting down one of his fighters, and asked if his pilots would refrain from throwing grenades at his men!

Two days later Ewald was wounded when his aircraft was hit by Soviet anti-aircraft fire and he was forced to bail out and landed about 12 miles south-east of Gardony. It took him 23 hours to reach the German lines. He was wounded again on 3 April, when his aircraft was damaged by US Mustangs and he was forced to make a belly-landing near Vienna. He claimed his 80th victory on 14 April and claimed his final two victories of the war the next day. On the 20th he was awarded the Knight's Cross and three weeks later on 8 May he surrendered to US forces in Bavaria. He was held as a prisoner-of-war until 22 June 1945 and then returned home to Coburg where he died in on 14 March 2002.

Alfred GROSS

Leutnant

Knight's Cross: Awarded on 20 April 1945 as *Staffelführer* of the 5th Squadron of the 26th Fighter Wing for actions over the Soviet Union and the Western Front and for claiming a total of fifty-one victories.

Alfred Gross claimed fifty-one aerial victories of which thirty-eight were achieved over the Eastern Front during the Second World War. He was born on 4 October 1919 in Alt-Placht, Templin in the district of Brandenburg, Germany and began his career with the *Luftwaffe* as a flight instructor with Advanced Training Group East in 1942.

From October 1943 he served as a *Feldwebel* with the 5th Squadron of the 54th Fighter Wing and claimed his first victory on 5 October, a Yakovlev Yak-9 fighter over Gorostaipol. Three days later he claimed three more victories and shortly after was awarded the Iron Cross 2nd Class. During October he claimed another ten victories, which included four on the 21st, and was awarded the Iron Cross 1st Class towards the

(Deutsches Wehrkundearchiv)

end of the month. He claimed his 15th victory on 3 November and claimed two more victories on the 30th and soon after his Group moved to Vinnitsa, and it was during this time he was wingman to *Oberleutnant* Horst Ademeit (Knight's Cross with Oakleaves). He claimed his 20th victory on 11 February 1944, and went on to claim a total of nine victories between 19 and 25 March. On 2 April he claimed his 30th aerial victory, a Lavochkin La-5 fighter south-west of Selo, and by the end of the month he had achieved his 38th victory and had been awarded the *Luftwaffe* Honour Goblet.

In May he was transferred to the 8th Squadron of the 54th Fighter Wing based on the Western Front, shortly after being promoted to *Oberfeldwebel*. He claimed a P-38 on 19 May and two P-47s on 12 June, which included his 40th victory and was commissioned as a *Leutnant* a few weeks later. He claimed a Spitfire over Caen on 23 June and he claimed two victories on 5 July, a Spitfire and a P-47, his 45th aerial victory. He was awarded the German Cross in Gold on 10 July in recognition of his success as a fighter pilot, and claimed his 50th victory on 28 July, being appointed *Staffelkapitän* of 11th Squadron on 15 August. By the 27th he was once again transferred this time to the 2nd Group of the 16th Fighter Wing flying from Mons-en-Chausee in northern France.

On 3 September he had just taken off from St. Trond when he was attacked by several Spitfires and was severely wounded and had to bail out, but not before he had shot down the fighter being flown by Warrant Officer Peter W. Chattin who was subsequently killed. Gross landed safely but he was so badly wounded that he never flew again. He was awarded the Knight's Cross on 20 April 1945, but there are doubts to whether the award is legal as no citation was issued. Gross died from Tuberculosis on 19 September 1947 in Tönning, Holstein.

Karl-Heinz LANGER

Major

Knight's Cross: Awarded on 20 April 1945 as *Major* and commander of the 3rd Group of the 3rd Fighter Wing '*Udet*' for operations over the Western and Eastern Fronts.

Karl-Heinz Langer claimed twenty-nine aerial victories of which nineteen were claimed over the Eastern Front and ten, of which four were four-engined bombers, over the Western Front during the Second World War. He was born on 19 April 1914 in Gorlitz, a small town in the German state of Saxony, and after completing his fighter pilots training at Fighter Pilots School 5 he was assigned as an *Oberleutnant* and Staff Officer to the 3rd Group of the 3rd Fighter Wing in May 1941. He was later appointed adjutant to the group and saw action over the Soviet Union during the summer.

Langer claimed his first aerial victory on 14 July, an Ilyushin I-153 fighter. He made a forced landing in his Bf 109F-4 west of Golubinskaja on 5 September, after engine damage during a dogfight. He claimed his second victory on 5 October, a DB-3 long-range bomber, and he claimed two more victories in March 1942 and two on 24 August. He claimed his 10th victory near the Bassargino railway on 26 October and had by this time been awarded the Iron Cross 1st and 2nd Class. On 17 December, inside the Stalingrad encirclement he inadvertently taxied over an unexploded bomb buried in the snow at Pitomnik airfield when it exploded, and he was lucky to escape with only minor wounds.

On 1 June 1943 Langer took over as *Staffelkapitän* of the 7th Squadron of the 3rd Fighter Wing. He had by this time only scored eleven victories, as adjutant of the 3rd Group his staff duties had kept him away from flying, it wasn't until now that he could take part in some sustained action. In early August, now with fifteen victories, his Squadron transferred back to Germany, and where on 14 October he claimed a B-17 Flying Fortress over Hammelburg. Shortly after this Langer was himself shot down and slightly wounded, and once he had recovered he served as wingman to *Kommodore Oberst* Wolf-Dietrich Wilcke until the latter's death in March 1944. He did a short stint as an instructor with Fighter Group East from February 1944 and returned to combat a few weeks later.

(Deutsches Wehrkundearchiv)

In March he returned to combat duty and on 21 May 1944 he was appointed the last *Gruppenkommandeur* of the 3rd Group of the 3rd Fighter Wing in Ansbach, now with the rank of *Hauptmann*. On 27 May he claimed a B-17, and he shot down two more just three days later and on 21 June Langer claimed a P-47 Thunderbolt over the Houdan area and a P-51 Mustang near Dreux, his 20th and 21st aerial victories. On 26 July he claimed a P-38 Lightning and the same day he was awarded the German Cross in Gold. On 8 August he was awarded the *Luftwaffe* Honour Goblet and the following week he claimed another P-47.

On 1 January 1945 during Operation Bodenplatte, an attempt by the *Luftwaffe* to cripple Allied air forces in the Low Countries, Langer destroyed two Spitfires on the ground at Eindhoven, Holland. He returned with his Group to the Eastern Front in February where he claimed a Boston on the 19th and an Ilyushin Il-2 ground-attack aircraft on 6 and 18 March. He claimed another Il-2 on 19 April and the following day he was also made adjutant of the 3rd Group. On 20 April he was awarded the Knight's Cross in recognition of claiming over twenty aerial victories and for destroying five aircraft on the ground, as well as over forty vehicles, three rocket launchers and one locomotive. He claimed his final aerial victory on 23 April, a Yakovlev Yak-3 single-engined fighter. Langer died on 6 May 1955 in Remscheid, a city in North Rhine-Westphalia.

Walter LOOS

Oberfeldwebel

Knight's Cross: Awarded as *Oberfeldwebel* and fighter pilot attached to the Staff Squadron of the 300th Fighter Wing on 20 April 1945 for operations over the Western Front.

(Deutsches Wehrkundearchiv)

Walter Loos claimed over fourteen aerial victories during the Second World War of which at least ten were four-engined bombers claimed over the Western Front. He was born on 11 April 1923 in Oppenheim, a town in the Mainz-Bingen district of Rhineland-Palatinate in Germany, and upon qualifying as a fighter pilot he joined the 3rd Fighter Wing in January 1944.

He was at first assigned to the 3rd Group of the 3rd Fighter Wing, as an *Unteroffizier*, but shortly after transferred to the *Sturmgruppe*, a Group of heavily armed and armoured Focke-Wulf Fw 190s charged with breaking up the massed formations of the USAAF four-engined daylight bombers. The Germans suffered many loses and Loos himself was shot down nine times during his career. He claimed his first victory on 6 March 1944 and went onto to claim two more on the 8th and two more in April but these were all unconfirmed victories. Nevertheless he was awarded the Iron Cross 2nd Class on 9th march and on 11 April he claimed two B-17 Flying Fortresses over Germany and these have been accepted as his first two victories of the war. He claimed two more victories, both four-engined bombers, in April and he claimed his fifth victory, a B-24 Liberator on 8 May, and the next day he was awarded the Iron Cross 1st Class.

By June he had been promoted to *Feldwebel* and now flew with the Staff Squadron of the 300th Fighter Wing and claimed another B-24 on 7 July. He flew as wingman to *Kommodore* Walther Dahl whilst flying the Focke-Wulf Ta 152 high-altitude fighter during air defence flights over Germany. On 8 August he was awarded the *Luftwaffe* Goblet and a week later claimed a B-17 over the area of Koblenz, and on 23 August claimed a P-51 Mustang over Murzzuschlag, and on the 29th he claimed another B-17 over Czechoslovakia. He was awarded the German Cross in Gold on 29 September and from December he flew with the Advanced Fighter Training Group East as an instructor.

From early 1945 he flew with the 301st Fighter Wing, now with the rank of *Oberfeldwebel*, and during April he claimed three Yak-9 fighters over Berlin, his 12th to 14th victories. During the chaotic last weeks of the war it is very possible that Loss had claimed more than is officially recorded. Some sources have claimed that he achieved as many as thirty-eight victories, but only around fourteen have been officially recorded. He was awarded the Knight's Cross on 20 April in recognition of his success as a four-engined bomber ace, after claiming at least eleven. After the war he joined the *Bundesluftwaffe* and reached the rank of *Hauptmann* before retiring, and he died on 27 October 2004 in Penzing, Vienna.

Willi RESCHKE

Oberfeldwebel

Knight's Cross: Awarded on 20 April 1945 as *Oberfeldwebel* and fighter pilot and staff officer with the 301st Fighter Wing for operations over the Western and Eastern Front.

(Deutsches Wehrkundearchiv)

Willi Reschke claimed twenty aerial victories during the Second World War, eighteen, which included fourteen four-engined bombers, over the Western Front. He was born on 3 February 1922 in Mühlow, Brandenburg in Germany and joined the *Luftwaffe* in February 1941. After completing his fighter-pilot training, he was attached to Fighter Group 102 at Zerbst from June 1943 as an *Unteroffizier*.

On 22 June 1944 he joined the 1st Squadron of the 302nd Fighter Wing in Götzendorf, a village in Austria. His first combat mission was on the 26th, flying the Bf 109G-6, and he was almost shot down by escorting fighters and landed his damaged Messerschmitt at Deutsch-Wagram, a small village in Austria, but he wasn't injured. He claimed his first two victories on 2 July, and both were B-24 Liberator four-engined bombers, shot down south-west of Budapest. But during combat his Bf 109 was hit in the radiator resulting in a forced landing in a field near Erd and on 13 and 14 July he claimed a B-17 Flying Fortress and a B-24, however both remain unconfirmed. He claimed two more victories on the 18th, but again both were unconfirmed, but the following day he claimed a B-17 over Starnberg in Bavaria, his fourth official victory. He had by this time been awarded both the Iron Cross 1st and 2nd Classes. On 24 August he claimed a B-24 near Neuhaus but during the attack on a second aircraft his Bf 109 was hit by return fire and as he attempted to make a forced landing he was attacked by P-51 Mustangs and had to bail out.

He claimed his eighth victory on 29 August, another B-17 bomber, and his Group was redesignated the 3rd Group of the 301st Fighter Wing and Resch now flew with the 9th Squadron. He was equipped with the Fw 190A-8 and had been promoted to *Feldwebel* and was now flying combat missions over his homeland in 'Defence of the Reich' missions. He claimed a B-24 on 26 November near Hildesheim and claimed another B-24 and a P-51 over south Göttingen on 17 December. A week later, on Christmas Eve the US 8th Air Force launched its largest aerial attack of the war, sending over 2,000 bombers against *Luftwaffe* airfields and infrastructure. The *Luftwaffe* managed to shoot down just twelve of the attacking bombers, two being claimed by Reschke. On 31 December he claimed a B-24 near Hamburg and on New Year's Day 1945 he claimed a B-17 near Gardelegen but his Fw 190 was hit by return fire and he had to bail out. He wasn't injured and returned to combat the next day, and on 14 January he claimed two aerial victories, a P-51 and a P-47 Thunderbolt.

From late January 1945 his Group was equipped with the new Focke-Wulf Ta 152 H-O, intended for medium to high-altitude operations against the large formations of enemy bombers. Reschke flew one of these new aircraft for the first time on 2 March. On the 13th he joined the Staff Squadron of the 301st Fighter Wing and that same day he was awarded the German Cross in Gold. The presentation was made by the *Kommodore*, *Oberstleutnant* Fritz Auffhammer. On 10 April his Group moved to an airfield at Neustadt-Glewe, and four days later two pilots were scrambled, one being Reschke, when Hawker Tempest fighters were reported attacking at Ludwigslust railway yards in Mecklenburg-Vorpommern, Reschke claiming one of the fighters. On 20 April he was awarded the Knight's Cross and on the 14th he claimed two Yak-9s over Berlin and then his Squadron moved to Leck airfield. Shortly after this the British arrived and Reschke and his Group surrendered.

Reschke had been wounded five times and had flown a total of seventy combat missions and ended the war with the rank of *Oberfeldwebel*. He died on 5 July 2017 in Thüringen, Germany at the age of 95.

Hermann WOLF

Leutnant

Knight's Cross: Awarded as *Leutnant* and pilot attached to the 9th Squadron of the 11th Fighter Wing on 24 April 1945 for operations over the Soviet Union and the Western Front.

Hermann Wolf claimed fifty-five aerial victories, of which all but three were achieved over the Eastern Front, whilst flying 586 combat missions during the Second World War. He was born on 27 December 1919 in Frankfurt am Main, Germany and he joined the *Luftwaffe* and trained as a fighter pilot. From April 1942 he served with the Advanced Training Group East in Cracow, Poland flying the Messerschmitt Bf 109E.

(Deutsches Wehrkundearchiv)

Wolf joined the 9th Squadron of the 52nd Fighter Wing at the beginning of May 1942 as an *Unteroffizier*. He flew during the German attack in the Crimea in support of the 17th Army and he made a forced landing near Kharkov on 14 May but wasn't hurt. After a successful breakthrough by ground forces his Group moved to Kharkov where he took part in the counter-attack. He claimed his first aerial victory on 22 May, a MiG-1 fighter, and then on the 31st his aircraft was hit in the radiator and he had to make an emergency landing at the Barvinkove airstrip in the Ukraine without injury. He claimed his second victory, another MiG-1, on 5 August and his third he achieved the following day. A few days later he was awarded the Iron Cross 2nd Class and then flew as part of the German advance towards the Caucasus and Stalingrad. By 10 August his Group had reached Armavir, a city in Krasnodar Krai located on the banks of the Kuban River. Soon after he flew in support of the 17th Army and from 23 August flew in support of the attack on Stalingrad. By this time he had claimed eight victories, and by the end of August he claimed a total of eleven victories and had been awarded the Iron Cross 1st Class. During the aerial battles over Stalingrad and the surrounding area he claimed almost twenty victories and by the end of September had claimed a total of twenty-nine. He was awarded the *Luftwaffe* Honour Goblet on 20 November in recognition of his success during the important offensive.

Wolf was promoted to *Feldwebel* in early 1943 and was now flying the Bf 109G-2 over the southern sector of the Soviet Front. From 15 March he was flying from Kerch and from April from Taman and by early July he was flying from Ugrim in the Belgorodsky District of the Soviet Union. He claimed two victories on 5 July and three the following day, and claimed his 40th on 9 July over north Prokhorovka, part of the Prokhorovsky District of Belgorod Oblast, and shortly after was then deployed over the Kharkov area. On the 22nd he made an emergency belly-landing in his Bf 109 at the Uman airfield but wasn't injured, and the next day he was awarded the German Cross in Gold in recognition of achieving his 40th aerial victory. He claimed another five victories in October and November and by the end of the year his Group had moved to Apostolovo west of Nikopol in the Ukraine.

He was still flying over the Ukraine in early 1944, claiming three P-39s between 15 and 17 January, which included his 50th victory. On 27 February he flew as instructor with Advanced Training Group East, based in Legnica, Poland, until the beginning of July. He was then promoted to *Leutnant* and took over as *Staffelkapitän* of the 4th Squadron of the 11th Fighter Wing in Beille, France. Towards the end of July the Group relocated to Mönchengladbach, Germany where it was renamed the 8th Squadron of the 11th Fighter Wing. Shortly afterwards his Squadron, part of the 2nd Group, moved to a new base in France but due to inadequate training some of the young pilots crashed upon landing. After an Allied air raid in early August in which he had claimed a Spitfire over south Corbeil-Essonnes, his Group moved again, this time to Marolles-en-Brie, south of Paris, and from early September the Group relocated to Cologne where Wolf flew 'Defence of the Reich' missions.

Between 17 and 27 September he flew combat missions over Holland as part of the air defence during Operation Market Garden, the Allied assault in the Netherlands through to Germany, and during that time he claimed a Curtiss P-38 on 19 September. After the offensive his Group returned to Germany where on 6 October his airfield at Breitscheid was attacked by Allied fighter-bombers, destroying nine aircraft and damaging five others. Two more were shot down on landing and by the 13th the 2nd Group had moved to Wunstorf to be refreshed. On 17 December his Group moved to Zellhausen in preparation for the Ardennes Offensive, the Battle of the Bulge. He claimed a B-26 Marauder twin-engined medium bomber over south-east Daun on 23 December, and by 23 January 1945 the Germans were in full retreat in the Ardennes. At the same time his Group's missions ended and they moved to Strausberg in Brandenburg and on 20 February Wolf claimed his 55th and last aerial victory, a Bell P-39 Airacobra fighter.

In March he transferred as an instructor with the 3rd Group of the Fighter Replacement Training Wing 2, under the command of *Major* Heinz Bär, flying from Munich. On 21 April he transferred to the 3rd Group of the 7th Fighter Wing, flying the Me 262 jet fighter from his base in Prague, Czechoslovakia. On 24 April he was awarded the Knight's Cross in recognition of his success and service as a fighter pilot. The following day he flew with other pilots on their very last combat mission of the war against the American heavy bombers. Less than two weeks later Germany surrendered to the Allies. After the war Wolf settled in his home town of Frankfurt am Main, where he died on 21 October 1996.

Friedrich HAAS

Leutnant

Knight's Cross: Awarded posthumously as *Leutnant* and *Staffelführer* of the 5th Squadron of the 52nd Fighter Wing on 26 April 1945 for operations over the Soviet Union and the Eastern Front.

Friedrich Haas achieved approximately seventy-four aerial victories in just over 12 months over the Eastern Front during the Second World War. He was born on 10 January 1924 in Dillenburg, a small town in the Hesse Giessen region of Germany.

After completion of his training as a fighter pilot *Feldwebel* Haas was assigned to the 5th Squadron of the 52nd Fighter Wing and began service on the Russian Front from December 1943. He claimed his first aerial victory on 6 December, a Yakovlev Yak-1 fighter over north-west Cap Tulsa. Soon after he was promoted to *Unteroffizier* and on 29 December he claimed a P-39 fighter over south-east Kertsch. He claimed two more P-39s in January 1944 and was awarded the Iron Cross 2nd Class. From early April he was flying combat missions over Sevastopol during the Crimean Offensive where he claimed seven victories, earning the Iron Cross 1st Class.

(Deutsches Wehrkundearchiv)

During May Haas was even more successful, and in the first week he claimed a total of nine victories, which included five on 7 May to become an 'ace-in-a-day'. By the end of the month Haas had claimed his 30th aerial victory, an Il-2 ground-attack aircraft over south Lasi. On 10 July he was slightly wounded when his Bf 109G-6 was damaged during a transfer flight and he had to make a forced landing just west of Stryi. He was awarded the German Cross in Gold on 26 July in recognition of his 35th aerial victory and returned to duty in September. Now with the rank of *Leutnant* Haas claimed his 40th victory on 1 November and then the dates of his victories become less known, although we know he claimed six Yak-9s in December, and these included his 50th victory.

In February 1945 Haas was appointed *Staffelkapitän* of the 4th Squadron of the 52nd Fighter Wing which had previously been led by Germany's top ace, *Hauptmann* Erich Hartmann. In March it was redesignated the 5th Squadron and was attached to the 2nd Group now stationed in Veszprem which it vacated three weeks later and by the end of the Group had settled in Austria. On 9 April Haas was shot down in his Messerschmitt Bf 109G-6, and was forced to bail out over Vienna, but at only 260ft there was insufficient altitude for his parachute to fully open and he slammed into his rudder and was killed. He was posthumously awarded the Knight's Cross on 26 April and although his actual score was unknown it has been estimated at least seventy-four victories. His body lies today at the War Graves Cemetery in Oberwölbing, Lower Austria, its location is Block 2, Row 9, Grave No. 401.

Alfons KLEIN

Oberleutnant

Knight's Cross: Awarded on 27 April 1945 as *Oberleutnant* and *Staffelkapitän* of the 10th Squadron of the 11th Fighter Wing for operations over the Soviet Union, the Western and Eastern Fronts.

Alfons Klein claimed thirty-one victories over the Eastern Front and another six over the Western Front, flying a total of 480 combat missions during the Second World War. He was born on 6 February 1921 in Dieringhausen in Gummersbach, Germany and joined the *Luftwaffe* in 1940 and trained as a fighter pilot.

On completion of his in training, in July 1943 he was assigned to the 2nd Squadron of the 1st Group part of the 52nd Fighter Wing, on the Eastern Front, where he flew the Bf 109G-2. At this time *Unteroffizier* Klein flew in the Belgorod area and in the course of the German retreat that began in early August he moved to Kharkov-Rogan and continued to withdraw into September. He claimed his first victory on the 1st, an

(Deutsches Wehrkundearchiv)

Ilyushin Il-2 ground-attack aircraft, and claimed his second victory on 22 September a Petlyakov Pe-2 dive-bomber over south Tamanj. On 3 October he claimed his third victory and on the 11th his Group moved to Novo-Zaporozhye, from where he was deployed in the defensive battles in southern Zaporozhye. He was soon after awarded the Iron Cross 2nd Class and by the end of the month had claimed his eighth victory and had been awarded the Iron Cross 1st Class. His Squadron was later deployed over the Crimea and from 14 November he flew from Kirovograd-East and from early December into the New Year he flew from Mala Wyska, west of Kirovograd.

On the morning of 9 January 1944 his Group had to move quickly from its base because of the fast approaching Soviet armour. They managed to relocate and flew missions between Ingul and Dnieper Rivers before moving again in March to avoid the Soviet advance. They had to move again in late March due to Soviet artillery fire and by late April they were based in Romania where they stayed for the next few weeks. Klein, who had by this time been promoted to *Feldwebel*, claimed another Il-2 on 10 March and claimed his 10th victory on the 23rd, yet another Il-2. He claimed another three victories in April and seven during May, claiming his 20th aerial victory over south Tiraspol on 21 May.

On 9 June Klein transferred to the 12th Squadron of the 10th Fighter Wing as a newly-promoted *Leutnant*. He continued to see action over the Eastern Front and claimed two victories on 26 June and later flew fighter-bomber missions over Bobruisk and Vitebsk. From mid-July his Group had moved to about 30 miles south-east of Lublin and a few days later had to move again because of the advancing Soviets. He claimed his 25th victory on 18 July and the next day he claimed his 26th, a Yak-9 fighter

From 20 August Klein was *Staffelkapitän* of the 4th Squadron of the 11th Fighter Wing and was now stationed on the Western Front in Paris. He claimed two P-47 Thunderbolts over Paris on 27 August and from 2 September his Squadron was relocated to Cologne and from there moved to Gymnich on the 4th to be deployed in 'Defence of the Reich' missions. He claimed his 29th victory over south-west Hahn on 12 September and that same day his Fw 190 was shot down by a P-51 Mustang of the 4th Fighter Group and he was injured, crashing near Wiesbaden. From 17 to 27 September he flew missions over Holland against the Allied Operation Market Garden, the unsuccessful attempt to break through to Germany and end the war in 1944. He had been awarded the German Cross in Gold on 19 September after claiming his 25th victory. He claimed his 30th victory on 17 December, a P-38 Lightning during air support for the Ardennes Offensive, and on the 23rd he claimed two victories over the area of Koblenz.

From early February 1945 he flew as *Staffelkapitän* of the 10th Squadron, attached to the 3rd Group of the 11th Fighter Wing and was still involved with the Ardennes Offensive. From 23 January the Group's mission in the West ended and he moved once again to the Eastern Front where he claimed a Yak-3 on 5 February, and he claimed another three victories during March and he claimed his 38th and last victory on 18 April and his Group moved to Döberitz that same day. They relocated to Lärz on 22 April and a few days later he was awarded the Knight's Cross. The war ended for him on 2 May 1945 at Leck when he and most of his Group were captured by US troops. After the war he lived for a long time in America before moving back to his home town where he died on 25 November 1992.

Heinz KNOKE

Hauptmann

Knight's Cross: Awarded on 27 April 1945 as *Hauptmann* and commander of the 3rd Group of the 11th Fighter Wing for operations over the Western Front.

Heinz Knoke was credited with fifteen confirmed aerial victories during the Second World War of which thirteen were four-engined bombers and a further nineteen victories were claimed but never confirmed. He was born in Hameln near Weser in Lower Saxony on 24 March 1921, the son of a policeman, and joined the *Luftwaffe* in July 1938 after he took a ride in a transport aircraft.

Knoke underwent training as a pilot from August 1940 in Berlin and attended pilot's school in Werneuchen and from there was assigned to the 52nd Fighter Wing in early 1941. He was attached to the 6th Squadron of the 2nd Group where his comrades included the future aces Gerhard Barkhorn, Günther Rall and Walter Krupinski. After

(Deutsches Wehrkundearchiv)

briefly serving during the invasion of the Soviet Union he transferred in July 1941 as a *Leutnant* to the 2nd Squadron of the 1st Fighter Wing. In February 1942 he took part in Operation Thunderbolt, the code name given to the German operation to give aerial protection to the battleships *Scharnhorst* and *Gneisenau* and the heavy cruiser *Prinz Eugen* in the Channel and later in Norway. On 6 March he ran out of fuel and had to make an emergency landing on a frozen lake near Alvdal, Norway and had to be rescued. From October he flew as *Staffelkapitän* of the 2nd Squadron of the 1st Fighter Wing and claimed his first victory on the 31st, an RAF Blenheim, and on 6 November he claimed his second victory, a Mosquito north-west of Helgoland, and was awarded the Iron Cross 2nd Class. However, after post-war scrutiny both victories have been reclassified as unconfirmed. On 24 February he claimed a B-24 Liberator over Bad Zwischenahn, his first confirmed victory of the war and shortly after he was awarded the Iron Cross 1st Class. He said that after initially hitting the aircraft he went in for a second pass head-on, 'I kept firing until I had to break away to avoid colliding with the bomber. I saw flames spreading along the bottom of its fuselage. I followed it down and attacking twice more … I watched my cannon shells hit the top of the fuselage and right wing.' On 18 March he claimed his second victory, another B-24 over south-east Heligoland, and during the attack his wingman, *Leutnant* Dieter Gerhardt's aircraft was hit by return fire and crashed. He later died from his wounds.

As the US daylight bomber offensive intensified throughout 1943 operations against them increased. Knoke came up with a new idea of dropping bombs on the US bomber formations. The theory was that Bf 109s would ascend to an altitude of about 30,000ft, position themselves over a group of bombers and release their bombs, set to explode on a 15-second time delay. This method was used by Knoke for the first time on 22 March 1943. He later said in his memoir,

> I could see the American bombers high above me at 23,000 feet. The battle was already in progress, the unaccustomed heavy load was making my aircraft sluggish. It took me almost twenty-five minutes to climb to 29,500 feet. The Americans had already dropped their bombs … I crept forward above the formation … I fused the bomb, took aim and pressed the bomb-release button on the control stick. The bomb plummeted downwards. Climbing steeply, I banked so that I could watch the bomb fall. It exploded in the middle of the group of three B-17s; a wing is torn off of one of them and the other two dived away in alarm. The B-17 bomber without its wing plunges into the sea.

Upon landing Knoke was ordered to report to *Kommodore, Oberstleutnant* Erich Mix who had been in the air and witnessed everything. He congratulated Knoke and said that he should try it with the whole squadron. Knoke replied that was the plan. Later word spread and Knoke received a call from *Reichsmarschall* Hermann Göring who was delighted by Knoke's initiative and congratulated him. Later a test run was ordered at Rechlin air base to establish proper tactics and several missions were reported in the Mediterranean area. However, they proved to a complete failure: the US bombers did not fly in such tight formations and had fighter protection. It wasn't long before this idea was abandoned.

On 17 April 1943 Knoke claimed his fourth victory, another B-17 Flying Fortress over Bremen, and soon after was appointed *Staffelkapitän* of the 5th Squadron with the newly-formed 11th Fighter Wing. He claimed his fifth victory on 15 May, another B-17. On 1 June he was promoted to *Oberleutnant* and claimed two more victories and was wounded on 25 June when his Bf 109G-1 was hit after combat. During 1943 Knoke claimed a total of seventeen victories of which only seven were ever confirmed. On 17 May he was awarded the German Cross in Gold and on 4 October he was shot down by return fire from a B-24. He bailed out of his damaged fighter into the icy waters of the North Sea. An inflatable raft was dropped by a Focke-Wulf Fw 58 which he climbed into and was rescued two hours later. Then on 4 January he was again shot down near Münster by a P-47 of the 78th Fighter Group, and he bailed out but fractured his spine and skull. Seven days later he was again shot down but wasn't hurt and on the 30th he crashed due to engine failure following combat near Hilversum, Holland, but again was uninjured.

On 10 February he claimed his 12th victory, a B-17 over Osnabrück, Germany, and ten days later he claimed another over the Hameln area. In early March he claimed three more B-17s but all remain unconfirmed victories, and then on the 8th he was involved in an accident during take-off at Wunstorf but wasn't injured. He claimed his 14th victory on 29 April, a P-51 Mustang over the Braunschweig area. On 1 May he was promoted to *Hauptmann* and on 13 August was appointed *Gruppenkommandeur* of the 3rd Group of the 1st Fighter Wing, becoming the youngest *Gruppenkommandeur* in the *Luftwaffe*. He led his Group over the Normandy front, flying from Brétigny-sur-Orge in the southern suburbs of Paris. He claimed seven victories in August, and all were later reclassified as unconfirmed. On the 25th he claimed a P-51 over La Fére in northern France and was later shot down by return fire. He bailed out of his Bf 109 near Soissons and was captured, but managed to escape back to the German lines.

From 15 to 20 April 1944 he was attached to the Experimental Station at Lechfeld where he flew the Me 262A jet fighter. On 29 April he was shot down by a P-47 piloted by Captain James Canon and upon returning to base Knoke developed a fever and what later turned out to be a serious brain haemorrhage. Following this he had a nervous breakdown and was grounded until mid-August. On 9 October during a car journey he was injured in the legs by a landmine planted by partisans near Prague and was hospitalized until March 1945. When he was well enough he returned to active service at Jever as the airbase commander, arriving on crutches, and oversaw the defensive fortifications around Wilhelmshaven. On 27 April Knoke was awarded the Knight's Cross in recognition of his success as a fighter pilot against US four-engined bombers.

He survived the war and in 1951 he was a member of the Socialist Reich Party of Lower Saxony, although the Supreme Court declared the party illegal in 1952. He remained in politics for some years with the Liberal Democratic Party and was returned to office in March 1961, September 1964 and September 1968. He retired in October 1972 and was described as inventive and articulate. According to his diary which he published in 1950 he stated that he agreed with the war but by 1945 he was willing to enter into an armistice with the Western Allies but continue the fight with the Soviet Union. He lived in Bad Iburg, Westfalen in his later years where he died on 18 May 1993.

Erwin LASKOWSKI

Oberfeldwebel

Knight's Cross: Awarded on 27 April 1945 as *Oberfeldwebel* attached to the 8th Squadron of the 11th Fighter Wing for operations over the Soviet Union and the Western Front.

Erwin Laskowski claimed fifteen aerial victories during the Second World War of which ten were over the Eastern Front and five over the Western Front, all four-engined bombers. He was born on 27 May 1914 in Bochum in North Rhine-Westphalia and upon joining the *Luftwaffe* he was assigned to the 4th Anti-Aircraft Regiment from November 1936.

From November 1939 he attended pilot training, first with Fighter School 5 in Vienna and then from June 1941 in Magdeburg. He was assigned to the Replacement Group of the 52nd Fighter Wing from August 1941and then later moved to the 51st Fighter Wing in the Soviet Union. From November Laskowski flew as part of the 2nd Squadron, being attached to the 1st Group in Staraja Russa.

(Deutsches Wehrkundearchiv)

He flew the Bf 109E-7, mostly on fighter-bomber missions, and from February 1942 he was transferred as an *Unteroffizier* into the 1st Squadron. Between March and April taking off and landing was difficult because of the amount of mud as the snow had begun to melt, and flying was difficult. However, combat missions had to proceed and he managed to claim his first victory on 1 April, a Polikarpov R-5 reconnaissance aircraft. He claimed two more victories during April, and claimed his fourth on 2 May, being awarded the Iron Cross 2nd Class on the 25th. On 5 June he crashed his Bf 109 whilst landing at Tuleblja but wasn't wounded, and the following day he made a belly landing at Morino after running out of fuel. Now with the rank of *Feldwebel* he claimed two LaGG-2 fighters over Weretejka on 20 July, his fifth and sixth victories. He was shot down on 28 July by anti-aircraft fire and was able to make an emergency landing at Rykalowj airfield, and again wasn't wounded. During early August he flew missions in protection of ground troops with Army Group Centre and that same month his Group re-equipped with the Focke-Wulf Fw 190A. He returned to the front by mid-September and for a time operated over Leningrad until 17 October when his Squadron was withdrawn and relocated to Vyazma South. He claimed another LaGG-3 on 9 November and six days later he was awarded the Iron Cross 1st Class. He claimed his eighth and ninth victories on 14 November, and again both were LaGG-3s.

He claimed a single victory on 15 January 1943 and in early February his Squadron moved to Vitebsk and he flew from a frozen lake and then moved to the Velikiye Luki area. In March the Group moved to Bryansk and in May moved again to Orel where he stayed for the next few weeks. In the autumn of 1943 he transferred to the 8th Squadron of the 11th Fighter Wing and as part of the 3rd Group he flew from Oldenburg whilst flying the Bf 109G-6. He claimed a B-17 Flying Fortress on 11 January over Goslar, his 11th aerial victory, and had by this time been promoted to *Oberfeldwebel* and was now flying over Germany in 'Defence of the Reich' missions. He claimed two B-24 Liberators on 18 March 1944 over East Freiburg, and in May he claimed two more B-17s, his 14th and 15th victories – in fact his last victories of the war. By the end of November his Group had converted to the Fw 190 and by the end of the year his Group had claimed forty-five aircraft, of which thirty-five were four-engined bombers. In June, shortly after D-Day his Group moved to France, but after being bombed several times they moved to Étricourt-Manancourt in the northern part of the country. From July he flew from Mondésir just west of Paris and on the 10th Laskowski was awarded the German Cross in Gold.

Laskowski spent the last few months of the war flying with Fighter Group West until March 1945 when he flew as part of Fighter Replacement Group East in Mühldorf, Bavaria. He was credited with over 300 combat missions and was awarded the Knight's Cross on 27 April, and shortly after receiving his award in May his unit surrendered to the Western Allies. Laskowski died in his home town of Bochum on 13 October 1983.

Fritz LOSIGKEIT

Major

Knight's Cross: Awarded on 28 April 1945 as *Major* and commander of the 51st Fighter Wing '*Mölders*' for operations over France, England and the Eastern Front.

Fritz Losigkeit claimed fifty-one aerial victories, of which forty-four were over the Eastern Front, and flew over 750 combat missions during the Second World War,. He was born on 17 November 1913 in Berlin-Tegel and joined the police in 1934 before joining the *Luftwaffe* two years later.

From October 1936 until March 1938 he flew with the 88th Fighter Group as part of the Condor Legion in Spain, during the Civil War, flying the Heinkel He 51 whilst attached to the 3rd Squadron in ground-attack missions. On 31 March 1938, he took off from his air base in Zaragaza, his second mission that day, and he saw a line of trucks close to the enemy lines and assumed they were carrying munitions. The trucks were travelling fast and he soon realized they were making for cover. He approached at low level and anti-aircraft guns opened fire and his aircraft was hit. He bailed out and was unhurt upon landing and was immediately taken prisoner, spending eight months in captivity in Valencia and Barcelona. He was released in February 1939, and he was awarded the Spanish Cross in Silver with Swords two months later.

(Author's collection)

He began his career in the Second World War as an *Oberleutnant* with the 26th Fighter Wing and was appointed *Staffelkapitän* of the 2nd Squadron on 23 September 1939. He saw action during the invasion of France, claiming his first victory on 28 May 1940, an RAF Spitfire over Calais. He claimed his second victory on 1 June, another Spitfire near Dunkirk and was awarded the Iron Cross 2nd Class. During August he claimed a Hurricane and a Spitfire, being awarded the Iron Cross 1st Class and he claimed his fifth victory on 15 September, another Spitfire over south-east London. In December his Squadron moved to Abbeville in France and from February 1941 was relocated to Dortmund, Germany to be converted to the Bf 109E-7 fighter. On 17 May Losigkeit was transferred to Japan as Attaché to the German Mission in Tokyo with the rank of *Hauptmann*.

He returned to combat duty in early 1942, and took command of *Kommando Losigket*, formed to provide temporary air cover for German ships in Norwegian waters until more significant air cover could be deployed to the country. By March he was tasked with the reorganization of the new 4th Group of the 1st Fighter Wing at Döberitz and was then assigned to combat duty in France. A few weeks later his Group was incorporated into the 5th Fighter Wing and he flew fighter protection missions over Trondheim, Norway. From April 1943 his Group was redesignated 1st Group of the 1st Fighter Wing seeing action over the Netherlands, now with the rank of *Major*. He claimed a B-17 Flying Fortress (one of seventeen claimed by the 1st and 11th Fighter Wings that day) on 17 April and a Ventura medium bomber over Haarlem on 2 May. From early June he was *Gruppenkommandeur* of the 1st Group of the 26th Fighter Wing and three weeks later he transferred as *Gruppenkommandeur* of the 3rd Group of the 51st Fighter Wing, and from June over the Eastern Front. He flew from Bryansk from July and later transferred to Poltava, claiming his 10th victory on the 6th and by the end of the month had claimed his 19th victory. He claimed two victories on 1 August, both LaGG-3 fighters, and went on to claim a total of fifteen victories during August, which included his 30th victory. He claimed his 37th victory on 15 September and was awarded the *Luftwaffe* Honour Goblet on 11 October and seven days later was awarded the German Cross in Gold. He claimed his 40th victory on 16 January 1944, a Yak-7 fighter over south Paritschi.

In April he was appointed *Kommodore* of the 51st Fighter Wing and continued to score victories over the Eastern Front. He claimed his 50th victory, a Pe-2 dive-bomber over the area of Zolocev on 16 July, and claimed his 51st and last victory of the war on 24 July 1944. Towards the end of the year his Fighter Wing returned to Germany and flew fighter protection missions over the Reich. On 1 April 1945 Losigkeit was transferred and became the last *Kommodore* of the 77th Fighter Wing and was awarded the Knight's Cross on 28 April. He spent the final few weeks in Czechoslovakia flying occasional sorties, before surrendering to the Allies on 8 May 1945.

In 1946 he became Secretary of the *Freie Demokratische Partei* and held posts as a business representative until 1978. He died in Hünxe, North Rhine-Westphalia in Germany on 14 January 1994.

Alfred RAUCH

Leutnant

Knight's Cross: Awarded as *Fahnenjunker-Oberfeldwebel* as pilot with the Staff Squadron of the 51st Fighter Wing '*Molders*' on 28 April 1945 for operations over England, the Soviet Union, North Africa and the Eastern Front.

Alfred Rauch claimed approximately fifty-nine aerial victories, all apart from five over the Eastern Front during the Second World War. He was born on 29 December 1917 in Eltmann, Bavaria, joined the *Luftwaffe* in 1938 and after training was assigned to the 4th Squadron of the 51st Fighter Wing in June 1940. As an *Unteroffizier* he later transferred to the 5th Squadron and saw action during the Battle of Britain from July, and he claimed an RAF Hurricane over the Thames Estuary on 11 August but this was unconfirmed.

In early 1941 he transferred and became a test pilot, then a fighter instructor until August when he returned to his Squadron, now on the Eastern Front. On 4 October, now with the rank of *Feldwebel* he claimed his first confirmed victory, an Ilyushin DB-3 long-range bomber over Orel. He claimed his second victory on 7 October, and claimed his third the next day when he was awarded the Iron Cross 2nd Class. he continued to fly over the Eastern Front into 1942 and claimed two victories on 18 February and two more, both MiG-1s, on 6 March and with ten victories to his name was awarded the Iron Cross 1st Class. He claimed a Pe-2 dive-bomber north-east of Dugino on 29 March and claimed two MiG-3 fighters the following day. Soon afterwards he fell ill and was hospitalized for a time and removed from combat until August, when he returned to combat on the Eastern Front. He claimed five more victories during the last two weeks of August and claimed another three in September, which included his 20th.

On 2 November Rauch was awarded the *Luftwaffe* Honour Goblet and claimed his 25th victory, a B-26 Marauder twin-engined bomber on 15 January 1943. From March he flew with the Staff Squadron and was promoted to *Oberfeldwebel*. He was awarded the German Cross in Gold on 23 July after achieving his 27th aerial victory. On 20 and 28 October he claimed two victories and on 15 December he claimed three more. From May 1944 he flew as an instructor with the Replacement and Training Fighter Group East under the command of *Major* Viktor Bauer in Lignitz.

Rauch returned to the 51st Fighter Wing in October, claiming his 35th victory on the 24th, a Yak-9 fighter over south-east Gumbinnen, East Prussia. During the last months of the war he flew with the 4th Group of the 51st Fighter Wing, flying from Mödlin in Austria and later from Danzig. In April he was commissioned as a *Leutnant* and on the 25th claimed eight aerial victories to become an 'ace-in-a-day'. Four were Il-2 ground-attack aircraft, shot down over Stettin, and the others were a Boston, two Yak-3s and a P-39. Finally on 28 April he was awarded the Knight's Cross, the recommendation read, 'he brought relief to our hard pressed ground troops by flying 102 fighter-bomber missions during which he achieved 100 hits on ground enemy facilities and artillery positions'. He claimed his final victory of the war over Neubrandenburg, a Lavochkin La-7 fighter, on 29 April. Rauch had flown 681 combat missions and 102 as a fighter-bomber pilot and had claimed at least fifty-four aerial victories over the Eastern Front, probably more. He died on 25 March 1991 in Bad Kissingen in Bavaria, Germany.

(Deutsches Wehrkundearchiv)

Appendix

Top Aces of the Luftwaffe

Erich Hartmann	352	Friedrich-Karl Müller	139
Gerhard Barkhorn	301	Karl Gratz	138
		Otto Fönnekold	134
Günther Rall	274	Joachim Müncheberg	134
Otto Kittel	265+	Walter Wolfrum	134
Walter Nowotny	256	Franz Schall	133
Wilhelm Batz	233	Heinrich Setz	133
Erich Rudorffer	219	Adolf Borchers	132
Oskar-Heinz Bär	208	Adolf Dickfeld	132
Theodor Weissenberger	208	Rudolf Trenkel	132
Hermann Graf	206	Karl-Heinz Weber	132
Anton Hafner	203	Wilhelm Lemke	131
Helmut Lipfert	200	Hans-Peter Waldemann	131
		Gerhard Hoffmann	130
Walter Krupinski	197	Franz Eisenach	129
Johannes Philipp	193	Alfred Grislawski	127
Joachim Brendel	189	Walter Oesau	127
Heinrich Ehrler	182+	Dietrich Hrabak	125
Maximilian Stotz	182	Heinrich Sturm	123
Joachim Kirschner	181	Josef Zwernemann	123
Walter Schuck	181	Franz Dörr	122
Anton Hackl	180+	Herbert Ihlefeld	122
Günther Josten	178	Robert Weiss	122
Günther Schack	174	Wolf-Udo Ettel	121
Heinz Schmidt	173	Erich Leie	121
Emil Lang	172	Heinz Marquardt	121
Kurt-Werner Brändle	170	Wolfgang Tonne	120
Ernst-Wilhelm Reinert	168	Heinz Wernicke	118
Johannes Steinhoff	168	Johannes Wiese	118
Horst Ademeit	160	Hans-Joachim Birkner	117
Gerhard Thyben	157	Wilhelm Crinius	114
Wolf-Dietrich Wilcke	155	Kurt Bühligen	112
Hans-Joachim Marseille	152	Friedrich Obleser	112
Hans Beisswenger	150	Franz-Josef Beerenbrock	111
		Günther Lützow	109
Peter Düttmann	147	Reinhard Seiler	109
Gordon M. Gollob	146	Berthold Korts	108
Fritz Tegtmeier	146	Werner Mölders	108
Albin Wolf	142	Heinrich Sterr	108

Top Aces of the Luftwaffe

Bernhard Vechtel	108	Adolf Galland	103
Emil Bitsch	106	Josef Wurmheller	103
Werner Schroer	106	Egon Mayer	102
Viktor Bauer	104	Max-Hellmuth Ostermann	102
Jakob Norz	104	Ulrich Wernitz	101
Heinz Sachsenberg	104	Erwin Clausen	100
Hans Hahn	105	Paul-Heinrich Dahne	100
Werner Lucas	105	Rudolf Miethig	100
Hans Dammers	103	Josef Priller	100

There were 387 *Luftwaffe* day fighter pilots who won the Knight's Cross during the Second World War, and shown below are their different ranks and how many of each rank, with the British RAF equivalent.

2	*Feldwebel*	Sergeant
31	*Oberfeldwebel*	Flight Sergeant
80	*Leutnant*	Pilot Officer
77	*Oberleutnant*	Flying Officer
81	*Hauptmann*	Flight Lieutenant
83	*Major*	Squadron Leader
16	*Oberstleutnant*	Wing Commander
16	*Oberst*	Group Captain
1	*Generalleutnant*	Air Vice-Marshal

Claims made by Luftwaffe pilots during the Spanish Civil War in 1936.

Werner Mölders	14	Johannes Trautloft	5
Wolfgang Schellmann	12	Hubertus von Bonin	4
Otto Bertram	9	Karl-Wolfgang Redlich	4
Herbert Ihlefeld	9	Josef Fözo	3
Walter Oesau	9	Lothar Keller	3
Reinhard Seiler	9	Joachim Schlichting	3
Horst Tietzen	7	Heinz Bretnütz	2
Hans-Karl Mayer	6	Walter Adolph	1
Rolf Peter Pingel	6	Wolfgang Ewald	1
Wolfgang Lippert	5	Rudolf Resch	1
Günther Lützow	5		

Claims made by Luftwaffe pilots who claimed more than five victories against four-engined bombers during the Second World War.

Egon Mayer	27	Anton-Rudolf Piffer	21
Friedrich-Karl Müller	24	Werner Gerth	20
Georg-Peter Eder	23+	Hans-Heinrich Koenig	19
Werner Schroer	23	Hermann Staiger	19
Walther Dahl	22	Willy Unger	18
Hans Ehlers	22	Adolf Glunz	17
Hans Weik	22	Rolf Hermichen	17

Herbert Huppertz	17	Walter Loos	10
Klaus Neumann	17	Walter Matoni	10
Anton Hackl	16	Leopold Münster	10
Willy Kientsch	16	Johann Pichler	10
Klaus Bretschneider	15	Josef Priller	10
Hugo Frey	15	Herbert Rollwage	10
Günther Specht	15	Siegfried Schnell	10
Otto Wessling	15	Eugen-Ludwig Zweigart	10
Oskar-Heinz Bär	14	Ernst Düllberg	9
Ernst Börngen	14	Wilhelm-Ferdinand Galland	9
Alfred Grislawski	14	Ernst-Erich Hirschfeld	9
Will Reschke	14	Fritz Karch	9
Gerhard Sommer	14	Wilhelm Moritz	9
Rudolf Zwesken	14	Karl Schnörrer	9
Konrad Bauer	13	Peter Werfft	9
Kurt Bühlingen	13	Fritz Gromotka	8
Heinz Knocke	13	Erich Hohagen	8
Klaus Mietusch	13	Karl Rammelt	8
Walter Oesau	13	Hans Remmer	8
Franz Ruhl	13	Oskar Romm	8
Waldemar Radener	12	Günther Seeger	8
Gerhard Michalski	11	Gerhard Vogt	8
Rudolf Rademacher	11	Heinrich Ehrler	7
Gustav Rödel	11	Peter Jenne	7
Erich Rudorffer	11	Wilhelm Mayer	7
Karl-Heinz Willius	11	Johannes Naumann	7
Oskar Zimmermann	11	Otto Schultz-Wittner	7
Anton Benning	10	Theodor Weissenberger	7
Erwin Clausen	10	Heinz Gossow	6
Hans Grünberg	10	Walter Hoeckner	6
Horst Haase	10	Karl-Wilhelm Hofmann	6
Jürgen Harder	10	Armin Köhler	6
Rudolf Klemm	10	Josef Wurmheller	6

Claims made by pilots who flew the Me 262 jet fighter during the Second World War.

Georg-Peter Eder	21	Johannes Steinhoff	6
Rudolf Rademacher	16	Hans Grünberg	5
Franz Schall	16	Wolfgang Späte	5
Oskar-Heinz Bär	15	Klaus Neumann	3
Erich Rudorffer	12	Walter Krupinski	2
Karl Schnörrer	11	Hans Waldemann	2
Heinrich Ehrler	8	Günther Lützow	1
Walter Schuck	8	Walter Nowotny	1
Theodor Weissenberger	8		
Walther Dahl	7	Franz-Walter Woidich	1 with the Me 163B
Adolf Galland	6		

German Awards and Decorations

Knight's Cross with Oakleaves, Swords and Diamonds: Instituted by Hitler on 15 July 1941. The Diamonds could only be awarded to previous winners of the Swords. There were just twenty-seven recipients of this prized award. With the Diamonds came a lavish document, printed on high-grade parchment in gold. The diamonds were hand-crafted by a jeweller using real diamonds set in the Oakleaves and on the handles of the Swords. All recipients were presented with the award personally by Hitler.

Knight's Cross with Oakleaves and Swords: Instituted by Hitler on 28 September 1941, and could only be awarded to previous winners of the Oakleaves. The Swords was presented to the recipient in a box and was attached below the Oakleaves crossed at a 40-degree angle, with the right sword overlapping the left. The band clip on the back was slightly larger than the one attached to the Oakleaves. There were 159 confirmed recipients of the Swords.

Knight's Cross with Oakleaves: Instituted by Hitler on 3 June 1940 and was worn above the Knight's Cross and held in place by means of a silver loop that would also secure the neck ribbon. The decoration consisted of a cluster of three oak leaves with the centre leaf superimposed on the two lower leaves. The original clasp had the digits 800 or 900 added, like the Knight's Cross to show it was made from 800-grade silver and measured 2cm in diameter. Hitler frequently made the presentations of the Oakleaves to the recipients personally, either at the Reich Chancellery in Berlin or at the Berghof on the Obersalzburg near Berchtesgaden. There were 890 recipients of the Oakleaves.

Knight's Cross of the Iron Cross: The Knight's Cross was instituted by Hitler on 30 September 1939, and is probably one of the most recognizable decorations of the Second World War. It was similar in design to the Iron Cross except it was larger. It measured 48mm x 48mm with a silver ring on top which measured 6mm. At the top of the cross there was an elongated ribbon top which went through the silver ring and this is where the ribbon went that was used to hold it in position around the recipient's neck. With the Knight's Cross came an impressive-looking citation presented in a red leather binder and stamped with an embossed German Eagle in gold on the front cover and signed by Hitler. There were over 7,000 recipients of the Knight's Cross.

German Cross: The award was created in two classes: Gold and Silver, independent of one another, and was instituted on 28 September 1941. The Gold type was awarded in recognition of repeated acts of bravery or exceptional command not justifying the award of the Knight's Cross. The Silver type was to reward significant performance in military conduct of the war. A total of 24,204 Gold and 1,114 Silver types were awarded.

Iron Cross 1st Class: Instituted on 1 September 1939, for three to five acts of bravery above and beyond the call of duty. Approximately 450,000 were awarded.

Iron Cross 2nd Class: Instituted on 1 September 1939, for one act of bravery above and beyond the call of duty. Approximately 3,000,000 were awarded.

Luftwaffe Honour Goblet: Instituted on 27 February 1940 by *Reichsmarschall* Hermann Göring, it was awarded 'For Special achievement in the Air War' and was given to both pilots and aircrew. Although German war records show that almost 58,000 were given 'on paper' only about 13,000 to 15,000 were actually presented. The first airman to receive the Goblet was Oberstleutnant Johann Schalk on 21 August 1940.

Bibliography

Angolia, John R., *On the Field of Honor Volume 1*, San Jose, California, USA: Roger James Bender Publications, 1979.
——, *On the Field of Honor Volume 2*, San Jose, California, USA: Roger James Bender Publications, 1980.
Baker, David, *Adolf Galland. The Authorised Biography*, The Crowood Press Ltd, 1998.
Baumbach, Werner, *The Life and Death of the Luftwaffe*, Coward-McCann, 1960.
Beevor, Anthony, *The Battle for Spain: The Spanish Civil War 1936-1939*, London: Phoenix, 2006
Bekker, Cajus, *The Luftwaffe War Diaries*, New York: Doubleday, 1964.
Bergström, Christer, *Luftwaffe Pilots in World War II. The Veteran's Stories Volume 1*. Sweden: Vaktel Books, 2018.
——, *Max-Hellmuth Ostermann. Ace Profiles: The Men and Their Aircraft.* East Sussex, England: Air Power Editions, 2007.
——, and Andrey Mikhailov, *Black Cross Red Star. The Air War Over the Eastern Front Resgurence January-June 1942, Volume 2*, Pacifica Military History, 2001.
Boehme, Manfred, *JG7. The World's First Jet Fighter Unit 1944-1945*, Atglen, PA: Schiffer Military History, 1992.
Caldwell, Donald, *Day Fighters in Defence of the Reich: A War Diary, 1942-45*, South Yorkshire: Frontline Books, 2011.
——, *JG26 Top Guns of the Luftwaffe. The Epic Saga of Germany's Legendary Fighter Wing*, New York: Orion Books, 1991.
——, *The JG26 War Diary Volume One 1939-1942*, London: Grub Street, 1996.
——, *The JG26 War Diary Volume Two 1943-1945*, London: Grub Street, 1998.
—— and Richard Muller. *The Luftwaffe Over Germany. Defense of the Reich*, London: Greenhill Books, 2007.
Collier, Richard, *Eagle Day: The Battle of Britain August 6 – September 15, 1940*, New York: E.P. Dutton, 1966.
Cooper, Matthew, *The German Air Force 1933-1945*, London: Jane's, 1981.
Dildy, Douglas C. and Paul F. Crickmore, *To Defeat The Few. The Lufwaffe's Campaign to Destroy RAF Fighter Command August–September 1940*, Oxford: Osprey Publishing, 2020.
Dixon, Jeremy, *Luftwaffe Generals: The Knight's Cross Holders 1939-1945*, Agten, PA, USA: Schiffer Military History, 2009.
——, *The Knight's Cross with Oakleaves 1940-1945 Volumes 1 & 2*, Agten, PA, USA: Schiffer Military History, 2012.
Forsgren, Jan, *Sinking the Beast. The RAF 1944 Lancaster Raids against Tirpitz*, Fonthill Media Ltd, 2014.
Forsyth, Robert, *Aces of the Legion Condor*, Oxford: Osprey Publishing, 2011.
——, *Jagdgeschwader 1 'Oesau' Aces 1939-45*, Oxford: Osprey Publishing, 2017.

——, *Jagdgeschwader 7 'Nowotny'*, Oxford: Osprey Publishing, 2008.
——, *Luftwaffe Viermot Aces 1942-45*. Oxford: Osprey Publishing, 2011.
Fraschka, Günther, *Knights of the Reich*, Atglen, PA: Schiffer Military Publishing, 1989.
Galland, Adolf, *The First and the Last*, London: Methuen, 1955.
——, et al. (edited by David C. Isby), *The Luftwaffe Fighter Force: The View from the Cockpit*, London: Greenhill Books, 1998.
Gerbig, Werner, *Jagdgeschwader 5: The Luftwaffe's JG 5 'Eismeerjager' in World War II*, Atglen, PA: Schiffer Military Publishing, 2012.
——, *Six Months to Oblivion: The Defeat of the Luftwaffe Fighter Force over the Western Front 1944-1945*, Atglen, PA: Schiffer Military Publishing, 2004.
Goralski, Robert, *World War II Almanac 1931-1945. A Political and Military Record*, London: Hamish Hamilton, 1981.
Goss, Chris, *Jagdgeschwader 53 'Pik-As' Bf 109 Aces of 1940*, Oxford: Osprey Publishing, 2017.
——, *Knights of the Battle of Britain: Luftwaffe Aircrew Awarded the Knight's Cross in 1940*. London: Frontline Books, 2018.
——, *Luftwaffe Aces in the Battle of Britain*, South Yorkshire: Air World Books (Pen & Sword), 2020.
——, *The Luftwaffe Fighters. Battle of Britain. The inside story: July-October 1940*. Manchester, Crecy Publishing, 2000.
Green, William, *Warplanes of the Third Reich*, New York: Doubleday, 1972.
Griehl, Manfred, *Last Days of the Luftwaffe. German Luftwaffe Combat Units 1944-1945*, London: Frontline Books, 2009.
Heaton, Colin D. and Anne-Marie Lewis, *The German Aces Speak. Vol. I & II*, USA: Quatro Publishing, 2018.
Held, Werner, *German Fighter Ace Walter Nowotny: An Illustrated Biography*, Atglen, PA: Schiffer Military Publishing, 2006.
Held, Werner, *Reichsverteidigung – Die Deutsche Tagjagd 1943-1945*, Friedberg: Podzun-Pallas Verlag, 1988.
Hildebrand, Karl Friedrich, *Die Generale der Deutschen Luftwaffe 1935-1945*, Osnabrück: Biblio Verlag, Band 1-3, 1990–2.
Hooton, E.R., *Eagle in Flames: The Fall of the Luftwaffe*. London: Brockhampton Press, 1999.
——, *Phoenix Triumphant: The Rise and Fall of the Luftwaffe*. London: Brockhampton Press, 1999.
Irving, David, *Göring. A Biography*, London: Macmillan, 1989.
——, *The Rise and Fall of the Luftwaffe: the Life of Erhard Milch*. London: Weidenfeld & Nicolson, 1973.
Jacobs, Peter, *Aces of the Luftwaffe. The Jagdflieger in the Second World War*, London: Frontline Books, 2014.
Kaplan, Philip, *Fighter Aces of the Luftwaffe in World War II*, Auldgirth, Dumfriesshire: Pen & Sword Aviation, 2007.
Kay, Antony L. & Richard Smith, *German Aircraft of the Second World War*, Annapolis, MD: Naval Institute Press, 2002.
Knoke, Heinz, *I Flew for the Führer*, London: Evans, 1953.
Konstam, Angus, *Sink the Tirpitz 1942-1944. The RAF and Fleet Air Arm duel with Germany's mighty battleship*, Oxford: Osprey Publishing, 2018.
Kurowski, Franz, *German Fighter Ace: Hans-Joachim Marseille: Star of Africa*, Atglen, PA: Schiffer Publishing, 1994.

Kurowski, Franz, *Knight's Cross Holders of the Afrika Korps*, Atglen, PA: Schiffer Military, 1996.
Lipfert, Helmut and Werner Girbig, *The War Diary of Hauptmann Helmut Lipfert: JG52 on the Russian Front 1943-1945*. Atglen, PA: Schiffer Publishing, 1993.
MacLean, French L., *Luftwaffe Efficiency & Promotion Reports for the Knight's Cross Winners Vol: 1 & 2*, Atglen, PA: Schiffer Military History, 2007.
Mason, Francis K., *Battle Over Britain*, New York: Doubleday, 1969.
Mathews, Andrew Johannes and John Foreman, *Luftwaffe Aces: Biographies and Victory Claims*, Volumes 1-4, Red Kite, 2014
Mitcham, Samuel W., *Men of the Luftwaffe*, Novato CA: Presidio Press, 1988.
Mombeek, Eric, *Defending the Reich: The History of Jagdgeschwader 1 'Oesau'*, Norwich: JAC Publications, 1992.
Mosley, Leonard, *The Reich Marshal: A Biography of Hermann Goering*, London: Weidenfeld & Nicolson, 1974.
Muller, Richard, *The German Air War in Russia*, Baltimore, MD: Nautical & Aviation, 1992.
Obermaier, Ernst, *Die Ritterkreuzträger der Luftwaffe 1939-1945. Band I. Jagdflieger*, Verlag Dieter Hoffmann, 1989.
——, *German Fighter Ace Werner Mölders: An Illustrated Biography*, Atglen, PA: Schiffer Military Publishing, 2006.
Page, Neil, *Day Fighter Aces of the Luftwaffe 1939-1942*, Casemate Publishers, 2020.
——, *Day Fighter Aces of the Luftwaffe 1943-1945*, Casemate Publishers, 2020.
Patzwall, Claus and Veit Scherzer, *Das Deutsche Kreuz 1941-1945. Geschichte und Inhaber Band II*, Norderstedt: Verlag Klaus D. Patzwall, 2001.
Price, Alfred, *Battle over the Reich*, London: Ian Allen, 1973.
——, *Blitz on Britain, 1939-1945*, London: Ian Allen, 1977.
——, *Luftwaffe Handbook 1939-1945*, New York: Chas. Scribner's Sons, 1976.
Proctor, Raymond L., *Hitler's Luftwaffe in the Spanish Civil War*, Westport, Conn.: ABC-CLIO, 1983.
Reschke, Willi, *Jagdgeschwader 301/302 'Wilde Sau'. In Defense of the Reich with the Bf 109, Fw 190 and Ta 152*, Atglen, PA: Schiffer Military Publishing, 2005.
Ringlstetter, Herbert, *Helmut Wick: An Illustrated Biography of the Luftwaffe Ace and Commander of Jagdgeschwader 2 during the Battle of Britain*, Atglen, PA: Schiffer Military Publishing, 2013.
Roba, Jean-Louis, *The Luftwaffe in Africa 1941-1943*, Casemate Publishers, 2019.
Scherzer, Veit, *Die Ritterkreuzträger, Die Inhaber des Ritterkreuzes des Eisernen Kreuzes 1939 von Heer, Luftwaffe, Kriegsmarine, Waffen-SS, Volkssturm, Ranis*, Scherzers Militaer-Verlag, 2007.
Scutts, Jerry, *Bf 109 Aces of North Africa and the Mediterranean*, Oxford: Osprey Publishing, 1994.
——, *JG54 Jagdgeschwader 54 Grünherz. Aces of the Eastern Front*, Shrewsbury: Airlife, 1992.
Spick, Mike, *Aces of the Reich. The Making of a Luftwaffe Fighter Pilot*, London: Greenhill Books, 2006.
——, *Fighter Pilot Tactics*, Cambridge: Patrick Stephens, 1983.
——, *Luftwaffe Fighter Aces. The Jagdflieger and their Combat Tactics and Techniques*, London: Greenhill Books, 1996.
Steinhoff, Johannes, *The Last Chance*, London: Hutchinson & Co., 1977.
Stockert, Peter, *Die Eichenlaubträger 1940-1945*, 4 volumes, Verlag Friedrichshaller Rundblick GmbH, 1996–8.
Take, Robert, *Hans-Joachim Marseille: An illustrated Tribute to the Luftwaffe's 'Star of Africa'*, Atglen, PA: Schiffer Publishing. 2008.

Thomas, Franz, *Die Eichenlaubträger 1940-1945, Band 1: A-K*, Osnabrück: Biblio Verlag, 1997.

——, *Die Eichenlaubträger 1940-1945, Band 2: L-Z*, Osnabrück: Biblio Verlag, 1998.

Toliver, Col. Raymond, USAF (Ret.) & Trevor J. Constable, *German Fighter Ace Erich Hartmann: The Life Story of the World's Highest Scoring Ace*, Atglen, PA: Schiffer Publishing, 1996.

——, *Horrido! Fighter Aces of the Luftwaffe*, New York: Ballantine, 1968.

——, *The Life of Adolf Galland. The Official Biography*, Atglen, PA: Schiffer Publishing, 1998.

Trigg, Jonathan, *The Defeat of the Luftwaffe. The Eastern Front 1941-45. A Strategy for Disaster*, Gloucestershire: Amberley Publishing, 2016.

Weal, John, *Bf 109 'Defence of the Reich' Aces*, Oxford: Osprey Publishing, 2006.

——, *Bf 109 D/E Aces 1939-41*, Oxford: Osprey Publishing, 2001.

——, *Bf 109F/G/K Aces of the Western Front*, Oxford: Osprey Publishing, 1999.

——, *Aces of Jagdgeschwader 3 'Udet'*, Oxford: Osprey Publishing, 2013.

——, *Focke-Wulf Fw 190 Aces of the Russian Front*, Oxford: Osprey Publishing, 1996.

——, *Focke-Wulf Fw 190 Aces of the Western Front*, Oxford: Osprey Publishing, 1996.

——, *Fw 190 'Defence of the Reich' Aces,* Oxford: Osprey Publishing, 2011.

——, *Jagdgeschwader 2 'Richthofen'*, Oxford: Osprey Publishing, 2000.

——, *Jagdgeschwader 27 'Afrika'*, Oxford: Osprey Publishing, 2003.

——, *Jagdgeschwader 51 'Mölders'*, Oxford: Osprey Publishing, 2006.

——, *Jagdgeschwader 52 The Experten*, Oxford: Osprey Publishing, 2004.

——, *Jagdgeschwader 53 'Pik-As'*, Oxford: Osprey Publishing, 2007.

——, *Jagdgeschwader 54 'Grünherz'*, Oxford: Osprey Publishing, 2001.

——, *Luftwaffe Sturmgruppen*, Oxford: Osprey Publishing, 2005.

——, *More Bf 109 Aces of the Russian Front*, Oxford: Osprey Publishing, 2007.

Williamson, Gordon, *Aces of the Reich*, London: Arms & Armour Press, 1989.

Williamson, Murray, *Strategy for Defeat: The Luftwaffe 1933-1945*, Royston, Herts: Eagle Editions, 2003.

—— *Die Wehrmacht berichte 1939-1945* Band 1-3, Deutscher Taschenbuch Verlag, 1985.

Index

Ademeit, Horst 'Adomaitis' 20

Bachnick, Herbert 133
Barten, Franz 161
Batz, Wilhelm 'Willi' 77
Bauer, Konrad 'Pitt' 173
Benning, Anton Hermann 215
Berres, Heinz-Edgar 35
Birkner, Hans-Joachim 133
Bitsch, Emil 31
Borchers, Adolf 48
Börngen, Ernst 134
Borris, Karl 181
Böwing-Treuding, Wolfgang 15
Brandt, Paul 149
Brandt, Walter 15
Brendel, Joachim 'Achim' 50
Bretschneider, Klaus Karl Theobald 176
Broch, Hugo 204
Brönnle, Herbert 7
Brunner, Albert 28
Bunzek, Johannes 101

Dahl, Walther 74
Dähne, Paul-Heinrich 'Sarotti' 104
Denk, Gustav 8
Döbele, Anton 'Toni' 78
Döbrich, Hans Heinrich 36
Dörr, Franz 143
Dortenmann, Hans 218
Düllberg, Ernst 131
Düttmann, Peter 'Bonifazius' 113

Ebener, Kurt 18
Eder, Georg-Peter 'Schorsch' 128
Ehlers, Johann 'Hans' 115
Ehrenberger, Rudolf 94

Eichel-Streiber, Diethelm von 95
Eisenach, Franz 153
Ettel, Wolf-Udo 24
Ewald, Heinz 'Esau' 219

Fassong, Horst-Günther von 136
Fink, Günter 9
Fönnekold, Otto 79
Freuwörth, Wilhelm 'Willi' 1
Frey, Hugo 110
Friebel, Herbert 5
Frielinghaus, Gustav 64

Gaiser, Otto 116
Galland, Wilhelm-Ferdinand 'Wutz' 22
Gerth, Werner 171
Glunz, Adolf 'Addi' 32
Goltzsch, Kurt 65
Gossow, Heinz 162
Grollmus, Helmut 152
Gromotka, Fritz 195
Gross, Alfred 221
Grünberg, Hans 'Specker' 117

Haas, Friedrich 226
Haase, Horst 163
Hackler, Heinrich 'Heinz' 144
Haiböck, Josef 118
Harder, Jürgen Hans Eberhard 56
Hartmann, Erich Alfred 'Bubi' 37
Hermichen, Rolf-Günther 80
Hirschfeld, Ernst-Erich 164
Hoeckner, Walter 101
Hoffmann, Gerhard 112
Hoffmann, Reinhold 196
Hofmann, Karl-Wilhelm 165
Hrdlicka, Franz 158
Hübner, Wilhelm 203

Isken, Eduard 193

Jenne, Peter 200
Jennewein, Josef 'Pepi' 58
Josten, Günther 66
Jung, Heinrich 45

Kaiser, Herbert 9
Kalden, Peter 185
Karch, Friedrich 'Fritz' 216
Kientsch, Wilhelm 'Willy' 51
Kittel, Otto 'Bruno' 41
Klein, Alfons 227
Klemm, Rudolf 177
Knoke, Heinz 228
Koall, Gerhard 'Knall' 154
Koenig, Hans-Heinrich 'Kira' 146
Köhler, Armin 201
Kolbow, Hans 137
Korts, Berthold 34
Kroschinski, Hans-Joachim 217

Lang, Emil 'Bully' 52
Lange, Heinz 178
Langer, Karl-Heinz 221
Laskowski, Erwin 230
Leber, Heinz 71
Lemke, Siegfried 'Wumm' 125
Lindner, Anton 'Toni' 105
Linz, Rudolf 'Rudi' 205
Lipfert, Helmut 96
Litjens, Stefan 26
Loos, Gerhard 68
Loos, Walter 223
Losigkeit, Fritz 231
Lücke, Max-Hermann 'Anatol' 103
Lüddecke, Fritz 'Paulo' 179

Marquardt, Heinz 'Negus' 180
Matoni, Walter 189
Mayer, Wilhelm 206
Mayerl, Maximilian 54
Meier, Johann-Hermann 190
Meimberg, Julius 'Jule' 167
Mietusch, Klaus Dietrich Wilhelm 'Kurt' 82
Missner, Helmut 156

Moritz, Wilhelm 130
Mors, August 168

Naumann, Johannes (Hans) 'Focke' 174
Nemitz, Willi 'Altvater' 17
Neumann, Helmut 183
Neumann, Klaus 207
Norz, Jakob 'Jockel' 84

Obleser, Friedrich 85

Petermann, Viktor 72
Philipp, Wilhelm 86
Pichler, Johann 147
Piffer, Anton-Rudolf 'Toni' 159
Puschmann, Herbert 'Puschi' 98

Quaet-Faslem, Klaus 120
Quast, Werner 'Quax' 62

Rademacher, Rudolf 'Rudi' 150
Radener, Waldemar 'Waldi' 208
Rammelt, Karl 169
Rauch, Alfred 233
Remmer, Hans 'Bubi' 121
Resch, Anton 'Toni' 214
Reschke, Willi 224
Rollwage, Herbert 99
Romm, Oskar 73
Rübell, Günther 11
Ruhl, Franz 138
Rupp, Friedrich Albert Ragnar 6

Sachsenberg, Heinz 'Heino' 122
Schack, Günther 43
Schall, Franz 157
Scheel, Günther 59
Schiess, Franz 'Nawratil' 27
Schleinhege, Hermann 197
Schnörrer, Karl 'Quax' 211
Schönfelder, Helmut 213
Schuck, Walter 'Sohndel' 106
Schuhmacher, Leo 203
Schultz-Wittmer, Otto 19
Schumann, Heinz 13
Seeger, Günther 'Hupatz' 87